Introduction to
finite mathematics

PRENTICE-HALL MATHEMATICS SERIES

Introduction to finite mathematics

JOHN G. KEMENY

Professor of Mathematics, Dartmouth College

J. LAURIE SNELL

Professor of Mathematics, Dartmouth College

GERALD L. THOMPSON

*Professor of Mathematics and Industrial Administration,
Carnegie Institute of Technology*

SECOND EDITION

Englewood Cliffs, N.J., PRENTICE-HALL, INC.

Current printing (last digit):

11   10   9   8   7   6   5   4

Library of Congress Catalog Card Number: 66-19894

PRINTED IN THE UNITED STATES OF AMERICA

C—48379

Preface to
the second edition

THE FIRST EDITION of this book was published in January, 1957. Since that time we and our colleagues at various institutions have had experience teaching its material to a large number of students. We therefore felt it appropriate that a second edition should be prepared that would reflect the experience we have had.

The changes to the basic core (the unasterisked sections) of the book are minor, and involved the rewriting of a few sections and the addition of supplementary exercises. We have also added between ten to fifteen percent of new material, most of it in asterisked (optional) sections. A brief summary of the more important changes is as follows: the section on logical possibilities has been rewritten; a new section on counting techniques has been added; Bayes theorem replaces geometric probabilities; the section on the law of large numbers and central limit theorem has been split in two; the section on linear equations has been rewritten and a flow diagram added; the section on the inverse of a matrix has been rewritten; the material on Markov chains has been expanded; the material on linear programming has been completely rewritten; game theory has had minor rewriting; the section on equivalence classes in communication networks is new; and the section on computer simulation is new.

Our objectives in the present edition of the book are the same as for the first edition; namely, to present a course in elementary modern mathematics which can appear early in a student's career. The applications discussed in the course are primarily to the biological and social sciences and hence provide a point of view, other than that given by physics—the application stressed in calculus courses—concerning the possible uses of mathematics.

The only prerequisite for this book is the mathematical maturity obtained from two and a half or more years of high school mathematics.

Without being dogmatic about the way the book should be used, we make the following suggestions for possible courses to be taught from it:

1. *A basic mathematics course*, covering the unasterisked sections of Chapters I–V and supplemented by some of the asterisked sections from these Chapters as well as selected sections of Chapter VI.

2. *A mathematics course for behavioral scientists*, covering the unasterisked sections of Chapters I–V and selected sections from Chapters VI and VII.

In addition to these courses it is possible to derive a brief introduction to probability and its applications from Chapters I–IV and VII; and it is also possible to derive a brief introduction to matrix theory and its applications from Chapters II, V, VI, and VII. We have included a bibliography at the end of each chapter to guide those interested in further reading.

At the end of each section there are a number of exercises. We have tried to grade them in order of increasing difficulty, and to provide two of each kind, one with and the other without an answer printed in the text. There are also supplementary exercises at the end of some of the sections. Some of these exercises are easier and some are more difficult than the earlier ones. They were added to help provide variety.

We wish to thank our colleagues, in many different institutions, who sent us suggestions for revisions. In particular, we are grateful to Professor A. W. Tucker, who has shown a strong and continuing interest in our work. We would also like to thank F. Mosteller and H. Roberts, whose stimulating criticisms of our computer simulation section helped us to improve it. To Dartmouth College and Carnegie Institute of Technology we offer our appreciation for providing facilities which made the preparation of this book possible. And, finally, we thank the staff of Prentice-Hall for their careful attention to editorial details.

J.G.K., J.L.S., G.L.T.

Preface to
the first edition

IN THE USUAL undergraduate mathematical curriculum, the courses which a student takes during his first two years are those leading up to the calculus and the calculus itself. A few years ago, the department of mathematics at Dartmouth College decided to introduce a different kind of freshman course, which students could elect along with these more traditional ones. The new course was to be designed to introduce a student to some concepts in modern mathematics early in his college career. While primarily a mathematics course, it was to include applications to the biological and social sciences and thus provide a point of view, other than that given by physics, concerning the possible uses of mathematics.

In planning the proposed course, we found that there was no textbook available to fulfill our needs and, therefore, we decided to write such a book. Our aim was to choose topics which are initially close to the students' experience, which are important in modern day mathematics, and which have interesting and important applications. To guide us in the latter we asked for the opinions of a number of behavioral scientists about the kinds of mathematics a future behavioral scientist might need. The main topics of the book were chosen from this list.

Our purpose in writing the book was to develop several topics from

:entral point of view. In order to accomplish this on an elementary vel, we restricted ourselves to the consideration of *finite* problems, hat is, problems which do not involve infinite sets, limiting processes, continuity, etc. By so doing it was possible to go further into the subject matter than would otherwise be possible, and we found that the basic ideas of finite mathematics were easier to state and theorems about them considerably easier to prove than their infinite counterparts.

The first five chapters form a natural unit. The discussion of the set of logical possibilities (in Chapter I) leads to the idea of the truth set associated with a statement which, in turn, gives a natural way of defining the probability that a statement is true (in Chapter IV). The correspondence that exists among logical operations (Chapter I), set operations (Chapter II), and probability operations (Chapter IV) becomes especially transparent in the finite case. A very useful pedagogical device, that of a "tree" (a special type of diagram) is used in these chapters and in the rest of the book to illustrate and clarify ideas. In particular, this allows an introduction to the theory of stochastic processes in an elementary manner. The Markov chains here introduced help to motivate vector and matrix theory, which is presented in Chapter V.

In Chapter VI the student is introduced to two recent branches of mathematics that have proved useful in applications, namely, linear programming and the theory of games. We are able to explain the basic ideas of both relatively quickly because of the mathematical preparation given in the earlier chapters.

In our concluding Chapter VII we discuss several significant applications of mathematics to the behavioral sciences. These were selected for their interest both to mathematicians and to behavioral scientists. One topic was chosen from each of five sciences: sociology, genetics, psychology, anthropology, and economics. A reader may find it more difficult to read parts of this chapter than the earlier chapters, but it was found necessary to make it so in order that nontrivial applications could be taken up and pursued far enough to see the contributions mathematics makes. In teaching a course from our book we would not expect that all of the topics from this chapter would be used. We hope, however, that Chapter VII will serve as reference and self-study material for ambitious students.

The Committee on the undergraduate program of the Mathematical Association of America was planning a new freshman mathematics program at the same time we were planning our book. They had already written Part I of *Universal Mathematics*, which is an introduction to analytic geometry and the calculus, and were making plans for Part II. When the chairman of that committee learned of the similarity of the plans for our book to those for Part II of *Universal Mathematics*, he invited one of us to join his committee. We believe that our book agrees with the spirit of their recommendations. We are grateful for their permission to use some of their illustrations, of which the applications to voting problems are the principal ones.

The report of the Committee on Mathematical Training of Social Scientists of the Social Science Research Council appeared after our plans were completed. We were pleased to note that on many questions we had reached the same conclusions as had that committee. They recommend two years of training, about half in the calculus and half along the lines here discussed. A semester course based on our book together with a semester of calculus would give the student a distribution in the proportions recommended by that committee.

The basic core of the book consists of the unasterisked sections of Chapters I-V. This material should be covered in every course. Flexibility is provided by the inclusion of additional material, the optional (asterisked) sections of these chapters, Chapter VI, and Chapter VII. By emphasizing the first five chapters, the course would be a basic mathematics course. By aiming at Chapter VII and taking up several of these applications, the course can be designed as a mathematics course suited for the behavioral scientist. Chapter VI is appropriate as supplementary material for either type of course. We have included a bibliography at the end of each chapter to guide those interested in further reading.

The only prerequisite for this book is the mathematical maturity obtained from two and a half or more years of high school mathematics. Our book has been tried successfully in a freshman course at Dartmouth College and for supplementary reading in other courses. It has also been used in a mathematics course for faculty members in the behavioral sciences.

We wish to thank Dartmouth College for releasing us from part of our teaching duties to enable us to prepare this book. Thanks are also due to A. W. Tucker for his valuable advice and to our colleagues in the mathematics department at Dartmouth for their many helpful estions. We are also grateful to James K. Schiller for reading the nuscript and for providing the reactions of a student. Finally we sh to thank Joan Snell, Margaret P. Andrews, and Stephen Russell or their invaluable aid in the preparation of the manuscript.

J.G.K., J.L.S., G.L.T.

Contents

I

Compound statements

xi

II

Sets and subsets

III

Partitions and counting

IV

Probability theory

V

Vectors and matrices

VI

* Linear programming
and the theory of games

VII

* Applications to
behavioral science problems

Compound statements

1. PURPOSE OF THE THEORY

A *statement* is a verbal or written assertion. In the English language such assertions are made by means of declarative sentences. For example, "It is snowing" and "I made a mistake in signing up for this course" are statements.

The two statements quoted above are *simple statements*. A combination of two or more simple statements is a *compound statement*. For example, "It is snowing, and I wish that I were out of doors, but I made the mistake of signing up for this course," is a compound statement.

It might seem natural that one should make a study of simple statements first, and then proceed to the study of compound ones. However, the reverse order has proved to be more useful. Because of the tremendous variety of simple statements, the theory of such statements is very complex. It has been found in mathematics that it is often fruitful to assume for the moment that a difficult problem has been solved and then to go on to the next problem. Therefore we shall proceed as if we knew all about simple statements and study only the way they are compounded. The latter is a relatively easy problem.

While the first systematic treatment of such problems is found in the writings of Aristotle, mathematical methods were first employed by George Boole about 100 years ago. The more polished techniques now available are the product of twentieth century mathematical logicians.

The fundamental property of any statement is that it is either true or false (and that it cannot be both true and false). Naturally, we are interested in finding out which is the case. For a compound statement it is sufficient to know which of its components are true, since the truth values (i.e., the truth or falsity) of the components determine in a way to be described later the truth value of the compound.

Our problem then is twofold: (1) In how many different ways can statements be compounded? (2) How do we determine the truth value of a compound statement given the truth values of its components?

Let us prepare our mathematical tools. In any mathematical formula we find three kinds of symbols: *constants, variables,* and *auxiliary symbols.* For example, in the formula $(x + y)^2$ the plus sign and the exponent are constants, the letters x and y are variables, and the parentheses are auxiliary symbols. Constants are symbols whose meanings in a given context are fixed. Thus in the formula given above, the plus sign indicates that we are to form the sum of the two numbers x and y, while the exponent 2 indicates that we are to multiply $(x + y)$ by itself. Variables always stand for entities of a given kind, but they allow us to leave open just which particular entity we have in mind. In our example above the letters x and y stand for unspecified numbers. Auxiliary symbols function somewhat like punctuation marks. Thus if we omit the parentheses in the expression above we obtain the formula $x + y^2$, which has quite a different meaning than the formula $(x + y)^2$.

In this chapter we shall use variables of only one kind. We indicate these variables by the letters p, q, r, etc., which will stand for unspecified statements. These statements frequently will be simple statements but may also be compound. In any case we know that, since each variable stands for a statement, it has an (unknown) truth value.

The constants that we shall use will stand for certain connectives used in the compounding of statements. We will have one symbol for forming the negation of a statement and several symbols for combining two statements. It will not be necessary to introduce symbols for the compounding of three or more statements, since we can show that the same combination can also be formed by compounding them two at a time. In practice only a small number of basic constants are used and the others are defined in terms of these. It is even possible to use only a single connective! (See Section 4, Exercises 10 and 11.)

The auxiliary symbols that we shall use are, for the most part, the same ones used in elementary algebra. Any case where the usage is different will be explained.

Examples. As examples of simple statements, let us take "The weather is nice" and "It is very hot." We will let p stand for the former and q for the latter.

Suppose we wish to make the compound statement that both are true, "The weather is nice *and* it is very hot." We shall symbolize this statement by $p \wedge q$. The symbol $\wedge$, which can be read "and," is our first connective.

In place of the strong assertion above we might want to make the weak (cautious) assertion that one or the other of the statements is true. "The weather is nice *or* it is very hot." We symbolize this assertion by $p \vee q$. The symbol $\vee$, which can be read "or," is the second connective which we shall use.

Suppose we believed that one of the statements above was false, for example, "It is *not* very hot." Symbolically we would write $\sim q$. Our third connective is then $\sim$, which can be read "not."

More complex compound statements can now be made. For example, $p \wedge \sim q$ stands for "The weather is nice *and* it is *not* very hot."

EXERCISES

1. The following are compound statements or may be so interpreted. Find their simple components.
   (a) It is hot and it is raining.
   (b) It is hot but it is not very humid.
   > [*Ans.* "It is hot"; "it is very humid."]
   (c) It is raining or it is very humid.
   (d) Jack and Jill went up the hill.
   (e) The murderer is Jones or Smith.
   (f) It is neither necessary nor desirable.
   (g) Either Jones wrote this book or Smith did not know who the author was.

2. In Exercise 1 assign letters to the various components, and write the statements in symbolic form.   [*Ans.* (b) $p \wedge \sim q$.]

3. Write the following statements in symbolic form, letting p be "Fred is smart" and q be "George is smart."

(a) Fred is smart and George is stupid.

(b) George is smart and Fred is stupid.

(c) Fred and George are both stupid.

(d) Either Fred is smart or George is stupid.

(e) Neither Fred nor George is smart.

(f) Fred is not smart, but George is stupid.

(g) It is not true that Fred and George are both stupid.

4. Assume that Fred and George are both smart. Which of the seven compound statements in Exercise 3 are true?

5. Write the following statements in symbolic form.

(a) Fred likes George. (Statement p.)

(b) George likes Fred. (Statement q.)

(c) Fred and George like each other.

(d) Fred and George dislike each other.

(e) Fred likes George, but George does not reciprocate.

(f) George is liked by Fred, but Fred is disliked by George.

(g) Neither Fred nor George dislikes the other.

(h) It is not true that Fred and George dislike each other.

6. Suppose that Fred likes George and George dislikes Fred. Which of the eight statements in Exercise 5 are true?

7. For each statement in Exercise 5 give a condition under which it is false.   [*Ans.* (c) Fred does not like George.]

8. Let p be "Stock prices are high" and q be "Stocks are rising." Give a verbal translation for each of the following.

(a) $p \wedge q$.

(b) $p \wedge \sim q$.

(c) $\sim p \wedge \sim q$.

(d) $p \vee \sim q$.

(e) $\sim(p \wedge q)$.

(f) $\sim(p \vee q)$.

(g) $\sim(\sim p \vee \sim q)$.

9. Using your answers to Exercise 8, parts (e), (f), (g), find simpler symbolic statements expressing the same idea.

10. Let p be "I have a dog" and q be "I have a cat." Translate into English and simplify: $\sim[\sim p \vee \sim\sim q] \wedge \sim\sim p$.

2. THE MOST COMMON CONNECTIVES

The truth value of a compound statement is determined by the truth values of its components. When discussing a connective we will want to know just how the truth of a compound statement made from this connective depends upon the truth of its components. A very convenient way of tabulating this dependency is by means of a *truth table*.

Let us consider the compound $p \wedge q$. Statement p could be either true or false and so could statement q. Thus there are four possible pairs of truth values for these statements and we want to know in each case whether or not the statement $p \wedge q$ is true. The answer is straightforward: If p and q are both true, then $p \wedge q$ is true, and otherwise $p \wedge q$ is false. This seems reasonable since the assertion $p \wedge q$ says no more and no less than that p and q are both true.

p	q	$p \wedge q$
T	T	T
T	F	F
F	T	F
F	F	F

Figure 1

Figure 1 gives the truth table for $p \wedge q$, the *conjunction* of p and q. The truth table contains all the information that we need to know about the connective $\wedge$, namely it tells us the truth value of the conjunction of two statements given the truth values of each of the statements.

p	q	$p \vee q$
T	T	?
T	F	T
F	T	T
F	F	F

Figure 2

We next look at the compound statement $p \vee q$, the *disjunction* of p and q. Here the assertion is that one or the other of these statements is true. Clearly, if one statement is true and the other false, then the disjunction is true, while if both statements are false, then the disjunction is certainly false. Thus we can fill in the last three rows of the truth table for disjunction (see Figure 2).

Observe that one possibility is left unsettled, namely, what happens if both components are true? Here we observe that the everyday usage of "or" is ambiguous. Does "or" mean "one or the other or both" or does it mean "one or the other but not both"?

Let us seek the answer in examples. The sentence "This summer I will date Jean or Pat" allows for the possibility that the speaker may date both girls. However the sentence "I will go to Dartmouth or to Princeton" indicates that only one of these schools will be chosen. "I will buy a TV set or a phonograph next year" could be used in either sense; the speaker may mean that he is trying to make up his mind which one of the two to buy, but it could also mean that he will buy *at least one* of these—possibly both. We see that sometimes the context makes the meaning clear, but not always.

A mathematician would never waste his time on a dispute as to which usage "should" be called the disjunction of two statements. Rather he recognizes two perfectly good usages, and calls one the *inclusive disjunction* (p or q or both) and the other the *exclusive disjunction* (p or q but not both). The symbol $\vee$ will be used for inclusive disjunction, and the symbol $\underline{\vee}$ will be used for exclusive disjunction. The truth tables for each of these are found in Figures 3 and 4. Unless we state otherwise, our disjunctions will be inclusive disjunctions.

p	q	$p \vee q$
T	T	T
T	F	T
F	T	T
F	F	F

Figure 3

p	q	$p \underline{\vee} q$
T	T	F
T	F	T
F	T	T
F	F	F

Figure 4

The last connective which we shall discuss in this section is *negation*. If p is a statement, the symbol $\sim p$, called the negation of p, asserts that p is false. Hence $\sim p$ is true when p is false, and false when p is true. The truth table for negation is shown in Figure 5.

p	$\sim p$
T	F
F	T

Figure 5

Besides using these basic connectives singly to form compound statements, several can be used to form a more complicated compound statement, in much the same way that complicated algebraic expressions can be formed by means of the basic arithmetic operations. For example, $\sim(p \wedge q)$, $p \wedge \sim p$, and $(p \vee q) \vee \sim p$ are all compound statements. They are to be read "from the inside out" in the same way that algebraic expressions are, namely, quantities inside the innermost parentheses are first grouped together, then these parentheses are grouped together, etc. Each compound statement has a truth table which can be constructed in a routine way. The following examples show how to construct truth tables.

Example 1. Consider the compound statement $p \vee \sim q$. We begin the construction of its truth table by writing in the first two columns the four possible pairs of truth values for the statements p and q.

Then we write the proposition in question, leaving plenty of space between symbols so that we can fill in columns below. Next we copy the truth values of p and q in the columns below their occurrences in the proposition. This completes step 1; see Figure 6.

p	q	p	$\vee$	$\sim q$
T	T	T		T
T	F	T		F
F	T	F		T
F	F	F		F
Step No.		1		1

Figure 6

Next we treat the innermost compound, the negation of the variable q, completing step 2, see Figure 7.

p	q	p	$\vee$	$\sim$	q
T	T	T		F	T
T	F	T		T	F
F	T	F		F	T
F	F	F		T	F
Step No.		1		2	1

Figure 7

Finally we fill in the column under the disjunction symbol, which gives us the truth value of the compound statement for various truth values of its variables. To indicate this we place two parallel lines on each side of the final column, completing step 3 as in Figure 8.

p	q	p	$\vee$	$\sim$	q
T	T	T	T	F	T
T	F	T	T	T	F
F	T	F	F	F	T
F	F	F	T	T	F
Step No.		1	3	2	1

Figure 8

The next two examples show truth tables of more complicated compounds worked out in the same manner. There are only two basic rules which the student must remember when working these: first, work from the "inside out"; second, the truth values of the compound statement are found in the last column filled in during this procedure.

Example 2. The truth table for the statement $(p \lor \sim q) \land \sim p$ together with the numbers indicating the order in which the columns are filled in appears in Figure 9.

p	q	$(p$	$\lor$	$\sim$	$q)$	$\land$	$\sim$	p
T	T	T	T	F	T	F	F	T
T	F	T	T	T	F	F	F	T
F	T	F	F	F	T	F	T	F
F	F	F	T	T	F	T	T	F
Step No.		1	3	2	1	4	2	1

Figure 9

Example 3. The truth table for the statement $\sim[(p \land q) \lor (\sim p \land \sim q)]$ together with the numbers indicating the order in which the columns are filled appears in Figure 10. We note that the compound statement has the same truth table as $p \underline{\lor} q$. These two statements are *equivalent* (see Section 7).

p	q	$\sim$	$[(p$	$\land$	$q)$	$\lor$	$(\sim$	p	$\land$	$\sim$	$q)]$
T	T	F	T	T	T	T	F	T	F	F	T
T	F	T	T	F	F	F	F	T	F	T	F
F	T	T	F	F	T	F	T	F	F	F	T
F	F	F	F	F	F	T	T	F	T	T	F
Step No.		5	1	2	1	4	2	1	3	2	1

Figure 10

EXERCISES

1. Give a compound statement which symbolically states "p or q but not both," using only $\sim$, $\lor$, and $\land$.

2. Construct the truth table for your answer to Exercise 1, and compare this with Figure 4.

3. Construct the truth table for the symbolic form of each statement in Exercise 3 of Section 1. How does Exercise 4 of Section 1 relate to these truth tables?

4. Construct a truth table for each of the following.
    (a) $\sim(p \wedge q)$.   [*Ans.* FTTT.]
    (b) $p \wedge \sim p$.   [*Ans.* FF.]
    (c) $(p \vee q) \vee \sim p$.   [*Ans.* TTTT.]
    (d) $\sim[(p \vee q) \wedge (\sim p \vee \sim q)]$.   [*Ans.* TFFT.]

5. Let p stand for "Jones passed the course" and q stand for "Smith passed the course" and translate into symbolic form the statement "It is not the case that Jones and Smith both failed the course." Construct a truth table for this compound statement. State *in words* the circumstances under which the statement is true.

6. Construct a simpler statement about Jones and Smith that has the same truth table as the one in Exercise 5.

7. Let $p \mid q$ express that "p and q are not both true." Write a symbolic expression for $p \mid q$ using $\sim$ and $\wedge$.

8. Write a truth table for $p \mid q$.

9. Write a truth table for $p \mid p$.   [*Ans.* Same as Figure 5.]

10. Write a truth table for $(p \mid q) \mid (p \mid q)$.   [*Ans.* Same as Figure 1.]

11. Construct a truth table for each of the following.
    (a) $\sim(p \vee q) \vee \sim(q \vee p)$.   [*Ans.* FFFT.]
    (b) $\sim(p \vee q) \wedge p$.   [*Ans.* FFFF.]
    (c) $\sim(p \veebar q)$.   [*Ans.* TFFT.]
    (d) $\sim(p \mid q)$.   [*Ans.* TFFF.]

12. Construct two symbolic statements, using only $\sim$, $\vee$, and $\wedge$, which have the following truth tables (a) and (b), respectively.

p	q	(a)	(b)
T	T	T	T
T	F	F	F
F	T	T	F
F	F	T	T

13. Using only $\sim$ and $\underline{\vee}$, construct a compound statement having the same truth table as:

  (a) $p \leftrightarrow q$.

  (b) $p \wedge q$.

3. OTHER CONNECTIVES

Suppose we did not wish to make an outright assertion but rather an assertion containing a condition. As examples, consider the following sentences. "If the weather is nice, I will take a walk." "If the following statement is true, then I can prove the theorem." "If the cost of living continues to rise, then the government will impose rigid curbs." Each of these statements is of the form *"if p then q."* The *conditional* is then a new connective which is symbolized by the arrow $\rightarrow$.

Of course the precise definition of this new connective must be made by means of a truth table. If both p and q are true, then $p \rightarrow q$ is certainly true, and if p is true and q false, then $p \rightarrow q$ is certainly false. Thus the first two lines of the truth table can easily be filled in, see Figure 11a. Suppose now that p is false; how shall we fill in the last two lines of the truth table in Figure 11a? At first thought one might suppose that it would be best to leave it completely undefined. However, to do so would violate our basic principle that a statement is either true or false.

p	q	$p \rightarrow q$
T	T	T
T	F	F
F	T	?
F	F	?

p	q	$p \rightarrow q$
T	T	T
T	F	F
F	T	T
F	F	T

Figure 11a   *Figure 11b*

Therefore we make the completely arbitrary decision that the conditional, $p \rightarrow q$, is *true* whenever p is false, regardless of the truth value of q. This decision enables us to complete the truth table for the conditional and it is given in Figure 11b. A glance at this truth table shows that the conditional $p \rightarrow q$ is considered false only if p is true and q is false. If we wished, we might rationalize the arbitrary decision made above by saying that if statement p happens to be false, then we give the conditional $p \rightarrow q$ the "benefit of the doubt" and consider it true. (For another reason, see Exercise 1.)

In everyday conversation it is customary to combine simple statements only if they are somehow related. Thus we might say "It is raining today and I will take an umbrella," but we would not say "I read a good book and I will take an umbrella." However, the rather ill-defined concept of relatedness is difficult to enforce. Concepts related to each other in one person's mind need not be related in another's. In our study of compound statements no requirement of relatedness is imposed on two statements in order that they be compounded by any of the connectives. This freedom sometimes produces strange results in the use of the conditional. For example, according to the truth table in Figure 11b, the statement "If $2 \times 2 = 5$, then black is white" is true, while the statement "If $2 \times 2 = 4$, then cows are monkeys" is false. Since we use the "if . . . then . . ." form usually only when there is a causal connection between the two statements, we might be tempted to label both of the above statements as nonsense. At this point it is important to remember that no such causal connection is intended in the usage of $\rightarrow$; the meaning of the conditional is contained in Figure 11b and nothing more is intended. This point will be discussed again in Section 7 in connection with implication.

Closely connected to the conditional connective is the *biconditional* statement, $p \leftrightarrow q$, which may be read "*p if and only if q.*" The biconditional statement asserts that if p is true, then q is true, and if p is false, then q is false. Hence the biconditional is true in these cases and false in the others, so that its truth table can be filled in as in Figure 12.

p	q	$p \leftrightarrow q$
T	T	T
T	F	F
F	T	F
F	F	T

Figure 12

The biconditional is the last of the five connectives which we shall use in this chapter. The table below gives a summary of them together with the numbers of the figures giving their truth tables. Remem-

Name	Symbol	Translated as	Truth Table
Conjunction	$\wedge$	"and"	Figure 1
Disjunction (inclusive)	$\vee$	"or"	Figure 3
Negation	$\sim$	"not"	Figure 5
Conditional	$\rightarrow$	"if . . . then . . ."	Figure 11b
Biconditional	$\leftrightarrow$	". . . if and only if . . ."	Figure 12

ber that the complete definition of each of these connectives is given by its truth table. The examples below show the use of the two new connectives.

Examples. In Figures 13 and 14 the truth tables of two statements are worked out following the procedure of Section 2.

p	q	p	$\rightarrow$	$(p$	$\vee$	$q)$
T	T	T	T	T	T	T
T	F	T	T	T	T	F
F	T	F	T	F	T	T
F	F	F	T	F	F	F
Step No.		1	3	1	2	1

Figure 13

p	q	$\sim$	p	$\leftrightarrow$	$(p$	$\rightarrow$	$\sim$	$q)$
T	T	F	T	T	T	F	F	T
T	F	F	T	F	T	T	T	F
F	T	T	F	T	F	T	F	T
F	F	T	F	T	F	T	T	F
Step No.		2	1	4	1	3	2	1

Figure 14

It is also possible to form compound statements from three or more simple statements. The next example is a compound formed from three simple statements p, q, and r. Notice that there will be a total of eight possible triples of truth values for these three statements so that the truth table for our compound will have eight rows as shown in Figure 15.

p	q	r	$[p$	$\rightarrow$	$(q$	$\lor$	$r)]$	$\land$	$\sim$	$[p$	$\leftrightarrow$	$\sim$	$r]$
T	T	T	T	T	T	T	T	T	T	T	F	F	T
T	T	F	T	T	T	T	F	F	F	T	T	T	F
T	F	T	T	T	F	T	T	T	T	T	F	F	T
T	F	F	T	F	F	F	F	F	F	T	T	T	F
F	T	T	F	T	T	T	T	F	F	F	T	F	T
F	T	F	F	T	T	T	F	T	T	F	F	T	F
F	F	T	F	T	F	T	T	F	F	F	T	F	T
F	F	F	F	T	F	F	F	T	T	F	F	T	F
Step No.			1	3	1	2	1	5	4	1	3	2	1

Figure 15

EXERCISES

1. One way of filling in the question-marked squares in Figure 11a is given in Figure 11b. There are three other possible ways.
   (a) Write the three other truth tables.
   (b) Show that each one of these truth tables has an interpretation in terms of the connectives now available to us.

2. Write truth tables for $q \lor p, q \land p, q \rightarrow p, q \leftrightarrow p$. Compare these with the truth tables in Figures 3, 1, 11b, and 12, respectively.

3. Construct truth tables for
   (a) $p \rightarrow (q \lor r)$.   [*Ans.* TTTFTTTT.]
   (b) $(p \lor r) \land (p \rightarrow q)$.   [*Ans.* TTFFTFTF.]
   (c) $(p \lor q) \leftrightarrow (q \lor p)$.   [*Ans.* TTTT.]
   (d) $p \land \sim p$.   [*Ans.* FF.]
   (e) $(p \rightarrow p) \lor (p \rightarrow \sim p)$.   [*Ans.* TT.]
   (f) $(p \lor \sim q) \land r$.   [*Ans.* TFTFFFTF.]
   (g) $[p \rightarrow (q \rightarrow r)] \rightarrow [(p \rightarrow q) \rightarrow (p \rightarrow r)]$.   [*Ans.* TTTTTTTT.]

4. For each of the following statements (i) find a symbolic form, and (ii) construct the truth table. Use the notation: p for "Joe is smart," q for "Jim is stupid," r for "Joe will get the prize."

(a) If Joe is smart and Jim is stupid, then Joe will get the prize.

[*Ans.* TFTTTTTT.]

(b) Joe will get the prize if and only if either he is smart or Jim is stupid.

[*Ans.* TFTFTFFT.]

(c) If Jim is stupid but Joe fails to get the prize, then Joe is not smart.

[*Ans.* Same as (a).]

5. Construct truth tables for each of the following, and give an interpretation.

(a) $(p \rightarrow q) \wedge (q \rightarrow p)$. (Compare with Figure 12.)

(b) $(p \wedge q) \rightarrow p$.

(c) $q \rightarrow (p \vee q)$.

(d) $(p \rightarrow q) \leftrightarrow (\sim p \vee q)$.

6. The truth table for a statement compounded from two simple statements has four rows, and the truth table for a statement compounded from three simple statements has eight rows. How many rows would the truth table for a statement compounded from four simple statements have? How many for five? For n? Devise a systematic way of writing down these latter truth tables.

7. Let p be "It is raining" and q be "The wind is blowing." Translate each of the following into symbolic form.

(a) If it rains, then the wind blows.

(b) If the wind blows, then it rains.

(c) The wind blows if and only if it rains.

(d) If the wind blows, then it does not rain.

(e) It is not the case that the wind blows if and only if it does not rain.

8. Construct truth tables for the statements in Exercise 7.

[*Ans.* TFTT; TTFT; TFFT; FTTT; TFFT.]

9. Construct truth tables for

(a) $(p \vee q) \leftrightarrow (\sim r \wedge \sim s)$.

(b) $(p \wedge q) \rightarrow \sim [\sim p \wedge (r \vee s)]$.

10. Construct a truth table for $\sim [(\sim p \wedge \sim q) \wedge (p \vee r)]$.

[*Ans.* TTTTTTFT.]

11. Find a simpler statement having the same truth table as the one found in Exercise 10.

SUPPLEMENTARY EXERCISES

12. A compound statement in p and q must have one of 16 possible truth tables. Find all of these tables.

13. For the 16 truth tables found in Exercise 12, show that eight represent negations of eight others.

14. Find a simple compound statement for each of the 16 truth tables found in Exercise 12. [*Hint:* Use the result of Exercise 13.]

15. Construct the truth table of

$$p \to ((r \lor q) \leftrightarrow \sim (r \land s))$$

16. Show that the truth table in Exercise 15 can be constructed much more quickly by identifying the cases in which the statement is false.

[*Ans.* False in cases TTTT, TFTT, TFFT, TFFF.]

*4. STATEMENTS HAVING GIVEN TRUTH TABLES

In the preceding two sections we showed how to construct the truth table for any compound statement. It is also interesting to consider the converse problem, namely, given a truth table to find one or more statements having this truth table. The converse problem always has a solution and, in fact, a solution using only the connectives $\land$, $\lor$, and $\sim$. The discussion which we give here is valid only for a truth table in three variables but can easily be extended to cover the case of n variables.

As observed in the last section, a truth table with three variables has eight rows, one for each of the eight possible triples of truth values. Suppose that our given truth table has its last column consisting entirely of F's. Then it is easy to check that the truth table of the statement $p \land \sim p$ also has only F's in its last column, so that this statement serves as an answer to our problem. We now need consider only truth tables having one or more T's. The method that we shall use is to construct statements that are true in one case only, and then to construct the desired statement as a disjunction of these.

It is not hard to construct statements that are true in only one case. In Figure 16 are listed eight such statements, each true in exactly

p	q	r	Basic Conjunctions
T	T	T	$p \wedge q \wedge r$
T	T	F	$p \wedge q \wedge \sim r$
T	F	T	$p \wedge \sim q \wedge r$
T	F	F	$p \wedge \sim q \wedge \sim r$
F	T	T	$\sim p \wedge q \wedge r$
F	T	F	$\sim p \wedge q \wedge \sim r$
F	F	T	$\sim p \wedge \sim q \wedge r$
F	F	F	$\sim p \wedge \sim q \wedge \sim r$

Figure 16

one case. We shall call such statements *basic conjunctions*. Such a basic conjunction contains each variable or its negation, depending on whether the line on which it appears in Figure 16 has a T or an F under the variable. Observe that the disjunction of two such basic conjunctions will be true in exactly two cases, the disjunction of three in three cases, etc. Therefore, to find a statement having a given truth table simply form the disjunction of those basic conjunctions which occur in Figure 16 on the rows where the given truth table has T's.

Example 1. Find a statement whose truth table has T's in the first, second, and last rows, and F's in the other rows. The required statement is the disjunction of the first, second, and eighth basic conjunctions, that is,

$$(p \wedge q \wedge r) \vee (p \wedge q \wedge \sim r) \vee (\sim p \wedge \sim q \wedge \sim r).$$

Exercise 2 asks the student to show that this statement has the required truth table.

Example 2. A logician is captured by a tribe of savages and placed in a jail having two exits. The savage chief offers the captive the following chance to escape: "One of the doors leads to certain death and the other to freedom. You can leave by either door. To help you in making a decision, two of my warriors will stay with you and answer any one question which you wish to ask of them. I must warn you, however, that one of my warriors is completely truthful while the other always lies." The chief then leaves, believing that he has given his captive only a sporting chance to escape.

After thinking a moment, our quick-witted logician asks one question and then chooses the door leading to freedom. What question did he ask?

Let p be the statement "The first door leads to freedom" and q be the statement "You are truthful." It is clear that p and q are useless questions in themselves, so let us try compound statements. We want to ask a single question for which a "yes" answer means that p is true and a "no" answer means that p is false, regardless of which warrior is asked the question. The answers desired to these questions are listed in Figure 17.

p	q	Desired Answer	Truth Table of Question
T	T	yes	T
T	F	yes	F
F	T	no	F
F	F	no	T

Figure 17

The next thing to consider is, what would be the truth table of a question having the desired answers. If the warrior answers "yes" and if he is truthful, that is, if q is true, then the truth value is T. But if he answers "yes" and he is a liar, that is, if q is false, then the truth value is F. A similar analysis holds if the answer is "no." The truth values of the desired question are shown in Figure 17.

Therefore we have reduced the problem to that of finding a statement having the truth table of Figure 17. Following the general method outlined above, we see that the statement

$$(p \wedge q) \vee (\sim p \wedge \sim q)$$

will do. Hence the logician asks the question: "Does the first door lead to freedom and are you truthful, or does the second door lead to freedom and are you lying?" The reader can show (Exercise 3) that the statement $p \leftrightarrow q$ also has the truth table given in Figure 17, hence a shorter equivalent question would be: "Does the first door lead to freedom if and only if you are truthful?"

As can be seen in Example 2, the method does not necessarily yield the simplest possible compound statement. However it has two advantages: (1) It gives us a mechanical method of finding a statement that solves the problem. (2) The statement appears in a standard form. The latter will be made use of in designing switching circuits (see Section 12).

EXERCISES

1. Show that each of the basic conjunctions in Figure 16 has a truth table consisting of one T appearing in the row in which the statement appears in Figure 16, and all the rest F's.

2. Find the truth table of the compound statement constructed in Example 1.

3. Show in Example 2 that the statement $p \leftrightarrow q$ has the truth table of Figure 17.

4. Construct one or more compound statements having each of the following truth tables, (a), (b), and (c).

p	q	r	(a)	(b)	(c)
T	T	T	T	F	T
T	T	F	F	F	T
T	F	T	T	F	T
T	F	F	F	T	F
F	T	T	F	F	T
F	T	F	F	F	T
F	F	T	T	F	F
F	F	F	F	F	T

5. Using only $\vee$, $\wedge$, and $\sim$, write a statement equivalent to each of the following.
   (a) $p \leftrightarrow q$.
   (b) $p \rightarrow q$.
   (c) $\sim(p \rightarrow q)$.

6. Using only $\vee$ and $\sim$, write down a statement equivalent to $p \wedge q$. Use this result to prove that any truth table can be represented by means of the two connectives $\vee$ and $\sim$.

In Exercises 7–10 we will study the new connective $\downarrow$, where $p \downarrow q$ expresses "neither p nor q."

7. Construct the truth table of $p \downarrow q$.

8. Construct the truth table for $p \downarrow p$. What other compound has this truth table?   [*Ans.* Same as Figure 5.]

9. Construct the truth table for $(p \downarrow q) \downarrow (p \downarrow q)$. What other compound has this truth table?   [*Ans.* Same as Figure 3.]

10. Use the results of Exercises 6, 8, and 9 to show that any truth table can be represented by means of the single connective $\downarrow$.

11. Use the results of Exercises 9 and 10 following Section 2 to show that any truth table can be represented by means of the single connective $|$.

12. Write down a compound of p, q, r which is true if and only if exactly one of the three components is true.

13. The "basic conjunctions" for statements having only one variable are p and $\sim p$. Discuss the various compound statements that can be formed by disjunctions of these. How do these relate to the possible truth tables for statements of one variable? What can be asserted about an arbitrary compound, no matter how long, that contains only the variable p?
                    [*Partial Ans.* There are four possible truth tables.]

14. In Example 2 there is a second question, having a different truth table than that in Figure 17, which the logician can ask. What is it?

15. A student is confronted with a true-false exam, consisting of five questions. He knows that his instructor always has more true than false questions, and that he never has three questions in a row with the same answer. From the nature of the first and last questions he knows that these must have the opposite answer. The only question to which he knows the answer is number two. And this *assures* him of having all answers correct. What did he know about question two? What is the answer to the five questions?
                                                                [*Ans.* TFTTF.]

5. LOGICAL POSSIBILITIES

One of the most important contributions that mathematics can make to the solution of a scientific problem is to provide an exhaustive analysis of the logical possibilities for the problem. The role of science is then to discover facts which will eliminate all but one possibility. Or, if this cannot be achieved, at least science tries to estimate the probabilities of the various possibilities.

So far we have considered only a very special case of the analysis of logical possibilities, namely truth tables. We started with a small number of given statements, say p, q, and r, and we assumed that all the truth table cases were possible. This amounts to assuming that the three statements are logically unrelated (see Section 8). Then we could determine the truth or falsity of every compound statement formed from p, q, and r for every truth table case (every logical possibility).

But there are many more statements whose truth cannot be analyzed in terms of the eight truth table cases discussed above. For example, $\sim p \vee (q \wedge r \wedge \sim s)$ requires a finer analysis, a truth table with 16 cases.

Many of these ideas are applicable in a more general setting. Let us suppose that we have an analysis of logical possibilities. That is, we have a list of eventualities, such that one and only one of them can possibly be true. We know this partly from the framework in which the problem is considered, and partly as a matter of pure logic. We then consider *statements relative to this set of possibilities.* These are statements whose truth or falsity can be determined for each logical possibility. For example, the set of possibilities may be the eight truth table cases, and the statements relative to these possibilities are the compound statements formed from p, q, and r. But we should consider a more typical example.

Example 1. Let us consider the following problem, which is of a type often studied in probability theory. "There are two urns; the first contains two black balls and one white ball, while the second contains one black ball and two white balls. Select an urn at random and draw two balls in succession from it. What is the probability

Case	Urn	First Ball	Second Ball
1	1	black	black
2	1	black	white
3	1	white	black
4	2	black	white
5	2	white	black
6	2	white	white

Figure 18

that . . . ?" Without raising questions of probability, let us ask what
the possibilities are. Figures 18 and 19 give us two ways of analyzing
the logical possibilities.

Case	Urn	First Ball	Second Ball
1	1	black no. 1	black no. 2
2	1	black no. 2	black no. 1
3	1	black no. 1	white
4	1	black no. 2	white
5	1	white	black no. 1
6	1	white	black no. 2
7	2	black	white no. 1
8	2	black	white no. 2
9	2	white no. 1	black
10	2	white no. 2	black
11	2	white no. 1	white no. 2
12	2	white no. 2	white no. 1

Figure 19

In Figure 18 we have analyzed the possibilities as far as colors of
balls drawn was concerned. Such an analysis may be sufficient for
many purposes. In Figure 19 we have carried out a finer analysis, in
which we distinguished between balls of the same color in an urn.
For some purposes the finer analysis may be necessary.

It is important to realize that the possibilities in a given problem may
be analyzed in many different ways, from a very rough grouping to a
highly refined one. The only requirements on an analysis of logical
possibilities are:

(1) That under any conceivable circumstances one and only one of these possibilities must be the case, and

(2) that the analysis is fine enough so that the truth value of each statement under consideration in the problem is determined in each case.

It is easy to verify that both analyses (Figures 18 and 19) satisfy the first condition. Whether the rougher analysis will satisfy the second condition depends on the nature of the problem. If we can limit ourselves to statements like "Two black balls are drawn from the first urn," then it suffices. But if we wish to consider "The first black ball is drawn after the second black ball from the first urn," then the finer analysis is needed.

Given the analysis of logical possibilities, we can ask for each assertion about the problem, and for each logical possibility, whether the assertion is true in this case. Normally, for a given statement there will be many cases in which it is true and many in which it is false. Logic will be able to do no more than to point out the cases in which the statement is true. In Example 1, the statement "One white ball and one black ball is drawn" is true (in Figure 18) in cases 2, 3, 4, and 5, and false in cases 1 and 6. However, there are two notable exceptions, namely, a statement that is true in every logically possible case, and one that is false in every case. Here logic alone suffices to determine the truth value.

A statement that is true in every logically possible case is said to be *logically true.* The truth of such a statement follows from the meaning of the words and the form of the statement, together with the context of the problem about which the statement is made. We will see several examples of logically true statements below. A statement that is false in every logically possible case is said to be *logically false*, or to be a *self-contradiction.* For example, the conjunction of any statement with its own negation will always be a self-contradiction, since it cannot be true under any circumstances.

In Example 1, the statement "At most two black balls are drawn" is true in every case, in either analysis. Hence this statement is logically true. It follows from the very definition of the problem that we cannot draw more than two balls. Hence, also, the statement "Draw three white balls" is logically false.

What the logical possibilities are for a given set of statements will depend on the context, i.e., on the problem that is being considered. Unless we know what the possibilities are, we have not understood the task before us. This does not preclude that there may be several ways of analyzing the logical possibilities. In Example 1 above, for example, we gave two different analyses, and others could be found. In general, the question "How many cases are there in which p is true" will depend on the analysis given. (This will be of importance in our study of probability theory.) However, note that a statement that is logically true (false) according to one analysis will be logically true (false) according to every other analysis of the given problem.

The truth table analysis is often the roughest possible analysis. There may be hundreds of logical possibilities, but if all we are interested in are compounds formed from p and q, we need only know when p and q are true or false. For example, a statement of the form $p \rightarrow (p \lor q)$ will have to be true in every conceivable case. We may have a hundred cases, giving varying truth values for p and q, but every such case must correspond to one of the four truth table cases, as far as the compound is concerned. In each of these four cases the compound is true, and therefore such a statement is logically true. An example of it is "If Jones is smart, then he is smart or lucky."

However, if the components are logically related, then a truth table analysis may not be adequate. Let p be the statement "Jim is taller than Bill," while q is "Bill is taller than Jim." And consider the statement, "Either Jim is not taller than Bill or Bill is not taller than Jim," i.e., $\sim p \lor \sim q$. If we work the truth table of this compound, we find that it is false in the first case. But this case is not logically possible, since under no circumstances can p and q both be true! Our compound is logically true, but a truth table will not show this. Had we made a careful analysis of the possibilities as to the heights of the two men, we would have found that the compound statement is true in every case. (Such relations will be considered in Section 8. This particular pair of statements will be considered in Exercise 11 in that section.)

Example 2. The Miracle Filter Company conducts an annual survey of the smoking habits of adult Americans. The results of the survey are organized into 25 files, corresponding to the 25 cases in Figure 20.

Case	Sex	Educational Level	Occupation
1	male	0	prof.
2	male	0	non-prof.
3	male	1	prof.
4	male	1	non-prof.
5	male	2	prof.
6	male	2	non-prof.
7	male	3	prof.
8	male	3	non-prof.
9	male	4	prof.
10	male	4	non-prof.
11	female	0	housewife
12	female	0	prof.
13	female	0	non-prof.
14	female	1	housewife
15	female	1	prof.
16	female	1	non-prof.
17	female	2	housewife
18	female	2	prof.
19	female	2	non-prof.
20	female	3	housewife
21	female	3	prof.
22	female	3	non-prof.
23	female	4	housewife
24	female	4	prof.
25	female	4	non-prof.

Figure 20

First, figures are kept separately for men and women. Secondly, the educational level is noted according to the following code:

0 did not finish high school
1 finished high school, no college
2 some college, but no degree
3 college graduate, but no graduate work
4 did some graduate work

Finally, there is a rough occupational classification: housewife, salaried professional, or salaried non-professional.

They have found that this classification is adequate for their purposes. For instance, to get figures on all adults in their survey who did not go beyond high school, they pull out the files numbered 1, 2, 3, 4, 11, 12, 13, 14, 15, and 16. Or they can locate data on male professional workers by looking at files 1, 3, 5, 7, and 9.

According to their analysis, the statement "The person is a housewife, professional, or non-professional" is logically true, while the statement "The person has educational level greater than 3, is neither professional nor non-professional, but not a female with graduate education" is a self-contradiction. The former statement is true about all 25 files, the latter about none.

Of course, they may at some time be forced to consider a finer analysis of logical possibilities. For instance, "The person is a male with annual income over $10,000" is *not* a statement relative to the given possibilities. We could choose a case—say case 6—and the given statement may be either true or false in this case. Thus the analysis is not fine enough.

Of all the logical possibilities, one and only one represents the facts as they are. That is, for a given person, one and only one of the 25 cases is a correct description. To know which one, we need factual information. When we say that a certain statement is "true," without qualifying it, we mean that it is true in this one case. But, as we have said before, what the case actually is lies outside the domain of logic. Logic can tell us only what the circumstances (logical possibilities) are under which a statement is true.

EXERCISES

1. Prove that the negation of a logically true statement is logically false, and the negation of a logically false statement is logically true.

2. Classify the following as (i) logically true, (ii) a self-contradiction, (iii) neither.

    (a) $p \leftrightarrow p$.   [*Ans.* Logically true.]

    (b) $p \rightarrow \sim p$.

    (c) $(p \vee q) \leftrightarrow (p \wedge q)$.   [*Ans.* Neither.]

    (d) $(p \rightarrow \sim q) \rightarrow (q \rightarrow \sim p)$.

    (e) $(p \rightarrow q) \wedge (q \rightarrow r) \wedge \sim(p \rightarrow r)$.   [*Ans.* Self-contradiction.]

    (f) $(p \rightarrow q) \rightarrow p$.

    (g) $[(p \rightarrow q) \rightarrow p] \rightarrow p$.

3. Figure 20 gives the possible classifications of one person in the survey. How many cases do we get if we classify two people jointly?   [*Ans.* 625.]

4. For each of the 25 cases in Figure 20 state whether the following statement is true: "The person has had some college education, and if the person is female then she is a housewife."

5. In Example 1, with the logical possibilities given by Figure 18, state the cases in which the following statements are true.
   (a) Urn one is selected.
   (b) At least one white ball is drawn.
   (c) At most one white ball is drawn.
   (d) If the first ball drawn is white, then the second is black.
   (e) Two balls of different color are drawn if and only if urn one is selected.

6. In Example 1 give two logically true and two logically false statements (other than those in the text).

7. In a college using grades A, B, C, D, and F, how many logically possible report cards are there for a student taking four courses?   [*Ans.* 625.]

8. A man has nine coins totaling 78 cents. What are the logical possibilities for the distribution of the coins? [*Hint:* There are three possibilities.]

9. In Exercise 8, which of the following statements are logically true and which are logically false?
   (a) He has at least one penny.   [*Ans.* Logically true.]
   (b) He has at least one nickel.   [*Ans.* Neither.]
   (c) He has exactly two nickels.   [*Ans.* Logically false.]
   (d) He has exactly three nickels if and only if he has exactly one dime.
                                                  [*Ans.* Logically true.]

10. In Exercise 8 we are told that the man has no nickel in his possession. What can we infer from this?

11. Two dice are rolled. Which of the following analyses satisfy the first condition for logical possibilities? What is wrong with the others?
   The sum of the numbers shown is:
   (a): (1) 6, (2) not 6.
   (b): (1) an even number, (2) less than 6, (3) greater than 6.
   (c): (1) 2, (2) 3, (3) 4, (4) more than 4.
   (d): (1) 7 or 11, (2) 2, 3, or 12, (3) 4, 5, 6, 8, 9, or 10.
   (e): (1) 2, 4, or 6, (2) an odd number, (3) 10 or 12.
   (f): (1) less than 5 or more than 8, (2) 5 or 6, (3) 7, (4) 8.
   (g): (1) more than 5 and less than 10, (2) at most 4, (3) 7, (4) 11 or 12.
                     [*Ans.* (a), (c), (d), (f) satisfy the condition.]

SUPPLEMENTARY EXERCISES

Note: These exercises refer to the following example: There are three urns. The first one contains two black balls. The second one contains one black and two white balls, while the third contains two black and two white balls. We select an urn, and draw two balls.

12. Construct a table of the logical possibilities, similar to Figure 18.

[*Partial Ans.* There are eight cases.]

13. In which cases is the statement "One black and one white ball is drawn" true?

14. What is the status of the statement "Urn 1 is selected, and two different color balls are drawn"? [*Ans.* Logically false.]

15. Find the cases in which the statement "Urn 1 is selected if and only if two black balls are drawn" is true.

16. How does the list of possibilities change if we don't care about the order in which the balls are drawn?

6. TREE DIAGRAMS

A very useful tool for the analysis of logical possibilities is the drawing of a "tree." This device will be illustrated by several examples.

Example 1. Consider again the survey of the Miracle Filter Company. They keep two large filing cabinets, one for men and one for women. Each cabinet has five drawers, corresponding to the five educational levels. Each drawer is subdivided according to occupations; drawers in the filing cabinet for men have two large folders, while in the other cabinet each drawer has three folders.

When a clerk files a new piece of information, he first has to find the right cabinet, then the correct drawer, and then the appropriate folder. This three-step process of filing is shown in Figure 21. For obvious reasons we shall call a figure like this, which starts at a point and branches out, a *tree*.

Observe that the tree contains all the information relevant to classifying a person interviewed. There are 25 ways of starting at the bottom and following a path to the top. The 25 paths represent the 25 cases in Figure 20. The order in which we performed the classification is

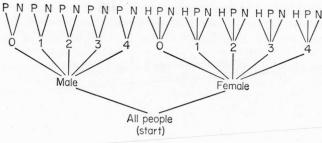

Figure 21

arbitrary. We might as well have classified first according to educational level, then according to occupation, and then according to sex. We would still obtain a tree representing the 25 logical possibilities, but the tree would look quite different. (See Exercise 1.)

Example 2. Next let us consider the example of Figure 18. This is a three-stage process; first we select an urn, then draw a ball and then draw a second ball. The tree of logical possibilities is shown in Figure 22. We note that six is the correct number of logical possibili-

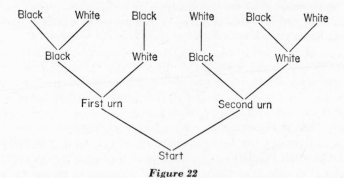

Figure 22

ties. The reason for this is: If we choose the first urn (which contains two black balls and one white ball) and draw from it a black ball, then the second draw may be of either color; however, if we draw a white ball first, then the second ball drawn is necessarily black. Similar remarks apply if the second urn is chosen.

Example 3. As a final example, let us construct the tree of logical possibilities for the outcomes of a World Series played between the Dodgers and the Yankees. In Figure 23 is shown half of the tree,

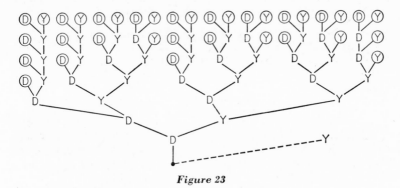

Figure 23

corresponding to the case when the Dodgers win the first game (the dotted line at the bottom leads to the other half of the tree). In the figure a "D" stands for a Dodger win and "Y" for a Yankee win. There are 35 possible outcomes (corresponding to the circled letters) in the half-tree shown, so that the World Series can end in 70 ways.

This example is different from the previous two in that the paths of the tree end at different levels, corresponding to the fact that the World Series ends whenever one of the teams has won four games.

Not always do we wish as detailed an analysis as that provided in the examples above. If, in Example 2, we wanted to know only the color and order in which the balls were drawn and not which urn they came from, then there would be only four logical possibilities instead of six. Then in Figure 22 the second and fourth paths (counting from the left) represent the same outcome, namely, a black ball followed by a white ball. Similarly, the third and fifth paths represent the same outcome. Finally, if we cared only about the color of the balls drawn, not the order, then there are only three logical possibilities: two black balls, two white balls, or one black and one white ball.

A less detailed analysis of the possibilities for the World Series is also possible. For example, we can analyze the possibilities as follows: Dodgers in four, five, six, or seven games, and Yankees in four, five, six, or seven games. The new classification reduced the number of possibilities from 70 to eight. The other possibilities have not been eliminated but merely grouped together. Thus the statement "Dodgers in four games" can happen in only one way, while "Dodgers in seven games" can happen in 20 ways (see Figure 23). A still less detailed analysis would be a classification according to the number of games in the series. Here there are only four logical possibilities.

The student will find that it often requires several trials before the "best" way of listing logical possibilities is found for a given problem.

EXERCISES

1. Construct a tree for Example 1, if people are first classified according to educational level, then according to profession, and finally according to sex. Is the shape of the tree the same as in Figure 21? Does it represent the same possibilities?

2. In 1965 the Dodgers lost the first two games of the World Series, but won the series in the end. In how many ways can the series go so that the losing team wins the first two games?   [*Ans.* 10.]

3. The following is a typical process in genetics: Each parent has two genes for a given trait, AA or Aa or aa. The child will inherit one gene from each parent. What are the possibilities for a child if both parents are AA? What if one is AA and the other aa? What if one is AA and the other Aa? What if both are Aa? Construct a tree for each process. [Let stage one be the choice of a gene from the first parent, stage two from the second parent. Then see how many different types the resulting branches represent.]

4. It is often the case that types AA and Aa (see Exercise 3) are indistinguishable from the outside, but easily distinguishable from type aa. What are the logical possibilities if the two parents are of noticeably different types?

5. In nominating candidates for President and Vice President, a major party takes into account the sex of the candidate, and the part of the country from which he comes. For the latter purpose they identify four regions: East, Midwest, South, and West. Draw a tree for the various possibilities in selecting a pair of candidates.

    (a) How many cases are there?

    (b) How many are there if the two candidates must not come from the same part of the country?

    (c) How many are there if, in addition, the party refuses to nominate two women?   [*Ans.* (c) 36.]

6. We set up an experiment similar to that of Figure 18, but urn 1 has two black balls and two white balls, while urn 2 has one white ball and four black balls. We select an urn, and draw three balls from it. Construct the tree of logical possibilities. How many cases are there? [*Ans.* 10.]

7. From the tree constructed in Exercise 6 answer the following questions.
   (a) In how many cases do we draw three black balls?
   (b) In how many cases do we draw two black balls and one white ball?
   (c) In how many cases do we draw three white balls?
   (d) How many cases does this leave? What cases are these?

   [*Partial Ans.* 3.]

8. In how many ways can the World Series be played (see Figure 23) if the Dodgers win the first game and
   (a) No team wins two games in a row. [*Ans.* 1.]
   (b) The Dodgers win at least the odd-numbered games. [*Ans.* 5.]
   (c) The winning team wins four games in a row. [*Ans.* 4.]
   (d) The losing team wins four games. [*Ans.* 0.]

9. A man is considering the purchase of one of four types of stocks. Each stock may go up, go down, or stay the same after his purchase. Draw the tree of logical possibilities.

10. For the tree constructed in Exercise 9 give a statement which
    (a) Is true in half the cases.
    (b) Is false in all but one case.
    (c) Is true in all but one case.
    (d) Is logically true.
    (e) Is logically false.

11. In Exercise 6 we wish to make a rougher classification of logical possibilities. What branches (in the tree there constructed) become identical if
    (a) We do not care about the order in which the balls are drawn.
    (b) We care neither about the order of balls, nor about the number of the urn selected.
    (c) We care only about what urn is selected, and whether the balls drawn are all the same color.

12. Work Exercise 7 of the last section by sketching a tree diagram.

13. A menu lists a choice of soup or orange juice for an appetizer, a choice of steak, chicken, or fish for the entree, and a choice of pie or cake for dessert. A complete dinner consists of one choice in each case. Draw the tree for the possible complete dinners.
    (a) How many different complete dinners are possible? [*Ans.* 12.]
    (b) How many complete dinners are there which have chicken for the entree? [*Ans.* 4.]
    (c) How many complete dinners are there available for a man who will eat pie only if he had steak for the entree? [*Ans.* 8.]

SUPPLEMENTARY EXERCISES

14. In how many different ways can 55 cents change be given, using quarters, dimes, and nickels? Draw a tree. [*Hint:* To eliminate duplication, require that larger coins be handed out before smaller ones. Let the branches of the tree be labelled with the number of coins of each type handed out.]

[*Ans.* 11.]

15. Redraw the tree of Exercise 14, requiring that smaller coins be handed out before larger ones.

16. What is the answer to Exercise 14 if only one nickel is available?

17. Draw a tree for Exercise 12 in Section 5.

18. In electing the chairman of a small committee, candidate A receives two votes, and candidate B receives one. Draw a tree to represent the possible orders in which the three ballots are counted. In what fraction of the cases is A ahead all the way?

19. Redo Exercise 18 for the election in which A receives four votes and B receives two.   [*Ans.* $\frac{1}{3}$ of the cases.]

7. LOGICAL RELATIONS

Until now we have considered statements in isolation. Sometimes, however, we want to consider the relationship between pairs of statements. The most interesting such relation is that one statement (logically) *implies* the other one. If r implies s we also say that s follows from r, or that s is (logically) deducible from r. For instance, in any mathematical theorem the hypothesis implies the conclusion.

If we have listed all logical possibilities, then we shall characterize implication as follows: r implies s if s is true whenever r is true, i.e., if s is true in all the logically possible cases in which r is true.

For compound statements having the same components, truth tables provide a convenient method for testing this relation. In Figure 24 we illustrate this method. Let us take $p \leftrightarrow q$ as our hypothesis r. Since it is true only in the first and fourth cases, and $p \rightarrow q$ is true in both these cases, we see that the statement $p \leftrightarrow q$ implies $p \rightarrow q$. On the other hand, the statement $p \lor q$ is false in the fourth case and hence it is not implied by $p \leftrightarrow q$. Again, a comparison of the last two columns of Figure 24 shows that the statement $p \rightarrow q$ does not imply and is not implied by $p \lor q$.

The relation of implication has a close affinity to the conditional statement, but it is important not to confuse the two. The conditional is a new *statement* compounded from two given statements, while implication is a *relation* between the two statements. The connection is the following: r implies s if and only if the conditional $r \rightarrow s$ is logically true.

That this is the case is shown by a simple argument. The statement r implies the statement s if s is true whenever r is true. This means that there is no case in which r is true and s false, i.e., no case in which $r \rightarrow s$ is false. But this in turn means that $r \rightarrow s$ is logically true. In Exercise 1 this result will be applied to Figure 24.

p	q	$p \leftrightarrow q$	$p \rightarrow q$	$p \vee q$
T	T	T	T	T
T	F	F	F	T
F	T	F	T	T
F	F	T	T	F

Figure 24

Let us now take up the "paradoxes" of the conditional. Conditional statements sound paradoxical when the components are not related. For example, it sounds strange to say that "If it is a nice day then chalk is made of wood" is true on a rainy day. It must be remembered that the conditional statement just quoted means no more and no less than that one of the following holds: (1) It is a nice day and chalk is made of wood, or (2) It is not a nice day and chalk is made of wood, or (3) It is not a nice day and chalk is not made of wood. [See Figure 11b.] And on a rainy day number (3) happens to be correct.

But it is by no means true that "It is a nice day" implies that "Chalk is made of wood." It is logically possible for the former to be true and for the latter to be false (indeed, this is the case on a nice day, with the usual method of chalk manufacture), hence the implication does not hold. Thus, while the conditional quoted in the previous paragraph is true on a given day, it is not logically true.

In common parlance "if . . . then . . ." is usually asserted on logical grounds. Hence any usage in which such an assertion happens to be true, but is not logically true, sounds paradoxical. Similar remarks apply to the common usage of "if and only if."

If the biconditional $r \leftrightarrow s$ is not only true but logically true, then this establishes a relation between r and s. If $r \leftrightarrow s$ is true in every logically possible case, then the statements r and s have the same truth value in every case. We say, under these circumstances, that r and s are (logically) *equivalent*. For compound statements having the same components, the truth table provides a convenient means of testing for equivalence. We merely have to verify that the compounds have the same truth table. Figure 25 establishes that $\sim p \wedge \sim q$ is equivalent

p	q	$\sim p \wedge \sim q$	$\sim(p \vee q)$
T	T	F	F
T	F	F	F
F	T	F	F
F	F	T	T

Figure 25

to $\sim(p \vee q)$. This is one of the so-called *De Morgan laws*. (See Exercise 13.)

A third important relationship is that of inconsistency. Statements r and s are *inconsistent* if it is impossible for both of them to be true, in other words, if $r \wedge s$ is a self-contradiction. For example, the statements $p \wedge q$ and $\sim q$ are inconsistent. An important use of logic is to check for inconsistencies in a set of assumptions or beliefs.

EXERCISES

1. Show that $(p \leftrightarrow q) \rightarrow (p \rightarrow q)$ is logically true, but that $(p \leftrightarrow q) \rightarrow (p \vee q)$ is not logically true.

2. Prove that r is equivalent to s just in case r implies s and s implies r.

3. Construct truth tables for the following compounds, and test for implications and equivalences.

(a) $p \wedge q$.

(b) $p \rightarrow \sim q$.

(c) $\sim p \vee \sim q$.

(d) $\sim p \vee q$.

(e) $p \wedge \sim q$.   [*Ans.* (b) equiv. (c); (a) impl. (d); (e) impl. (b), (c).]

4. Construct truth tables for the following compounds, and arrange them in order so that each compound implies all the following ones.

(a) $\sim p \leftrightarrow q$.

(b) $p \rightarrow (\sim p \rightarrow q)$.

(c) $\sim[p \rightarrow (q \rightarrow p)]$.

(d) $p \vee q$.

(e) $\sim p \wedge q$.   [*Ans.* (c); (e); (a); (d); (b).]

5. Construct a compound equivalent to $p \wedge q$, using only the connectives $\sim$ and $\vee$.

6. Construct a compound equivalent to $p \leftrightarrow q$, using only the connectives $\rightarrow$ and $\wedge$. (Cf. Exercise 2.)

7. Construct a compound statement equivalent to $p \vee q$, using only the connectives $\sim$ and $\wedge$.

8. If p is logically true, prove that

(a) $p \vee q$ is logically true.

(b) $\sim p \wedge q$ is logically false.

(c) $p \wedge q$ is equivalent to q.

(d) $\sim p \vee q$ is equivalent to q.

9. If p and q are logically true and r is logically false, what is the status of $(p \vee \sim q) \wedge \sim r$?   [*Ans.* Logically true.]

10. Pick out an inconsistent pair from among the following four compound statements.

$$r:\quad p \vee q.$$
$$s:\quad p \rightarrow q.$$
$$t:\quad \sim q.$$
$$u:\quad \sim(q \rightarrow p).$$

11. What implications hold between pairs of statements in Exercise 10?   [*Ans. u* implies r and s.]

12. In Exercise 10, is there an inconsistent pair among r, s, and t? Is it possible that all three statements are true?

13. One of the De Morgan laws is established in Figure 25. The other one states that $\sim(p \wedge q)$ is equivalent to $\sim p \vee \sim q$. Prove this.

14. What relation exists between two logically true statements? Between two self-contradictions?

15. Prove that

(a) A logically true statement is implied by every statement, and that a self-contradiction implies every statement.

(b) The conjunction or disjunction of a statement with itself is equivalent to the statement.

(c) The double negation of a statement is equivalent to the statement.

(d) A statement which implies its own negation is a self-contradiction.

16. Using the results of Section 4, Exercises 10 and 11, prove that for any compound statement there is an equivalent compound statement

    (a) Whose only connective is $\downarrow$.

    (b) Whose only connective is $|$.

17. What is the status of a statement equivalent to its own negation?

[*Ans.* Impossible.]

*8. A SYSTEMATIC ANALYSIS OF LOGICAL RELATIONS

The relation of implication is characterized by the fact that it is impossible for the hypothesis to be true and the conclusion to be false. If two statements are equivalent, it is impossible for one to be true and the other to be false. Thus we see that for an implication one truth table case must not occur, and for an equivalence two of the four truth table cases must not occur. The absence of one or more truth table cases is thus characteristic of logical relations. In this section we shall investigate all conceivable relations that can exist between two statements.

p	q	Case No.
T	T	1
T	F	2
F	T	3
F	F	4

Figure 26

We shall say that two statements are *unrelated* if each of the four truth table cases (see Figure 26) can occur. The two statements are *related* if one or more of the four cases in Figure 26 cannot occur. [Cf. Section 5.]

If p and q are statements such that exactly one of the cases in Figure 26 is excluded, then we say that there is a *onefold* relation between them. Obviously there are four possible onefold relations which we list below. (a) If case 1 is excluded, the two statements cannot both be true. In this case p and q are said to be a pair of *contraries* or are said to be *inconsistent*. (b) If case 2 is excluded, then (cf. Section 7) p implies q. (c) If case 3 is excluded, it is false that q is true and p is false, that is, q implies p. (d) If case 4 is excluded, both statements cannot be false, i.e., at least one of them is true. Such a pair of statements is called a pair of *subcontraries*.

If p and q are statements such that exactly two of the cases in Figure 26 are excluded, then we say that there is a *twofold* relation between them. There are six ways in which two cases can be selected from four, but several of these do not produce interesting relations. For example, suppose cases 1 and 2 are excluded; then p cannot be true, i.e., it is logically false. Similarly, if cases 1 and 3 are excluded, then q is logically false. On the other hand, if cases 3 and 4 are excluded, then p is logically true; and if 2 and 4 are excluded, then q is logically true. Hence we see that these choices do not give us new relations; they merely indicate that one of the two statements is logically true or false. We now have only two alternatives remaining: (A) cases 2 and 3 are excluded, which means that the two statements are equivalent; and (B) cases 1 and 4 are excluded, which means that the two statements cannot both be true and cannot both be false, in other words, one must be true and the other false. We shall then say that p and q are *contradictories*, or a *pair of alternatives*.

It is not hard to see that there are no threefold relations, for if three of the cases in Figure 26 are excluded, then there is only one possibility for each of the two statements, so that each must be either logically true or logically false.

We have already discussed implication and equivalence and have noted their connection to the conditional and the biconditional, respectively. We can do the same for the three remaining relations. If p and q are subcontraries, then they cannot both be false; since this is the only case in which their disjunction is false, we see that p and q are subcontraries if and only if $p \lor q$ is logically true. If p and q are contraries, then they cannot both be true; since this is the only case in which their conjunction is true, we see that p and q are contraries if and only if $p \land q$ is logically false. Finally, if p and q are contradictories, then cases 1 and 4 of Figure 26 are excluded, hence $p \leftrightarrow q$ is logically false. (Note also that, if p and q are contradictories, then $p \lor q$ is logically true.) The table in Figure 27 gives a summary of the relevant facts about the six relations we have derived.

Subcontraries are not of great theoretical importance, but contraries and contradictories are very important. Each of these relations can be generalized to hold for more than two statements. If we have n different statements, not all of which can be true, then we say that they are *inconsistent*. Then the conjunction of these statements must be false. Special cases of inconsistent statements are the following: if $n = 1$,

Case(s) Excluded	Relation	Alternate Definition
T-T	Contraries	$p \wedge q$ logically false
F-F	Subcontraries	$p \vee q$ logically true
T-F	First implies second	$p \rightarrow q$ logically true
F-T	Second implies first	$q \rightarrow p$ logically true
T-F and F-T	Equivalents	$p \leftrightarrow q$ logically true
T-T and F-F	Contradictories	$p \leftrightarrow q$ logically false

Figure 27

then we have a single self-contradictory statement; and if $n = 2$, then we have a pair of inconsistent statements (i.e., a pair of contraries).

If we have n different statements such that one and only one of them can be true, then we say they form a *complete set of alternatives*. Again the special cases are: if $n = 1$, then we have a single logically true statement; and if $n = 2$, then we have a pair of contradictories.

Truth tables again furnish a method for recognizing when relations hold between statements. The examples below show how the method works.

Examples. Consider the five compound statements, all having the same components, which appear in Figure 28. Find all relations which exist between pairs of these statements.

p	q	$p \wedge q$	$\sim p \vee \sim q$	$\sim p \vee q$	$\sim p$	$p \rightarrow q$
T	T	T	F	T	F	T
T	F	F	T	F	F	F
F	T	F	T	T	T	T
F	F	F	T	T	T	T
Statement Number		1	2	3	4	5

Figure 28

First of all we note that statements 3 and 5 have identical truth tables, hence they are equivalent. Therefore we need consider only one of them, say statement 3. Statements 1 and 2 have exactly opposite truth tables, hence they are contradictories. Upon comparing statements 1 and 3 we find no T-F case, so that 1 implies 3. Since numbers 1 and 4 are never both true, they are contraries, while numbers 2 and 3 are never both false, so that they are subcontraries. Finally, upon comparing either 2 or 3 to 4 we find no F-T case and hence both are implied by 4. Thus the six relations we found above are all exemplified in Figure 28. Observe also that statements $\sim p$ and q give an example of a pair of unrelated statements. [Cf. Section 5.]

EXERCISES

1. Construct truth tables for the following four statements and state what relation (if any) holds between each of the six pairs formable.
   (a) $\sim p$.
   (b) $\sim q$.
   (c) $p \wedge \sim q$.
   (d) $\sim(\sim p \vee q)$.
   [*Ans.* (a) and (b) unrelated; (a) and (c), (d) contraries; (c), (d) imply (b); (c) equiv. (d).]

2. Construct truth tables for each of the following six statements. Give an example of an unrelated pair, and an example of each of the six possible relations among these.
   (a) $p \leftrightarrow q$.
   (b) $p \rightarrow q$.
   (c) $\sim p \wedge \sim q$.
   (d) $(p \wedge q) \vee (\sim p \wedge \sim q)$.
   (e) $\sim q$.
   (f) $p \wedge \sim q$.

3. Prove the following assertions.
   (a) The disjunction of two contradictory statements is logically true.
   (b) The contradictories of two contraries are subcontraries.

4. What is the relation between the following pair of statements?
   (a) $p \rightarrow [p \wedge \sim(q \vee r)]$.
   (b) $\sim p \vee (\sim q \wedge \sim r)$.   [*Ans.* Equivalent.]

5. At most how many of the following assertions can one person consistently believe?
   (a) Joe is smart.
   (b) Joe is unlucky.
   (c) Joe is lucky but not smart.

(d) If Joe is smart, then he is unlucky.

(e) Joe is smart if and only if he is lucky.

(f) Either Joe is smart, or he is lucky, but not both.   [*Ans.* 4.]

6. Prove the following assertions.

(a) The contradictories of two equivalent statements are equivalent.

(b) In a complete set of alternatives any two statements are contraries.

(c) If p and q are subcontraries, and if each implies r, then r is logically true.

7. Pick out a complete set of (four) alternatives from the following.

(a) It is raining but the wind is not blowing.

(b) It rains if and only if the wind blows.

(c) It is not the case that it rains and the wind blows.

(d) It is raining and the wind is blowing.

(e) It is neither raining nor is the wind blowing.

(f) It is not the case that it is raining or the wind is not blowing.

[*Ans.* (a); (d); (e); (f).]

8. What is the relation between $[p \vee \sim(q \vee r) \vee (p \wedge s)]$ and $\sim(p \wedge q \wedge r \wedge s)$?   [*Ans.* Subcontraries.]

9. Suppose that p and q are contraries. What is the relation between

(a) p and $\sim q$.

(b) $\sim p$ and q.

(c) $\sim p$ and $\sim q$.

(d) p and $\sim p$.

10. Let p, q, and r be three statements such that any two of them are unrelated. Discuss the possible relations among the three statements. [*Hint:* If we ignore the order of the statements, there are 16 such relations. The relations are at most fourfold. There are two fourfold relations, and 12 relations are found from these by excluding fewer cases. There are two other possible relations.]

11. In Section 5 we considered an example comparing the height of two men. Suppose that we allow for the possibilities: below 5 ft. 9 in., 5 ft. 9 in., 5 ft. 10 in., 5 ft. 11 in., 6 ft. 0 in., above 6 ft. We will, for the purpose of this problem, consider two men of the same height if they fall into the same category according to the above analysis.

(a) Construct the set of all possibilities for a pair of men, Jim and Bill.

(b) Find the cases in which "Jim is taller than Bill" is true.

(c) Find the cases where "Bill is taller than Jim" is true.

(d) Are all four truth table cases present?

(e) What is the relation between the two statements?

12. Construct the set of logical possibilities which classify a person with respect to sex and marital status.

(a) Show that "If the person is a bachelor, then he is unmarried" is logically true.

(b) Show that "If a person is an old maid, then the person is a man" is not logically false.

(c) Find the relation between "The person is a man" and "The person is a bachelor."

(d) Find a simple statement that is a subcontrary of "The person is a man" and is consistent with it.

*9. VARIANTS OF THE CONDITIONAL

The conditional of two statements differs from the biconditional and from disjunctions and conjunctions of these two in that it lacks symmetry. Thus $p \lor q$ is equivalent to $q \lor p$, $p \land q$ is equivalent to $q \land p$, and $p \leftrightarrow q$ is equivalent to $q \leftrightarrow p$; *but $p \to q$ is not equivalent to $q \to p$.* The latter statement, $q \to p$, is called the *converse* of $p \to q$. Many of the most common fallacies in thinking arise from a confusion of a statement with its converse.

It is of interest to consider conditionals formed from the statements p and q and their negations. The truth tables of four such conditionals together with their names are tabulated in Figure 29. We note that

		Conditional	Converse of Conditional	Converse of Contra- positive	Contra- positive
p	q	$p \to q$	$q \to p$	$\sim p \to \sim q$	$\sim q \to \sim p$
T	T	T	T	T	T
T	F	F	T	T	F
F	T	T	F	F	T
F	F	T	T	T	T

Figure 29

$p \to q$ is equivalent to $\sim q \to \sim p$. The latter is called the *contrapositive* of the former. For many arguments the contrapositive is a very useful form of the conditional. In the same manner the statement $\sim p \to \sim q$ is the converse of the contrapositive. Since the contrapositive is equivalent to $p \to q$, the converse of the former is equivalent to the converse of the latter as can be seen in Figure 29.

The use of conditionals seems to cause more trouble than the use of the other connectives, perhaps because of the lack of symmetry, but also perhaps because there are so many different ways of expressing conditionals. In many cases only a careful analysis of a conditional statement shows whether the person making the assertion means the given conditional or its converse. Indeed, sometimes he means both of these, i.e., he means the biconditional. (See Exercise 5.)

The statement "I will go for a walk only if the sun shines" is a variant of a conditional statement. A statement of the form "p only if q" is closely related to the statement "If p then q," but just how? Actually the two express the same idea. The statement "p only if q" states that "If $\sim q$ then $\sim p$" and hence is equivalent to "If p then q." Thus the statement at the beginning of the paragraph is equivalent to the statement, "If I go for a walk, then the sun will be shining."

Other phrases, in common use by mathematicians, which indicate a conditional statement are: "a necessary condition" and "a sufficient condition." To say that p is a sufficient condition for q means that if p takes place, then q will also take place. Hence the sentence "p is a sufficient condition for q" is equivalent to the sentence "If p then q."

Similarly, the sentence "p is a necessary condition for q" is equivalent to "q only if p." Since we know that the latter is equivalent to "If q then p," it follows that the assertion of a necessary condition is the converse of the assertion of a sufficient condition.

Finally, if both a conditional statement and its converse are asserted, then effectively the biconditional statement is being asserted. Hence the assertion "p is a necessary and sufficient condition for q" is equivalent to the assertion "p if and only if q."

These various equivalences are summarized in Figure 30.

Basic Statement	Equivalent Forms
If p then q	p only if q p is a sufficient condition for q
If q then p	q only if p p is a necessary condition for q
p if and only if q	p is a necessary and sufficient condition for q

Figure 30

EXERCISES

1. Let p stand for "I will pass this course" and q for "I will do homework regularly." Put the following statements into symbolic form.
- (a) I will pass the course only if I do homework regularly.
- (b) Doing homework regularly is a necessary condition for me to pass this course.
- (c) Passing this course is a sufficient condition for me to do homework regularly.
- (d) I will pass this course if and only if I do homework regularly.
- (e) Doing homework regularly is a necessary and sufficient condition for me to pass this course.

2. Take the statement in part (a) of the previous exercise. Form its converse, its contrapositive, and the converse of the contrapositive. For each of these give both a verbal and a symbolic form.

3. Let p stand for "It snows" and q for "The train is late." Put the following statements into symbolic form.
- (a) Snowing is a sufficient condition for the train to be late.
- (b) Snowing is a necessary and sufficient condition for the train to be late.
- (c) The train is late only if it snows.

4. Take the statement in part (a) of the previous exercise. Form its converse, its contrapositive, and the converse of its contrapositive. Give a verbal form of each of them.

5. Prove that the conjunction of a conditional and its converse is equivalent to the biconditional.

6. To what is the conjunction of the contrapositive and its converse equivalent? Prove it.

7. Prove that
- (a) $\sim\sim p$ is equivalent to p.
- (b) The contrapositive of the contrapositive is equivalent to the original conditional.

8. "For a matrix to have an inverse it is necessary that its determinant be different from zero." Which of the following statements follow from this? [No knowledge of matrices is required.]
- (a) For a matrix to have an inverse it is sufficient that its determinant be zero.
- (b) For its determinant to be different from zero it is sufficient for the matrix to have an inverse.

  (c) For its determinant to be zero it is necessary that the matrix have no inverse.

  (d) A matrix has an inverse if and only if its determinant is not zero.

  (e) A matrix has a zero determinant only if it has no inverse.

$[Ans.$ (b); (c); (e).]

9. "A function that is differentiable is continuous." This statement is true for all functions, but its converse is not always true. Which of the following statements are true for all functions? [No knowledge of functions is required.]

  (a) A function is differentiable only if it is continuous.

  (b) A function is continuous only if it is differentiable.

  (c) Being differentiable is a necessary condition for a function to be continuous.

  (d) Being differentiable is a sufficient condition for a function to be continuous.

  (e) Being differentiable is a necessary and sufficient condition for a function to be differentiable. $[Ans.$ (a); (d); (e).]

10. Prove that the negation of "p is a necessary and sufficient condition for q" is equivalent to "p is a necessary and sufficient condition for $\sim q$."

*10. VALID ARGUMENTS

One of the most important tasks of a logician is the checking of *arguments*. By an argument we shall mean the assertion that a certain statement (the *conclusion*) follows from other statements (the *premises*). An argument will be said to be *valid* if and only if the conjunction of the premises implies the conclusion, i.e., if the premises are all true, the conclusion *must* also be true.

It is important to realize that the truth of the conclusion is irrelevant as far as the test of the validity of the argument goes. A true conclusion is neither necessary nor sufficient for the validity of the argument. The two examples below show this, and they also show the form in which we shall state arguments, i.e., first we state the premises, then draw a line, and then state the conclusion.

Example 1.

If the United States is a democracy, then its
citizens have the right to vote.
Its citizens do have the right to vote.
Therefore the United States is a democracy.

The conclusion is, of course, true. However, the argument is not valid since the conclusion does not follow from the two premises.

Example 2.

> To pass this Math course you must be a genius.
> Every player on the football team has passed this course.
> The captain of the football team is not a genius.
> Therefore the captain of the football team does not
> play on the team.

Here the conclusion is false, but the argument is valid since the conclusion follows from the premises. If we observe that the first premise is false, the paradox disappears. There is nothing surprising in the correct derivation of a false conclusion from false premises.

If an argument is valid, then the conjunction of the premises implies the conclusion. Hence if all the premises are true, then the conclusion is also true. However, if one or more of the premises is false, so that the conjunction of all the premises is false, then the conclusion may be either true or false. In fact, all the premises could be false, the conclusion true, and the argument valid, as the following example shows.

Example 3.

> All dogs have two legs.
> All two-legged animals are carnivorous.
> Therefore, all dogs are carnivorous.

Here the argument is valid and the conclusion is true, but both premises are false!

Each of these examples underlines the fact that neither the truth value nor the content of the statements appearing in an argument affect the validity of the argument. In Figures 31a and 31b are two valid forms of arguments.

$$p \rightarrow q \qquad\qquad p \rightarrow q$$
$$\underline{p} \qquad\qquad\qquad \underline{\sim q}$$
$$\therefore q \qquad\qquad\quad \therefore \sim p$$

Figure 31a   *Figure 31b*

The symbol $\therefore$ means "therefore." The truth tables for these argument forms appear in Figure 32.

p	q	$p \to q$	p	q	$p \to q$	$\sim q$	$\sim p$
T	T	T	T	T	T	F	F
T	F	F	T	F	F	T	F
F	T	T	F	T	T	F	T
F	F	T	F	F	T	T	T

Figure 32

For the argument of Figure 31a, we see in Figure 32 that there is only one case in which both premises are true, namely, the first case, and in this case the conclusion is true, hence the argument is valid. Similarly, in the argument of Figure 31b, both premises are true in the fourth case only, and in this case the conclusion is also true, hence the argument is valid.

An argument that is not valid is called a *fallacy*. Two examples of fallacies are the following argument forms.

$$
\begin{array}{ccc}
\begin{array}{c} p \to q \\ \underline{q} \\ \therefore p \end{array} & \text{\emph{Fallacies}} & \begin{array}{c} p \to q \\ \underline{\sim p} \\ \therefore \sim q \end{array}
\end{array}
$$

In the first fallacy, both premises are true in the first and third cases of Figure 32, but the conclusion is false in the third case, so that the argument is invalid. (This is the form of Example 1.) Similarly, in the second fallacy we see that both premises are true in the last two cases, but the conclusion is false in the third case.

We say that an argument depends only upon its form in that it does not matter what the components of the argument are. The truth tables in Figure 32 show that if both premises are true, then the conclusions of the arguments in Figures 31a and 31b are also true. For the fallacies above, the truth tables show that it is possible to choose both premises true without making the conclusion true, namely, choose a false p and a true q.

Example 4. Consider the following argument.

$$
\begin{array}{c}
p \to q \\
\underline{q \to r} \\
\therefore p \to r
\end{array}
$$

The truth table of the argument appears in Figure 33.

p	q	r	$p \rightarrow q$	$q \rightarrow r$	$p \rightarrow r$
T	T	T	T	T	T
T	T	F	T	F	F
T	F	T	F	T	T
T	F	F	F	T	F
F	T	T	T	T	T
F	T	F	T	F	T
F	F	T	T	T	T
F	F	F	T	T	T

Figure 33

Both premises are true in the first, fifth, seventh, and eighth rows of the truth table. Since in each of these cases the conclusion is also true, the argument is valid. (Example 3 can be written in this form.)

Once we have discovered that a certain form of argument is valid, we can use it in drawing conclusions. It is then no longer necessary to compute truth tables. Presumably, this is what we do when we reason in everyday life; we apply a variety of valid forms known to us from previous experience. However, the truth table method has one great advantage: It is always applicable and purely automatic. We can even get a computer to test the validity of arguments involving compound statements.

EXERCISES

1. Test the validity of the following arguments.

(a) $p \leftrightarrow q$ (b) $p \lor q$ (c) $p \land q$

     $\underline{\quad p \quad}$ $\underline{\quad \sim p \quad}$ $\underline{\sim p \rightarrow q}$

   $\therefore q$ $\therefore \quad q$ $\therefore \sim q$

[*Ans.* (a), (b) are valid.]

2. Test the validity of the following arguments.

(a) $p \rightarrow \quad q$ (b) $p \rightarrow \quad q$

     $\underline{\sim q \rightarrow \sim r}$ $\underline{\sim r \rightarrow \sim q}$

   $\therefore \quad r \rightarrow \quad p$ $\therefore \sim r \rightarrow \sim p$

[*Ans.* (b) is valid.]

3. Test the validity of the argument

$$p \leftrightarrow q$$
$$q \vee r$$
$$\underline{\sim r}$$
$$\therefore \quad \sim p$$

[*Ans.* Not valid.]

4. Test the validity of the argument

$$p \veebar \quad q$$
$$\sim q \rightarrow \quad r$$
$$\underline{\sim p \vee \sim r}$$
$$\therefore \qquad \sim p$$

5. Test the validity of the argument

$$p \rightarrow \quad q$$
$$\sim p \rightarrow \sim q$$
$$\underline{\quad p \wedge \sim r}$$
$$\therefore \qquad s$$

6. Given are the premises $\sim p \rightarrow q$ and $\sim r \rightarrow \sim q$. We wish to find a valid conclusion involving p and r (if there is any).
    (a) Construct truth tables for the two premises.
    (b) Note the cases in which the conclusion must be true.
    (c) Construct a truth table for a combination of p and r only, filling in T wherever necessary.
    (d) Fill in the remainder of the truth table, making sure that you do not end up with a logically true statement.
    (e) What combination of p and r has this truth table? This is a valid conclusion.   [*Ans.* $p \vee r$.]

7. Translate the following argument into symbolic form, and test its validity.

> If this is a good course, then it is worth taking.
> Either the grading is lenient, or the course is not worth taking.
> But the grading is not lenient.
> Therefore, this is not a good course.   [*Ans.* Valid.]

8. Write the following argument in symbolic form, and test its validity.

> "For the candidate to win, it is sufficient that he carry New York. He will carry New York only if he takes a strong stand on civil rights. He will not take a strong stand on civil rights. Therefore, he will not win."

9. Write the following argument in symbolic form and test its validity.

"Father praises me only if I can be proud of myself. Either I do well in sports or I cannot be proud of myself. If I study hard, then I cannot do well in sports. Therefore, if father praises me, then I do not study hard."

10. Supply a conclusion to the following argument, making it a valid argument. [Adapted from Lewis Carroll.]

"If he goes to a party, he does not fail to brush his hair.
To look fascinating it is necessary to be tidy.
If he is an opium eater, then he has no self-command.
If he brushes his hair, he looks fascinating.
He wears white kid gloves only if he goes to a party.
Having no self-command is sufficient to make one look untidy.
Therefore . . ."

SUPPLEMENTARY EXERCISES

11. Show that the following method may be used for testing the validity of an argument: Find the cases in which the conclusion is false, and show that in each case at least one premise is false.

12. Use the method of Exercise 11 to test Example 4.

13. Redo Exercise 1 using the method of Exercise 11.

14. Redo Exercise 4 using the method of Exercise 11.

15. Draw a valid conclusion from the following premises.

Either he is a man or a mouse.
He has no skill in athletics.
To be a man it is necessary to command respect.
A man can command respect only if he has some athletic skill.

16. Draw a valid conclusion from the following premises.

Either he will go to graduate school, or he will be drafted.
If he does not go to graduate school, he will get married.
If he gets married, he will need a good income.
He will not have a good income in the Army.

*11. THE INDIRECT METHOD OF PROOF

A proof is an argument which shows that a conditional statement of the form $p \rightarrow q$ is logically true. (Namely, p is the conjunction of the premises, and q is the conclusion of the argument.) Sometimes it is more convenient to show that an equivalent conditional statement is logically true.

Example 1. Let x and y be positive integers.

Theorem. If xy is an odd number, then x and y are both odd.

Proof. Suppose, on the contrary, that they are not both odd. Then one of them is even, say $x = 2z$. Then $xy = 2zy$ is an even number, contrary to hypothesis. Hence we have proved our theorem.

Example 2. "He did not know the first name of the president of the Jones Corporation, hence he cannot be an employee of that firm. Why? Because every employee of that firm calls the boss by his first name (behind his back). Therefore, if he were really an employee of Jones, then he would know Jones's first name."

These are simple examples of a very common form of argument, frequently used both in mathematics and in everyday discussions. Let us try to unravel the form of the argument.

Given:	xy is an odd number.	He doesn't know Jones's first name.	p
To prove:	x and y are both odd numbers.	He doesn't work for Jones.	q
Suppose:	x and y are not both odd numbers.	He does work for Jones.	$\sim q$
Then:	xy is an even number.	He must know what Jones's first name is.	$\sim p$

In each case we assume the contradictory to the conclusion and derive, by a valid argument, a result contradictory to the hypothesis. This is one form of the *indirect* method of proof.

To restate, what we want to do is to show that the conditional $p \to q$ is logically true; what we actually show is that the contrapositive

$$(1) \qquad \sim q \to \sim p$$

is logically true. Since these two statements are equivalent our procedure is valid. (See Section 9.)

There are several other important variants of this method of proof.

It is easy to check that the following statements have the same truth table as (are equivalent to) the conditional $p \rightarrow q$.

(2) $(p \wedge \sim q) \rightarrow \sim p$.
(3) $(p \wedge \sim q) \rightarrow q$.
(4) $(p \wedge \sim q) \rightarrow (r \wedge \sim r)$.

Statement (2) shows that in the indirect method of proof we may make use of the original hypothesis in addition to the contradictory assumption $\sim q$. Statement (3) shows that we may also use this double hypothesis in the direct proof of the conclusion q. Statement (4) shows that if, from the double hypothesis p and $\sim q$ we can arrive at a contradiction of the form $r \wedge \sim r$, then the proof of the original statement is complete. This last form of the method is often referred to as *reductio ad absurdum*.

These last forms of the method are very useful for the following reasons: First of all we see that we can always take $\sim q$ as a hypothesis in addition to p. Second we see that besides q there are two other conclusions ($\sim p$ or a contradiction) which are just as good.

EXERCISES

1. Construct indirect proofs for the following assertions.
   (a) If x^2 is odd, then x is odd (x an integer).
   (b) If I am to pass this course, I must do homework regularly.
   (c) If he earns a great deal of money (more than \$30,000), he is **not a** college professor.

2. Give a symbolic analysis of the following argument.

   "If he is to succeed, he must be both competent and lucky. Because, if he is not competent, then it is impossible for him to succeed. If he is not lucky, something is sure to go wrong."

3. Construct indirect proofs for the following assertions.
   (a) If $p \vee q$ and $\sim q$, then p.
   (b) If $p \leftrightarrow q$ and $q \rightarrow \sim r$ and r, then $\sim p$.

4. Give a symbolic analysis of the following argument.

   "If Jones is the murderer, then he knows the exact time of death and the murder weapon. Therefore, if he does not know the exact time or does not know the weapon, then he is not the murderer."

5. Verify that forms (2), (3), and (4) given above are equivalent to $p \rightarrow q$.

6. Give an example of an indirect proof of some statement in which from p and $\sim q$ a contradiction is derived.

7. Give a statement equivalent to $(p \wedge q) \to r$, which is in terms of $\sim p$, $\sim q$, and $\sim r$. Show how this can be used in a proof where there are two hypotheses given.

8. Use the indirect method to establish the validity of the following argument.

$$p \veebar q$$
$$\sim p \to r$$
$$r \to s$$
$$q \to \sim s$$
$$\therefore p$$

9. Use the indirect method on Exercise 7 of Section 10.

*12. APPLICATIONS TO SWITCHING CIRCUITS

The theory of compound statements has many applications to subjects other than pure mathematics. As an example we shall develop a theory of simple switching networks.

A switching network is an arrangement of wires and switches which connect together two terminals T_1 and T_2. Each switch can be either "open" or "closed." An open switch prevents the flow of current, while a closed switch permits flow. The problem that we want to solve is the following: Given a network and given the knowledge of which switches are closed, determine whether or not current will flow from T_1 to T_2.

Figure 34 shows the simplest kind of a network in which the terminals are connected by a single wire containing a switch P. If P is closed, then current will flow between the terminals; otherwise it does not.

Figure 34   **Figure 35**

The network in Figure 35 has two switches P and Q in "series." Here the current flows only if both P and Q are closed.

To see how our logical analysis can be used to solve the problem stated above, let us associate a statement with each switch. Let p be the statement "Switch P is closed" and let q be the statement "Switch

Q is closed." Then in Figure 34 current will flow if and only if p is true. Similarly, in Figure 35 the current will flow if and only if both p and q are true, that is, if and only if $p \wedge q$ is true. Thus the first circuit is represented by p and the second by $p \wedge q$.

In Figure 36 is shown a network with switches P and Q in "parallel." In this case the current flows if either of the switches is closed, so the circuit is represented by the statement $p \vee q$.

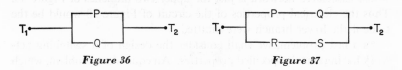

Figure 36   Figure 37

The network in Figure 37 combines the series and parallel types of connections. The upper branch of the network is represented by the statement $p \wedge q$ and the lower by $r \wedge s$; hence the entire circuit is represented by $(p \wedge q) \vee (r \wedge s)$. Since there are four switches and each one can be either open or closed, there are $2^4 = 16$ possible settings for these switches. Similarly, the statement $(p \wedge q) \vee (r \wedge s)$ has four variables, so that its truth table has 16 rows in it. The switch settings for which current flows correspond to the entries in the truth table for which the above compound statement is true.

Switches need not always act independently of each other. It is possible to couple two or more switches together so that they open and close simultaneously, and we shall indicate this in diagrams by giving all such switches the same letter. It is also possible to couple two switches together, so that if one is closed, the other is open. We shall indicate this by giving the first switch the letter P and the second the letter P'. Then the statement "P is closed" is true if and only if the statement "P' is closed" is false. Therefore if p is the statement "P is closed," then $\sim p$ is equivalent to the statement "P' is closed."

Such a circuit is illustrated in Figure 38. The associated compound statement is $[p \vee (\sim p \wedge \sim q)] \vee [p \wedge q]$. Since this statement is false only if p is false and q is true, the current will flow unless P is open and Q is closed. We can also check directly. If P is closed, current will flow through the top branch regardless of Q's setting. If both switches are open, then P' and Q' will be closed, so that current will flow through the middle branch. But if P is open and Q is closed, none of the branches will pass current.

Notice that we never had to consider current flow through the bottom branch. The logical counterpart of this fact is that the statement associated with the network is equivalent to $[p \lor (\sim p \land \sim q)]$ whose associated network is just the upper two branches of Figure 38. Thus the electrical properties of the circuit of Figure 38 would be the same if the lower branch were omitted.

As a last problem, we shall consider the design of a switching network having certain specified properties. An equivalent problem, which we solved in Section 4, is that of constructing a compound statement having a given truth table. As in that section, we shall limit ourselves to statements having three variables, although our methods could easily be extended.

In Section 4 we developed a general method for finding a statement having a given truth table not consisting entirely of F's. (The circuit which corresponds to a statement whose truth table consists entirely of F's is one in which current never flows, and hence is not of interest.) Each such statement could be constructed as a disjunction of basic conjunctions. Since the basic conjunctions were of the form $p \land q \land r$, $p \land q \land \sim r$, etc., each will be represented by a circuit consisting of three switches in series and will be called a *basic series circuit*. The disjunction of certain of these basic conjunctions will then be represented by the circuit obtained by putting several basic series circuits in parallel. The resulting network will not, in general, be the simplest possible such network fulfilling the requirements, but the method always suffices to find one.

Example. A three-man committee wishes to employ an electric circuit to record a secret simple majority vote. Design a circuit so that each member can push a button for his "yes" vote (not push it for a "no" vote), and so that a signal light will go on if a majority of the committee members vote yes.

Let p be the statement "Committee member 1 votes yes," let q be the statement "Member 2 votes yes," and let r be "Member 3 votes yes." The truth table of the statement "Majority of the members

p	q	r	Desired Truth Value	Corresponding Basic Conjunction
T	T	T	T	$p \wedge q \wedge r$
T	T	F	T	$p \wedge q \wedge \sim r$
T	F	T	T	$p \wedge \sim q \wedge r$
T	F	F	F	$p \wedge \sim q \wedge \sim r$
F	T	T	T	$\sim p \wedge q \wedge r$
F	T	F	F	$\sim p \wedge q \wedge \sim r$
F	F	T	F	$\sim p \wedge \sim q \wedge r$
F	F	F	F	$\sim p \wedge \sim q \wedge \sim r$

Figure 39

vote yes" appears in Figure 39. From that figure we can read off the desired compound statement as

$$(p \wedge q \wedge r) \vee (p \wedge q \wedge \sim r) \vee (p \wedge \sim q \wedge r) \vee (\sim p \wedge q \wedge r).$$

The circuit desired for the voting procedure appears in Figure 40.

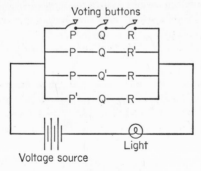

Figure 40

EXERCISES

1. What kind of a circuit has a logically true statement assigned to it? Give an example.

2. Construct a network corresponding to

$$[(p \wedge \sim q) \vee (\sim p \wedge q)] \vee (\sim p \wedge \sim q).$$

3. What compound statement represents the following circuit?

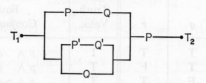

4. Work out the truth table of the statement in Exercise 3. What does this tell us about the circuit?

5. Design a simpler circuit than the one in Exercise 3, having the same properties.

6. Construct a network corresponding to

$$[(p \lor q) \land \sim r] \lor [(\sim p \land r) \lor q].$$

7. Design a circuit for an electrical version of the game of matching pennies: At a given signal each of the two players either opens or closes a switch under his control. If they both do the same, A wins; if they do the opposite, then B wins. Design the circuit so that a light goes on if A wins.

8. In a large hall it is desired to turn the lights on or off from any one of four switches on the four walls. This can be accomplished by designing a circuit which turns the light on if an even number of switches are closed, and off if an odd number are closed. (Why does this solve the problem?) Design such a circuit.

9. A committee has five members. It takes a majority vote to carry a measure, except that the chairman has a veto (i.e., the measure carries only if he votes for it). Design a circuit for the committee, so that each member votes for a measure by pressing a button, and the light goes on if and only if the measure is carried.

10. A group of candidates is asked to take a true-false exam, with four questions. Design a circuit such that a candidate can push the buttons of those questions to which he wants to answer "true," and that the circuit will indicate the number of correct answers. [*Hint:* Have five lights, corresponding to 0, 1, 2, 3, 4 correct answers, respectively.]

11. Devise a scheme for working truth tables by means of switching circuits.

12. Figure 40 uses 12 switches. Find a circuit that accomplishes the same goal with only 5 switches. Check that the corresponding truth table agrees with Figure 39.

SUGGESTED READING

Tarski, A., *Introduction to Logic*, Oxford University Press, New York, 2d rev. ed., 1946, Chapters I, II.

Suppes, P., *Introduction to Logic*, D. Van Nostrand, Princeton, 1957, Chapters 1, 2, 3.

Cohen, M. R., and E. Nagel, *An Introduction to Logic and Scientific Method*, Harcourt, Brace, New York, 1934.

Church, A., *Introduction to Mathematical Logic*, Volume I, Princeton University Press, 1956.

Hilbert, D., and W. Ackermann, *Principles of Mathematical Logic*, Chelsea, New York, 2d ed., 1950.

Allendoerfer, C. B., and C. O. Oakley, *Principles of Mathematics*, McGraw-Hill, New York, 1955, Chapter I.

Johnstone, H. W., Jr., *Elementary Deductive Logic*, Crowell, New York, 1954. Parts One and Two.

Hohn, Franz, "Some Mathematical Aspects of Switching," *The American Mathematical Monthly*, **62** (1955), pp. 75–90.

Sets and subsets

1. INTRODUCTION

A well-defined collection of objects is known as a *set*. This concept, in its complete generality, is of great importance in mathematics since all of mathematics can be developed by starting from it.

The various pieces of furniture in a given room form a set. So do the books in a given library, or the integers between 1 and 1,000,000, or all the ideas that mankind has had, or the human beings alive between one billion B.C. and ten billion A.D. These examples are all examples of *finite* sets, that is, sets having a finite number of elements. All the sets discussed in this book will be finite sets.

There are two essentially different ways of specifying a set. One can give a rule by which it can be determined whether or not a given object is a member of the set, or one can give a complete list of the elements in the set. We shall say that the former is a *description* of the set and the latter is a *listing* of the set. For example, we can define a set of four people as (a) the members of the string quartet which played in town last night, or (b) four particular persons whose names are Jones, Smith, Brown, and Green. It is customary to use braces to surround the listing of a set; thus the set above should be listed {Jones, Smith, Brown, Green}.

We shall frequently be interested in sets of logical possibilities, since the analysis of such sets is very often a major task in the solving of a problem. Suppose, for example, that we were interested in the successes of three candidates who enter the presidential primaries (we assume there are no other entries). Suppose that the key primaries will be held in New Hampshire, Minnesota, Wisconsin, and California. Assume that candidate A enters all the primaries, that B does not contest in New Hampshire's primary, and C does not contest in Wisconsin's. A list of the logical possibilities is given in Figure 1. Since the New Hampshire and Wisconsin primaries can each end in two ways, and the Minnesota and California primaries can each end in three ways, there are in all $2 \cdot 2 \cdot 3 \cdot 3 = 36$ different logical possibilities as listed in Figure 1.

A set that consists of some members of another set is called a *subset* of that set. For example, the set of those logical possibilities in Figure 1 for which the statement "Candidate A wins at least three primaries" is true, is a subset of the set of all logical possibilities. This subset can also be defined by listing its members: {P1, P2, P3, P4, P7, P13, P19}.

In order to discuss all the subsets of a given set, let us introduce the following terminology. We shall call the original set the *universal set*, one-element subsets will be called *unit sets*, and the set which contains no members the *empty set*. We do not introduce special names for other kinds of subsets of the universal set. As an example, let the universal set $\mathfrak{U}$ consist of the three elements $\{a, b, c\}$. The *proper subsets* of $\mathfrak{U}$ are those sets containing some but not all of the elements of $\mathfrak{U}$. The proper subsets consist of three two-element sets namely, $\{a, b\}$, $\{a, c\}$, and $\{b, c\}$ and three unit sets, namely, $\{a\}$, $\{b\}$, and $\{c\}$. To complete the picture, we also consider the universal set a subset (but not a proper subset) of itself, and we consider the empty set $\mathcal{E}$, that contains no elements of $\mathfrak{U}$, as a subset of $\mathfrak{U}$. At first it may seem strange that we should include the sets $\mathfrak{U}$ and $\mathcal{E}$ as subsets of $\mathfrak{U}$, but the reasons for their inclusion will become clear later.

We saw that the three-element set above had $8 = 2^3$ subsets. In general, a set with n elements has 2^n subsets, as can be seen in the following manner. We form subsets P of $\mathfrak{U}$ by considering each of the elements of $\mathfrak{U}$ in turn and deciding whether or not to include it in the subset P. If we decide to put every element of $\mathfrak{U}$ into P, we get the universal set, and if we decide to put no element of $\mathfrak{U}$ into P, we get the empty set. In most cases we will put some but not all the

Possibility Number	Winner in New Hampshire	Winner in Minnesota	Winner in Wisconsin	Winner in California
P1	A	A	A	A
P2	A	A	A	B
P3	A	A	A	C
P4	A	A	B	A
P5	A	A	B	B
P6	A	A	B	C
P7	A	B	A	A
P8	A	B	A	B
P9	A	B	A	C
P10	A	B	B	A
P11	A	B	B	B
P12	A	B	B	C
P13	A	C	A	A
P14	A	C	A	B
P15	A	C	A	C
P16	A	C	B	A
P17	A	C	B	B
P18	A	C	B	C
P19	C	A	A	A
P20	C	A	A	B
P21	C	A	A	C
P22	C	A	B	A
P23	C	A	B	B
P24	C	A	B	C
P25	C	B	A	A
P26	C	B	A	B
P27	C	B	A	C
P28	C	B	B	A
P29	C	B	B	B
P30	C	B	B	C
P31	C	C	C	A
P32	C	C	C	B
P33	C	C	A	C
P34	C	C	B	A
P35	C	C	B	B
P36	C	C	C	C

Figure 1

elements into P and thus obtain a proper subset of $\mathfrak{U}$. We have to make n decisions, one for each element of the set, and for each decision we have to choose between two alternatives. We can make these decisions in $2 \cdot 2 \cdot \ldots \cdot 2 = 2^n$ ways, and hence this is the number of different subsets of $\mathfrak{U}$ that can be formed. Observe that our formula would not have been so simple if we had not included the universal set and the empty set as subsets of $\mathfrak{U}$.

In the example of the voting primaries above there are 2^{36} or about 70 billion subsets. Of course, we cannot deal with this many subsets in a practical problem, but fortunately we are usually interested in only a few of the subsets. The most interesting subsets are those which can be defined by means of a simple rule such as "the set of all logical possibilities in which C loses at least two primaries." It would be difficult to give a simple description for the subset containing the elements {P1, P4, P14, P30, P34}. On the other hand, we shall see in the next section how to define new subsets in terms of subsets already defined.

Examples. We illustrate the two different ways of specifying sets in terms of the primary voting example. Let the universal set $\mathfrak{U}$ be the logical possibilities given in Figure 1.

1. What is the subset of $\mathfrak{U}$ in which candidate B wins more primaries than either of the other candidates? *Answer:* {P11, P12, P17, P23, P26, P28, P29}.

2. What is the subset in which the primaries are split two and two? *Answer:* {P5, P8, P10, P15, P21, P30, P31, P35}.

3. Describe the set {P1, P4, P19, P22}. *Answer:* The set of possibilities for which A wins in Minnesota and California.

4. How can we describe the set {P18, P24, P27}? *Answer:* The set of possibilities for which C wins in California, and the other primaries are split three ways.

EXERCISES

1. In the primary example, give a listing for each of the following sets.
   (a) The set in which C wins at least two primaries.
   (b) The set in which the first three primaries are won by the same candidate.
   (c) The set in which B wins all four primaries.

2. The primaries are considered decisive if a candidate can win three primaries, or if he wins two primaries including California. List the set in which the primaries are decisive.

3. Give simple descriptions for the following sets (referring to the primary example).

    (a) {P33, P36}.

    (b) {P10, P11, P12, P28, P29, P30}.

    (c) {P6, P20, P22}.

4. Joe, Jim, Pete, Mary, and Peg are to be photographed. They want to line up so that boys and girls alternate. List the set of all possibilities.

5. In Exercise 4, list the following subsets.

    (a) The set in which Pete and Mary are next to each other.

    (b) The set in which Peg is between Joe and Jim.

    (c) The set in which Jim is in the middle.

    (d) The set in which Mary is in the middle.

    (e) The set in which a boy is at each end.

6. Pick out all pairs in Exercise 5 in which one set is a subset of the other.

7. A TV producer is planning a half-hour show. He wants to have a combination of comedy, music, and commercials. If each is allotted a multiple of five minutes, construct the set of possible distributions of time. (Consider only the total time allotted to each.)

8. In Exercise 7, list the following subsets.

    (a) The set in which more time is devoted to comedy than to music.

    (b) The set in which no more time is devoted to commercials than to either music or comedy.

    (c) The set in which exactly five minutes is devoted to music.

    (d) The set in which all three of the above conditions are satisfied.

9. In Exercise 8, find two sets, each of which is a proper subset of the set in (a) and also of the set in (c).

10. Let $\mathfrak{u}$ be the set of paths in Figure 22 of Chapter I. Find the subset in which

    (a) Two balls of the same color are drawn.

    (b) Two different color balls are drawn.

11. A set has 101 elements. How many subsets does it have? How many of the subsets have an odd number of elements?   [*Ans.* 2^{101}; 2^{100}.]

12. Do Exercise 11 for the case of a set with 102 elements.

2. OPERATIONS ON SUBSETS

In Chapter I we considered the ways in which one could form new statements from given statements. Now we shall consider an analogous procedure, the formation of new sets from given sets. We shall assume that each of the sets that we use in the combination is a subset of some universal set, and we shall also want the newly formed set to be a subset of the same universal set. As usual, we can specify a newly formed set either by a description or by a listing.

If P and Q are two sets, we shall define a new set $P \cap Q$, called the *intersection* of P and Q as follows: $P \cap Q$ is the set which contains those and only those elements which belong to both P and Q. As an example, consider the logical possibilities listed in Figure 1. Let P be the subset in which candidate A wins at least three primaries, i.e., the set {P1, P2, P3, P4, P7, P13, P19} ; let Q be the subset in which A wins the first two primaries, i.e., the set {P1, P2, P3, P4, P5, P6}. Then the intersection $P \cap Q$ is the set in which both events take place, i.e., where A wins the first two primaries *and* wins at least three primaries. Thus $P \cap Q$ is the set {P1, P2, P3, P4}.

If P and Q are two sets, we shall define a new set $P \cup Q$ called the *union* of P and Q as follows: $P \cup Q$ is the set that contains those and only those elements that belong either to P or to Q (or to both). In the example in the paragraph above, the union $P \cup Q$ is the set of possibilities for which either A wins the first two primaries *or* wins at least three primaries, i.e., the set {P1, P2, P3, P4, P5, P6, P7, P13, P19}.

To help in visualizing these operations we shall draw diagrams, called Venn diagrams, which illustrate them. We let the universal set be a rectangle and let subsets be circles drawn inside the rectangle.

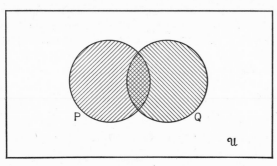

Figure 2

In Figure 2 we show two sets P and Q as shaded circles. Then the doubly crosshatched area is the intersection $P \cap Q$ and the total shaded area is the union $P \cup Q$.

If P is a given subset of the universal set $\mathcal{U}$, we can define a new set $\tilde{P}$ called the *complement* of P as follows: $\tilde{P}$ is the set of all elements of $\mathcal{U}$ that are *not* contained in P. For example, if, as above, Q is the set in which candidate A wins the first two primaries, then $\tilde{Q}$ is the set $\{P7, P8, \ldots, P36\}$. The shaded area in Figure 3 is the complement of the set P. Observe that the complement of the empty set $\mathcal{E}$ is the universal set $\mathcal{U}$, and also that the complement of the universal set is the empty set.

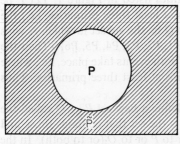

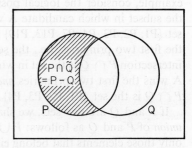

Figure 3   **Figure 4**

Sometimes we shall be interested in only part of the complement of a set. For example, we might wish to consider the part of the complement of the set Q that is contained in P, i.e., the set $P \cap \tilde{Q}$. The shaded area in Figure 4 is $P \cap \tilde{Q}$.

A somewhat more suggestive definition of this set can be given as follows: Let $P - Q$ be the *difference* of P and Q, that is, the set that contains those elements of P that do not belong to Q. Figure 4 shows that $P \cap \tilde{Q}$ and $P - Q$ are the same set. In the primary voting example above, the set $P - Q$ can be listed as $\{P7, P13, P19\}$.

The complement of a subset is a special case of a difference set, since we can write $\tilde{Q} = \mathcal{U} - Q$. If P and Q are nonempty subsets whose intersection is the empty set, i.e., $P \cap Q = \mathcal{E}$, then we say that they are *disjoint* subsets.

Examples. In the primary voting example let R be the set in which A wins the first three primaries, i.e., the set $\{P1, P2, P3\}$; let S be the set in which A wins the last two primaries, i.e., the set $\{P1, P7, P13, P19, P25, P31\}$. Then $R \cap S = \{P1\}$ is the set in which A wins the first three primaries and also the last two, that is, he wins all the primaries. We also have

$$R \cup S = \{P1, P2, P3, P7, P13, P19, P25, P31\},$$

which can be described as the set in which A wins the first three primaries or the last two. The set in which A does not win the first three primaries is $\tilde{R} = \{P4, P5, \ldots, P36\}$. Finally, we see that the difference set $R - S$ is the set in which A wins the first three primaries but not both of the last two. This set can be found by taking from R the element P1 which it has in common with S, so that $R - S = \{P2, P3\}$.

EXERCISES

1. Draw Venn diagrams for $P \cap Q, P \cap \tilde{Q}, \tilde{P} \cap Q, \tilde{P} \cap \tilde{Q}$.

2. Give a step-by-step construction of the diagram for $(\tilde{P} - Q) \cup (P \cap \tilde{Q})$.

3. Venn diagrams are also useful when three subsets are given. Construct such a diagram, given the subsets P, Q, and R. Identify each of the eight resulting areas in terms of P, Q, and R.

4. In testing blood, three types of antigens are looked for: A, B, and Rh. Every person is classified doubly. He is Rh positive if he has the Rh antigen, and Rh negative otherwise. He is type AB, A, or B depending on which of the other antigens he has, with type O having neither A nor B. Draw a Venn diagram, and identify each of the eight areas.

5. Considering only two subsets, the set X of people having antigen A, and the set Y of people having antigen B, define (symbolically) the types AB, A, B, and O.

6. A person can receive blood from another person if he has all the antigens of the donor. Describe in terms of X and Y the sets of people who can give to each of the four types. Identify these sets in terms of blood types.

7.

	Liked Very Much	Liked Slightly	Disliked Slightly	Disliked Very Much
Men	1	3	5	10
Women	6	8	3	1
Boys	5	5	3	2
Girls	8	5	1	1

This tabulation records the reaction of a number of spectators to a television show. All the categories can be defined in terms of the following four: M (male), G (grown-up), L (liked), Vm (very much). How many people fall into each of the following categories?

(a) M. [*Ans.* 34.]

(b) $\bar{L}$.

(c) Vm.

(d) $M \cap \bar{G} \cap \bar{L} \cap Vm$. [*Ans.* 2.]

(e) $\tilde{M} \cap G \cap L$.

(f) $(M \cap G) \cup (L \cap Vm)$.

(g) $\widetilde{(M \cap G)}$. [*Ans.* 48.]

(h) $(\tilde{M} \cup \tilde{G})$.

(i) $(M - G)$.

(j) $[\tilde{M} - (G \cap L \cap \widetilde{Vm})]$.

8. In a survey of 100 students, the numbers studying various languages were found to be: Spanish, 28; German, 30; French, 42; Spanish and German, 8; Spanish and French, 10; German and French, 5; all three languages, 3.

(a) How many students were studying no language? [*Ans.* 20.]

(b) How many students had French as their only language?

[*Ans.* 30.]

(c) How many students studied German if and only if they studied French? [*Ans.* 38.]

[*Hint:* Draw a Venn diagram with three circles, for French, German, and Spanish students. Fill in the numbers in each of the eight areas, using the data given above. Start from the end of the list and work back.]

9. In a later survey of the 100 students (see Exercise 8), numbers studying the various languages were found to be: German only, 18; German but not Spanish, 23; German and French, 8; German, 26; French, 48; French and Spanish, 8; no language, 24.

(a) How many students took Spanish? [*Ans.* 18.]

(b) How many took German and Spanish but not French?

[*Ans.* None.]

(c) How many took French if and only if they did not take Spanish? [*Ans.* 50.]

10. The report of one survey of the 100 students (see Exercise 8) stated that the numbers studying the various languages were: all three languages, 5; German and Spanish, 10; French and Spanish, 8; German and French, 20; Spanish, 30; German, 23; French, 50. The surveyor who turned in this report was fired. Why?

11. A recent survey of 100 Dartmouth students has revealed the information about their dates that is summarized in the following table.

	Beautiful and Intelligent	Plain and Intelligent	Beautiful and Dumb	Plain and Dumb
Blonde	6	9	10	20
Brunette	7	11	15	9
Redhead	2	3	8	0

Let BL = blondes, BR = brunettes, R = redheads, BE = beautiful girls, D = dumb girls. Determine the number of girls in each of the following classes.

    (a) $BL \cap BE \cap D$.   [*Ans.* 10.]

    (b) BR.

    (c) $R \cap \tilde{D}$.

    (d) $(BR \cup R) \cap (BE \cup \tilde{D})$.   [*Ans.* 46.]

    (e) $\widetilde{BL} \cup (\widetilde{BE \cap D})$.

12. In Exercise 11, which set of each of the following pairs has more girls as members?

    (a) $(\widetilde{BL \cup BR})$ or R.

    (b) $D \cap \widetilde{BE}$ or $BL - (D \cap \widetilde{BE})$.

    (c) ε or $R \cap \widetilde{BE} \cap D$.

3. THE RELATIONSHIP BETWEEN SETS AND COMPOUND STATEMENTS

The reader may have observed several times in the preceding sections that there was a close connection between sets and statements, and between set operations and compounding operations. In this section we shall formalize these relationships.

If we have a number of statements relative to a set of logical possibilities, there is a natural way of assigning a set to each statement. First of all, we take the set of logical possibilities as our universal set. Then to each statement we assign the subset of logical possibilities of the universal set for which that statement is true. This idea is so important that we embody it in a formal definition.

DEFINITION. Let 𝔲 be a set of logical possibilities, let p be a statement relative to it, and let P be that subset of the possibilities for which p is true; then we call P the *truth set* of p.

If p and q are statements, then $p \vee q$ and $p \wedge q$ are also statements and hence must have truth sets. To find the truth set of $p \vee q$, we observe that it is true whenever p is true or q is true (or both). Therefore we must assign to $p \vee q$ the logical possibilities which are in P or in Q (or both); that is, we must assign to $p \vee q$ the set $P \cup Q$. On the other hand, the statement $p \wedge q$ is true only when both p and q are true, so that we must assign to $p \wedge q$ the set $P \cap Q$.

Thus we see that there is a close connection between the logical operation of disjunction and the set operation of union, and also between conjunction and intersection. A careful examination of the definitions of union and intersection shows that the word "or" occurs in the definition of union and the word "and" occurs in the definition of intersection. Thus the connection between the two theories is not surprising.

Since the connective "not" occurs in the definition of the complement of a set, it is not surprising that the truth set of $\sim p$ is $\tilde{P}$. This follows since $\sim p$ is true when p is false, so that the truth set of $\sim p$ contains all logical possibilities for which p is false, that is, the truth set of $\sim p$ is $\tilde{P}$.

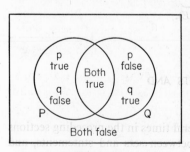

The truth sets of two propositions p and q are shown in Figure 5. Also marked on the diagram are the various logical possibilities for these two statements. The reader

Figure 5

should pick out in this diagram the truth sets of the statements $p \vee q$, $p \wedge q$, $\sim p$, and $\sim q$.

The connection between a statement and its truth set makes it possible to "translate" a problem about compound statements into a problem about sets. It is also possible to go in the reverse direction. Given a problem about sets, think of the universal set as being a set of logical possibilities and think of a subset as being the truth set of a statement. Hence we can "translate" a problem about sets into a problem about compound statements.

So far we have discussed only the truth sets assigned to compound statements involving $\vee$, $\wedge$, and $\sim$. All the other connectives can be defined in terms of these three basic ones, so that we can deduce what truth sets should be assigned to them. For example, we know that $p \rightarrow q$ is equivalent to $\sim p \vee q$ (see Figure 28 of Chapter I). Hence the truth set of $p \rightarrow q$ is the same as the truth set of $\sim p \vee q$, that is, it is

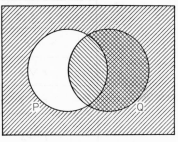

Figure 6

$\bar{P} \cup Q$. The Venn diagram for $p \rightarrow q$ is shown in Figure 6, where the shaded area is the truth set for the statement. Observe that the un-shaded area in Figure 6 is the set $P - Q = P \cap \bar{Q}$, which is the truth set of the statement $p \wedge \sim q$. Thus the shaded area is the set $\widetilde{(P - Q)}$ $= \widetilde{P \cap \bar{Q}}$, which is the truth set of the statement $\sim[p \wedge \sim q]$. We have thus discovered the fact that $(p \rightarrow q)$, $(\sim p \vee q)$, and $\sim(p \wedge \sim q)$ are equivalent. It is always the case that two compound statements are equivalent if and only if they have the same truth sets. Thus we can test for equivalence by checking whether they have the same Venn diagram.

Suppose that p is a statement that is logically true. What is its truth set? Now p is logically true if and only if it is true in every logically possible case, so that the truth set of p must be $\mathfrak{U}$. Similarly, if p is logically false, then it is false for every logically possible case, so that its truth set is the empty set $\mathcal{E}$.

Finally, let us consider the implication relation. Recall that p implies q if and only if the conditional $p \rightarrow q$ is logically true. But $p \rightarrow q$ is logically true if and only if its truth set is $\mathfrak{U}$, that is, $\widetilde{(P - Q)} = \mathfrak{U}$, or $(P - Q) = \mathcal{E}$. From Figure 4 we see that if $P - Q$ is empty, then P is contained in Q. We shall symbolize the containing relation as follows: $P \subset Q$ means "P is a subset of Q." We conclude that $p \rightarrow q$ is logically true if and only if $P \subset Q$.

Statement Language	Set Language
r	R
s	S
$\sim r$	$\tilde{R}$
$r \vee s$	$R \cup S$
$r \wedge s$	$R \cap S$
$r \rightarrow s$	$\widetilde{(R - S)}$
r implies s	$R \subset S$
r is equivalent to s	$R = S$

Figure 7

Figure 7 supplies a "dictionary" for translating from statement language to set language, and back. To each statement relative to a set of possibilities $\mathfrak{U}$ there corresponds a subset of $\mathfrak{U}$, namely the truth set of the statement. This is shown in lines 1 and 2 of the figure. To each connective there corresponds an operation on sets, as illustrated in the next four lines. And to each relation between statements there

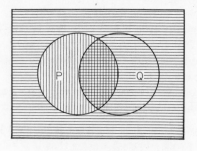

Figure 8

corresponds a relation between sets, examples of which are shown in the last two lines of the figure.

Example 1. Prove by means of a Venn diagram that the statement $[p \lor (\sim p \lor q)]$ is logically true. The assigned set of this statement is $[P \cup (\tilde{P} \cup Q)]$, and its Venn diagram is shown in Figure 8. In that figure the set P is shaded vertically, and the set $\tilde{P} \cup Q$ is shaded horizontally. Their union is the entire shaded area, which is $\mathfrak{U}$, so that the compound statement is logically true.

Example 2. Prove by means of Venn diagrams that $p \lor (q \land r)$ is equivalent to $(p \lor q) \land (p \lor r)$. The truth set of $p \lor (q \land r)$ is the entire shaded area of Figure 9a, and the truth set of $(p \lor q) \land (p \lor r)$

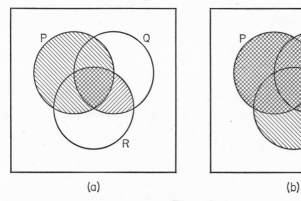

(a)   (b)

Figure 9

is the doubly shaded area in Figure 9b. Since these two sets are equal, we see that the two statements are equivalent.

Example 3. Show by means of a Venn diagram that q implies $p \rightarrow q$. The truth set of $p \rightarrow q$ is the shaded area in Figure 6. Since this shaded area includes the set Q, we see that q implies $p \rightarrow q$.

EXERCISES

Note: In Exercises 1, 2, and 3, find first the truth set of each statement.

1. Use Venn diagrams to test which of the following statements are logically true or logically false.

   (a) $p \vee \sim p$.
   (b) $p \wedge \sim p$.
   (c) $p \vee (\sim p \wedge q)$.
   (d) $p \rightarrow (q \rightarrow p)$.
   (e) $p \wedge \sim (q \rightarrow p)$.

   [*Ans.* (a), (d) logically true; (b), (e) logically false.]

2. Use Venn diagrams to test the following statements for equivalences.
   (a) $p \vee \sim q$.
   (b) $\sim (p \wedge q)$.
   (c) $\sim (q \wedge \sim p)$.
   (d) $p \rightarrow \sim q$.
   (e) $\sim p \vee \sim q$.

   [*Ans.* (a) and (c) equivalent; (b) and (d) and (e) equivalent.]

3. Use Venn diagrams for the following pairs of statements to test whether one implies the other.
   (a) p; $p \wedge q$.
   (b) $p \wedge \sim q$; $\sim p \rightarrow \sim q$.
   (c) $p \rightarrow q$; $q \rightarrow p$.
   (d) $p \wedge q$; $p \wedge \sim q$.

4. Devise a test for inconsistency of p and q, using Venn diagrams.

5. Three or more statements are said to be inconsistent if they cannot all be true. What does this state about their truth sets?

6. In the following three compound statements (a) assign variables to the components, (b) bring the statements into symbolic form, (c) find the truth sets, and (d) test for consistency.

   If this is a good course, then I will work hard in it.
   If this is not a good course, then I shall get a bad grade in it.
   I will not work hard, but I will get a good grade in this course.

   [*Ans.* Inconsistent.]

Note: In Exercises 7–9 assign to each set a statement having it as a truth set.

7. Use truth tables to find which of the following sets are empty.
   (a) $(P \cup Q) \cap (\bar{P} \cup \bar{Q})$.
   (b) $(P \cap Q) \cap (\bar{Q} \cap R)$.
   (c) $(P \cap Q) - P$.
   (d) $(P \cup R) \cap (\bar{P} \cup \bar{Q})$.   [*Ans.* (b) and (c).]

8. Use truth tables to find out whether the following sets are all different.
   (a) $P \cap (Q \cup R)$.
   (b) $(R - Q) \cup (Q - R)$.
   (c) $(R \cup Q) \cap (R \cap Q)$.

(d) $(P \cap Q) \cup (P \cap R)$.

(e) $(P \cap Q \cap \tilde{R}) \cup (P \cap \tilde{Q} \cap R) \cup (\tilde{P} \cap Q \cap \tilde{R}) \cup (\tilde{P} \cap \tilde{Q} \cap R)$.

9. Use truth tables for the following pairs of sets to test whether one is a subset of the other.

     (a) $P; P \cap Q$.

     (b) $P \cap \tilde{Q}; Q \cap \tilde{P}$.

     (c) $P - Q; Q - P$.

     (d) $\tilde{P} \cap \tilde{Q}; P \cup Q$.

10. Show, both by the use of truth tables and by the use of Venn diagrams, that $p \wedge (q \vee r)$ is equivalent to $(p \wedge q) \vee (p \wedge r)$.

11. The *symmetric difference* of P and Q is defined to be $(P - Q) \cup (Q - P)$. What connective corresponds to this set operation?

12. Let p, q, r be a complete set of alternatives (see Chapter I, Section 8). What can we say about the truth sets P, Q, R?

*4. THE ABSTRACT LAWS OF SET OPERATIONS

The set operations which we have introduced obey some very simple abstract laws, which we shall list in this section. These laws can be proved by means of Venn diagrams or they can be translated into statements and checked by means of truth tables.

The abstract laws given below bear a close resemblance to the elementary algebraic laws with which the student is already familiar. The resemblance can be made even more striking by replacing $\cup$ by $+$ and $\cap$ by $\times$. For this reason, a set, its subsets, and the laws of combination of subsets are considered an algebraic system, called a Boolean algebra—after the British mathematician George Boole who was the first person to study them from the algebraic point of view. Any other system obeying these laws, for example, the system of compound statements studied in Chapter I, is also known as a Boolean algebra. We can study any of these systems from either the algebraic or the logical point of view.

Below are the basic laws of Boolean algebras. The proofs of these laws will be left as exercises.

The laws governing union and intersection:

     A1. $A \cup A = A$.

     A2. $A \cap A = A$.

A3. $A \cup B = B \cup A.$
A4. $A \cap B = B \cap A.$
A5. $A \cup (B \cup C) = (A \cup B) \cup C.$
A6. $A \cap (B \cap C) = (A \cap B) \cap C.$
A7. $A \cap (B \cup C) = (A \cap B) \cup (A \cap C).$
A8. $A \cup (B \cap C) = (A \cup B) \cap (A \cup C).$
A9. $A \cup \mathcal{U} = \mathcal{U}.$
A10. $A \cap \mathcal{E} = \mathcal{E}.$
A11. $A \cap \mathcal{U} = A.$
A12. $A \cup \mathcal{E} = A.$

The laws governing complements:

B1. $\tilde{\tilde{A}} = A.$
B2. $A \cup \tilde{A} = \mathcal{U}.$
B3. $A \cap \tilde{A} = \mathcal{E}.$
B4. $\widetilde{(A \cup B)} = \tilde{A} \cap \tilde{B}.$
B5. $\widetilde{(A \cap B)} = \tilde{A} \cup \tilde{B}.$
B6. $\tilde{\mathcal{U}} = \mathcal{E}.$

The laws governing set-differences:

C1. $A - B = A \cap \tilde{B}.$
C2. $\mathcal{U} - A = \tilde{A}.$
C3. $A - \mathcal{U} = \mathcal{E}.$
C4. $A - \mathcal{E} = A.$
C5. $\mathcal{E} - A = \mathcal{E}.$
C6. $A - A = \mathcal{E}.$
C7. $(A - B) - C = A - (B \cup C).$
C8. $A - (B - C) = (A - B) \cup (A \cap C).$
C9. $A \cup (B - C) = (A \cup B) - (C - A).$
C10. $A \cap (B - C) = (A \cap B) - (A \cap C).$

EXERCISES

1. Test laws in the group A1–A12 by means of Venn diagrams.

2. "Translate" the A-laws into laws about compound statements. Test these by truth tables.

3. Test the laws in groups B and C by Venn diagrams.

4. "Translate" the B- and C-laws into laws about compound statements. Test these by means of truth tables.

5. Derive the following results from the 28 basic laws.
(a) $A = (A \cap B) \cup (A \cap \bar{B})$.
(b) $A \cup B = (A \cap B) \cup (A \cap \bar{B}) \cup (\bar{A} \cap B)$.
(c) $A \cap (A \cup B) = A$.
(d) $A \cup (\bar{A} \cap B) = A \cup B$.

6. From the A- and B-laws and from C1, derive C2–C6.

7. Use A1–A12 and C2–C10 to derive B1, B2, B3, and B6.

SUPPLEMENTARY EXERCISES

Note: Use the following definitions in these exercises: Let $+$ be symmetric difference (see Section 3, Exercise 11), $\times$ be intersection, let 0 be ε and 1 be $\mathfrak{u}$.

8. From A2, A4, and A6 derive the properties of multiplication.

9. Find corresponding properties for addition.

10. Set up addition and multiplication tables for 0 and 1.

11. What do $A \times 0$, $A \times 1$, $A + 0$, and $A + 1$ equal?
[*Ans.* $0; A; A; \bar{A}$.]

12. Show that

$$A \times (B + C) = (A \times B) + (A \times C).$$

13. Show that the following equation is not always true.

$$A + (B \times C) = (A + B) \times (A + C).$$

*5. TWO-DIGIT NUMBER SYSTEMS

In the decimal number system one can write any number by using only the ten digits, 0, 1, 2, . . . , 9. Other number systems can be constructed which use either fewer or more digits. Probably the simplest number system is the *binary number system* which uses only the digits 0 and 1. We shall consider all the possible ways of forming number systems using only these two digits.

The two basic arithmetical operations are addition and multiplication. To understand any arithmetic system, it is necessary to know how to add or multiply any two digits together. Thus to understand the decimal system, we had to learn a multiplication table and an

addition table, each of which had 100 entries. To understand the
binary system, we have to learn a multiplication and an addition
table, each of which has only four
entries. These are shown in Figure
10.

+	0	1
0	0	1
1	1	?

•	0	1
0	0	0
1	0	1

Figure 10

The multiplication table given
there is completely determined by
the two familiar rules that multiplying a number by zero gives zero,
and multiplying a number by one leaves it unchanged. For addition,
we have only the rule that the addition of zero to a number does not
change that number. The latter rule is sufficient to determine all but
one of the entries in the addition table in Figure 10. We must still
decide what shall be the sum $1 + 1$.

What are the possible ways in which we can complete the addition
table? The only one-digit numbers that we can use are 0 and 1, and
these lead to interesting systems. Of the possible two-digit numbers,
we see that 00 and 01 are the same as 0 and 1 and so do not give anything new. The number 11 or any greater number would introduce a
"jump" in the table, hence the only other possibility is 10. The addition tables of these three different number systems are shown in Figure 11, and they all have the multiplication table shown in Figure 10.
Each of these systems is interesting in itself as the interpretations below
show.

Let us say that the *parity* of a positive integer is the fact of it being
odd or even. Consider now the number system having the addition
table in Figure 11a and let 0 represent "even" and 1 represent "odd."

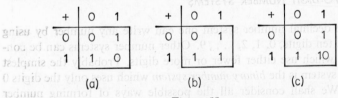

+	0	1
0	0	1
1	1	0

+	0	1
0	0	1
1	1	1

+	0	1
0	0	1
1	1	10

(a)   (b)   (c)

Figure 11

The tables above now tell how the parity of a combination of two
positive integers is related to the parity of each. Thus $0 \cdot 1 = 0$ tells us
that the product of an even number and an odd number is even, while
$1 + 1 = 0$ tells us that the sum of two odd numbers is even, etc. Thus

the first number system is that which we get from the arithmetic of the positive integers if we consider only the parity of numbers.

The second number system, which has the addition table in Figure 11b, has an interpretation in terms of sets. Let 0 correspond to the empty set $\mathcal{E}$ and 1 correspond to the universal set $\mathcal{u}$. Let the addition of numbers correspond to the union of sets and let the multiplication of sets correspond to the intersection of sets. Then $0 \cdot 1 = 0$ tells us that $\mathcal{E} \cap \mathcal{u} = \mathcal{E}$ and $1 + 1 = 1$ tells us that $\mathcal{u} \cup \mathcal{u} = \mathcal{u}$. The student should give the interpretations for the other arithmetic computations possible for this number system.

Finally, the third number system, which has the addition table in Figure 11c, is the so-called *binary number system*. Every ordinary integer can be written as a binary integer. Thus the binary 0 corresponds to the ordinary 0, and the binary unit 1 to the ordinary single unit. The binary number 10 means a "unit of higher order" and corresponds to the ordinary number two (not to ten). The binary number 100 then means two times two or four. In general, if $b_n b_{n-1} \ldots b_2 b_1 b_0$ is a binary number, where each digit is either 0 or 1, then the corresponding ordinary integer I is given by the formula

$$I = b_n \cdot 2^n + b_{n-1} \cdot 2^{n-1} + \ldots + b_2 \cdot 2^2 + b_1 \cdot 2 + b_0.$$

Thus the binary number 11001 corresponds to $2^4 + 2^3 + 1 = 16 + 8 + 1 = 25$. The table in Figure 12 shows some binary numbers and their decimal equivalents.

Binary number	1	10	11	100	101	110	111	1000	10000	100000
Decimal equiv.	1	2	3	4	5	6	7	8	16	32

Figure 12

Because electronic circuits are particularly well adapted to performing computations in the binary system, modern high-speed electronic computers are frequently constructed to work in the binary system.

Example. As an example of a computation, let us multiply 5 by 5 in the binary system. Since the binary equivalent of 5 is the number 101, the multiplication is done as follows.

$$\begin{array}{r} 101 \\ 101 \\ \hline 101 \\ 000 \\ 101 \\ \hline 11001 \end{array}$$

The answer is the binary number 11001, which we saw above was equivalent to the decimal integer 25, the answer we expected to get.

EXERCISES

1. Complete the interpretations of the addition and multiplication tables for the number systems representing (a) parity, (b) the sets $\mathfrak{u}$ and $\mathcal{E}$.

2. (a) What are the binary numbers corresponding to the integers 11, 52, 64, 98, 128, 144?   [*Partial Ans.* 1100010 corresponds to 98.]
   (b) What decimal integers correspond to the binary numbers 1111, 1010101, 1000000, 11011011?

   [*Partial Ans.* 1010101 corresponds to 85.]

3. Carry out the following operations in the binary system. Check your answer.
   (a) $29 + 20$.
   (b) $9 \cdot 7$.

4. Of the laws listed below, which apply to each of the three systems?
   (a) $x + y = y + x$.
   (b) $x + x = x$.
   (c) $x + x + x = x$.

5. Interpret $a + b$ to be the larger of the two numbers a and b, and $a \cdot b$ to be the smaller of the two. Write tables of "addition" and "multiplication" for the digits 0 and 1. Compare the result with the three systems given above.
   [*Ans.* Same as the $\mathfrak{u}$, $\mathcal{E}$ system.]

6. What do the laws A1–A10 of the last section tell us about the second number system established above?

7. The first number system above (about parity) can be interpreted to deal with the remainders of integers when divided by 2. An even number leaves 0, an odd number leaves 1. Construct tables of addition and multiplication for remainders of integers when divided by 3. [*Hint:* These will be 3×3 tables.]

8. Given a set of four elements, suppose that we want to number its subsets. For a given subset, write down a binary number as follows: The first digit is 1 if and only if the first element is in the subset, the second digit is 1 if and only if the second element is in the subset, etc. Prove that this assigns a unique number, from 0 to 15, to each subset.

9. In a multiple choice test the answers were numbered 1, 2, 4, and 8. The students were told that there might be no correct answer, or that one or more answers might be correct. They were told to *add* together the numbers of the correct answers (or to write 0 if no answer was correct).

    (a) By using the result of Exercise 8, show that the resulting number gives the instructor all the information he wants.

    (b) On a given question the correct sum was 7. Three students put down 4, 8, and 15, respectively. Which answer was most nearly correct? Which answer was worst?   [*Ans.* 15 best, 8 worst.]

10. In the ternary number system, numbers are expressed to the base 3, so that 201 in this system stands for $2 \cdot 3^2 + 0 \cdot 3 + 1 \cdot 1 = 19$.

    (a) Write the numbers from 1 through 30 in this notation.

    (b) Construct a table of addition and multiplication for the digits 0, 1, 2.

    (c) Carry out the multiplication of $5 \cdot 5$ in this system. Check your answer.

11. Explain the meaning of the numeral "2907" in our ordinary (base 10) notation, in analogy to the formula *I* given for the binary system.

12. Show that the addition and multiplication tables set up in Section 4, Exercise 10 correspond to one of our three systems.

*6. VOTING COALITIONS

As an application of our set concepts, we shall consider the significance of voting coalitions in voting bodies. Here the universal set is a set of human beings which form a decision-making body. For example, the universal set might be the members of a committee, or of a city council, or of a convention, or of the House of Representatives, etc. Each member can cast a certain number of votes. The decision as to whether or not a measure is passed can be decided by a simple majority rule, or $\frac{2}{3}$ majority, etc.

Suppose now that a subset of the members of the body forms a coalition in order to pass a measure. The question is whether or not they have enough votes to guarantee passage of the measure. If they have enough votes to carry the measure, then we say they form a *winning coalition*. If the members *not* in the coalition can pass a measure of their own, then we say that the original coalition is a *losing coalition*. Finally, if the members of the coalition cannot carry their measure, and if the members not in the coalition cannot carry their measure, then the coalition is called a *blocking coalition*.

Let us restate these definitions in set-theoretic terms. A coalition C is winning if they have enough votes to carry an issue; coalition C is losing if the coalition $\tilde{C}$ is winning; and coalition C is blocking if neither C nor $\tilde{C}$ is a winning coalition.

The following facts are immediate consequences of these definitions. The complement of a winning coalition is a losing coalition. The complement of a losing coalition is a winning coalition. The complement of a blocking coalition is a blocking coalition.

Example 1. A committee consists of six men each having one vote. A simple majority vote will carry an issue. Then any coalition of four or more members is winning, any coalition with one or two members is losing, and any three-person coalition is blocking.

Example 2. Suppose in Example 1 one of the six members (say the chairman) is given the additional power to break ties. Then any three-person coalition of which he is a member is winning, while the other three-person coalitions are losing; hence there are no blocking coalitions. The other coalitions are as in Example 1.

Example 3. Let the universal set $\mathfrak{U}$ be the set $\{x, y, w, z\}$, where x and y each has one vote, w has two votes, and z has three votes. Suppose it takes five votes to carry a measure. Then the winning coalitions are: $\{z, w\}$, $\{z, x, y\}$, $\{z, w, x\}$, $\{z, w, y\}$, and $\mathfrak{U}$. The losing coalitions are the complements of these sets. Blocking coalitions are: $\{z\}$, $\{z, x\}$, $\{z, y\}$, $\{w, x\}$, $\{w, y\}$, and $\{w, x, y\}$.

The last example shows that it is not always necessary to list all members of a winning coalition. For example, if the coalition $\{z, w\}$ is winning, then it is obvious that the coalition $\{z, w, y\}$ is also winning. In general, if a coalition C is winning, then any other set that has C as a subset will also be winning. Thus we are led to the notion of a *minimal winning coalition*. A minimal winning coalition is a winning coalition which contains no smaller winning coalition as a subset. Another way of stating this is that a minimal winning coalition is a winning coalition such that, if any member is lost from the coalition, then it ceases to be a winning coalition.

If we know the minimal winning coalitions, then we know everything that we need to know about the voting problem. The winning coalitions are all those sets that contain a minimal winning coalition, and the losing coalitions are the complements of the winning coalitions. All other sets are blocking coalitions.

In Example 1 the minimal winning coalitions are the sets containing four members. In Example 2 the minimal winning coalitions are the three-member coalitions that contain the tie-breaking member and the four-member coalitions that do not contain the tie-breaking member. The minimal winning coalitions in the third example are the sets $\{z, w\}$ and $\{z, x, y\}$.

Sometimes there are committee members who have special powers or lack of power. If a member can pass any measure he wishes without needing anyone else to vote with him, then we call him a *dictator*. Thus member x is a dictator if and only if $\{x\}$ is a winning coalition. A somewhat weaker but still very powerful member is one who can by himself block any measure. If x is such a member, then we say that x has *veto power*. Thus x has veto power if and only if $\{x\}$ is a blocking coalition. Finally if x is not a member of any minimal winning coalition, we shall call him a *powerless* member. Thus x is powerless if and only if any winning coalition of which x is a member is a winning coalition without him.

Example 4. An interesting example of a decision-making body is the Security Council of the United Nations. The Security Council has eleven members consisting of the five permanent large-nation members called the Big Five, and six small-nation members. In order that a measure be passed by the Council, seven members including all of the Big Five must vote for the measure. Thus the seven-member sets made up of the Big Five plus two small nations are the minimal winning coalitions. Then the losing coalitions are the sets that contain at most four small nations. The blocking coalitions are the sets that are neither winning nor losing. In particular, a unit set that contains one of the Big Five as a member is a blocking coalition. This is the sense in which a Big Five member has a veto. [The possibility of "abstaining" is immaterial in the above discussion.]

In 1966 the number of small-nation members was increased to 10. A measure now requires the vote of nine members, including all of the Big Five. (See Exercise 11.)

EXERCISES

1. A committee has w, x, y, and z as members. Member w has two votes, the others have one vote each. List the winning, losing, and blocking coalitions.

2. A committee has n members, each with one vote. It takes a majority vote to carry an issue. What are the winning, losing, and blocking coalitions?

3. The Board of Estimate of New York City consists of eight members with voting strength as follows:

s.	Mayor	4 votes
t.	Controller	4
u.	Council President	4
v.	Brooklyn Borough President	2
w.	Manhattan Borough President	2
x.	Bronx Borough President	2
y.	Richmond Borough President	2
z.	Queens Borough President	2

A simple majority is needed to carry an issue. List the minimal winning coalitions. List the blocking coalitions. Do the same if we give the mayor the additional power to break ties.

4. A company has issued 100,000 shares of common stock and each share has one vote. How many shares must a stockholder have to be a dictator? How many to have a veto?   [*Ans.* 50,001; 50,000.]

5. In Exercise 4, if the company requires a $\frac{2}{3}$ majority vote to carry an issue, how many shares must a stockholder have to be a dictator or to have a veto?   [*Ans.* At least 66,667; at least 33,334.]

6. Prove that if a committee has a dictator as a member, then the remaining members are powerless.

7. We can define a maximal losing coalition in analogy to the minimal winning coalitions. What is the relation between the maximal losing and minimal winning coalitions? Do the maximal losing coalitions provide all relevant information?

8. Prove that any two minimal winning coalitions have at least one member in common.

9. Find all the blocking coalitions in the Security Council example.

10. Prove that if a man has veto power and if he together with any one other member can carry a measure, then the distribution of the remaining votes is irrelevant.

11. Find the winning, losing, and blocking coalitions in the Security Council, using the revised (1966) structure.

SUGGESTED READING

Birkhoff, G., and S. MacLane, *A Survey of Modern Algebra*, Macmillan, New York, 1953, Chapter XI.

Tarski, A., *Introduction to Logic*, Oxford University Press, New York, 2d rev. ed., 1946, Chapter IV.

Allendoerfer, C. B., and C. O. Oakley, *Principles of Mathematics*, McGraw-Hill, New York, 1955, Chapter V.

Johnstone, H. W., Jr., *Elementary Deductive Logic*, Crowell, New York, 1954, Part Three.

Breuer, Joseph, *Introduction to the Theory of Sets*, Prentice-Hall, Englewood Cliffs, N. J., 1958.

Fraenkel, A. A., *Abstract Set Theory*, North-Holland Publishing Co., Amsterdam, 1953.

Kemeny, John G., Hazleton Mirkil, J. Laurie Snell, and Gerald L. Thompson, *Finite Mathematical Structures*, Prentice-Hall, Englewood Cliffs, N. J., 1959, Chapter 2.

Partitions and counting

1. PARTITIONS

The problems to be studied in this chapter can be most conveniently described in terms of partitions of a set. A *partition* of a set $\mathfrak{U}$ is a subdivision of the set into subsets that are disjoint and exhaustive, i.e., every element of $\mathfrak{U}$ must belong to one and only one of the subsets. The subsets A_i in the partition are called *cells*. Thus $[A_1, A_2, \ldots, A_r]$ is a partition of $\mathfrak{U}$ if two conditions are satisfied: (1) $A_i \cap A_j = \mathcal{E}$ if $i \neq j$ (the cells are disjoint) and (2) $A_1 \cup A_2 \cup \ldots \cup A_r = \mathfrak{U}$ (the cells are exhaustive).

Example 1. If $\mathfrak{U} = \{a, b, c, d, e\}$, then $[\{a, b\}, \{c, d, e\}]$ and $[\{b, c, e\}, \{a\}, \{d\}]$ and $[\{a\}, \{b\}, \{c\}, \{d\}, \{e\}]$ are three different partitions of $\mathfrak{U}$. The last is a partition into unit sets.

The process of going from a fine to a less fine analysis of a set of logical possibilities is actually carried out by means of a partition. For example, let us consider the logical possibilities for the first three games of the World Series if the Yankees play the Dodgers. We can list the possibilities in terms of the winner of each game as

$$\{YYY, YYD, YDY, DYY, YDD, DDY, DYD, DDD\}.$$

We form a partition by putting all the possibilities with the same number of wins for the Yankees in a single cell,

$$[\{YYY\}, \{YYD, YDY, DYY\}, \{YDD, DDY, DYD\}, \{DDD\}].$$

Thus, if we wish the possibilities to be Yankees win three games, win two, win one, win zero, then we are considering a less detailed analysis obtained from the former analysis by identifying the possibilities in each cell of the partition.

If $[A_1, A_2, \ldots, A_r]$ and $[B_1, B_2, B_3, \ldots, B_s]$ are two partitions of the same set $\mathfrak{U}$, we can obtain a new partition by considering the collection of all subsets of $\mathfrak{U}$ of the form $A_i \cap B_j$ (see Exercise 7). This new partition is called the *cross-partition* of the original two partitions.

Example 2. A common use of cross-partitions is in the problem of classification. For example, from the set $\mathfrak{U}$ of all life forms we can form the partition $[P, A]$ where P is the set of all plants and A is the set of all animals. We may also form the partition $[E, F]$ where E is the set of extinct life forms and F is the set of all existing life forms. The cross-partition

$$[P \cap E, \quad P \cap F, \quad A \cap E, \quad A \cap F]$$

gives a complete classification according to the two separate classifications.

Many of the examples with which we shall deal in the future will relate to processes which take place in stages. It will be convenient to use partitions and cross-partitions to represent the stages of the process. The graphical representation of such a process is, of course, a tree. For example, suppose that the process is such that we learn in succession the truth values of a series of statements relative to a given situation. If $\mathfrak{U}$ is the set of logical possibilities for the situation, and p is a statement relative to $\mathfrak{U}$, then the knowledge of the truth value of p amounts to knowing which cell of the partition $[P, \tilde{P}]$ contains the actual possibility. Recall that P is the truth set of p, and $\tilde{P}$ is the truth set of $\sim p$. Suppose now we discover the truth value of a second statement q. This information can again be described by a partition, namely, $[Q, \tilde{Q}]$. The two statements together give us information which can be represented by the cross-partition of these two partitions,

$$[P \cap Q, \quad P \cap \tilde{Q}, \quad \tilde{P} \cap Q, \quad \tilde{P} \cap \tilde{Q}].$$

That is, if we know the truth values of p and q, we also know which of the cells of this cross-partition contains the particular logical possibility describing the given situation. Conversely, if we knew which cell contained the possibility, we would know the truth values for the statements p and q.

The information obtained by the additional knowledge of the truth value of a third statement r, having a truth set R, can be represented by the cross-partition of the three partitions $[P, \tilde{P}]$, $[Q, \tilde{Q}]$, $[R, \tilde{R}]$. This cross-partition is

$$[P \cap Q \cap R, \quad P \cap Q \cap \tilde{R}, \quad P \cap \tilde{Q} \cap R, \quad \tilde{P} \cap Q \cap R,$$
$$P \cap \tilde{Q} \cap \tilde{R}, \quad \tilde{P} \cap Q \cap \tilde{R}, \quad \tilde{P} \cap \tilde{Q} \cap R, \quad \tilde{P} \cap \tilde{Q} \cap \tilde{R}].$$

Notice that now we have the possibility narrowed down to being in one of $8 = 2^3$ possible cells. Similarly, if we knew the truth values of n statements, our partition would have 2^n cells.

If the set $\mathcal{U}$ were to contain 2^{20} (approximately one million) logical possibilities, and if we were able to ask yes-no questions in such a way that the knowledge of the truth value of each question would cut the number of possibilities in half each time, then we could determine in 20 questions any given possibility in the set $\mathcal{U}$. We could accomplish this kind of questioning, for example, if we had a list of all the possibilities and were allowed to ask "Is it in the first half?" and, if the answer is yes, then "Is it in the first one-fourth?," etc. In practice we ordinarily do not have such a list, and we can only approximate this procedure.

Example 3. In the familiar radio game of twenty questions it is not unusual for a contestant to try to carry out a partitioning of the above kind. For example, he may know that he is trying to guess a city. He might ask, "Is the city in North America?" and if the answer is yes, "Is it in the United States?" and if yes, "Is it west of the Mississippi?" and if no, "Is it in the New England states?," etc. Of course, the above procedure does not actually divide the possibilities exactly in half each time. The more nearly the answer to each question comes to dividing the possibilities in half, the more certain one can be of getting the answer in twenty questions, if there are at most a million possibilities.

EXERCISES

1. If $\mathfrak{U}$ is the set of integers from 1 to 6, find the cross-partitions of the following pairs of partitions.

   (a) $[\{1, 2, 3\}, \{4, 5, 6\}]$ and $[\{1, 4\}, \{2, 3, 5, 6\}]$.

   (b) $[\{1, 2, 3, 4, 5\}, \{6\}]$ and $[\{1, 3, 5\}, \{2, 6\}, \{4\}]$.

                                            [Ans. (a) $\{1\}, \{2, 3\}, \{4\}, \{5, 6\}$.]

2. A coin is thrown three times. List the possibilities according to which side turns up each time. Give the partition formed by putting in the same cell all those possibilities for which the same number of heads occur.

3. Let p and q be two statements with truth set P and Q. What can be said about the cross-partition of $[P, \bar{P}]$ and $[Q, \bar{Q}]$ in the case that

   (a) p implies q.   *[Ans.* $P \cap \bar{Q} = \varepsilon$.]

   (b) p is equivalent to q.

   (c) p and q are inconsistent.

4. Consider the set of eight states consisting of Illinois, Colorado, Michigan, New York, Vermont, Texas, Alabama, and California.

   (a) Show that in three "yes" or "no" questions one can identify any one of the eight states.

   (b) Design a set of three "yes" or "no" questions which can be answered independently of each other and which will serve to identify any one of the states.

5. An unabridged dictionary contains about 600,000 words and 3000 pages. If a person chooses a word from such a dictionary, is it possible to identify this word by twenty "yes" or "no" questions? If so, describe the procedure that you would use and discuss the feasibility of the procedure.

   [Ans. One solution is the following. Use 12 questions to locate the page, but then you may need 9 questions to locate the word.]

6. Mr. Jones has two parents, each of his parents had two parents, each of these had two parents, etc. Tracing a person's family tree back 40 generations (about 1000 years) gives Mr. Jones 2^{40} ancestors, which is more people than have been on the earth in the last 1000 years. What is wrong with this argument?

7. Let $[A_1, A_2, A_3]$ and $[B_1, B_2]$ be two partitions. Prove that the cross-partition of the two given partitions really is a partition, that is, it satisfies requirements (1) and (2) for partitions.

8. The cross-partition formed from the truth sets of n statements has 2^n cells. As seen in Chapter I, the truth table of a statement compounded from n statements has 2^n rows. What is the relationship between these two facts?

9. Let p and q be statements with truth sets P and Q. Form the partition $[P \cap Q, P \cap \tilde{Q}, \tilde{P} \cap Q, \tilde{P} \cap \tilde{Q}]$. State in each case below which of the cells must be empty in order to make the given statement a logically true statement.

(a) $p \to q$.

(b) $p \leftrightarrow q$.

(c) $p \vee \sim p$.

(d) p.

10. A partition $[A_1, A_2, \ldots, A_n]$ is said to be a *refinement* of the partition $[B_1, B_2, \ldots, B_m]$ if every A_j is a subset of some B_k. Show that a cross-partition of two partitions is a refinement of each of the partitions from which the cross-partition is formed.

11. Consider the partition of the people in the United States determined by classification according to states. The classification according to county determines a second partition. Show that this is a refinement of the first partition. Give a third partition which is different from each of these and is a refinement of both.

12. What can be said concerning the cross-partition of two partitions, one of which is a refinement of the other?

13. Given nine objects, of which it is known that eight have the same weight and one is heavier, show how, in two weighings with a pan balance, the heavy one can be identified.

14. Suppose that you are given thirteen objects, twelve of which are the same, but one is either heavier or lighter than the others. Show that, with three weighings using a pan balance, it is possible to identify the odd object. [A complete solution to this problem is given on page 42 of *Mathematical Snapshots*, second edition, by H. Steinhaus.]

15. A subject can be completely classified by introducing several simple subdivisions and taking their cross-partition. Thus, courses in college may be partitioned according to subject, level of advancement, number of students, hours per week, interests, etc. For each of the following subjects, introduce five or more partitions. How many cells are there in the complete classification (cross-partition) in each case?

(a) Detective stories.

(b) Diseases.

16. Assume that in a given generation x men are Republicans and y are Democrats and that the total number of men remains at 50 million in each generation. Assume further that it is known that 20 per cent of the sons of Republicans are Democrats and 30 per cent of the sons of Democrats are Republicans in any generation. What conditions must x and y satisfy if there are to be the same number of Republicans in each generation? Is there more than one choice for x and y? If not, what must x and y be?

[*Partial Ans.* There are 30 million Republicans.]

17. Assume that there are 30 million Democratic and 20 million Republican men in the country. It is known that p per cent of the sons of Democrats are Republicans, and q per cent of the sons of Republicans are Democrats. If the total number of men remains 50 million, what condition must p and q satisfy so that the number in each party remains the same? Is there more than one choice of p and q?

2. THE NUMBER OF ELEMENTS IN A SET

The remainder of this chapter will be devoted to certain counting problems. For any set X we shall denote by $n(X)$ the number of elements in the set.

Suppose we know the number of elements in certain given sets and wish to know the number in other sets related to these by the operations of unions, intersections, and complementations. As an example, consider the following problem.

Suppose that we are told that 100 students take mathematics, and 150 students take economics. Can we then tell how many take either mathematics or economics? The answer is no, since clearly we would also need to know how many students take both courses. If we know that no student takes both courses, i.e., if we know that the two sets of students are disjoint, then the answer would be the sum of the two numbers or 250 students.

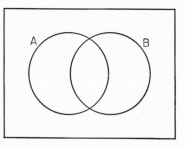

Figure 1

In general, if we are given disjoint sets A and B, then it is true that $n(A \cup B) = n(A) + n(B)$. Suppose now that A and B are not disjoint as shown in Figure 1. We can divide the set A into disjoint sets $A \cap \tilde{B}$ and $A \cap B$. Similarly, we can divide B into the disjoint sets $\tilde{A} \cap B$ and $A \cap B$. Thus,

$$n(A) = n(A \cap \bar{B}) + n(A \cap B)$$
$$n(B) = n(\bar{A} \cap B) + n(A \cap B).$$

Adding these two equations, we obtain

$$n(A) + n(B) = n(A \cap \bar{B}) + n(\bar{A} \cap B) + 2n(A \cap B).$$

Since the sets $A \cap \bar{B}$, $\bar{A} \cap B$, and $A \cap B$ are disjoint sets whose union is $A \cup B$, we obtain the formula

$$n(A \cup B) = n(A) + n(B) - n(A \cap B),$$

which is valid for any two sets A and B.

Example 1. Let p and q be statements relative to a set $\mathfrak{U}$ of logical possibilities. Denote by P and Q the truth sets of these statements. The truth set of $p \vee q$ is $P \cup Q$ and the truth set of $p \wedge q$ is $P \cap Q$. Thus the above formula enables us to find the number of cases where $p \vee q$ is true if we know the number of cases for which p, q, and $p \wedge q$ are true.

Example 2. *More than two sets.* It is possible to derive formulas for the number of elements in a set which is the union of more than two sets (see Exercise 6), but usually it is easier to work with Venn diagrams. For example, suppose that the registrar of a school reports the following statistics about a group of 30 students:

Figure 2

19   take mathematics.
17   take music.
11   take history.
12   take mathematics and music.
7   take history and mathematics.
5   take music and history.
2   take mathematics, history, and music.

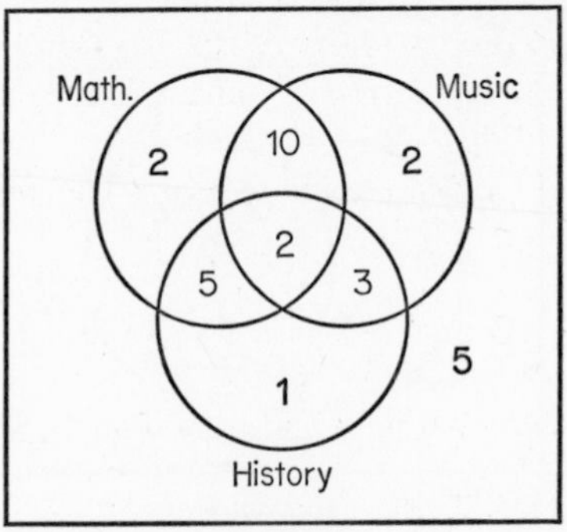

We draw the Venn diagram in Figure 2 and fill in the numbers for the number of elements in each subset working from the bottom of our list to the top. That is, since 2 students take all three courses, and 5 take music and history, then 3 take history and music but not mathematics, etc. Once the diagram is completed we can read off the number which take any combination of the courses. For example, the number which take history but not mathematics is $3 + 1 = 4$.

Example 3. Cancer studies. The following reasoning is often found in statistical studies on the effect of smoking on the incidence of lung cancer. Suppose a study has shown that the fraction of smokers among those who have lung cancer is greater than the fraction of smokers among those who do not have lung cancer. It is then asserted that the fraction of smokers who have lung cancer is greater than the fraction of nonsmokers who have lung cancer. Let us examine this argument.

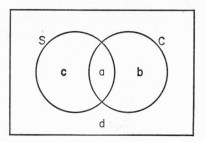

Figure 3

Let S be the set of all smokers in the population, and C be the set of all people with lung cancer. Let $a = n(S \cap C)$, $b = n(\tilde{S} \cap C)$, $c = n(S \cap \tilde{C})$, and $d = n(\tilde{S} \cap \tilde{C})$, as indicated in Figure 3. The fractions in which we are interested are

$$p_1 = \frac{a}{a+b}, \quad p_2 = \frac{c}{c+d}, \quad p_3 = \frac{a}{a+c}, \quad p_4 = \frac{b}{b+d},$$

where p_1 is the fraction of those with lung cancer that smoke, p_2 the fraction of those without lung cancer that smoke, p_3 the fraction of smokers who have lung cancer, and p_4 the fraction of nonsmokers who have cancer.

The argument above states that if $p_1 > p_2$, then $p_3 > p_4$. The hypothesis,

$$\frac{a}{a+b} > \frac{c}{c+d}$$

is true if and only if $ac + ad > ac + bc$, that is, if and only if $ad > bc$. The conclusion

$$\frac{a}{a+c} > \frac{b}{b+d}$$

is true if and only if $ab + ad > ab + bc$, that is, if and only if $ad > bc$. Thus the two statements $p_1 > p_2$ and $p_3 > p_4$ are in fact equivalent statements, so that the argument is valid.

EXERCISES

1. In Example 2, find
   (a) The number of students that take mathematics but do not take history.   [*Ans.* 12.]
   (b) The number that take exactly two of the three courses.
   (c) The number that take one or none of the courses.

2. In a chemistry class there are 20 students, and in a psychology class there are 30 students. Find the number in either the psychology class or the chemistry class if
   (a) The two classes meet at the same hour.   [*Ans.* 50.]
   (b) The two classes meet at different hours and 10 students are enrolled in both courses.   [*Ans.* 40.]

3. If the truth set of a statement p has 10 elements, and the truth set of a statement q has 20 elements, find the number of elements in the truth set of $p \vee q$ if
   (a) p and q are inconsistent.
   (b) p and q are consistent and there are two elements in the truth set of $p \wedge q$.

4. If p is a statement that is true in ten cases, and q is a statement that is true in five cases, find the number of cases in which both p and q are true if $p \vee q$ is true in ten cases. What relation holds between p and q?

5. Assume that the incidence of lung cancer is 16 per 100,000, and that it is estimated that 75 per cent of those with lung cancer smoke and 60 per cent of those without lung cancer smoke. (These numbers are fictitious.) Estimate the fraction of smokers with lung cancer, and the fraction of non-smokers with lung cancer.   [*Ans.* 20 and 10 per 100,000.]

6. Let A, B, and C be any three sets of a universal set $\mathfrak{U}$. Draw a Venn diagram and show that

$$n(A \cup B \cup C) = n(A) + n(B) + n(C) - n(A \cap B)$$
$$- n(B \cap C) - n(A \cap C) + n(A \cap B \cap C).$$

7. Analyze the data given below and draw a Venn diagram like that in Figure 2. Assuming that every student in the school takes one of the courses, find the total number of students in the school.

(a)	(b)	
28	36	students take English.
23	23	students take French.

23	13	students take German.
12	6	students take English and French.
11	11	students take English and German.
8	4	students take French and German.
5	1	students take all three courses.

Comment on the result in (b).

8. Suppose that in a survey concerning the reading habits of students it is found that:

> 60 per cent read magazine A.
> 50 per cent read magazine B.
> 50 per cent read magazine C.
> 30 per cent read magazines A and B.
> 20 per cent read magazines B and C.
> 30 per cent read magazines A and C.
> 10 per cent read all three magazines.

(a) What per cent read exactly two magazines?   [*Ans.* 50.]
(b) What per cent do not read any of the magazines?   [*Ans.* 10.]

9. If p and q are equivalent statements and $n(P) = 10$, what is $n(P \cup Q)$?

10. If p implies q, prove that $n(P \cup \tilde{Q}) = n(P) + n(\tilde{Q})$.

11. On a transcontinental airliner, there are 9 boys, 5 American children, 9 men, 7 foreign boys, 14 Americans, 6 American males, and 7 foreign females. What is the number of people on the plane?   [*Ans.* 33.]

SUPPLEMENTARY EXERCISES

12. Prove that $n(\tilde{A}) = n(\mathfrak{U}) - n(A)$.

13. Show that $n(\tilde{A} \cap \tilde{B}) = n(\widetilde{A \cup B}) = n(\mathfrak{U}) - n(A \cup B)$.

14. In a collection of baseball players there are ten who can play only outfield positions, five who can play only infield positions but cannot pitch, three who can pitch, four who can play any position but pitcher, and two who can play any position at all. How many players are there in all?

[*Ans.* 22.]

15. Ivyten College awarded 38 varsity letters in football, 15 in basketball, and 20 in baseball. If these letters went to a total of 58 men and only three of these men lettered in all three sports, how many men received letters in exactly two of the three sports?   [*Ans.* 9.]

16. Let $\mathfrak{U}$ be a finite set. For any two sets A and B define the "distance" from A to B to be $d(A, B) = n(A \cap \tilde{B}) + n(\tilde{A} \cap B)$.

(a) Show that $d(A, B) \geq 0$. When is $d(A, B) = 0$?

(b) If A, B, and C are nonintersecting sets, show that

$$d(A, C) \leq d(A, B) + d(B, C).$$

(c) Show that for any three sets A, B, and C

$$d(A, C) \leq d(A, B) + d(B, C).$$

3. PERMUTATIONS

We wish to consider here the number of ways in which a group of n different objects can be arranged. A listing of n different objects *in a certain order* is called a *permutation* of the n objects. We consider first the case of three objects, a, b, and c. We can exhibit all possible permu-

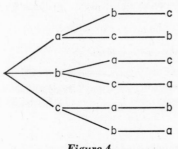

tations of these three objects as paths of a tree, as shown in Figure 4. Each path exhibits a possible permutation, and there are six such paths. We could also list these permutations as follows:

abc,	bca,
acb,	cab,
bac,	cba.

Figure 4

If we were to construct a similar tree for n objects, we would find that the number of paths could be found by multiplying together the numbers n, $n - 1$, $n - 2$, continuing down to the number 1. The number obtained in this way occurs so often that we give it a symbol, namely $n!$, which is read "n factorial." Thus, for example, $3! = 3 \cdot 2 \cdot 1 = 6$, $4! = 4 \cdot 3 \cdot 2 \cdot 1 = 24$, etc. For reasons which will be clear later, we define $0! = 1$. Thus we can say *there are $n!$ different permutations of n distinct objects.*

Example 1. In the game of Scrabble, suppose there are seven lettered blocks from which we try to form a seven-letter word. If the seven letters are all different, we must consider $7! = 5040$ different orders.

Example 2. A quarterback has a sequence of ten plays. Suppose his coach instructs him to run through the ten-play sequence without repetition. How much freedom is left to the quarterback? He may choose any one of 10! = 3,628,800 orders in which to call the plays.

Example 3. How many ways can *n* people be seated around a circular table? When this question is asked, it is usually understood that two arrangements are different only if at least one person has a different person next to him in the two arrangements. Consider then one person in a fixed position. There are (*n* − 1)! ways in which the other people may be seated. We have now counted all the arrangements we wish to consider different.

A general principle. There are many counting problems for which it is not possible to give a simple formula for the number of possible cases. In many of these the only way to find the number of cases is to draw a tree and count them (see Exercise 4). In some problems, the following general principle is useful.

If one thing can be done in exactly r different ways, for each of these a second thing can be done in exactly s different ways, for each of the first two, a third can be done in exactly t ways, etc., then the sequence of things can be done in the product of the numbers of ways in which the individual things can be done, i.e., r·s·t . . . ways.

The validity of the above general principle can be established by thinking of a tree representing all the ways in which the sequence of things can be done. There would be *r* branches from the starting position. From the ends of each of these *r* branches there would be *s* new branches, and from each of these *t* new branches, etc. The number of paths through the tree would be given by the product *r·s·t* . . . .

Example 4. The number of permutations of *n* distinct objects is a special case of this principle. If we were to list all the possible permutations, there would be *n* possibilities for the first, for each of these *n* − 1 for the second, etc., until we came to the last object, and for which there is only one possibility. Thus there are *n*(*n* − 1) . . . 1 = *n*! possibilities in all.

Example 5. If there are three roads from city x to city y and two roads from city y to city z, then there are $3 \cdot 2 = 6$ ways that a person can drive from city x to city z passing through city y.

Example 6. Suppose there are n applicants for a certain job. Three interviewers are asked independently to rank the applicants according to their suitability for the job. It is decided that an applicant will be hired if he is ranked first by at least two of the three interviewers. What fraction of the possible reports would lead to the acceptance of some candidate? We shall solve this problem by finding the fraction of the reports which do not lead to an acceptance and subtract this answer from 1. Frequently, an indirect attack of this kind on a problem is easier than the direct approach. The total number of reports possible is $(n!)^3$ since each interviewer can rank the men in $n!$ different ways. If a particular report does not lead to the acceptance of a candidate, it must be true that each interviewer has put a different man in first place. This can be done in $n(n - 1)(n - 2)$ different ways by our general principle. For each possible first choices, there are $[(n - 1)!]^3$ ways in which the remaining men can be ranked by the interviewers. Thus the number of reports which do not lead to acceptance is $n(n - 1)(n - 2)[(n - 1)!]^3$. Dividing this number by $(n!)^3$ we obtain

$$\frac{(n - 1)(n - 2)}{n^2}$$

as the fraction of reports which fail to accept a candidate. The fraction which leads to acceptance is found by subtracting this fraction from 1 which gives

$$\frac{3n - 2}{n^2}.$$

For the case of three applicants, we see that $\frac{7}{9}$ of the possibilities lead to acceptance. Here the procedure might be criticized on the grounds that even if the interviewers are completely ineffective and are essentially guessing there is a good chance that a candidate will be accepted on the basis of the reports. For n equal to ten, the fraction of acceptances is only .28, so that it is possible to attach more significance to the interviewers ratings, if they reach a decision.

EXERCISES

1. In how many ways can five people be lined up in a row for a group picture? In how many ways if it is desired to have three in the front row and two in the back row?   [*Ans.* 120; 120.]

2. Assuming that a baseball team is determined by the players and the position each is playing, how many teams can be made from 13 players if
    (a) Each player can play any position?
    (b) Two of the players can be used only as pitchers?

3. Grades of A, B, C, D, or E are assigned to a class of five students.
    (a) How many ways may this be done, if no two students receive the same grade?   [*Ans.* 120.]
    (b) Two of the students are named Smith and Jones. How many ways can grades be assigned if no two students receive the same grade and Smith must receive a higher grade than Jones?   [*Ans.* 60.]
    (c) How many ways may grades be assigned if only grades of A and E are assigned?   [*Ans.* 32.]

4. A certain club wishes to admit seven new members, four of whom are Republicans and three of whom are Democrats. Suppose the club wishes to admit them one at a time and in such a way that there are always more Republicans among the new members than there are Democrats. Draw a tree to represent all possible ways in which new members can be admitted, distinguishing members by their party only.

5. There are three different routes connecting city A to city B. How many ways can a round trip be made from A to B and back? How many ways if it is desired to take a different route on the way back?   [*Ans.* 9; 6.]

6. How many different ways can a ten-question multiple-choice exam be answered if each question has three possibilities, a, b, and c? How many if no two consecutive answers are the same?

7. Modify Example 6 so that, to be accepted, an applicant must be first in two of the interviewers' ratings and must be either first or second in the third interviewers' rating. What fraction of the possible reports lead to acceptance in the case of three applicants? In the case of n?   [*Ans.* $\frac{4}{9}$; $4/n^2$.]

8. A town has 1240 registered Republicans. It is desired to contact each of these by phone to announce a meeting. A committee of r people devise a method of phoning s people each and asking each of these to call t new people. If the method is such that no person is called twice,
    (a) How many people know about the meeting after the phoning?

(b) If the committee has 40 members and it is desired that all 1240 Republicans be informed of the meeting and that s and t should be the same, what should they be?

9. In the Scrabble example, suppose the letters are Q, Q, U, F, F, F, A. How many distinguishable arrangements are there for these seven letters?

[*Ans.* 420.]

10. How many different necklaces can be made
(a) If seven different sized beads are available? [*Ans.* 360.]
(b) If six of the beads are the same size and one is larger? [*Ans.* 1.]
(c) If the beads are of two sizes, five of the smaller size and two of the larger size? [*Ans.* 3.]

11. Prove that two people in Columbus, Ohio, have the same initials.

12. Find the number of arrangements of the five symbols that can be distinguished. (The same letters with different subscripts indicate distinguishable objects.)

(a) A_1, A_2, B_1, B_2, B_3. [*Ans.* 120.]
(b) A, A, B_1, B_2, B_3. [*Ans.* 60.]
(c) A, A, B, B, B. [*Ans.* 10.]

13. Show that the number of distinguishable arrangements possible for n objects, n_1 of type 1, n_2 of type 2, etc., for r different types is

$$\frac{n!}{n_1!\, n_2! \ldots, n_r!}.$$

SUPPLEMENTARY EXERCISES

14. (a) How many four digit numbers can be formed from the digits 1, 2, 3, 4, using each digit only once?
(b) How many of these numbers are less than 3000? [*Ans.* 12.]

15. How many license plates can be made if they are to contain five symbols, the first two being letters and the last three integers?

16. How many signals can a ship show if it has seven flags and a signal consists of five flags hoisted vertically on a rope? [*Ans.* 2520.]

17. We must arrange three green, two red, and four blue books on a single shelf.

(a) In how many ways can this be done if there are no restrictions?
(b) In how many ways if books of the same color must be grouped together?

(c) In how many ways if, in addition to the restriction in (b), the red books must be to the left of the blue books?

(d) In how many ways if, in addition to the restrictions in (b) and (c), the red and blue books must not be next to each other? [*Ans.* 288.]

18. A young lady has three shades of nail polish with which to paint her fingernails. In how many ways can she do this (each nail being one solid color) if there are no more than two different shades on each hand?

[*Ans.* 8649.]

4. COUNTING PARTITIONS

Up to now we have not had occasion to consider the partitions [{1, 2}, {3, 4}] and [{3, 4}, {1, 2}] of the integers from 1 to 4 as being different partitions. Here it will be convenient to do so, and to indicate this distinction we shall use the term *ordered partition*. An *ordered partition with r cells* is a partition with *r* cells (some of which may be empty), with a particular order specified for the cells.

We are interested in counting the number of possible ordered partitions with *r* cells that can be formed from a set of *n* objects having a prescribed number of elements in each cell. We consider first a special case to illustrate the general procedure.

Suppose that we have eight students, A, B, C, D, E, F, G, and H, and we wish to assign these to three rooms, Room 1, which is a triple room, Room 2, a triple room, and Room 3, a double room. In how many different ways can the assignment be made? One way to assign the students is to put them in the rooms in the order in which they arrive, putting the first three in Room 1, the next three in Room 2, and the last two in Room 3. There are 8! ways in which the students can arrive, but not all of these lead to different assignments. We can represent the assignment corresponding to a particular order of arrival as follows,

|BCA|DFE|HG|.

In this case, B, C, and A are assigned to Room 1, D, F, and E to Room 2, and H and G to Room 3. Notice that orders of arrival which simply change the order within the rooms lead to the same assignment. The number of different orders of arrival which lead to the same assignment as the one above is the number of arrangements which differ from the given one only in that the arrangement within the rooms is different. There are $3! \cdot 3! \cdot 2!$ such orders of arrival, since we can arrange the three in Room 1 in 3! different ways, for each of these the ones in Room 2 in 3! different ways, and for each of these, the ones in Room 3 in 2! ways. Thus we can divide the 8! different orders of arrival into groups of $3! \cdot 3! \cdot 2!$ different orders such that all the orders of arrival in a single group lead to the same room assignment. Since there are $3! \cdot 3! \cdot 2!$ elements in each group and 8! elements altogether, there are $\dfrac{8!}{3! \, 3! \, 2!}$ groups, or this many different room assignments.

The same argument could be carried out for n elements and r rooms, with n_1 in the first, n_2 in the second, etc. This would lead to the following result. Let $n_1, n_2, \ldots, n_r$ be nonnegative integers with

$$n_1 + n_2 + \ldots + n_r = n.$$

Then:

The number of ordered partitions with r cells $[A_1, A_2, A_3, \ldots, A_r]$ of a set of n elements with n_1 in the first cell, n_2 in the second, etc. is

$$\frac{n!}{n_1! \, n_2! \ldots n_r!}.$$

We shall denote this number by the symbol

$$\binom{n}{n_1, n_2, \ldots, n_r}.$$

Note that this symbol is defined only if $n_1 + n_2 + \ldots + n_r = n$.

The special case of two cells is particularly important. Here the problem can be stated equivalently as the problem of finding the number of subsets with r elements that can be chosen from a set of n elements. This is true because any choice defines a partition $[A, \bar{A}]$, where A is the set of elements chosen and $\bar{A}$ is the set of remaining elements. The number of such partitions is $\dfrac{n!}{r!(n-r)!}$ and hence this is also the number of subsets with r elements. Our notation $\binom{n}{r, n-r}$ for this case is shortened to $\binom{n}{r}$.

Notice that $\binom{n}{n-r}$ is the number of subsets with $n-r$ elements which can be chosen from n, which is the number of partitions of the form $[\bar{A}, A]$ above. Clearly, this is the same as the number of $[A, A]$ partitions. Hence $\binom{n}{r} = \binom{n}{n-r}$.

Example 1. A college has scheduled six football games during a season. How many ways can the season end in two wins, three losses, and one tie? From each possible outcome of the season, we form a partition, with three cells, of the opposing teams. In the first cell we put the teams which our college defeats, in the second the teams to which our college loses, and in the third cell the teams which our college ties. There are $\binom{6}{2, 3, 1} = 60$ such partitions, and hence 60 ways in which the season can end with two wins, three losses, and one tie.

Example 2. In the game of bridge, the hands N, E, S, and W determine a partition of the 52 cards having four cells, each with 13 elements. Thus there are $\dfrac{52!}{13!\ 13!\ 13!\ 13!}$ different bridge deals. This number is about $5.3645 \cdot 10^{28}$ or approximately 54 billion billion billion deals.

Example 3. The following example will be important in probability theory, which we take up in the next chapter. If a coin is thrown six times, there are 2^6 possibilities for the outcome of the six throws, since each throw can result in either a head or a tail. How many of these possibilities result in four heads and two tails? Each sequence of six heads and tails determines a two-cell partition of the numbers from one to six as follows: In the first cell put the numbers corresponding to throws which resulted in a head, and in the second put the numbers corresponding to throws which resulted in tails. We require that the first cell should contain four elements and the second two elements. Hence the number of the 2^6 possibilities which lead to four heads and two tails is the number of two-cell partitions of six elements which have four elements in the first cell and two in the second cell. The answer is $\binom{6}{4} = 15$. For n throws of a coin, a similar analysis shows that there are $\binom{n}{r}$ different sequences of H's and T's of length n which have exactly r heads and $n - r$ tails.

EXERCISES

1. Compute the following numbers.

(a) $\binom{7}{5}$ [*Ans.* 21.]   (e) $\binom{5}{0}$

(b) $\binom{3}{2}$ (f) $\binom{5}{1, 2, 2}$

(c) $\binom{7}{2}$ (g) $\binom{4}{2, 0, 2}$ [*Ans.* 6.]

(d) $\binom{250}{249}$ [*Ans.* 250.]   (h) $\binom{2}{1, 1, 1}$

2. Give an interpretation for $\binom{n}{0}$ and also for $\binom{n}{n}$. Can you now give a reason for making $0! = 1$?

3. How many ways can nine students be assigned to three triple rooms? How many ways if one particular pair of students refuse to room together? [*Ans.* 1680; 1260.]

4. A group of seven boys and ten girls attends a dance. If all the boys dance in a particular dance, how many choices are there for the girls who dance? For the girls who do not dance? How many choices are there for the girls who do not dance, if three of the girls are sure to be asked to dance?

5. Suppose that a course is given at three different hours. If fifteen students sign up for the course,

  (a) How many possibilities are there for the ways the students could distribute themselves in the classes?   [*Ans.* 3^{15}.]

  (b) How many of the ways would give the same number of students in each class?   [*Ans.* 756,756.]

6. A college professor anticipates teaching the same course for the next 35 years. So not to become bored with his jokes, he decides to tell exactly three jokes every year and in no two years to tell exactly the same three jokes. What is the minimum number of jokes that will accomplish this? What is the minimum number if he determines never to tell the same joke twice?

7. How many ways can you answer a ten-question true-false exam, marking the same number of answers true as you do false? How many if it is desired to have no two consecutive answers the same?

8. From three Republicans and three Democrats, find the number of committees of three which can be formed

  (a) With no restrictions.   [*Ans.* 20.]

(b) With three Republicans and no Democrats.   [*Ans.* 1.]
(c) With two Republicans and one Democrat.   [*Ans.* 9.]
(d) With one Republican and two Democrats.   [*Ans.* 9.]
(e) With no Republicans and three Democrats.   [*Ans.* 1.]

What is the relation between your answer in part (a) and the answers to the remaining four parts?

9. Exercise 8 suggests that the following should be true.

$$\binom{2n}{n} = \binom{n}{0}\binom{n}{n} + \binom{n}{1}\binom{n}{n-1} + \binom{n}{2}\binom{n}{n-2} + \cdots + \binom{n}{n}\binom{n}{0}$$
$$= \binom{n}{0}^2 + \binom{n}{1}^2 + \cdots + \binom{n}{n}^2.$$

Show that it is true.

10. A student needs to choose two electives from six possible courses.
    (a) How many ways can he make his choice?   [*Ans.* 15.]
    (b) How many ways can he choose if two of the courses meet at the same time?   [*Ans.* 14.]
    (c) How many ways can he choose if two of the courses meet at 10 o'clock, two at 11 o'clock, and there are no other conflicts among the courses?   [*Ans.* 13.]

SUPPLEMENTARY EXERCISES

11. Consider a town in which there are three plumbers, A, B, and C. On a certain day six residents of the town telephone for a plumber. If each resident selects a plumber from the telephone directory, in how many ways can it happen that
    (a) Three residents call A, two residents call B, and one resident calls C?   [*Ans.* 60.]
    (b) The distribution of calls to the plumbers is three, two, and one?   [*Ans.* 360.]

12. Two committees (a labor relations committee and a quality control committee) are to be selected from a board of nine men. The only rules are (1) the two committees must have no members in common, and (2) each committee must have at least four men. In how many ways can the two committees be appointed?

13. A group of ten people is to be divided into three committees of three, three, and six members, respectively. The chairman of the group is to serve on all three committees and is the only member of the group who serves on more than one committee. In how many ways can the committee assignments be made?   [*Ans.* 756.]

14. In a class of 20 students, grades of A, B, C, D, and F are to be assigned. Omit arithmetic details in answering the following.

(a) In how many ways can this be done if there are ño restrictions?

[*Ans.* 5^{20}.]

(b) In how many ways can this be done if the grades are assigned as follows: 2 A's, 3 B's, 10 C's, 3 D's, and 2 F's?

(c) In how many ways can this be done if the following rules are to be satisfied: exactly 10 C's; the same number of A's as F's; the same number of B's as D's; always more B's than A's?

$$\left[\textit{Ans.} \ \binom{20}{5, 10, 5} + \binom{20}{1, 4, 10, 4, 1} + \binom{20}{2, 3, 10, 3, 2}.\right]$$

15. Establish the identity

$$\binom{n}{r}\binom{r}{k} = \binom{n}{k}\binom{n-k}{r-k}$$

for $n \geq r \geq k$ in two ways, as follows:

(a) Replace each expression by a ratio of factorials and show that the two sides are equal.

(b) Consider the following problem: From a set of n people a committee of r is to be chosen, and from these r people a steering subcommittee of k people is to be selected. Show that the two sides of the identity give two different ways of counting the possibilities for this problem.

5. SOME PROPERTIES OF THE NUMBERS $\binom{n}{j}$

The numbers $\binom{n}{j}$ introduced in the previous section will play an important role in our future work. We give here some of the more important properties of these numbers.

A convenient way to obtain these numbers is given by the famous Pascal triangle, shown in Figure 5. To obtain the triangle we first write the 1's down the sides. Any of the other numbers in the triangle has the property that it is the sum of the two adjacent numbers in the row just above. Thus the next row in the triangle is 1, 6, 15, 20, 15, 6, 1. To find the number $\binom{n}{j}$ we look in the row corresponding to the number n and see where the diagonal line corresponding to the

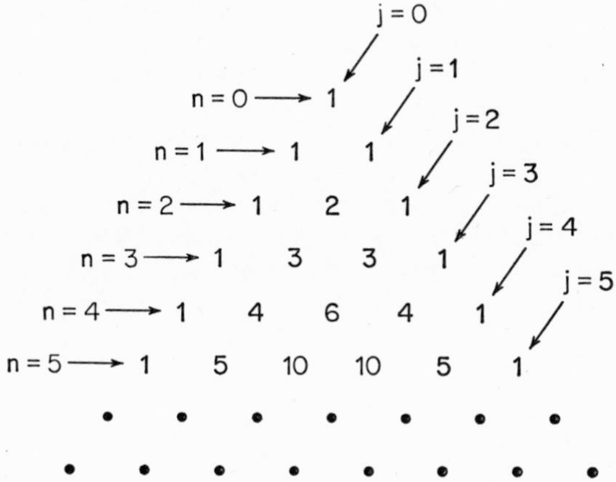

Figure 5

value of j intersects this row. For example, $\binom{4}{2} = 6$ is in the row marked $n = 4$ and on the diagonal marked $j = 2$.

The property of the numbers $\binom{n}{j}$ upon which the triangle is based is

$$\binom{n+1}{j} = \binom{n}{j-1} + \binom{n}{j}.$$

This fact can be verified directly (see Exercise 6), but the following argument is interesting in itself. The number $\binom{n+1}{j}$ is the number of subsets with j elements that can be formed from a set of $n + 1$ elements. Select one of the $n + 1$ elements, x. The $\binom{n+1}{j}$ subsets can be partitioned into those that contain x and those that do not. The latter are subsets of j elements formed from n objects, and hence there are $\binom{n}{j}$ such subsets. The former are constructed by adding x to a subset of $j - 1$ elements formed from n elements, and hence there are $\binom{n}{j-1}$ of them. Thus

$$\binom{n+1}{j} = \binom{n}{j-1} + \binom{n}{j}.$$

If we look again at the Pascal triangle, we observe that the numbers in a given row increase for a while, and then decrease. We can prove this fact in general by considering the ratio of two successive terms,

$$\frac{\binom{n}{j+1}}{\binom{n}{j}} = \frac{n!}{(j+1)!\,(n-j-1)!} \cdot \frac{j!\,(n-j)!}{n!} = \frac{n-j}{j+1}.$$

The numbers increase as long as the ratio is greater than 1, i.e., $n - j > j + 1$. This means that $j < \frac{1}{2}(n - 1)$. We must distinguish the case of an even n from an odd n. For example, if $n = 10$, j must be less than $\frac{1}{2}(10 - 1) = 4.5$. Hence for j up to 4 the terms are increasing, from $j = 5$ on, the terms decrease. For $n = 11$, j must be less than $\frac{1}{2}(11 - 1) = 5$. For $j = 5$, $(n - j)/(j + 1) = 1$. Hence, up to $j = 5$ the terms increase, then $\binom{11}{5} = \binom{11}{6}$, and then the terms decrease.

EXERCISES

1. Extend the Pascal triangle to $n = 16$. Save the result for later use.

2. Prove that

$$\binom{n}{0} + \binom{n}{1} + \binom{n}{2} + \ldots + \binom{n}{n} = 2^n,$$

using the fact that a set with n elements has 2^n subsets.

3. For a set of ten elements prove that there are more subsets with five elements than there are subsets with any other fixed number of elements.

4. Using the fact that $\binom{n}{r+1} = \frac{n-r}{r+1} \cdot \binom{n}{r}$, compute $\binom{30}{s}$ for $s = 1$, 2, 3, 4 from the fact that $\binom{30}{0} = 1$.   [*Ans.* 30; 435; 4060; 27,405.]

5. There are $\binom{52}{13}$ different possible bridge hands. Assume that a list is made showing all these hands, and that in this list the first card in every hand is crossed out. This leaves us with a list of twelve-card hands. Prove that at least two hands in the latter list contain exactly the same cards.

6. Prove that

$$\binom{n+1}{j} = \binom{n}{j-1} + \binom{n}{j},$$

using only the fact that

$$\binom{n}{j} = \frac{n!}{j!\,(n-j)!}.$$

7. Construct a triangle in the same way that the Pascal triangle was constructed, except that whenever you add two numbers, use the addition table in Chapter II, Figure 11a. Construct the triangle for 16 rows. What does this triangle tell you about the numbers in the Pascal triangle? Use this result to check your triangle in Exercise 1.

8. In the triangle obtained in Exercise 7, what property do the rows 1, 2, 4, 8, and 16 have in common? What does this say about the numbers in the corresponding rows of the Pascal triangle? What would you predict for the terms in the 32nd row of the Pascal triangle?

9. For the following table state how one row is obtained from the preceding row and give the relation of this table to the Pascal triangle.

1	1	1	1	1	1	1
1	2	3	4	5	6	7
1	3	6	10	15	21	28
1	4	10	20	35	56	84
1	5	15	35	70	126	210
1	6	21	56	126	252	462
1	7	28	84	210	462	924

10. Referring to the table in Exercise 9, number the columns starting with 0, 1, 2, . . . and number the rows starting with 1, 2, 3, ... Let $f(n, r)$ be the element in the nth column and the rth row. The table was constructed by the rule

$$f(n, r) = f(n-1, r) + f(n, r-1)$$

for $n > 0$ and $r > 1$, and $f(n, 1) = f(0, r) = 1$ for all n and r. Verify that

$$f(n, r) = \binom{n+r-1}{n}$$

satisfies these conditions and is in fact the only choice for $f(n, r)$ which will satisfy the conditions.

11. Consider a set $\{a, a, a\}$ of three objects which cannot be distinguished from one another. Then the ordered partitions with two cells which could be distinguished are

$$[\{a, a, a\}, \varepsilon]$$
$$[\{a, a\}, \{a\}]$$
$$[\{a\}, \{a, a\}]$$
$$[\varepsilon, \{a, a, a\}].$$

List all such ordered partitions with three cells. How many are there?

[*Ans.* 10.]

12. Let $f(n, r)$ be the number of distinguishable ordered partitions with r cells which can be formed from a set of n indistinguishable objects. Show that $f(n, r)$ satisfies the conditions

$$f(n, r) = f(n - 1, r) + f(n, r - 1)$$

for $n > 0$ and $r > 1$, and $f(n, 1) = f(0, r) = 1$ for all n and r. [*Hint:* Show that $f(n, r - 1)$ is the number of partitions which have the last cell empty and $f(n - 1, r)$ is the number which have at least one element in the last cell.]

13. Using the results of Exercises 10 and 12, show that the number of distinguishable ordered partitions with r cells which can be formed from a set of n indistinguishable objects is

$$\binom{n + r - 1}{n}.$$

14. Assume that a mailman has seven letters to put in three mail boxes. How many ways can this be done if the letters are not distinguished?

[*Ans.* 36.]

15. For $n \geq r \geq k \geq s$ show that the identity

$$\binom{n}{r}\binom{r}{k}\binom{k}{s} = \binom{n}{s}\binom{n - s}{k - s}\binom{n - k}{r - k}$$

holds by replacing each binomial coefficient by a ratio of factorials.

16. Establish the identity in Exercise 15 in another way by showing that the two sides of the expression are simply two different ways of counting the number of solutions to the following problem: From a set of n people a subset of r is to be chosen; from the set of r people a subset of k is to be chosen; and from the set of k people a subset of s people is to be chosen.

17. Generalize the identity in Exercises 15 and 16 to solve the problem of finding the number of ways of selecting a t-element subset from an s-element subset from a k-element subset from an r-element subset of an n-element set, where $n \geq r \geq k \geq s \geq t$.

6. BINOMIAL AND MULTINOMIAL THEOREMS

It is sometimes necessary to expand products of the form $(x + y)^3$, $(x + 2y + 11z)^5$, etc. In this section we shall consider systematic ways of carrying out such expansions.

Consider first the special case $(x + y)^3$. We write this as

$$(x + y)^3 = (x + y)(x + y)(x + y).$$

To perform the multiplication, we choose either an x or a y from each of the three factors and multiply our choices together; we do this for all possible choices and add the results. We represent a particular set of choices by a two-cell partition of the numbers 1, 2, 3. In the first cell we put the numbers which correspond to factors from which we chose an x. In the second cell we put the numbers which correspond to factors from which we chose a y. For example, the partitions $[\{1, 3\}, \{2\}]$ correspond to a choice of x from the first and third factors and y from the second. The product so obtained is $xyx = x^2y$. The coefficient of x^2y in the expansion of $(x + y)^3$ will be the number of partitions which lead to a choice of two x's and one y, that is, the number of two-cell partitions of three elements with two elements in the first cell and one in the second, which is $\binom{3}{2} = 3$. More generally, the coefficient of the term of the form $x^j y^{3-j}$ will be $\binom{3}{j}$ for $j = 0, 1, 2, 3$.

Thus we can write the desired expansion as

$$(x + y)^3 = \binom{3}{3} x^3 + \binom{3}{2} x^2 y + \binom{3}{1} xy^2 + \binom{3}{0} y^3$$
$$= x^3 + 3x^2 y + 3xy^2 + y^3.$$

The same argument carried out for the expansion $(x + y)^n$ leads to the binomial theorem of algebra.

Binomial theorem. The expansion of $(x + y)^n$ is given by

$$(x + y)^n = x^n + \binom{n}{n-1} x^{n-1} y + \binom{n}{n-2} x^{n-2} y^2$$
$$+ \ldots + \binom{n}{1} xy^{n-1} + y^n.$$

Example 1. Let us find the expansion for $(a - 2b)^3$. To fit this into the binomial theorem, we think of x as being a and y as being $-2b$. Then we have

$$(a - 2b)^3 = a^3 + 3a^2(-2b) + 3a(-2b)^2 + (-2b)^3$$
$$= a^3 - 6a^2b + 12ab^2 - 8b^3.$$

We turn now to the problem of expanding the trinomial $(x + y + z)^3$. Again we write

$$(x + y + z)^3 = (x + y + z)(x + y + z)(x + y + z).$$

This time we choose either an x or y or z from each of the three factors. Our choice is now represented by a three-cell partition of the set of numbers $\{1, 2, 3\}$. The first cell has the numbers corresponding to factors from which we choose an x, the second cell the numbers corresponding to factors from which we choose a y, and the third those from which we choose a z. For example, the partition $[\{1, 3\}, \mathcal{E}, \{2\}]$ corresponds to a choice of x from the first and third factors, no y's, and a z from the second factor. The term obtained is $xzx = x^2z$. The coefficient of the term x^2z in the expansion is thus the number of three-cell partitions with two elements in the first cell, none in the second, and one in the third. There are $\begin{pmatrix} 3 \\ 2, 0, 1 \end{pmatrix} = 3$ such partitions. In general, the coefficient of the term of the form $x^ay^bz^c$ in the expansion of $(x + y + z)^3$ will be

$$\begin{pmatrix} 3 \\ a, b, c \end{pmatrix} = \frac{3!}{a! \, b! \, c!}.$$

Finding this way the coefficient for each possible a, b, and c, we obtain

$$(x + y + z)^3 = x^3 + y^3 + z^3 + 3x^2y + 3xy^2$$
$$+ 3yz^2 + 3y^2z + 3xz^2 + 3x^2z + 6xyz.$$

The same method can be carried out in general for finding the expansion of $(x_1 + x_2 + \ldots + x_r)^n$. From each factor we choose either an x_1, or x_2, or $x_3, \ldots,$ or x_r, form the product and add these products for all n possible choices. We will have r^n products, but many will be equal. A particular choice of one term from each factor determines an r-cell partition of the numbers from 1 to n. In the first cell we put the numbers of the factors from which we choose an x_1, in the second cell those from which we choose x_2, etc. A particular choice gives us a term of the form $x_1^{n_1} x_2^{n_2} \ldots x_r^{n_r}$ with $n_1 + n_2 + \ldots + n_r = n$. The corresponding partition has n_1 elements in the first cell, n_2 in the second, etc. For each such partition we obtain one such term. Hence the number of these terms which we obtain is the number of such partitions, which is

$$\binom{n}{n_1, n_2, \ldots, n_r} = \frac{n!}{n_1! \, n_2! \ldots n_r!}.$$

Thus we have the multinomial theorem.

Multinomial theorem. The expansion of $(x_1 + x_2 + \ldots + x_r)^n$ is found by adding all terms of the form

$$\binom{n}{n_1, n_2, \ldots, n_r} x_1^{n_1} x_2^{n_2} \ldots x_r^n$$

where $n_1 + n_2 + \ldots + n_r = n$.

EXERCISES

1. Expand by the binomial theorem
   (a) $(x + y)^4$.
   (b) $(1 + x)^5$.
   (c) $(x - y)^3$.
   (d) $(2x + a)^4$.
   (e) $(2x - 3y)^3$.
   (f) $(100 - 1)^5$.

2. Expand
   (a) $(x + y + z)^4$.
   (b) $(2x + y - z)^3$.
   (c) $(2 + 2 + 1)^3$. (Evaluate two ways.)

3. (a) Find the coefficient of the term $x^2 y^3 z^2$ in the expansion of $(x + y + z)^7$. [*Ans.* 210.]
   (b) Find the coefficient of the term $x^6 y^3 z^2$ in the expression $(x - 2y + 5z)^{11}$. [*Ans.* −924,000.]

4. Using the binomial theorem prove that

   (a) $\binom{n}{0} + \binom{n}{1} + \binom{n}{2} + \ldots + \binom{n}{n} = 2^n$.

   (b) $\binom{n}{0} - \binom{n}{1} + \binom{n}{2} - \binom{n}{3} + \ldots \pm \binom{n}{n} = 0$ for $n > 0$.

5. Using an argument similar to the one in Section 6, prove that

$$\binom{n+1}{i,j,k} = \binom{n}{i-1,j,k} + \binom{n}{i,j-1,k} + \binom{n}{i,j,k-1}.$$

6. Let $f(n, r)$ be the number of terms in the multinomial expansion of

$$(x_1 + x_2 + \ldots + x_r)^n$$

and show that

$$f(n, r) = \binom{n+r-1}{n}.$$

[*Hint:* Show that the conditions of Section 5, Exercise 10 are satisfied by showing that $f(n, r-1)$ is the number of terms which do not have x_r and $f(n-1, r)$ is the number which do.]

7. How many terms are there in each of the expansions:
    (a) $(x + y + z)^6$?   [*Ans.* 28.]
    (b) $(a + 2b + 5c + d)^4$?   [*Ans.* 35.]
    (c) $(r + s + t + u + v)^6$?   [*Ans.* 210.]

8. Prove that k^n is the sum of the numbers $\binom{n}{r_1, r_2, \ldots, r_k}$ for all choices of $r_1, r_2, \ldots, r_k$ such that $r_1 + r_2 + \ldots + r_k = n$.

SUPPLEMENTARY EXERCISES

9. Show that the problem given in Exercise 15(b) of Section 4 can also be solved by a multinomial coefficient, and hence show that

$$\binom{n}{n-r, r-k, k} = \binom{n}{r}\binom{r}{k} = \binom{n}{k}\binom{n-k}{r-k}.$$

10. Show that the problem given in Exercise 16 of Section 5 can also be solved by a multinomial coefficient, and hence show that

$$\binom{n}{n-r, r-k, k-s, s} = \binom{n}{r}\binom{r}{k}\binom{k}{s} = \binom{n}{s}\binom{n-s}{k-s}\binom{n-k}{r-k}.$$

11. If $a + b + c = n$, show that

$$\binom{n}{a, b, c} = \binom{n}{a}\binom{n-a}{b}.$$

12. If $a + b + c + d = n$, show that

$$\binom{n}{a, b, c, d} = \binom{n}{a}\binom{n-a}{b}\binom{n-a-b}{c}.$$

13. If $n_1 + n_2 + \ldots + n_r = n$, guess a formula that relates the multinomial coefficient

$$\binom{n}{n_1, n_2, \ldots, n_r}$$

to a product of binomial coefficients. [*Hint:* Use the formulas in Exercises 11 and 12 to guide you.]

14. Use Exercises 11–13 to show that the multinomial coefficients can always be obtained by taking products of suitable numbers in the first n rows of the Pascal triangle.

*7. VOTING POWER

We return to the problem raised in Section 6 of Chapter II. Now we are interested not only in coalitions, but also in the power of individual members. We will develop a numerical measure of voting power that was suggested by L. S. Shapley and M. Shubik. While the measure will be explained in detail below, for the reasons for choosing this particular measure the reader is referred to the original paper.

First of all we must realize that the number of votes a man controls is not in itself a good measure of his power. If x has three votes and y has one vote, it does not necessarily follow that x has three times the power that y has. Thus if the committee has just three members {x, y, z} and z also has only one vote, then x is a dictator and y is powerless.

The basic idea of the power index is found in considering various alignments of the committee members on a number of issues. The n members are ordered $x_1, x_2, \ldots, x_n$ according to how likely they are to vote for the measure. If the measure is to carry, we must persuade x_1 and x_2 up to x_i to vote for it until we have a winning coalition. If $\{x_1, x_2, \ldots, x_i\}$ is a winning coalition but $\{x_1, x_2, \ldots, x_{i-1}\}$ is not winning, then x_i is the crucial member of the coalition. We must persuade him to vote for the measure, and he is the one hardest to persuade of the i necessary members. We call x_i the *pivot*.

For a purely mathematical measure of the power of a member we do not consider the views of the members. Rather we consider all possible ways that the members could be aligned on an issue, and see how often a given member would be the pivot. That means considering all permutations, and there will be $n!$ of them. In each permutation one member will be the pivot. The frequency with which a man is the pivot of an alignment is a good measure of his voting power.

DEFINITION. The voting power of a member of a committee is the number of alignments in which he is pivotal divided by the total number of alignments. (The total number of alignments, of course, is $n!$ for a committee of n members.)

Example 1. If all n members have one vote each, and it takes a majority vote to carry a measure, it is easy to see (by symmetry) that each member is pivot in $1/n$ of the alignments. Hence each member has power $= 1/n$. Let us illustrate this for $n = 3$. There are $3! = 6$ alignments. It takes two votes to carry a measure; hence the second member is always the pivot. The alignments are: 1**2**3, 1**3**2, 2**1**3, 2**3**1, 3**1**2, 3**2**1. The pivots are in **boldface**. Each member is pivot twice, hence has power $\frac{2}{6} = \frac{1}{3}$.

Example 2. Reconsider Chapter II, Section 6, Example 3 from this point of view. There are 24 permutations of the four members. We will list them, with the pivot in **boldface**:

w**x**yz	w**x**zy	w**y**xz	w**y**zx	w**z**xy	w**z**yx
x**w**yz	x**w**zy	x**y**wz	x**y**zw	x**z**wy	x**z**yw
y**x**wz	y**x**zw	y**w**xz	y**w**xz	y**z**xw	y**z**wx
z**x**yw	z**x**wy	z**y**xw	z**y**xw	z**w**xy	z**w**yx

We see that z has power of $\frac{14}{24}$, w has $\frac{6}{24}$, x and y have $\frac{2}{24}$ each. (Or, simplified, they have $\frac{7}{12}, \frac{3}{12}, \frac{1}{12}, \frac{1}{12}$ power, respectively.) We note that these ratios are much further apart than the ratio of votes which is $3:2:1:1$. Here three votes are worth seven times as much as the single vote and more than twice as much as two votes.

Example 3. Reconsider Chapter II, Section 6, Example 4. By an analysis similar to the ones used so far (but too long to be included here) it can be shown that in the Security Council of the United Nations each of the Big Five has $\frac{76}{385}$ or approximately .197 power, while each of the small nations has approximately .002 power. This reproduces our intuitive feeling that, while the small nations in the Security Council are not powerless, nearly all the power is in the hands of the Big Five.

The voting powers according to the 1966 revision will be worked out in the exercises.

Example 4. In a committee of five each member has one vote, but the chairman has veto power. Hence the minimal winning coalitions are three-member coalitions including the chairman. There are 5! = 120 permutations. The pivot cannot come before the chairman, since without the chairman we do not have a winning coalition. Hence, when the chairman is in place number 3, 4, or 5, he is the pivot. This happens in $\frac{3}{5}$ of the permutations. When he is in position 1 or 2, then the number 3 man is pivot. The number of permutations in which the chairman is in one of the first two positions and a given man is third is 2·3! = 12. Hence the chairman has power $\frac{3}{5}$, and each of the others has power $\frac{1}{10}$.

EXERCISES

1. A committee of three makes decisions by majority vote. Write out all permutations, and calculate the voting powers if the three members have

    (a) One vote each.   [*Ans.* $\frac{1}{3}$, $\frac{1}{3}$, $\frac{1}{3}$.]

    (b) One vote for two of them, two votes for the third. [*Ans.* $\frac{1}{6}$, $\frac{1}{6}$, $\frac{2}{3}$.]

    (c) One vote for two of them, three votes for the third. [*Ans.* 0, 0, 1.]

    (d) One, two, and three votes, respectively.   [*Ans.* $\frac{1}{6}$, $\frac{1}{6}$, $\frac{2}{3}$.]

    (e) Two votes each for two of them, and three votes for the third.

                                                        [*Ans.* $\frac{1}{3}$, $\frac{1}{3}$, $\frac{1}{3}$.]

2. Prove that in any decision-making body the sum of the powers of the members is 1.

3. What is the power of a dictator? What is the power of a "powerless" member? Prove that your answers are correct.

4. A large company issued 100,000 shares. These are held by three stockholders, who have 50,000, 49,999, and one share, respectively. Calculate the powers of the three members.   [*Ans.* $\frac{2}{3}$, $\frac{1}{6}$, $\frac{1}{6}$.]

5. A committee consists of 100 members having one vote each, plus a chairman who can break ties. Calculate the power distribution. (Do *not* try to write out all permutations!)

6. In Exercise 5, give the chairman a veto instead of the power to break ties. How does this change the power distribution?

                         [*Ans.* The chairman has power $\frac{50}{101}$.]

7. How are the powers in Exercise 1 changed if the committee requires a $\frac{3}{4}$ vote to carry a measure?

8. If in a committee of five, requiring majority decisions, each member has one vote, then each has power $\frac{1}{5}$. Now let us suppose that two members team up, and always vote the same way. Does this increase their power? (The best way to represent this situation is by allowing only those permutations in which these two members are next to each other.)

[*Ans.* Yes, the pair's power increases from .4 to .5.]

9. If the minimal winning coalitions are known, show that the power of each member can be determined without knowing anything about the number of votes that each member controls.

10. Answer the following questions for a three-man committee.
   (a) Find all possible sets of minimal winning coalitions.
   (b) For each set of minimal winning coalitions find the distribution of voting power.
   (c) Verify that the various distributions of power found in Exercises 1 and 7 are the only ones possible.

11. In Exercise 1, parts (a) and (e) have the same answer, and parts (b) and (d) and Exercise 4 also have the same answer. Use the results of Exercise 9 to find a reason for these coincidences.

12. Compute the voting power of one of the Big Five in the Security Council of the United Nations as follows:
   (a) Show that for the nation to be pivotal it must be in the number 7 spot or later.
   (b) Show that there are $\binom{6}{2}$ 6! 4! permutations in which the nation is pivotal in the number 7 spot.
   (c) Find similar formulas for the number of permutations in which it is pivotal in the number 8, 9, 10, or 11 spot.
   (d) Use this information to find the total number of permutations in which it is pivotal, and from this compute the power of the nation.

13. Apply the method of Exercise 12 to the revised voting scheme in the Security Council (10 small-nation members, and 9 votes required to carry a measure). What is the power of a large nation? Has the power of one of the small nations increased or decreased?

[*Ans.* $\frac{421}{2145}$ (nearly the same as before); decreased.]

*8. TECHNIQUES FOR COUNTING

We know that there is no single method or formula for solving all counting problems. There are, however, some useful techniques that can be learned. In this section we shall discuss two problems that illustrate important techniques.

The first problem illustrates the importance of looking for a general pattern in the examination of special cases. We have seen in Section 2 of this chapter, and Exercise 6 of that section, that the following formulas hold for the number of elements in the union of two and three sets, respectively.

$$n(A_1 \cup A_2) = n(A_1) + n(A_2) - n(A_1 \cap A_2)$$

$$n(A_1 \cup A_2 \cup A_3) = n(A_1) + n(A_2) + n(A_3) - n(A_1 \cap A_2)$$
$$- n(A_1 \cap A_3) - n(A_2 \cap A_3) + n(A_1 \cap A_2 \cap A_3).$$

On the basis of these formulas we might conjecture that the number of elements in the union of any finite number of sets could be obtained by adding the numbers in each of the sets, then subtracting the numbers in each possible intersection of two sets, then adding the numbers in each possible intersection of three sets, etc. If this is correct, the formula for the intersection of four sets should be

$$(1) \quad n(A_1 \cup A_2 \cup A_3 \cup A_4)$$
$$= n(A_1) + n(A_2) + n(A_3) + n(A_4) - n(A_1 \cap A_2) - n(A_1 \cap A_3)$$
$$- n(A_1 \cap A_4) - n(A_2 \cap A_3) - n(A_2 \cap A_4) - n(A_3 \cap A_4)$$
$$+ n(A_1 \cap A_2 \cap A_3) + n(A_1 \cap A_2 \cap A_4) + n(A_1 \cap A_3 \cap A_4)$$
$$+ n(A_2 \cap A_3 \cap A_4) - n(A_1 \cap A_2 \cap A_3 \cap A_4).$$

Let us try to establish this formula. We must show that if u is an element of at least one of the four sets, then it is counted exactly once on the right-hand side of (1). We consider separately the cases where u is in exactly 1 of the sets, exactly 2 of the sets, etc.

For instance, if u is in exactly two of the sets it will be counted twice in the terms of the right-hand side of (1) that involve single sets, once in the terms that involve the intersection of two sets, and not at all in the terms that involve the intersections of three or four sets. Again, if u is in exactly three of the sets it will be counted three times in the terms involving single sets, twice in the terms involving intersections of two sets, once in the terms involving the intersections of three sets, and not at all in the last term involving the intersection of all four sets. Considering each possibility we have the following table.

Number of sets that contain u	Number of times it is counted
1	1
2	$2 - 1$
3	$3 - 3 + 1$
4	$4 - 6 + 4 - 1$

We see from this that, in every case, u is counted exactly once on the right-hand side of (1). Furthermore, if we look closely, we detect a pattern in the numbers in the right-hand column of the above table. If we put a -1 in front of these numbers we have

$$
\begin{array}{cc}
1 & -1 + 1 \\
2 & -1 + 2 - 1 \\
3 & -1 + 3 + 3 - 1 \\
4 & -1 + 4 - 6 + 4 - 1
\end{array}
$$

We now recognize that these numbers are simply the numbers in the first four rows of the Pascal triangle, but with alternating $+$ and $-$ signs. Since we put a -1 in each row of the table, we want to show that the sum of each row is 0. If that is true, it should be a general property of the Pascal triangle. That is, if we put alternating signs in the jth row of the Pascal triangle, we should get a sum of 0. But this is indeed the case, since, by the binomial theorem, for $j > 0$,

$$
0 = \pm(1 - 1)^j = 1 - \binom{j}{1} + \binom{j}{2} - \binom{j}{3} + \ldots \pm 1
$$

$$
= -1 + \binom{j}{1} - \binom{j}{2} + \binom{j}{3} - \ldots \mp 1.
$$

Thus we have not only seen why the formula works for the case of four sets, but we have also found the method for proving the formula for the general case. That is, suppose we wish to establish that the number of elements in the union of n sets may be obtained as an alternating sum by adding the numbers of elements in each of the sets, subtracting the numbers of elements in each pairwise intersection of the sets, adding the numbers of elements in each intersection of three sets, etc. Consider an element u that is in exactly j of the sets. Let us see how many times u will be counted in the alternating sum. If it is in j of the sets, it will first be counted j times in the sum of the elements in the sets by themselves. For u to be in the intersection of two sets, we must choose two of the j sets to which it belongs. This can be done in $\binom{j}{2}$ different ways. Hence an amount $\binom{j}{2}$ will be subtracted from the sum. To be in the intersection of three sets, we must choose three of the j sets containing u. This can be done in $\binom{j}{3}$ different ways. Thus, an amount $\binom{j}{3}$ will be added to the sum, etc. Hence the total number of times u will be counted by the alternating sum is

$$\binom{j}{1} - \binom{j}{2} + \binom{j}{3} - \ldots \pm 1.$$

Since we have just seen that, if we add -1 to the sum, we obtain 0. Hence the sum itself must always be 1. That is, no matter how many sets u is in, it will be counted exactly once by the alternating sum, and this is true for every element u in the union. We have thus established the general formula

$$(2) \quad n(A_1 \cup A_2 \cup \ldots \cup A_n)$$
$$= n(A_1) + n(A_2) + \ldots + n(A_n)$$
$$- n(A_1 \cap A_2) - n(A_1 \cap A_3) - \ldots$$
$$+ n(A_1 \cap A_2 \cap A_3) + n(A_1 \cap A_2 \cap A_4) + \ldots$$
$$+ \ldots \pm n(A_1 \cap A_2 \cap \ldots \cap A_n).$$

This formula is called the *inclusion-exclusion formula* for the number of elements in the union of sets. It can be extended to formulas for counting the number of elements that occur in two of the sets, three of the sets, etc. See Exercises 21, 25, and 27.

Example 1. In a high school the following language enrollments are recorded for the senior class.

English	150
French	75
German	35
Spanish	50

Also, the following overlaps are noted.

Taking English and French	70
Taking English and German	30
Taking English and Spanish	40
Taking French and German	5
Taking English, French and German	2

If every student takes at least one language, how many seniors are there?

Let E, F, G, and S be the sets of students taking English, French, German, and Spanish, respectively. Using formula (1) and ignoring empty sets, we have

$$n(E \cup F \cup G \cup S)$$
$$= n(E) + n(F) + n(G) + n(S) - n(E \cap F) - n(E \cap G)$$
$$- n(E \cap S) - n(F \cap G) + n(E \cap F \cap G)$$
$$= 150 + 75 + 35 + 50 - 70 - 30 - 40 - 5 + 2$$
$$= 167.$$

Since every student takes at least one language, the total number of students is 167.

Example 2. The four words

TABLE, BASIN, CLASP, BLUSH

have the following interesting properties. Each word consists of five different letters. Any two words have exactly two letters in common. Any three words have one letter in common. No letter occurs in all four words. How many different letters are there?

Letting the words be sets of letters, there are $\binom{4}{1}$ ways of taking these sets one at a time, $\binom{4}{2}$ ways of taking them two at a time, etc. Hence formula (2) gives

$$\binom{4}{1} \cdot 5 - \binom{4}{2} \cdot 2 + \binom{4}{3} \cdot 1 - \binom{4}{4} \cdot 0 = 12$$

as the number of distinct letters. The reader should verify this answer by direct count.

It often happens that a counting problem can be formulated in a number of different ways that sound quite different but that are in fact equivalent. And in one of these ways the answer may suggest itself readily. To illustrate how a reformulation can make a hard sounding problem easy, we give an alternate method for solving the problem considered in Exercises 9–13 of Section 5.

The problem is to count the number of ways that n indistinguishable objects can be put into r cells. For instance, if there are three objects and three cells, the number of different ways can be enumerated as follows (using O for object and bars to indicate the sides of the cells):

```
|O O O|         |       |
|O O  |O        |       |
|O O  |         |O      |
|O    |O O      |       |
|O    |O        |O      |
|O    |         |O O    |
|     |O O O|    |       |
|     |O O      |O      |
|     |O        |O O    |
|     |         |O O O|
```

We see that in this case there are ten ways the task can be accomplished. But the answer for the general case is not clear.

If we look at the problem in a slightly different manner, the answer suggests itself. Instead of putting the objects *in* the cells, we imagine putting the cells *around* the objects. In the above case we see that three cells are constructed from four bars. Two of these bars must be placed at the ends. The two other bars together with the three objects we regard as occupying five intermediate positions. Of these five intermediate positions we must choose two of them for bars and three for the objects. Hence the total number of ways we can accomplish the task is $\binom{5}{2}$ = $\binom{5}{3}$ = 10, which is the answer we got by counting all the ways.

For the general case we can argue in the same manner. We have r cells and n objects. We need $r + 1$ bars to form the r cells, but two of these must be fixed on the ends. The remaining $r - 1$ bars together with the n objects occupy $r - 1 + n$ intermediate positions. And we must choose $r - 1$ of these for the bars and the remaining n for the objects. Hence our task can be accomplished in

$$\binom{n + r - 1}{r - 1} = \binom{n + r - 1}{n}$$

different ways.

Example 3. Seven people enter an elevator that will stop at five floors. In how many different ways can the people leave the elevator if we are interested only in the number that depart at each floor, and do not distinguish among the people? According to our general formula, the answer is

$$\binom{7 + 5 - 1}{7} = \binom{11}{7} = 330.$$

Suppose we are interested in finding the number of such possibilities in which at least one person gets off at each floor. We can then arbitrarily assign one person to get off at each floor, and the remaining two can get off at any floor. They can get off the elevator in

$$\binom{2 + 5 - 1}{2} = \binom{6}{2} = 15$$

different ways.

EXERCISES

1. The survey discussed in Exercise 8 of Section 2 has been enlarged to include a fourth magazine D. It was found that no one who reads either magazine A or magazine B reads magazine D. However, 10 per cent of the people read magazine D and 5 per cent read both C and D. What per cent of the people do not read any magazine?   [*Ans.* 5 per cent.]

2. A certain college administers three qualifying tests. They announce the following results: "Of the students taking the tests, 2 per cent failed all three tests, 6 per cent failed tests A and B, 5 per cent failed A and C, 8 per cent failed B and C, 29 per cent failed test A, 32 per cent failed B, and 16 per cent failed C." How many students passed all three qualifying tests?

3. Four partners in a game require a score of exactly 20 points to win. In how many ways can they accomplish this? $[Ans. \binom{23}{3}.]$

4. In how many ways can eight apples be distributed among four boys? In how many ways can this be done if each boy is to get at least one apple?

5. Suppose we have n balls and r boxes with $n \geq r$. Show that the number of different ways that the balls can be put into the boxes which insures that there is at least one ball in every box is $\binom{n - 1}{r - 1}$.

6. Identical prizes are to be distributed among five boys. It is observed that there are 15 ways that this can be done if each boy is to get at least one prize. How many prizes are there?   [*Ans.* 7.]

7. Let $p_1, p_2, \ldots, p_n$ be n statements relative to a possibility space $\mathcal{U}$. Show that the inclusion-exclusion formula gives a formula for the number of elements in the truth set of the disjunction $p_1 \vee p_2 \vee \ldots \vee p_n$ in terms of the numbers of elements in the truth sets of conjunctions formed from subsets of these statements.

8. A man asks his secretary to put letters written to seven different persons into addressed envelopes. Find the number of ways that this can be done so that at least one person gets his own letter. [*Hint:* Use the result of Exercise 7, letting p_i be the statement "The ith man gets his own letter."]

[*Ans.* 3186.]

9. Consider the numbers from 2 to 10 inclusive. Let A_2 be the set of numbers divisible by 2 and A_3 the set of numbers divisible by 3. Find $n(A_2 \cup A_3)$ by using the inclusion-exclusion formula. From this result find the number of prime numbers between 2 and 10 (where a prime number is a number divisible only by itself and by 1). [*Hint:* Be sure to count the numbers 2 and 3 among the primes.]

10. Use the method of Exercise 9 to find the number of prime numbers between 2 and 100 inclusive. [*Hint:* Consider first the sets $A_2, A_3, A_5,$ and A_7.]

[*Ans.* 25.]

11. Verify that the following formula gives the number of elements in the intersection of three sets.

$$n(A_1 \cap A_2 \cap A_3) = n(A_1) + n(A_2) + n(A_3) - n(A_1 \cup A_2) - n(A_1 \cup A_3)$$
$$- n(A_2 \cup A_3) + n(A_1 \cup A_2 \cup A_3).$$

12. Show that if we replace $\cap$ by $\cup$ and $\cup$ by $\cap$ in formula (2), we get a valid formula for the number of elements in the intersection of n sets. [*Hint:* Apply the inclusion-exclusion formula to the left-hand side of

$$n[A_1 \cup A_2 \cup \ldots \cup A_m) = n(\mathcal{U}) - n(A_1 \cap A_2 \cap \ldots \cap A_m).]$$

13. For $n \leq m$ prove that

$$\binom{m}{0}\binom{n}{0} + \binom{m}{1}\binom{n}{1} + \binom{m}{2}\binom{n}{2} + \ldots + \binom{m}{n}\binom{n}{n} = \binom{m+n}{n}$$

by carrying out the following two steps:

    (a) Show that the left-hand side counts the number of ways of choosing equal numbers of men and women from sets of m men and n women.

    (b) Show that the right-hand side also counts the same number by showing that we can select equal numbers of men and women by selecting any subset of n persons from the whole set, and then combining the men selected with the women not selected.

14. By an ordered partition of n with r elements we mean a sequence of nonnegative integers, possibly some 0, written in a definite order, and having n as their sum. For instance, $\{1, 0, 3\}$ and $\{3, 0, 1\}$ are two different ordered partitions of 4 with three elements. Show that the number of ordered partitions of n with r elements is $\binom{n + r - 1}{n}$.

15. Show that the number of different possibilities for the outcomes of rolling n dice is $\binom{n + 5}{n}$.

Note: Exercises 16–19 illustrate an important counting technique called the *reflection principle*. In Figure 6 we show a path from the point $(0, 2)$ to

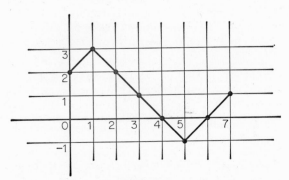

Figure 6

the point $(7, 1)$. We shall be interested in counting the number of paths of this type where at each step the path moves one unit to the right, and either one unit *up* or one unit *down*. We shall see that this model is useful for analyzing voting outcomes.

16. Show that the number of different paths leading from the point $(0, 2)$ to $(7, 1)$ is $\binom{7}{3}$. [*Hint:* Seven decisions must be made, of which three moves are up and the rest down.]

17. Show that the number of different paths from $(0, 2)$ to $(7, 1)$ which touch the x-axis at least once is the same as the total number of paths from the point $(0, -2)$ to the point $(7, 1)$. [*Hint:* Show that for every path to be counted from $(0, 2)$ that touches the x-axis, there corresponds a path from $(0, -2)$ to $(7, 1)$ obtained by reflecting the part of the path to the first touching point through the x-axis. A specific example is shown in Figure 7.]

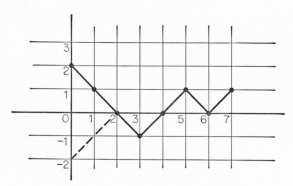

Figure 7

18. Use the results of Exercises 16 and 17 to find the number of paths from $(0, 2)$ to $(7, 1)$ that never touch the x-axis. [*Ans.* 14.]

19. Nine votes are cast in a race between two candidates A and B. Candidate A wins by one vote. Find the number of ways the ballots can be counted so that candidate A is leading throughout the entire count. [*Hint:* The first vote counted must be for A. Counting the remaining eight votes corresponds to a path from $(1, 1)$ to $(9, 1)$. We want the number of paths that never touch the x-axis.] [*Ans.* 14.]

20. Let the symbol $n_r^{(k)}$ stand for "the number of elements that are in k or more of the r sets $A_1, A_2, \ldots, A_r$." Show that $n_3^{(1)} = n(A_1 \cup A_2 \cup A_3)$.

21. Show that

$$n_3^{(2)} = n((A_1 \cap A_2) \cup (A_1 \cap A_3) \cup (A_2 \cap A_3))$$
$$= n(A_1 \cap A_2) + n(A_1 \cap A_3) + n(A_2 \cap A_3) - 2n(A_1 \cap A_2 \cap A_3)$$

by using the inclusion-exclusion formula. Also develop an independent argument for the last formula.

22. Use Exercise 21 to find the number of letters that appear two or more times in the three words TABLE, BASIN, and CLASP.

23. Give an interpretation for $n_3^{(1)} - n_3^{(2)}$.

24. Use Exercise 23 to find the number of letters that occur exactly once in the three words of Exercise 22.

25. Develop a general argument like that in Exercise 21 to show that

$$n_4^{(2)} = n(A_1 \cap A_2) + n(A_1 \cap A_3) + n(A_1 \cap A_4) + n(A_2 \cap A_3)$$
$$+ n(A_2 \cap A_4) + n(A_3 \cap A_4) - 2[n(A_1 \cap A_2 \cap A_3)$$
$$+ n(A_1 \cap A_2 \cap A_4) + n(A_1 \cap A_3 \cap A_4) + n(A_2 \cap A_3 \cap A_4)]$$
$$+ 3n(A_1 \cap A_2 \cap A_3 \cap A_4).$$

26. Use Exercise 25 to find the number of letters used two or more times in the four words of Example 2.

27. From the formulas in Exercises 21 and 25 guess the general formula for $n_r^{(2)}$ and develop a general argument to establish its correctness.

SUGGESTED READING

Shapley, L. S., and M. Shubik, "A Method for Evaluating the Distribution of Power in a Committee System," *The American Political Science Review*, XLVIII (1954), pp. 787–792.

Whitworth, W. A., *Choice and Chance, with 1000 Exercises*, Stechert, New York, 1934.

Goldberg, S., *Probability An Introduction*, Prentice-Hall, Englewood Cliffs, N. J., 1960.

Parzen, E., *Modern Probability Theory and Its Applications*, Wiley, New York, 1960.

Probability theory

1. INTRODUCTION

We often hear statements of the following kind: "It is likely to rain today," "I have a fair chance of passing this course," "There is an even chance that a coin will come up heads," etc. In each case our statement refers to a situation in which we are not certain of the outcome, but we express some degree of confidence that our prediction will be verified. The theory of probability provides a mathematical framework for such assertions.

Consider an experiment whose outcome is not known. Suppose that someone makes an assertion p about the outcome of the experiment, and we want to assign a probability to p. When statement p is considered in isolation, we usually find no natural assignment of probabilities. Rather, we look for a method of assigning probabilities to all conceivable statements concerning the outcome of the experiment. At first this might seem to be a hopeless task, since there is no end to the statements we can make about the experiment. However we are aided by a basic principle:

Fundamental assumption. Any two equivalent statements will be assigned the same probability.

As long as there are a finite number of logical possibilities, there are only a finite number of truth sets, and hence the process of assigning probabilities is a finite one. We proceed in three steps: (1) we first determine $\mathfrak{U}$, the possibility set, that is, the set of all logical possibilities, (2) to each subset X of $\mathfrak{U}$ we assign a number called the measure $m(X)$, (3) to each statement p we assign $m(p)$, the measure of its truth set, as a probability. The probability of statement p is denoted by $\Pr[p]$.

The first step, that of determining the set of logical possibilities, is one that we considered in the previous chapters. It is important to recall that there is no unique method for analyzing logical possibilities. In a given problem we may arrive at a very fine or a very rough analysis of possibilities, causing $\mathfrak{U}$ to have many or few elements.

Having chosen $\mathfrak{U}$, the next step is to assign a number to each subset X of $\mathfrak{U}$, which will in turn be taken to be the probability of any statement having truth set X. We do this in the following way.

Assignment of a measure. Assign a positive number (weight) to each element of $\mathfrak{U}$, so that the sum of the weights assigned is 1. Then the measure of a set is the sum of the weights of its elements. The measure of the set $\mathcal{E}$ is 0.

In applications of probability to scientific problems, the analysis of the logical possibilities and the assignment of measures may depend upon factual information and hence can best be done by the scientist making the application.

Once the weights are assigned, to find the probability of a particular statement we must find its truth set and find the sum of the weights assigned to elements of the truth set. This problem, which might seem easy, can often involve considerable mathematical difficulty. The development of techniques to solve this kind of problem is the main task of probability theory.

Example 1. An ordinary die is thrown. What is the probability that the number which turns up is less than four? Here the possibility set is $\mathfrak{U} = \{1, 2, 3, 4, 5, 6\}$. The symmetry of the die suggests that each face should have the same probability of turning up. To make this so, we assign weight $\frac{1}{6}$ to each of the outcomes. The truth set of the statement "The number which turns up is less than four" is $\{1, 2, 3\}$. Hence the probability of this statement is $\frac{3}{6} = \frac{1}{2}$, the sum of the weights of the elements in its truth set.

Example 2. A man attends a race involving three horses A, B, and C. He feels that A and B have the same chance of winning but that A (and hence also B) is twice as likely to win as C is. What is the probability that A or C wins? We take as $\mathfrak{u}$ the set $\{A, B, C\}$. If we were to assign weight a to the outcome C, then we would assign weight $2a$ to each of the outcomes A and B. Since the sum of the weights must be 1, we have $2a + 2a + a = 1$, or $a = \frac{1}{5}$. Hence we assign weights $\frac{2}{5}, \frac{2}{5}, \frac{1}{5}$ to the outcomes A, B, and C, respectively. The truth set of the statement "Horse A or C wins" is $\{A, C\}$. The sum of the weights of the elements of this set is $\frac{2}{5} + \frac{1}{5} = \frac{3}{5}$. Hence the probability that A or C wins is $\frac{3}{5}$.

EXERCISES

1. Assume that there are n possibilities for the outcome of a given experiment. How should the weights be assigned if it is desired that all outcomes be assigned the same weight?

2. Let $\mathfrak{u} = \{a, b, c\}$. Assign weights to the three elements so that no two have the same weight, and find the measures of the eight subsets of $\mathfrak{u}$.

3. In an election Jones has probability $\frac{1}{2}$ of winning, Smith has probability $\frac{1}{3}$, and Black has probability $\frac{1}{6}$.
   (a) Construct $\mathfrak{u}$.
   (b) Assign weights.
   (c) Find the measures of the eight subsets.
   (d) Give a pair of nonequivalent predictions which have the same probability.

4. Give the possibility set $\mathfrak{u}$ for each of the following experiments.
   (a) An election between candidates A and B is to take place.
   (b) A number from 1 to 5 is chosen at random.
   (c) A two-headed coin is thrown.
   (d) A student is asked for the day of the year on which his birthday falls.

5. For which of the cases in Exercise 4 might it be appropriate to assign the same weight to each outcome?

6. Suppose that the following probabilities have been assigned to the possible results of putting a penny in a certain defective peanut-vending machine: The probability that nothing comes out is $\frac{1}{2}$. The probability that either you get your money back or you get peanuts (but not both) is $\frac{1}{3}$.

(a) What is the probability that you get your money back and also get peanuts? [*Ans.* $\frac{1}{6}$.]

(b) From the information given, is it possible to find the probability that you get peanuts? [*Ans.* No.]

7. A die is loaded in such a way that the probability of each face is proportional to the number of dots on that face. (For instance, a 6 is three times as probable as a 2.) What is the probability of getting an even number in one throw? [*Ans.* $\frac{4}{7}$.]

8. If a coin is thrown three times, list the eight possibilities for the outcomes of the three successive throws. A typical outcome can be written (HTH). Determine a probability measure by assigning an equal weight to each outcome. Find the probabilities of the following statements.

(r) The number of heads that occur is greater than the number of tails. [*Ans.* $\frac{1}{2}$.]

(s) Exactly two heads occur. [*Ans.* $\frac{3}{8}$.]

(t) The same side turns up on every throw. [*Ans.* $\frac{1}{4}$.]

9. For the statements given in Exercise 8, which of the following equalities are true?

(a) $\Pr[r \lor s] = \Pr[r] + \Pr[s]$

(b) $\Pr[s \lor t] = \Pr[s] + \Pr[t]$

(c) $\Pr[r \lor \sim r] = \Pr[r] + \Pr[\sim r]$

(d) $\Pr[r \lor t] = \Pr[r] + \Pr[t]$

10. Which of the following pairs of statements (see Exercise 8) are inconsistent? (Recall that two statements are inconsistent if their truth sets have no element in common.)

(a) r, s (b) s, t

(c) $r, \sim r$ (d) r, t [*Ans.* (b) and (c).]

11. State a theorem suggested by Exercises 9 and 10.

12. An experiment has three possible outcomes, a, b, and c. Let p be the statement "the outcome is a or b," and q be the statement "the outcome is b or c." Assume that weights have been assigned to the three outcomes so that $\Pr[p] = \frac{2}{3}$ and $\Pr[q] = \frac{5}{6}$. Find the weights. [*Ans.* $\frac{1}{6}, \frac{1}{2}, \frac{1}{3}$.]

13. Repeat Exercise 12 if $\Pr[p] = \frac{1}{2}$ and $\Pr[q] = \frac{3}{8}$.

2. PROPERTIES OF A PROBABILITY MEASURE

Before studying special probability measures, we shall consider some general properties of such measures which are useful in computations and in the general understanding of probability theory.

Three basic properties of a probability measure are

(A) $m(X) = 0$ if and only if $X = \mathcal{E}$.

(B) $0 \leq m(X) \leq 1$ for any set X.

(C)   For two sets X and Y,

$$m(X \cup Y) = m(X) + m(Y)$$

if and only if X and Y are disjoint, i.e., have no elements in common.

The proofs of properties (A) and (B) are left as an exercise (see Exercise 16). We shall prove (C).

We observe first that $m(X) + m(Y)$ is the sum of the weights of the elements of X added to the sum of the weights of Y. If X and Y are disjoint, then the weight of every element of $X \cup Y$ is added once and only once, and hence $m(X) + m(Y) = m(X \cup Y)$.

Assume now that X and Y are not disjoint. Here the weight of every element contained in both X and Y, i.e., in $X \cap Y$, is added twice in the sum $m(X) + m(Y)$. Thus this sum is greater than $m(X \cup Y)$ by an amount $m(X \cap Y)$. By (A) and (B), if $X \cap Y$ is not the empty set, then $m(X \cap Y) > 0$. Hence in this case we have $m(X) + m(Y) > m(X \cup Y)$. Thus if X and Y are not disjoint, the equality in (C) does not hold. Our proof shows that in general we have

(C′)   For any two sets X and Y,

$$m(X \cup Y) = m(X) + m(Y) - m(X \cap Y).$$

Since the probabilities for statements are obtained directly from the probability measure $m(X)$, any property of $m(X)$ can be translated into a property about the probability of statements. For example, the above properties become, when expressed in terms of statements,

(a) $\Pr [p] = 0$ if and only if p is logically false.

(b) $0 \leq \Pr [p] \leq 1$ for any statement p.

(c)   The equality

$$\Pr [p \vee q] = \Pr [p] + \Pr [q]$$

holds if and only if p and q are inconsistent.

(c′)   For any two statements p and q,

$$\Pr [p \vee q] = \Pr [p] + \Pr [q] - \Pr [p \wedge q].$$

Another property of a probability measure which is often useful in computation is

(D) $m(\tilde{X}) = 1 - m(X)$,

or, in the language of statements,

(d) $\Pr[\sim p] = 1 - \Pr[p]$.

The proofs of (D) and (d) are left as an exercise (see Exercise 17).

It is important to observe that our probability measure assigns probability 0 only to statements which are logically false, i.e., which are false for every logical possibility. Hence, a prediction that such a statement will be true is certain to be wrong. Similarly, a statement is assigned probability 1 only if it is true in every case, i.e., logically true. Thus the prediction that a statement of this type will be true is certain to be correct. (While these properties of a probability measure seem quite natural, it is necessary, when dealing with infinite possibility sets, to weaken them slightly. We consider in this book only the finite possibility sets.)

We shall now discuss the interpretation of probabilities that are not 0 or 1. We shall give only some intuitive ideas that are commonly held concerning probabilities. While these ideas can be made mathematically more precise, we offer them here only as a guide to intuitive thinking.

Suppose that, relative to a given experiment, a statement has been assigned probability p. From this it is often inferred that if a sequence of such experiments is performed under identical conditions, the fraction of experiments which yield outcomes making the statement true would be approximately p. The mathematical version of this is the "law of large numbers" of probability theory (which will be treated in Section 10). In cases where there is no natural way to assign a probability measure, the probability of a statement is estimated experimentally. A sequence of experiments is performed and the fraction of the experiments which make the statement true is taken as the approximate probability for the statement.

A second and related interpretation of probabilities is concerned with betting. Suppose that a certain statement has been assigned probability p. We wish to offer a bet that the statement will in fact turn out to be true. We agree to give r dollars if the statement does not turn out to be true, provided that we receive s dollars if it does turn out to be true. What should r and s be to make the bet fair? If it were true that in a large number of such bets we would win s a fraction p of the times and lose r a fraction $1 - p$ of the time, then our average winning per bet would be $sp - r(1 - p)$. To make the bet fair we should make this average winning 0. This will be the case if $sp = r(1 - p)$ or if $r/s = p/(1 - p)$. Notice that this determines only the ratio of r and s. Such a ratio, written $r:s$, is said to give *odds* in favor of the statement.

DEFINITION. The *odds* in favor of an outcome are $r:s$ (r *to* s), if the probability of the outcome is p, and $r/s = p/(1 - p)$. Any two numbers having the required ratio may be used in place of r and s. Thus 6:4 odds are the same as 3:2 odds.

Example. Assume that a probability of $\frac{3}{4}$ has been assigned to a certain horse winning a race. Then the odds for a fair bet would be $\frac{3}{4}:\frac{1}{4}$. These odds could be equally well written as 3:1, 6:2 or 12:4, etc. A fair bet would be to agree to pay \$3 if the horse loses and receive \$1 if the horse wins. Another fair bet would be to pay \$6 if the horse loses and win \$2 if the horse wins.

EXERCISES

1. Let p and q be statements such that $\Pr [p \wedge q] = \frac{1}{4}$, $\Pr [\sim p] = \frac{1}{3}$, and $\Pr [q] = \frac{1}{2}$. What is $\Pr [p \vee q]$? [*Ans.* $\frac{11}{12}$.]

2. Using the result of Exercise 1, find $\Pr [\sim p \wedge \sim q]$.

3. Let p and q be statements such that $\Pr [p] = \frac{1}{2}$ and $\Pr [q] = \frac{2}{3}$. Are p and q consistent? [*Ans.* Yes.]

4. Show that, if $\Pr [p] + \Pr [q] > 1$, then p and q are consistent.

5. A student is worried about his grades in English and Art. He estimates that the probability of passing English is .4, that he will pass at least one course with probability .6, but that he has only probability .1 of passing both courses. What is the probability that he will pass Art? [*Ans.* .3.]

6. Given that a school has grades A, B, C, D, and F, and that a student has probability .9 of passing a course, and .6 of getting a grade lower than B, what is the probability that he will get a C or D? [*Ans.* $\frac{1}{2}$.]

7. What odds should a person give on a bet that a six will turn up when a die is thrown?

8. Referring to Example 2 of Section 1, what odds should the man be willing to give for a bet that either A or B will come in first?

9. Prove that if the odds in favor of a given statement are $r:s$, then the probability that the statement will be true is $r/(r + s)$.

10. Using the result of Exercise 9 and the definition of "odds," show that if the odds are $r:s$ that a statement is true, then the odds are $s:r$ that it is false.

11. A man is willing to give $5:4$ odds that the Dodgers will win the World Series. What must the probability of a Dodger victory be for this to be a fair bet? [*Ans.* $\frac{5}{9}$.]

12. A man has found through long experience that if he washes his car, it rains the next day 85 per cent of the time. What odds should he give that this will occur next time?

13. A man offers $1:3$ odds that A will occur, $1:2$ odds that B will occur. He knows that A and B cannot both occur. What odds should he give that A or B will occur? [*Ans.* $7:5$.]

14. A man offers $3:1$ odds that A will occur, $2:1$ odds that B will occur. He knows that A and B cannot both occur. What odds should he give that A or B will occur?

15. Show from the definition of a probability measure that $m(X) = 1$ if and only if $X = \mathfrak{u}$.

16. Show from the definition of a probability measure that properties (A), (B) of the text are true.

17. Prove property (D) of the text. Why does property (d) follow from this property?

18. Prove that if R, S, and T are three sets that have no element in common,
$$m(R \cup S \cup T) = m(R) + m(S) + m(T).$$

19. If X and Y are two sets such that X is a subset of Y, prove that $m(X) \leq m(Y)$.

20. If p and q are two statements such that p implies q, prove that $\Pr[p] \leq \Pr[q]$.

21. Suppose that you are given n statements and each has been assigned a probability less than or equal to r. Prove that the probability of the disjunction of these statements is less than or equal to nr.

22. The following is an alternative proof of property (C') of the text. Give a reason for each step.
 (a) $X \cup Y = (X \cap \tilde{Y}) \cup (X \cap Y) \cup (Y \cap \tilde{X})$.
 (b) $m(X \cup Y) = m(X \cap \tilde{Y}) + m(X \cap Y) + m(\tilde{X} \cap Y)$.
 (c) $m(X \cup Y) = m(X) + m(Y) - m(X \cap Y)$.

23. If X, Y, and Z are any three sets, prove that, for any probability measure,
$$m(X \cup Y \cup Z) = m(X) + m(Y) + m(Z) - m(X \cap Y)$$
$$- m(Y \cap Z) - m(X \cap Z) + m(X \cap Y \cap Z).$$

24. Translate the result of Exercise 23 into a result concerning three statements p, q, and r.

25. A man offers to bet "dollars to doughnuts" that a certain event will take place. Assuming that a doughnut costs a nickel, what must the probability of the event be for this to be a fair bet? [*Ans.* $\frac{20}{21}$.]

26. Show that the inclusion-exclusion formula [Chapter III, Section 8, formula (2)] is true if n is replaced by m. Apply this result to

$$\Pr(p_1 \vee p_2 \vee \ldots \vee p_n).$$

3. THE EQUIPROBABLE MEASURE

We have already seen several examples where it was natural to assign the same weight to all possibilities in determining the appropriate probability measure. The probability measure determined in this manner is called the *equiprobable measure*. The measure of sets in the case of the equiprobable measure has a very simple form. In fact, if $\mathfrak{U}$ has n elements and if the equiprobable measure has been assigned, then for any set X, $m(X)$ is r/n, where r is the number of elements in the set X. This is true since the weight of each element in X is $1/n$, and hence the sum of the weights of elements of X is r/n.

The particularly simple form of the equiprobable measure makes it easy to work with. In view of this, it is important to observe that a particular choice for the set of possibilities in a given situation may lead to the equiprobable measure, while some other choice will not. For example, consider the case of two throws of an ordinary coin. Suppose that we are interested in statements about the number of heads which occur. If we take for the possibility set the set $\mathfrak{U} = \{HH, HT, TH, TT\}$ then it is reasonable to assign the same weight to each outcome, and we are led to the equiprobable measure. If, on the other hand, we were to take as possible outcomes the set $\mathfrak{U} = \{$no H, one H, two H$\}$, it would not be natural to assign the same weight to each outcome, since one head can occur in two different ways, while each of the other possibilities can occur in only one way.

Example 1. Suppose that we throw two ordinary dice. Each die can turn up a number from 1 to 6; hence there are $6 \cdot 6$ possibilities. We assign weight $\frac{1}{36}$ to each possibility. A prediction that is true in j cases will then have probability $j/36$. For example, "The sum of the dice is 5" will be true if we get $1 + 4$, $2 + 3$, $3 + 2$, or $4 + 1$.

Hence the probability that the sum of the dice is 5 is $\frac{4}{36} = \frac{1}{9}$. The sum can be 12 in only one way, $6 + 6$. Hence the probability that the sum is 12 is $\frac{1}{36}$.

Example 2. Suppose that two cards are drawn successively from a deck of cards. What is the probability that both are hearts? There are 52 possibilities for the first card, and for each of these there are 51 possibilities for the second. Hence there are $52 \cdot 51$ possibilities for the result of the two draws. We assign the equiprobable measure. The statement "The two cards are hearts" is true in $13 \cdot 12$ of the $52 \cdot 51$ possibilities. Hence the probability of this statement is $13 \cdot 12/52 \cdot 51 = \frac{1}{17}$.

Example 3. Assume that, on the basis of a predictive index applied to students A, B, and C when entering college, it is predicted that after four years of college the scholastic record of A will be the highest, C the second highest, and B the lowest of the three. Suppose, in fact, that these predictions turn out to be exactly correct. If the predictive index has no merit at all and hence the predictions amount simply to guessing, what is the probability that such a prediction will be correct? There are $3! = 6$ orders in which the men might finish. If the predictions were really just guessing, then we would assign an equal weight to each of the six outcomes. In this case the probability that a particular prediction is true is $\frac{1}{6}$. Since this probability is reasonably large, we would hesitate to conclude that the predictive index is in fact useful, on the basis of this one experiment. Suppose, on the other hand, it predicted the order of six men correctly. Then a similar analysis would show that, by guessing, the probability is $\frac{1}{6!} = \frac{1}{720}$ that such a prediction would be correct. Hence, we might conclude here that there is strong evidence that the index has some merit.

EXERCISES

1. A letter is chosen at random from the word "random." What is the probability that it is an n? That it is a vowel? [*Ans.* $\frac{1}{6}$; $\frac{1}{3}$.]

2. An integer between 3 and 12 inclusive is chosen at random. What is the probability that it is an even number? That it is even and divisible by three?

3. A card is drawn at random from a pack of playing cards.

   (a) What is the probability that it is either a heart or the king of clubs?

                                               [*Ans.* $\frac{7}{26}$.]

   (b) What is the probability that it is either the queen of hearts or an honor card (i.e., ten, jack, queen, king, or ace)?   [*Ans.* $\frac{5}{13}$.]

4. A word is chosen at random from the set of words $\mathfrak{u} = \{$men, bird, ball, field, book$\}$. Let p, q, and r be the statements:

   p: The word has two vowels.

   q: The first letter of the word is b.

   r: The word rhymes with cook.

Find the probability of the following statements.

   (a) p.

   (b) q.

   (c) r.

   (d) $p \wedge q$.

   (e) $(p \vee q) \wedge \sim r$.

   (f) $p \rightarrow q$.   [*Ans.* $\frac{4}{5}$.]

5. A single die is thrown. Find the probability that

   (a) An odd number turns up.

   (b) The number which turns up is greater than two.

   (c) A seven turns up.

6. In the primary voting example of Chapter II, Section 1, assume that all 36 possibilities in the elections are equally likely. Find

   (a) The probability that candidate A wins more states than either of his rivals.   [*Ans.* $\frac{7}{18}$.]

   (b) That all the states are won by the same candidate.   [*Ans.* $\frac{1}{36}$.]

   (c) That every state is won by a different candidate.   [*Ans.* 0.]

7. A single die is thrown twice. What value for the sum of the two outcomes has the highest probability? What value or values of the sum has the lowest probability of occurring?

8. Two boys and two girls are placed at random in a row for a picture. What is the probability that the boys and girls alternate in the picture?

                                             [*Ans.* $\frac{1}{3}$.]

9. A certain college has 500 students and it is known that

                300 read French.

                200 read German.

                 50 read Russian.

                 20 read French and Russian.

                 30 read German and Russian.

                 20 read German and French.

                 10 read all three languages.

If a student is chosen at random from the school, what is the probability that the student

    (a) Reads two and only two languages?

    (b) Reads at least one language?

10. Suppose that three people enter a restaurant which has a row of six seats. If they choose their seats at random, what is the probability that they sit with no seats between them? What is the probability that there is at least one empty seat between any two of them?

11. Find the probability of obtaining each of the following poker hands. (A poker hand is a set of five cards chosen at random from a deck of 52 cards.)

    (a) Royal flush (ten, jack, queen, king, ace in a single suit).

$$[Ans.\ 4/(^{52}_{5}) = .0000015.]$$

    (b) Straight flush (five in a sequence in a single suit, but not a royal flush). $\quad [Ans.\ (40 - 4)/(^{52}_{5}) = .000014.]$

    (c) Four of a kind (four cards of the same face value).

$$[Ans.\ 624/(^{52}_{5}) = .00024.]$$

    (d) Full house (one pair and one triple of the same face value).

$$[Ans.\ 3744/(^{52}_{5}) = .0014.]$$

    (e) Flush (five cards in a single suit but not a straight or royal flush).

$$[Ans.\ (5148 - 40)/(^{52}_{5}) = .0020.]$$

    (f) Straight (five cards in a row, not all of the same suit).

$$[Ans.\ (10,240 - 40)/(^{52}_{5}) = .0039.]$$

    (g) Straight or better. $\hspace{5cm} [Ans.\ .0076.]$

12. If ten people are seated at a circular table at random, what is the probability that a particular pair of people are seated next to each other?

$$[Ans.\ \tfrac{2}{9}.]$$

13. A room contains a group of n people who are wearing badges numbered from 1 to n. If two people are selected at random, what is the probability that the larger badge number is a 3? Answer this problem assuming that $n = 5, 4, 3, 2$. $\hspace{2cm} [Ans.\ \tfrac{1}{5}; \tfrac{1}{4}; \tfrac{2}{3}; 0.]$

14. In Exercise 13, suppose that we observe two men leaving the room and that the larger of their badge numbers is 3. What might we guess as to the number of people in the room?

15. Find the probability that a bridge hand will have suits of

    (a) 5, 4, 3, and 1 cards. $\hspace{1cm} \left[Ans.\ \dfrac{4!(^{13}_{5})(^{13}_{4})(^{13}_{3})(^{13}_{1})}{(^{52}_{13})} \simeq .129.\right]$

    (b) 6, 4, 2, and 1 cards. $\hspace{3cm} [Ans.\ .047.]$

    (c) 4, 4, 3, and 2 cards. $\hspace{3cm} [Ans.\ .216.]$

    (d) 4, 3, 3, and 3 cards. $\hspace{3cm} [Ans.\ .105.]$

16. There are $\binom{52}{13} = 6.35 \times 10^{11}$ possible bridge hands. Find the probability that a bridge hand dealt at random will be all of one suit. Estimate *roughly* the number of bridge hands dealt in the entire country in a year. Is it likely that a hand of all one suit will occur sometime during the year in the United States?

SUPPLEMENTARY EXERCISES

17. Find the probability of *not* having a pair in a hand of poker.

18. Find the probability of a "bust" hand in poker. [*Hint:* A hand is a "bust" if there is no pair, and it is neither a straight nor a flush.]

[*Ans.* .5012.]

19. In poker, find the probability of having
    (a) Exactly one pair.   [*Ans.* .4226.]
    (b) Two pairs.   [*Ans.* .0475.]
    (c) Three of a kind.   [*Ans.* .0211.]

20. Verify from Exercises 11, 18, and 19 that the probabilities for all possible poker hands add up to one (within a rounding error).

21. A certain French professor announces that he will select three out of eight pages of text to put on an examination and that each student can choose one of these three pages to translate. What is the minimum number of pages that a student should prepare in order to be certain of being able to translate a page that he has studied?

Smith decides to study only four of the eight pages. What is the probability that one of these four pages will appear on the examination?

*4. TWO NONINTUITIVE EXAMPLES

There are occasions in probability theory when one finds a problem for which the answer, based on probability theory, is not at all in agreement with one's intuition. It is usually possible to arrange a few wagers that will bring one's intuition into line with the mathematical theory. A particularly good example of this is provided by the matching birthdays problem.

Assume that we have a room with r people in it and we propose the bet that there are at least two people in the room having the same birthday, i.e., the same month and day of the year. We ask for the value of r which will make this a fair bet. Few people would be willing to bet even money on this wager unless there were at least 100 people in the room. Most people would suggest 150 as a reasonable number. However, we shall see that with 150 people the odds are approximately 4,100,000,000,000,000, to 1 in favor of two people having the same birthday, and that one should be willing to bet even money with as few as 23 people in the room.

Let us first find the probability that in a room with r people, no two have the same birthday. There are 365 possibilities for each person's birthday (neglecting February 29). There are then 365^r possibilities for the birthdays of r people. We assume that all these possibilities are equally likely. To find the probability that no two have the same birthday we must find the number of possibilities for the birthdays which have *no* day represented twice. The first person can have any of 365 days for his birthday. For each of these, if the second person is to have a different birthday, there are only 364 possibilities for his birthday. For the third man, there are 363 possibilities if he is to have a different birthday than the first two, etc. Thus the probability that no two people have the same birthday in a group of r people is

$$q_r = \frac{365 \cdot 364 \cdot \ldots \cdot (365 - r + 1)}{365^r}.$$

The probability that at least two people have the same birthday is then $p_r = 1 - q_r$. In Figure 1 the values of p_r and the odds for a fair bet, $p_r : (1 - p_r)$, are given for several values of r.

We consider now a second problem in which intuition does not lead to the correct answer. A hat-check girl has checked n hats, but they have become hopelessly scrambled. She hands back the hats at random. What is the probability that at least one man gets his own hat? For this problem some people's intuition would lead them to guess that for a large number of hats this probability should be small, while others guess that it should be large. Few people guess that the probability is neither large nor small and essentially independent of the number of hats involved.

Let p_j be the statement "the jth man gets his own hat back." We wish to find $\Pr[p_1 \vee p_2 \vee \ldots \vee p_n]$. We know from Section 2, Exercise 26, that a probability of this form can be found from the inclusion-exclusion formula. We must add all probabilities of the form $\Pr[p_i]$, then subtract the sum of all probabilities of the form $\Pr[p_i \wedge p_j]$, then add the sum of all probabilities of the form $\Pr[p_i \wedge p_j \wedge p_k]$, etc.

Number of people in the room	Probability of at least two with same birthday	Approximate odds for a fair bet
5	.027	
10	.117	
15	.253	
20	.411	70:100
21	.444	80:100
22	.476	91:100
23	.507	103:100
24	.538	117:100
25	.569	132:100
30	.706	241:100
40	.891	819:100
50	.970	33:1
60	.994	170:1
70		1,200:1
80		12,000:1
90		160,000:1
100		3,300,000:1
125		31,000,000,000:1
150		4,100,000,000,000,000:1

Figure 1

However, each of these probabilities represents the probability that a particular set of men get their own hats back. These probabilities are very easy to compute.

Let us find the probability that out of n men some particular m of them get back their own hats. There are $n!$ ways that the hats can be returned. If a particular m of them are to get their own hats there are only $(n - m)!$ ways that it can be done. Hence the probability that a particular m men get their own hats back is

$$\frac{(n - m)!}{n!}.$$

There are $\binom{n}{m}$ different ways we can choose m men out of n. Hence the mth group of terms contributes

$$\binom{n}{m} \cdot \frac{(n - m)!}{n!} = \frac{1}{m!}$$

to the alternating sum. Thus

$$\Pr[p_1 \vee p_2 \vee \ldots \vee p_n] = 1 - \frac{1}{2!} + \frac{1}{3!} - \frac{1}{4!} \cdots \pm \frac{1}{n!},$$

where the $+$ sign is chosen if n is odd and the $-$ sign if n is even. In Figure 2, these numbers are given for the first few values of n.

Number of hats	Probability p_n that at least one man gets his own hat
2	.500000
3	.666667
4	.625000
5	.633333
6	.631944
7	.632143
8	.632118

Figure 2

It can be shown that, as the number of hats increases, the probabilities approach a number $1 - (1/e) = .632121 \ldots$, where the number $e = 2.71828 \ldots$ is a number that plays an important role in many branches of mathematics.

EXERCISES

1. What odds should you be willing to give on a bet that at least two people in the United States Senate have the same birthday?

[*Ans.* 3,300,000:1.]

2. What is the probability that in the House of Representatives at least two men have the same birthday?

3. What odds should you be willing to give on a bet that at least two of the Presidents of the United States have had the same birthday? Would you win the bet?

[*Ans.* More than 4:1; Yes. Polk and Harding were born on Nov. 2.]

4. What odds should you be willing to give on the bet that at least two of the Presidents of the United States have died on the same day of the year? Would you win the bet?

> [*Ans.* More than 2.7:1; Yes. Jefferson, Adams, and Monroe all died on July 4.]

5. Four men check their hats. Assuming that the hats are returned at random, what is the probability that *exactly* four men get their own hats? Calculate the answer for 3, 2, 1, 0 men.   [*Ans.* $\frac{1}{24}$; 0; $\frac{1}{4}$; $\frac{1}{3}$; $\frac{3}{8}$.]

6. A group of 50 men and their wives attend a dance. The partners for a dance are chosen by lot. What is the approximate probability that no man dances with his wife?

7. Show that the probability that, in a group of r people, *exactly* one pair has the same birthday is

$$t_r = \binom{r}{2} \frac{365 \cdot 364 \ldots (365 - r + 2)}{365^r}.$$

8. Show that $t_r = \binom{r}{2} \dfrac{q_r}{366 - r}$, where t_r is defined in Exercise 7, and q_r is the probability that no pair has the same birthday.

9. Using the result of Exercise 8 and the results given in Figure 1, find the probability of exactly one pair of people with the same birthday in a group of r people, for $r = 15, 20, 25, 30, 40$, and 50.

> [*Ans.* .22; .32; .38; .38; .26; .12.]

10. What is the approximate probability that there has been exactly one pair of Presidents with the same birthday?

SUPPLEMENTARY EXERCISES

11. Find a formula for the probability of having more than one coincidence of birthdays among n people, i.e., of having at least two pairs of identical birthdays, or of three or more people having the same birthday. [*Hint:* Take the probability of at least one coincidence, and subtract the probability of having exactly one pair.]

12. Compute the probability of having more than one coincidence of birthdays when there are 20, 25, 30, 40, or 50 people in the room.

13. What is the smallest number of people you need in order to have a better than even chance of finding more than one coincidence of birthdays?

> [*Ans.* 36.]

14. Is it very surprising that there was more than one coincidence of the dates on which Presidents died?

15. A game of solitaire is played as follows: A deck of cards is shuffled, and then the player turns the cards up one at a time. As he turns the cards, he calls out the names of the cards in a standard order—say "two of clubs," "three of clubs," etc. The object of the game is to go through the entire deck without once calling out the name of the card one turns up. What is the probability of winning? How does the probability change if one uses a single suit in place of a whole deck?

5. CONDITIONAL PROBABILITY

Suppose that we have a given $\mathfrak{U}$ and that measures have been assigned to all subsets of $\mathfrak{U}$. A statement p will have probability $\Pr[p] = m(P)$. Suppose we now receive some additional information, say that statement q is true. How does this additional information alter the probability of p?

The probability of p after the receipt of the information q is called its *conditional probability*, and it is denoted by $\Pr[p|q]$, which is read "the probability of p given q." In this section we will construct a method of finding this conditional probability in terms of the measure m.

If we know that q is true, then the original possibility set $\mathfrak{U}$ has been reduced to Q and therefore we must define our measure on the subsets of Q instead of on the subsets of $\mathfrak{U}$. Of course, every subset X of Q is a subset of $\mathfrak{U}$, and hence we know $m(X)$, its measure before q was discovered. Since q cuts down on the number of possibilities, its new measure $m'(X)$ should be larger.

The basic idea on which the definition of m' is based is that, while we know that the possibility set has been reduced to Q, we have no new information about subsets of Q. If X and Y are subsets of Q, and $m(X) = 2 \cdot m(Y)$, then we will want $m'(X) = 2 \cdot m'(Y)$. This will be the case if the measures of subsets of Q are simply increased by a proportionality factor $m'(X) = k \cdot m(X)$, and all that remains is to determine k. Since we know that $1 = m'(Q) = k \cdot m(Q)$, we see that $k = 1/m(Q)$ and our new measure on subsets of $\mathfrak{U}$ is determined by the formula

(1) $$m'(X) = \frac{m(X)}{m(Q)}.$$

How does this affect the probability of p? First of all, the truth set of p has been reduced. Because all elements of $\bar{Q}$ have been eliminated, the new truth set of p is $P \cap Q$ and therefore

$$(2) \qquad \Pr\,[p|q] = m'(P \cap Q) = \frac{m(P \cap Q)}{m(Q)} = \frac{\Pr\,[p \wedge q]}{\Pr\,[q]}.$$

Note that if the original measure m is the equiprobable measure, then the new measure m' will also be the equiprobable measure on the set Q.

We must take care that the denominators in (1) and (2) be different from zero. Observe that $m(Q)$ will be zero if Q is the empty set, which happens only if q is self-contradictory. This is also the only case in which $\Pr\,[q] = 0$, and hence we make the obvious assumption that our information q is not self-contradictory.

Example 1. In an election, candidate A has a .4 chance of winning, B has .3 chance, C has .2 chance, and D has .1 chance. Just before the election, C withdraws. Now what are the chances of the other three candidates? Let q be the statement that C will not win, i.e., that A or B or D will win. Observe that $\Pr\,[q] = .8$, hence all the other probabilities are increased by a factor of $1/.8 = 1.25$. Candidate A now has .5 chance of winning, B has .375, and D has .125.

Example 2. A family is chosen at random from the set of all families having exactly two children (not twins). What is the probability that the family has two boys, if it is known that there is a boy in the family? Without any information being given, we would assign the equiprobable measure on the set $\mathfrak{U} = \{BB, BG, GB, GG\}$, where the first letter of the pair indicates the sex of the younger child and the second that of the older. The information that there is a boy causes $\mathfrak{U}$ to change to $\{BB, BG, GB\}$, but the new measure is still the equiprobable measure. Thus the conditional probability that there are two boys given that there is a boy is $\frac{1}{3}$. If, on the other hand, we know that the first child is a boy, then the possibilities are reduced to $\{BB, BG\}$ and the conditional probability is $\frac{1}{2}$.

A particularly interesting case of conditional probability is that in which $\Pr\,\lfloor p|q \rfloor = \Pr\,\lfloor p \rfloor$. That is, the information that q is true has no effect on our prediction for p. If this is the case, we note that

$$(3) \qquad\qquad \Pr\,[p \wedge q] = \Pr\,[p]\,\Pr\,[q].$$

And the case $\Pr\,[q|p] = \Pr\,[q]$ leads to the same equation. Whenever equation (3) holds, we say that p and q are *independent*. Thus if q is not a self-contradiction, p and q are independent if and only if $\Pr[p|q] = \Pr[p]$.

Example 3. Consider three throws of an ordinary coin, where we consider the eight possibilities to be equally likely. Let p be the statement "A head turns up on the first throw" and q be the statement, "A tail turns up on the second throw." Then $\Pr[p] = \Pr[q] = \frac{1}{2}$ and $\Pr[p \wedge q] = \frac{1}{4}$ and therefore p and q are independent statements.

While we have an intuitive notion of independence, it can happen that two statements, which may not seem to be independent, are in fact independent. For example, let r be the statement "The same side turns up all three times." Let s be the statement "At most one head occurs." Then r and s are independent statements (see Exercise 10).

An important use of conditional probabilities arises in the following manner. We wish to find the probability of a statement p. We observe that there is a complete set of alternatives $q_1, q_2, \ldots, q_n$ such that the probability $\Pr[q_i]$ as well as the conditional probabilities $\Pr[p|q_i]$ can be found for every i. Then in terms of these we can find $\Pr[p]$ by

$$\Pr[p] = \Pr[q_1]\Pr[p|q_1] + \Pr[q_2]\Pr[p|q_2] + \ldots + \Pr[q_n]\Pr[p|q_n].$$

The proof of this assertion is left as an exercise (see Exercise 13).

Example 4. A psychology student once studied the way mathematicians solve problems and contended that at times they try too hard to look for symmetry in a problem. To illustrate this she asked a number of mathematicians the following problem: Fifty balls (25 white and 25 black) are to be put in two urns, not necessarily the same number of balls in each. How should the balls be placed in the urns so as to maximize the chance of drawing a black ball, if an urn is chosen at random and a ball drawn from this urn? A quite surprising number of mathematicians answered that you could not do any better than $\frac{1}{2}$, by the symmetry of the problem. In fact one can do a good deal better by putting one black ball in urn 1, and all the 49 other balls in urn 2. To find the probability in this case let p be the statement "A black ball is drawn," q_1 the statement "Urn 1 is drawn" and q_2 the statement "Urn 2 is drawn." Then q_1 and q_2 are a complete set of alternatives so

$$\Pr[p] = \Pr[q_1]\Pr[p|q_1] + \Pr[q_2]\Pr[p|q_2].$$

But $\Pr[q_1] = \Pr[q_2] = \frac{1}{2}$ and $\Pr[p|q_1] = 1$, $\Pr[p|q_2] = \frac{25}{49}$. Thus

$$\Pr[p] = \frac{1}{2} \cdot 1 + \frac{1}{2} \cdot \frac{25}{49} = \frac{74}{98} \approx .755.$$

When told the answer, a number of the mathematicians that had said $\frac{1}{2}$ replied that they thought there had to be the same number of balls in each urn. However, since this had been carefully stated not to be necessary, they also had fallen into the trap of assuming too much symmetry.

EXERCISES

1. A card is drawn at random from a pack of playing cards. What is the probability that it is a 5, given that it is between 2 and 7 inclusive?

2. A die is loaded in such a way that the probability of a given number turning up is proportional to that number (e.g., a 6 is three times as likely to turn up as a 2).

    (a) What is the probability of rolling a 3 given that an odd number turns up?　　　　　　　　　　　　　　　　　　　　　　[*Ans.* $\frac{1}{3}$.]

    (b) What is the probability of rolling an even number given that a number greater than three turns up?　　　　　　　　　　[*Ans.* $\frac{2}{3}$.]

3. A die is thrown twice. What is the probability that the sum of the faces which turn up is greater than 10, given that one of them is a 6? Given that the first throw is a 6?　　　　　　　　　　[*Ans.* $\frac{3}{11}$; $\frac{1}{3}$.]

4. Referring to Chapter IV, Section 3, Exercise 9, what is the probability that the man selected studies German if

    (a) He studies French?

    (b) He studies French and Russian?

    (c) He studies neither French nor Russian?

5. In the primary voting example of Chapter II, Section 1, assuming that the equiprobable measure has been assigned, find the probability that A wins at least two primaries, given that B drops out of the Wisconsin primary?

                                                            [*Ans.* $\frac{7}{9}$.]

6. If $\Pr[\sim p] = \frac{1}{4}$ and $\Pr[q|p] = \frac{1}{2}$, what is $\Pr[p \wedge q]$?　　[*Ans.* $\frac{3}{8}$.]

7. A student takes a five-question true-false exam. What is the probability that he will get all answers correct if

    (a) He is only guessing?

    (b) He knows that the instructor puts more true than false questions on his exams?

    (c) He also knows that the instructor never puts three questions in a row with the same answer?

(d) He also knows that the first and last questions must have the opposite answer?

(e) He also knows that the answer to the second problem is "false"?

8. Three persons, A, B, and C, are placed at random in a straight line. Let r be the statement "B is to the right of A" and let s be the statement "C is to the right of A."

    (a) What is the Pr $[r \wedge s]$?   [*Ans.* $\frac{1}{3}$.]

    (b) Are r and s independent?   [*Ans.* No.]

9. Let a deck of cards consist of the jacks and queens chosen from a bridge deck, and let two cards be drawn from the new deck. Find

    (a) The probability that the cards are both jacks, given that one is a jack.   [*Ans.* $\frac{3}{11} = .27$.]

    (b) The probability that the cards are both jacks, given that one is a red jack.   [*Ans.* $\frac{5}{13} = .38$.]

    (c) The probability that the cards are both jacks, given that one is the jack of hearts.   [*Ans.* $\frac{3}{7} = .43$.]

10. Prove that statements r and s in Example 3 are independent.

11. The following example shows that r may be independent of p and q without being independent of $p \wedge q$ and $p \vee q$. We throw a coin twice. Let p be "The first toss comes out heads," q be "The second toss comes out heads," and r be "The two tosses come out the same." Compute Pr $[r]$, Pr $[r|p]$, Pr $[r|q]$, Pr $[r|p \wedge q]$, Pr $[r|p \vee q]$.   [*Ans.* $\frac{1}{2}, \frac{1}{2}, \frac{1}{2}, 1, \frac{1}{3}$.]

12. Prove that for any two statements p and q,

$$\text{Pr } [p] = \text{Pr } [p \wedge q] + \text{Pr } [p \wedge \sim q].$$

13. Let p be any statement and q_1, q_2, q_3 be a complete set of alternatives. Prove that

$$\text{Pr } [p] = \text{Pr } [q_1] \text{ Pr } [p|q_1] + \text{Pr } [q_2] \text{ Pr } [p|q_2] + \text{Pr } [q_3] \text{ Pr } [p|q_3].$$

14. Prove that the procedure given in Example 4 does maximize the chance of getting a black ball. [*Hint:* Show that you can assume that one urn contains more black balls than white balls and then consider what is the best that could be achieved, first in the urn with more black than white balls, and then in the urn with more white than black balls.]

SUPPLEMENTARY EXERCISES

15. Assume that p and q are independent statements relative to a given measure. Prove that each of the following pairs of statements are independent relative to this same measure.

(a) p and $\sim q$.

(b) $\sim q$ and p.

(c) $\sim p$ and $\sim q$.

16. Prove that for any three statements p, q, and r,

$$\text{Pr } [p \wedge q \wedge r] = \text{Pr } [p] \cdot \text{Pr } [q|p] \cdot \text{Pr } [r|p \wedge q].$$

17. A coin is thrown twice. Let p be the statement "Heads turns up on the first toss" and q the statement "Heads turns up on the second toss." Show that it is possible to assign a measure to the possibility space {HH, HT, TH, TT} so that these statements are *not* independent.

18. A multiple-choice test question lists five alternative answers, of which just one is correct. If a student has done his homework, then he is certain to identify the correct answer; otherwise, he chooses an answer at random. Let p be the statement "A student does his homework" and q the statement "He answers the question correctly." Let Pr $[p] = a$.

(a) Find a formula for Pr $[p|q]$ in terms of a.

(b) Show that Pr $[p|q] \geq$ Pr $[p]$ for all values of a. When does the equality hold?

19. A coin is weighted so that heads has probability .7, tails has probability .2, and it stands on edge with probability .1. What is the probability that it does not come up heads, given that it does not come up tails?   [*Ans.* $\frac{1}{8}$.]

20. A card is drawn at random from a deck of playing cards. Are the following pairs of statements independent?

(a) p: A jack is drawn.

     q: A black card is drawn.

(b) p: An even numbered heart is drawn.

     q: A red card smaller than a five is drawn.

21. A simple genetic model for the color of a person's eyes is the following: There are two kinds of color-determining genes, B and b, and each person has two color-determining genes. If both are b, he has blue eyes; otherwise he has brown eyes. Assume that one-quarter of the people have two B genes, one-quarter of the people have two b genes, and the rest have one B gene and one b gene.

(a) If a man has brown eyes, what is the probability that he has two B genes?

Assume that a man has brown eyes and that his wife has blue eyes. A child born to this couple will get one gene from the man and one from his wife, the selection in each case being a random selection from the parent's two genes.

(b) What is the probability that the child will have brown eyes?

(c) If the child has brown eyes, what is the probability that the father has two B genes?   [*Ans.* (c) $\frac{1}{2}$.]

22. Three red, three green, and three blue balls are to be put into three urns, with at least two balls in each urn. Then an urn is selected at random and two balls withdrawn.

    (a) How should the balls be put in the urns in order to maximize the probability of drawing two balls of different color? What is the probability?   *[Partial Ans.* 1.]

    (b) How should the balls be put in the urns in order to maximize the probability of withdrawing a red and a green ball? What is the maximum probability?   *[Partial Ans.* $\frac{7}{10}$.]

6. FINITE STOCHASTIC PROCESSES

We consider here a very general situation which we will specialize in later sections. We deal with a sequence of experiments where the outcome on each particular experiment depends on some chance element. Any such sequence is called a *stochastic process.* (The Greek word "stochos" means "guess.") We shall assume a finite number of experiments and a finite number of possibilities for each experiment. We assume that, if all the outcomes of the experiments which precede a given experiment were known, then both the possibilities for this experiment and the probability that any particular possibility will occur would be known. We wish to make predictions about the process as a whole. For example, in the case of repeated throws of an ordinary coin we would assume that on any particular experiment we have two outcomes, and the probabilities for each of these outcomes is one-half regardless of any other outcomes. We might be interested, however, in the probabilities of statements of the form, "More than two-thirds of the throws result in heads," or "The number of heads and tails which occur is the same," etc. These are questions which can be answered only when a probability measure has been assigned to the process as a whole. In this section we show how probability measure can be assigned, using the given information. In the case of coin tossing, the probabilities (hence also the possibilities) on any given experiment do not depend upon the previous results. We will not make any such restriction here since the assumption is not true in general.

We shall show how the probability measure is constructed for a particular example, and the procedure in the general case is similar.

We assume that we have a sequence of three experiments, the possibilities for which are indicated in Figure 3. The set of all possible out-

comes which might occur on any of the experiments is represented by
the set $\{a, b, c, d, e, f\}$. Note that if we know that outcome b occurred
on the first experiment, then we
know that the possibilities on experiment two are $\{a, e, d\}$. Similarly, if we know that b occurred
on the first experiment and a on the
second, then the only possibilities
for the third are $\{c, f\}$. We denote
by p_a the probability that the first
experiment results in outcome a,
and by p_b the probability that
outcome b occurs in the first experiment. We denote by $p_{b,d}$ the
probability that outcome d occurs

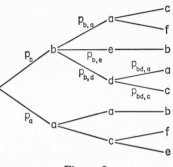

Figure 3

on the second experiment, which is the probability computed on the
assumption that outcome b occurred on the first experiment. Similarly
for $p_{b,a}, p_{b,e}, p_{a,a}, p_{a,c}$. We denote by $p_{bd,c}$ the probability that outcome
c occurs on the third experiment, the latter probability being com-
puted on the assumption that outcome b occurred on the first experiment
and d on the second. Similarly for $p_{ba,c}, p_{ba,f}$, etc. We have assumed
that these numbers are given and the fact that they are probabilities
assigned to possible outcomes would mean that they are positive and
that

$$p_a + p_b = 1, \quad p_{b,a} + p_{b,e} + p_{b,d} = 1, \quad \text{and} \quad p_{bd,a} + p_{bd,c} = 1, \text{etc.}$$

It is convenient to associate each probability with the branch of the tree
that connects the branch point representing the predicted outcome. We
have done this in Figure 3 for several branches. The sum of the numbers assigned to branches from a particular branch point is one, e.g.,

$$p_{b,a} + p_{b,e} + p_{b,d} = 1.$$

A possibility for the sequence of three experiments is indicated by a
path through the tree. We define now a probability measure on the set
of all paths. We call this a *tree measure*. To the path corresponding to
outcome b on the first experiment, d on the second, and c on the third,
we assign the weight $p_b \cdot p_{b,d} \cdot p_{bd,c}$. That is the *product* of the probabilities associated with each branch along the path being considered.
We find the probability for each path through the tree.

Before showing the reason for this choice, we must first show that it determines a probability measure, in other words, that the weights are positive and the sum of the weights is one. The weights are products of positive numbers and hence positive. To see that their sum is one we first find the sum of the weights of all paths corresponding to a particular outcome, say b, on the first experiment and a particular outcome, say d, on the second. We have

$$p_b \cdot p_{b,d} \cdot p_{bd,a} + p_b \cdot p_{b,d} \cdot p_{bd,c} = p_b \cdot p_{b,d}[p_{bd,a} + p_{bd,c}] = p_b \cdot p_{b,d}.$$

For any other first two outcomes we would obtain a similar result. For example, the sum of the weights assigned to paths corresponding to outcome a on the first experiment and c on the second is $p_a \cdot p_{a,c}$. Notice that when we have verified that we have a probability measure, this will be the probability that the first outcome results in a and the second experiment results in c.

Next we find the sum of the weights assigned to all the paths corresponding to the cases where the outcome of the first experiment is b. We find this by adding the sums corresponding to the different possibilities for the second experiment. But by our preceding calculation this is

$$p_b \cdot p_{b,a} + p_b \cdot p_{b,e} + p_b \cdot p_{b,d} = p_b[p_{b,a} + p_{b,e} + p_{b,d}] = p_b.$$

Similarly, the sum of the weights assigned to paths corresponding to the outcome a on the first experiment is p_a. Thus the sum of all weights is $p_a + p_b = 1$. Therefore we do have a probability measure. Note that we have also shown that the probability that the outcome of the first experiment is a has been assigned probability p_a in agreement with our given probability.

To see the complete connection of our new measure with the given probabilities, let $X_j = z$ be the statement "The outcome of the jth experiment was z." Then the statement $[X_1 = b \wedge X_2 = d \wedge X_3 = c]$ is a compound statement that has been assigned probability $p_b \cdot p_{b,d} \cdot p_{bd,c}$. The statement $[X_1 = b \wedge X_2 = d]$ we have noted has been assigned probability $p_b \cdot p_{b,d}$ and the statement $[X_1 = b]$ has been assigned probability p_b. Thus

$$\Pr\left[X_3 = c | X_2 = d \wedge X_1 = b\right] = \frac{p_b \cdot p_{b,d} \cdot p_{bd,c}}{p_b \cdot p_{b,d}} = p_{bd,c}$$

$$\Pr\left[X_2 = d | X_1 = b\right] = \frac{p_b \cdot p_{b,d}}{p_b} = p_{b,d}.$$

Thus we see that our probabilities, computed under the assumption that previous results were known, become the corresponding conditional probabilities when computed with respect to the tree measure. It can be shown that the tree measure which we have assigned is the only one which will lead to this agreement. We can now find the probability of any statement concerning the stochastic process from our tree measure.

Example 1. Suppose that we have two urns. Urn 1 contains two black balls and three white balls. Urn 2 contains two black balls and one white ball. An urn is chosen at random and a ball chosen from this urn at random. What is the probability that a white ball is chosen? A hasty answer might be $\frac{1}{2}$, since there are an equal number of black and white balls involved and everything is done at random. However, it is hasty answers like this (which is wrong) which show the need for a more careful analysis.

We are considering two experiments. The first consists in choosing the urn and the second in choosing the ball. There are two possibilities for the first experiment, and we assign $p_1 = p_2 = \frac{1}{2}$ for the probabilities of choosing the first and the second urn, respectively. We then assign $p_{1,W} = \frac{3}{5}$ for the probability that a white ball is chosen, under the assumption that urn 1 is chosen. Similarly we assign $p_{1,B} = \frac{2}{5}$, $p_{2,W} = \frac{1}{3}$, $p_{2,B} = \frac{2}{3}$. We indicate these probabilities on the possibility tree in Figure 4. The probability that a white ball is drawn is then found from the tree measure as the sum of the weights assigned to paths which lead to a choice of a white ball. This is $\frac{1}{2} \cdot \frac{3}{5} + \frac{1}{2} \cdot \frac{1}{3} = \frac{7}{15}$.

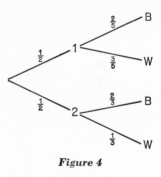

Figure 4

Example 2. Suppose that a man leaves a bar which is on a corner which he knows to be one block from his home. He is unable to remember which street leads to his home. He proceeds to try each of the streets at random without ever choosing the same street twice until he goes on the one which leads to his home. What possibilities are there for his trip home, and what is the probability for each of these possible trips? We label the streets A, B, C, and Home. The possibili-

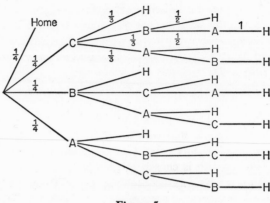

Figure 5

ties together with typical probabilities are given in Figure 5. The probability for any particular trip, or path, is found by taking the product of the branch probabilities.

Example 3. Assume that you are presented with two slot machines, A and B. Each machine pays the same fixed amount when it pays off.

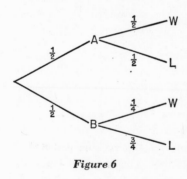

Figure 6

Machine A pays off each time with probability $\frac{1}{2}$, and machine B with probability $\frac{1}{4}$. You are not told which machine is A. Suppose that you choose a machine at random and win. What is the probability that you chose machine A? We first construct the tree (Figure 6) to show the possibilities and assign branch probabilities to determine a tree measure. Let p be the statement "Machine A was chosen" and q be the statement "The machine chosen paid off." Then we are asked for

$$\Pr\left[p|q\right] = \frac{\Pr\left[p \wedge q\right]}{\Pr\left[q\right]}.$$

The truth set of the statement $p \wedge q$ consists of a single path which has been assigned weight $\frac{1}{4}$. The truth set of the statement q consists of two paths, and the sum of the weights of these paths is $\frac{1}{2} \cdot \frac{1}{2} + \frac{1}{2} \cdot \frac{1}{4} = \frac{3}{8}$.

Thus Pr $[p|q] = \frac{2}{3}$. Thus if we win, it is more likely that we have machine A than B and this suggests that next time we should play the same machine. If we lose, however, it is more likely that we have machine B than A, and hence we would switch machines before the next play. (See Exercise 9.)

EXERCISES

1. The fractions of Republicans, Democrats, and Independent voters in cities A and B are

> City A: .30 Republican, .40 Democratic, .30 Independent;
> City B: .40 Republican, .50 Democratic, .10 Independent.

A city is chosen at random and two voters are chosen successively and at random from the voters of this city. Construct a tree measure and find the probability that two Democrats are chosen. Find the probability that the second voter chosen is an Independent voter.   [*Ans.* .205; .2.]

2. A coin is thrown. If a head turns up, a die is rolled. If a tail turns up, the coin is thrown again. Construct a tree measure to represent the two experiments and find the probability that the die is thrown and a six turns up.

3. A man wins a certain tournament if he can win two consecutive games out of three played alternately with two opponents A and B. A is a better player than B. The probability of winning a game when B is the opponent is $\frac{2}{3}$. The probability of winning a game when A is his opponent is only $\frac{1}{3}$. Construct a tree measure for the possibilities for three games, assuming that he plays alternately but plays A first. Do the same assuming that he plays B first. In each case find the probability that he will win two consecutive games. Is it better to play two games against the strong player or against the weaker player?   [*Ans.* $\frac{10}{27}$; $\frac{8}{27}$; better to play strong player twice.]

4. Construct a tree measure to represent the possibilities for four throws of an ordinary coin. Assume that the probability of a head on any toss is $\frac{1}{2}$ regardless of any information about other throws.

5. A student claims to be able to distinguish beer from ale. He is given a series of three tests. In each test he is given two cans of beer and one of ale and asked to pick out the ale. If he gets two or more correct we will admit his claim. Draw a tree to represent the possibilities (either right or wrong) for his answers. Construct the tree measure which would correspond to guessing and find the probability that his claim will be established if he guesses on every trial.

6. A box contains three defective light bulbs and seven good ones. Construct a tree to show the possibilities if three consecutive bulbs are drawn at random from the box (they are not replaced after being drawn). Assign a tree measure and find the probability that at least one good bulb is drawn out. Find the probability that all three are good if the first bulb is good.

[*Ans.* $\frac{119}{120}$; $\frac{5}{12}$.]

7. In Example 2 above, find the probability that the man reaches home after trying at most one wrong street.

8. In Example 3, find the probability that machine A was chosen, given that the player lost.

9. In Example 3, assume that the player makes two plays. Find the probability that he wins at least once under the assumption

    (a) That he plays the same machine twice.   [*Ans.* $\frac{19}{32}$.]

    (b) That he plays the same machine the second time if and only if he won the first time.   [*Ans.* $\frac{20}{32}$]

10. A chess player plays three successive games of chess. His psychological makeup is such that the probability of his winning a given game is $(\frac{1}{2})^{k+1}$, where k is the number of games he has won so far. (For instance, the probability of his winning the first game is $\frac{1}{2}$, the probability of his winning the second game *if he has already won the first game* is $\frac{1}{4}$, etc.) What is the probability that he will win at least two of the three games?

11. Before a political convention, a political expert has assigned the following probabilities. The probability that the President will be willing to run again is $\frac{1}{2}$. If he is willing to run, he and his Vice President are sure to be nominated and have probability $\frac{3}{5}$ of being elected again. If the President does not run, the present Vice President has probability $\frac{1}{10}$ of being nominated, and any other presidential candidate has probability $\frac{1}{2}$ of being elected. What is the probability that the present Vice President will be re-elected?

[*Ans.* $\frac{13}{40}$.]

12. There are two urns, A and B. Urn A contains one black and one red ball. Urn B contains two black and three red balls. A ball is chosen at random from urn A and put into urn B. A ball is then drawn at random from urn B.

    (a) What is the probability that both balls drawn are of the same color?

[*Ans.* $\frac{7}{12}$.]

    (b) What is the probability that the first ball drawn was red, given that the second ball drawn was black?   [*Ans.* $\frac{2}{5}$.]

SUPPLEMENTARY EXERCISES

13. Assume that in the World Series each team has probability one-half of winning each game, independently of the outcomes of any other game. Assign a tree measure. (See Chapter 1, Section 6 for the tree.) Find the probability that the series ends in four, five, six, and seven games, respectively.

14. Assume that in the World Series one team is stronger than the other and has probability .6 for winning each of the games. Assign a tree measure and find the following probabilities.

    (a) The probability that the stronger team wins in 4, 5, 6, and 7 games, respectively.

    (b) The probability that the weaker team wins in 4, 5, 6, and 7 games, respectively.

    (c) The probability that the series ends in 4, 5, 6, and 7 games, respectively.   [*Ans.* .16; .27; .30; .28.]

    (d) The probability that the strong team wins the series.   [*Ans.* .71.]

15. Redo Exercise 14 for the case of two poorly matched teams, where the better team has probability .9 of winning a game.

                            [*Ans.* (c) .66; .26; .07; .01.]
                            [*Ans.* (d) .997.]

16. In the World Series from 1905 through 1965 (excluding series of more than seven games) there were 11 four-game, 14 five-game, 13 six-game, and 20 seven-game series. Which of the assumptions in Exercises 13–15 comes closest to predicting these results? Is it a good fit?   [*Ans.* .6; no.]

17. Consider the following assumption concerning World Series: Ninety per cent of the time the two teams are evenly matched, while 10 per cent of the time they are poorly matched, with the better team having probability .9 of winning a game. Show that this assumption comes closer to predicting the actual outcomes than those considered in Exercise 16.

18. We are given three coins. Coin A is fair while coins B and C are loaded: B has probability .6 of heads and C has probability .4 of heads. A game is played by tossing a coin twice starting with coin B. If a head is obtained, B is tossed again, otherwise the second coin to be tossed is chosen at random from A and C.

    (a) Draw the tree for this game, assigning branch and path weights.

    (b) Let p be the statement "The first toss results in heads" and let q be the statement "The second toss results in heads." Find Pr $[p]$, Pr $[q]$, Pr $[q|p]$.   [*Ans.* (b) .6; .54; .6.]

19. A and B play a series of games for which they are evenly matched. A player wins the series either by winning two games in a row, or by winning a total of three games. Construct the tree and the tree measure.

(a) What is the probability that A wins the series?

(b) What is the probability that more than three games need to be played?

20. In a room there are three chests, each chest contains two drawers, and each drawer contains one coin. In one chest each drawer contains a gold coin; in the second chest each drawer contains a silver coin; and in the last chest one drawer contains a gold coin and the other contains a silver coin. A chest is picked at random and then a drawer is picked at random from that chest. When the drawer is opened, it is found to contain a gold coin. What is the probability that the other drawer of that same chest will also contain a gold coin?   [*Ans.* $\frac{2}{3}$.]

7. BAYES' PROBABILITIES

The following situation often occurs. Measures have been assigned in a possibility space $\mathfrak{U}$. A complete set of alternatives, $p_1, p_2, \ldots, p_n$ has been singled out. Their probabilities are determined by the assigned measure. (Recall that a complete set of alternatives is a set of statements such that for any possible outcome one and only one of the statements is true.) We are now given that a statement q is true. We wish to compute the new probabilities for the alternatives relative to this information. That is, we wish the conditional probabilities $\Pr[p_j|q]$ for each p_j. We shall give two different methods for obtaining these probabilities.

The first is by a general formula. We illustrate this formula for the case of four alternatives: p_1, p_2, p_3, p_4. Consider $\Pr[p_2|q]$. From the definition of conditional probability,

$$\Pr[p_2|q] = \frac{\Pr[p_2 \wedge q]}{\Pr[q]}.$$

But since p_1, p_2, p_3, p_4, are a complete set of alternatives,

$$\Pr[q] = \Pr[p_1 \wedge q] + \Pr[p_2 \wedge q] + \Pr[p_3 \wedge q] + \Pr[p_4 \wedge q].$$

Thus

$$\Pr[p_2|q] = \frac{\Pr[p_2 \wedge q]}{\Pr[p_1 \wedge q] + \Pr[p_2 \wedge q] + \Pr[p_3 \wedge q] + \Pr[p_4 \wedge q]}.$$

Since $\Pr[p_j \wedge q] = \Pr[p_j] \Pr[q|p_j]$, we have the desired formula

$$\Pr[p_2|q]$$
$$= \frac{\Pr[p_2] \cdot \Pr[q|p_2]}{\Pr[p_1] \cdot \Pr[q|p_1] + \Pr[p_2] \cdot \Pr[q|p_2] + \Pr[p_3] \cdot \Pr[q|p_3] + \Pr[p_4] \cdot \Pr[q|p_4]}.$$

Similar formulas apply for the other alternatives, and the formula generalizes in an obvious way to any number of alternatives. In its most general form it is called *Bayes' theorem*.

Example 1. Suppose that a freshman must choose among mathematics, physics, chemistry, and botany as his science course. On the basis of the interest he expressed, his adviser assigns probabilities of .4, .3, .2, and .1 to his choosing each of the four courses, respectively. His adviser does not hear which course he actually chose, but at the end of the term the adviser hears that he received A in the course chosen. On the basis of the difficulties of these courses the adviser estimates the probability of the student getting an A in mathematics to be .1, in physics .2, in chemistry .3, and in botany .9. How can the adviser revise his original estimates as to the probabilities of the student taking the various courses? Using Bayes' theorem we get

Pr [He took math|He got an A]
$$= \frac{(.4)(.1)}{(.4)(.1) + (.3)(.2) + (.2)(.3) + (.1)(.9)} = \frac{4}{25} = .16.$$

Similar computations assign probabilities of .24, .24, and .36 to the other three courses. Thus the new information, that he received an A, had little effect on the probability of his having taken physics or chemistry, but it has made it much less likely that he took mathematics, and much more likely that he took botany.

It is important to note that knowing the conditional probabilities of q relative to the alternatives is not enough. Unless we also know the probabilities of the alternatives at the start, we cannot apply Bayes' theorem. However, in some situations it is reasonable to assume that the alternatives are equally probable at the start. In this case the factors $\Pr[p_1], \ldots, \Pr[p_4]$ cancel from our basic formula, and we get the special form of the theorem:

If $\Pr[p_1] = \Pr[p_2] = \Pr[p_3] = \Pr[p_4]$, then

$$\Pr[p_2|q] = \frac{\Pr[q|p_2]}{\Pr[q|p_1] + \Pr[q|p_2] + \Pr[q|p_3] + \Pr[q|p_4]}.$$

Example 2. In a sociological experiment the subjects are handed four sealed envelopes, each containing a problem. They are told to open one envelope and try to solve the problem in ten minutes. From past experience, the experimenter knows that the probability of their being able to solve the hardest problem is .1. With the other problems, they have probabilities of .3, .5, and .8. Assume the group succeeds within the allotted time. What is the probability that they selected the hardest problem? Since they have no way of knowing which problem is in which envelope, they choose at random, and we assign equal probabilities to the selection of the various problems. Hence the above simple formula applies. The probability of their having selected the hardest problem is

$$\frac{.1}{.1 + .3 + .5 + .8} = \frac{1}{17}.$$

The second method of computing Bayes' probabilities is to draw a tree, and then to redraw the tree in a different order. This is illustrated in the following example.

Example 3. There are three urns. Each urn contains one white ball. In addition, urn I contains one black ball, urn II contains two, and urn

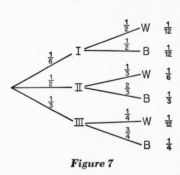

Figure 7

III contains 3. An urn is selected and one ball is drawn. The probability for selecting the three urns is $\frac{1}{6}$, $\frac{1}{2}$, and $\frac{1}{3}$, respectively. If we know that a white ball is drawn, how does this alter the probability that a given urn was selected?

First we construct the ordinary tree and tree measure, in Figure 7.

Next we redraw the tree, using the ball drawn as stage 1, and the urn selected as stage 2. We have the same paths as before, but in a different order. So the path weights are read off from the previous tree. The probability of drawing a white ball is

$$\frac{1}{12} + \frac{1}{6} + \frac{1}{12} = \frac{1}{3}.$$

This leaves the branch weights of the second stage to be computed (see Figure 8). But this is simply a matter of division. For example, the branch weights for the branches starting at "W" must be $\frac{1}{4}, \frac{1}{2}, \frac{1}{4}$ to yield the correct path weights. Thus, if a white ball is drawn, the probability of having selected urn I has increased to $\frac{1}{4}$, the probability of having picked urn III has fallen to $\frac{1}{4}$, while the probability of having chosen urn II is unchanged (see Figure 9).

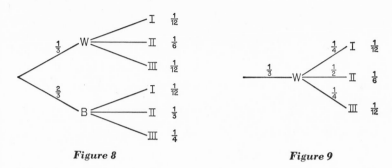

Figure 8   Figure 9

This method is particularly useful when we wish to compute all the conditional probabilities. We will apply the method next to Example 1. The tree and tree measure for this example in the natural order is shown in Figure 10. In that figure the letters M, P, C, and B stand for mathematics, physics, chemistry, and botany, respectively.

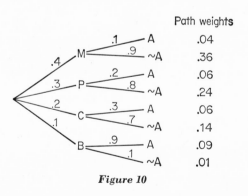

Figure 10

The tree drawn in reverse order is shown in Figure 11.

Each path in this tree corresponds to one of the paths in the original tree. Therefore the path weights for this new tree are the same as the weights assigned to the corresponding paths in the first tree. The two branch weights at the first level represent the probability that the student

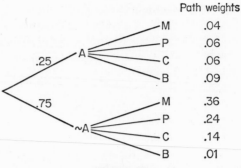

Figure 11

receives an A or that he does not receive an A. These probabilities are
also easily obtained from the first tree. In fact,

$$\Pr[A] = .04 + .06 + .06 + .09 = .25$$

and

$$\Pr[\sim A] = 1 - .25 = .75.$$

We have now enough information to obtain the branch weights at
the second level, since the product of the branch weights must be the
path weights. For example, to obtain $p_{A,M}$ we have

$$.25 \cdot p_{A,M} = .04 \quad \text{or} \quad p_{A,M} = .16.$$

But $p_{A,M}$ is also the conditional probability that the student took math
given that he got an A. Hence this is one of the new probabilities for
the alternatives in the event that the student received an A. The other
branch probabilities are found in the same way and represent the prob-

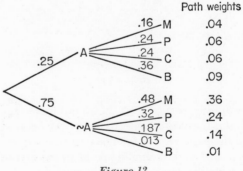

Figure 12

abilities for the other alternatives. By this method we obtain the new probabilities for all alternatives under the hypothesis that the student receives an A as well as the hypothesis that the student does not receive an A. The results are shown in the completed tree in Figure 12.

EXERCISES

1. Urn I contains 7 red and 3 black balls and urn II contains 6 red and 4 black balls. An urn is chosen at random and two balls are drawn from it in succession without replacement. The first ball is red and the second black. Show that it is more probable that urn II was chosen than urn I.

2. A gambler is told that one of three slot machines pays off with probability $\frac{1}{2}$, while each of the other two pays off with probability $\frac{1}{3}$.

(a) If the gambler selects one at random and plays it twice, what is the probability that he will lose the first time and win the second? [*Ans.* $\frac{25}{108}$.]

(b) If he loses the first time and wins the second, what is the probability he chose the favorable machine? [*Ans.* $\frac{9}{25}$.]

3. During the month of May the probability of a rainy day is .2. The Dodgers win on a clear day with probability .7, but on a rainy day only with probability .4. If we know that they won a certain game in May, what is the probability that it rained on that day? [*Ans.* $\frac{1}{8}$.]

4. Construct a diagram to represent the truth sets of various statements occurring in the previous exercise.

5. On a multiple-choice exam there are four possible answers for each question. Therefore, if a student knows the right answer, he has probability one of choosing correctly; if he is guessing, he has probability $\frac{1}{4}$ of choosing correctly. Let us further assume that a good student will know 90 per cent of the answers, a poor student only 50 per cent. If a good student has the right answer, what is the probability that he was only guessing? Answer the same question about a poor student, if the poor student has the right answer. [*Ans.* $\frac{1}{37}, \frac{1}{5}$.]

6. Three economic theories are proposed at a given time, which appear to be equally likely on the basis of existing evidence. The state of the American economy is observed the following year, and it turns out that its actual development had probability .6 of happening according to the first theory; and probabilities .4 and .2 according to the others. How does this modify the probabilities of correctness of the three theories?

7. Let p_1, p_2, p_3, and p_4 be a set of equally likely alternatives. Let Pr $[q|p_1]$ = a, Pr $[q|p_2]$ = b, Pr $[q|p_3]$ = c, Pr $[q|p_4]$ = d. Show that if $a + b + c + d = 1$, then the revised probabilities of the alternatives relative to q are a, b, c, and d, respectively.

8. In poker, Smith holds a very strong hand and bets a considerable amount. The probability that his opponent, Jones, has a better hand is .05. With a better hand Jones would raise the bet with probability .9, but with a poorer hand Jones would raise only with probability .2. Suppose that Jones raises, what is the new probability that he has a winning hand? [*Ans.* $\frac{9}{47}$.]

9. A rat is allowed to choose one of five mazes at random. If we know that the probabilities of his getting through the various mazes in three minutes are .6, .3, .2, .1, .1, and we find that the rat escapes in three minutes, how probable is it that he chose the first maze? The second maze? [*Ans.* $\frac{6}{13}$, $\frac{3}{13}$.]

10. Three men, A, B, and C, are in jail, and one of them is to be hanged the next day. The jailor knows which man will hang, but must not announce it. Man A says to the jailor, "Tell me the name of one of the other two who will not hang. If both are to go free, just toss a coin to decide which to say. Since I already know that at least one of them will go free, you are not giving away the secret." The jailor thinks a moment and then says, "No, this would not be fair to you. Right now you think the probability that you will hang is $\frac{1}{3}$; but if I tell you the name of one of the others who is to go free, your probability of hanging increases to $\frac{1}{2}$. You would not sleep as well tonight." Was the jailor's reasoning correct? [*Ans.* No.]

11. One coin in a collection of 8 million coins has two heads. The rest are fair coins. A coin chosen at random from the collection is tossed ten times and comes up heads every time. What is the probability that it is the two-headed coin?

12. Referring to Exercise 11, assume that the coin is tossed n times and comes up heads every time. How large does n have to be to make the probability approximately $\frac{1}{2}$ that you have the two-headed coin? [*Ans.* 23.]

13. A man will accept job a with probability $\frac{1}{2}$, job b with probability $\frac{1}{3}$, and job c with probability $\frac{1}{6}$. In each case he must decide whether to rent or buy a house. The probabilities of his buying are $\frac{1}{3}$ if he takes job a, $\frac{2}{3}$ if he takes job b, and 1 if he takes job c. Given that he buys a house, what are the probabilities of his having taken each job? [*Ans.* .3; .4; .3.]

14. Assume that chest X-rays for detecting tuberculosis have the following properties. For people having tuberculosis the test will detect the disease 90 out of every 100 times. For people not having the disease the test will in 1 out of every 100 cases diagnose the patient incorrectly as having the disease.

Assume that the incidence of tuberculosis is 5 persons per 10,000. A person is selected at random, given the X-ray test, and the radiologist reports the presence of tuberculosis. What is the probability that the person in fact has the disease?

8. INDEPENDENT TRIALS WITH TWO OUTCOMES

In the preceding section we developed a way to determine a probability measure for any sequence of chance experiments where there are only a finite number of possibilities for each experiment. While this provides the framework for the general study of stochastic processes, it is too general to be studied in complete detail. Therefore, in probability theory we look for simplifying assumptions which will make our probability measure easier to work with. It is desired also that these assumptions be such as to apply to a variety of experiments which would occur in practice. In this book we shall limit outselves to the study of two types of processes. The first, the independent trials process, will be considered in the present section. This process was the first one to be studied extensively in probability theory. The second, the Markov chain process, is a process that is finding increasing application, particularly in the social and biological sciences, and will be considered in Section 13.

A process of independent trials applies to the following situation. Assume that there is a sequence of chance experiments, each of which consists of a repetition of a single experiment, carried out in such a way that the results of any one experiment in no way affect the results in any other experiment. We label the possible outcome of a single experiment by $a_1, \ldots, a_r$. We assume that we are also given probabilities $p_1, \ldots, p_r$ for each of these outcomes occurring on any single experiment, the probabilities being independent of previous results. The tree representing the possibilities for the sequence of experiments will have the same outcomes from each branch point, and the branch probabilities will be assigned by assigning probability p_j to any branch leading to outcome a_j. The tree measure determined in this way is the measure of an *independent trials process*. In this section we shall consider the important case of two outcomes for each experiment. The more general case is studied in Section 11.

In the case of two outcomes we arbitrarily label one outcome "success" and the other "failure." For example, in repeated throws of a coin we might call heads success, and tails failure. We assume there is given a probability p for success and a probability $q = 1 - p$ for failure. The tree measure for a sequence of three such experiments is shown in Figure 13. The weights assigned to each path are indicated at the end of the path.

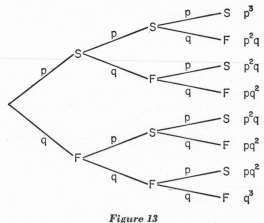

Figure 13

The question which we now ask is the following. Given an independent trials process with two outcomes, what is the probability of *exactly* x successes in n experiments? We denote this probability by $f(n, x; p)$ to indicate that it depends upon n, x, and p.

Assume that we had a tree for this general situation, similar to the tree in Figure 13 for three experiments, with the branch points labeled S for success and F for failure. Then the truth set of the statement "Exactly x successes occur" consists of all paths which go through x branch points labeled S and $n - x$ labeled F. To find the probability of this statement we must add the weights for all such paths. We are helped first by the fact that our tree measure assigns the same weight to any such path, namely $p^x q^{n-x}$. The reason for this is that every branch leading to an S is assigned probability p, and every branch leading to F is assigned probability q, and in the product there will be x p's and $(n - x)$ q's. To find the desired probability we need only find the number of paths in the truth set of the statement "Exactly x successes occur." To each such path we make correspond an ordered partition of the integers from 1 to n which has two cells, x elements in the first and $n - x$ in the second. We do this by putting the numbers of the experiments on which success occurred in the first cell and those for which failure occurred in the second cell. Since there are $\binom{n}{x}$ such partitions there are also this number of paths in the truth set of the statement considered. Thus we have proved:

In an independent trials process with two outcomes the probability of exactly x successes in n experiments is given by

$$f(n, x; p) = \binom{n}{x} p^x q^{n-x}.$$

Example 1. Consider n throws of an ordinary coin. We label heads "success" and tails "failure," and we assume that the probability is $\frac{1}{2}$ for heads on any one throw independently of the outcome of any other throw. Then the probability that exactly x heads will turn up is

$$f(n, x; \tfrac{1}{2}) = \binom{n}{x} \left(\frac{1}{2}\right)^n.$$

For example, in 100 throws the probability that exactly 50 heads will turn up is

$$f(100, 50; \tfrac{1}{2}) = \binom{100}{50} \left(\frac{1}{2}\right)^{100},$$

which is approximately .08. Thus we see that it is quite unlikely that exactly one-half of the tosses will result in heads. On the other hand, suppose that we ask for the probability that nearly one-half of the tosses will be heads. To be more precise, let us ask for the probability that the number of heads which occur does not deviate by more than 10 from 50. To find this we must add

$$f(100, x; \tfrac{1}{2}) \text{ for } x = 40, 41, \ldots, 60.$$

If this is done, we obtain a probability of approximately .96. Thus, while it is unlikely that exactly 50 heads will occur, it is very likely that the number of heads which occur will not deviate from 50 by more than 10.

Example 2. Assume that we have a machine which, on the basis of data given, is to predict the outcome of an election as either a Republican victory or a Democratic victory. If two identical machines are given the same data, they should predict the same result. We assume, however, that any such machine has a certain probability q of reversing

the prediction that it would ordinarily make, because of a mechanical
or electrical failure. To improve the accuracy of our prediction we give
the same data to r identical machines, and choose the answer which
the majority of the machines give. To avoid ties we assume that r is
odd. Let us see how this decreases the probability of an error due to a
faulty machine.

Consider r experiments, where the jth experiment results in success
if the jth machine produces the prediction which it would make when
operating without any failure of parts. The probability of success is
then $p = 1 - q$. The majority decision will agree with that of a perfectly operating machine if we have more than $r/2$ successes. Suppose,
for example, that we have five machines, each of which has a probability of .1 of reversing the prediction because of a parts failure. Then
the probability for success is .9, and the probability that the majority
decision will be the desired one is

$$f(5, 3; 0.9) + f(5, 4; 0.9) + f(5, 5; 0.9)$$

which is found to be approximately .991 (see Exercise 3).

Thus the above procedure decreases the probability of error due to
machine failure from .1 in the case of one machine to .009 for the case
of five machines.

EXERCISES

1. Compute for $n = 4$, $n = 8$, $n = 12$, and $n = 16$ the probability of
obtaining exactly $\frac{1}{2}$ heads when an ordinary coin is thrown.

[*Ans.* .375; .273; .226; .196.]

2. Compute for $n = 4$, $n = 8$, $n = 12$, and $n = 16$ the probability that
the fraction of heads deviates from $\frac{1}{2}$ by less than $\frac{1}{8}$.

[*Ans.* .375; .711; .854; .923.]

3. Verify that the probability .991 given in Example 2 is correct.

4. Assume that Peter and Paul match pennies four times. (In matching
pennies, Peter wins a penny with probability $\frac{1}{2}$, and Paul wins a penny with
probability $\frac{1}{2}$.) What is the probability that Peter wins more than Paul?
Answer the same for five throws. For the case of 12,917 throws.

[*Ans.* $\frac{5}{16}$; $\frac{1}{2}$; $\frac{1}{2}$.]

5. If an ordinary die is thrown four times, what is the probability that
exactly two sixes will occur?

6. In a ten-question true-false exam, what is the probability of getting 70 per cent or better by guessing? [*Ans.* $\frac{11}{64}$.]

7. Assume that, every time a batter comes to bat, he has probability .3 for getting a hit. Assuming that his hits form an independent trials process and that the batter comes to bat four times, what fraction of the games would he expect to get at least two hits? At least three hits? Four hits?
[*Ans.* .348; .084; .008.]

8. A coin is to be thrown eight times. What is the most probable number of heads that will occur? What is the number having the highest probability, given that the first four throws resulted in heads?

9. A small factory has ten workers. The workers eat their lunch at one of two diners, and they are just as likely to eat in one as in the other. If the proprietors want to be more than .95 sure of having enough seats, how many seats must each of the diners have? [*Ans.* Eight seats.]

10. Suppose that five people are chosen at random and asked if they favor a certain proposal. If only 30 per cent of the people favor the proposal, what is the probability that a majority of the five people chosen will favor the proposal?

11. In Example 2, if the probability for a machine reversing its answer due to a parts failure is .2, how many machines would have to be used to make the probability greater than .89 that the answer obtained would be that which a machine with no failure would give? [*Ans.* Three machines.]

12. Assume that it is estimated that a torpedo will hit a ship with probability $\frac{1}{3}$. How many torpedoes must be fired if it is desired that the probability for at least one hit should be greater than .9?

13. A student estimates that, if he takes four courses, he has probability .8 of passing each course. If he takes five courses he has probability .7 of passing each course, and if he takes six courses he has probability .5 for passing each course. His only goal is to pass at least four courses. How many courses should he take for the best chance of achieving his goal? [*Ans.* 5.]

SUPPLEMENTARY EXERCISES

14. In a certain board game players move around the board, and each turn consists of a player's rolling a pair of dice. If a player is on the square *Park Bench*, he must roll a seven or doubles before he is allowed to move out.
   (a) What is the probability that a player stuck on *Park Bench* will be allowed to move out on his next turn?
   (b) How many times must a player stuck on *Park Bench* roll before the chances of his getting out exceed $\frac{3}{4}$? [*Ans.* (a) $\frac{1}{3}$; (b) 4.]

15. A restaurant orders five pieces of apple pie and five pieces of cherry pie. Assume that the restaurant has ten customers, and the probability that a customer will ask for apple pie is $\frac{3}{4}$ and for cherry pie is $\frac{1}{4}$.

(a) What is the probability that the ten customers will all be able to have their first choice?

(b) What number of each kind of pie should the restaurant order if it wishes to order ten pieces of pie and wants to maximize the probability that the ten customers will all have their first choice?

16. Show that it is more probable to get at least one ace with 4 dice than at least one double ace in 24 throws of two dice.

17. A thick coin, when tossed, will land "heads" with a probability of $\frac{5}{12}$, "tails" with a probability of $\frac{5}{12}$, and will land on edge with a probability of $\frac{1}{6}$. If it is tossed six times, what is the probability that it lands on edge exactly two times?   [*Ans.* .2009.]

18. Without actually computing the probabilities, find the value of x for which $f(20, x; .3)$ is largest.

19. A certain team has probability $\frac{2}{3}$ of winning whenever it plays.

(a) What is the probability the team will win exactly four out of five games?

(b) What is the probability the team will win at most four out of five games?

(c) What is the probability the team will win exactly four games out of five if it has already won the first two games of the five?

[*Ans.* (a) $\frac{80}{243}$; (b) $\frac{211}{243}$; (c) $\frac{4}{9}$.]

*9. A PROBLEM OF DECISION

In the preceding sections we have dealt with the problem of calculating the probability of certain statements based on the assumption of a given probability measure. In a statistics problem, one is often called upon to make a decision in a case where the decision would be relatively easy to make if we could assign probabilities to certain statements, but we do not know how to assign these probabilities. For example, if a vaccine for a certain disease is proposed, we may be called upon to decide whether or not the vaccine should be used. We may decide that we could make the decision if we could compare the probability that a person vaccinated will get the disease with the probability that a person not vaccinated will get the disease. Statistical theory develops methods to obtain from experiments some information which will aid in estimating these probabilities, or will otherwise help in making the required decision. We shall illustrate a typical procedure.

Smith claims that he has the ability to distinguish ale from beer and has bet Jones a dollar to that effect. Now Smith does not mean that he can distinguish beer from ale with 100 per cent accuracy, but rather that he believes that he can distinguish them a proportion of the time which is significantly greater than $\frac{1}{2}$.

Assume that it is possible to assign a number p which represents the probability that Smith can pick out the ale from a pair of glasses, one containing ale and one beer. We identify $p = \frac{1}{2}$ with his having no ability, $p > \frac{1}{2}$ with his having some ability, and $p < \frac{1}{2}$ with his being able to distinguish, but having the wrong idea which is the ale. If we knew the value of p, we would award the dollar to Jones if p were $\leq \frac{1}{2}$, and to Smith if p were $> \frac{1}{2}$. As it stands, we have no knowledge of p and thus cannot make a decision. We perform an experiment and make a decision as follows.

Smith is given a pair of glasses, one containing ale and the other beer, and is asked to identify which is the ale. This procedure is repeated ten times, and the number of correct identifications is noted. If the number correct is at least eight, we award the dollar to Smith, and if it is less than eight, we award the dollar to Jones.

We now have a definite procedure and shall examine this procedure both from Jones' and Smith's points of view. We can make two kinds of errors. We may award the dollar to Smith when in fact the appropriate value of p is $\leq \frac{1}{2}$, or we may award the dollar to Jones when the appropriate value for p is $> \frac{1}{2}$. There is no way that these errors can be completely avoided. We hope that our procedure is such that each of the bettors will be convinced that, if he is right, he will very likely win the bet.

Jones believes that the true value of p is $\frac{1}{2}$. We shall calculate the probability of Jones winning the bet if this is indeed true. We assume that the individual tests are independent of each other and all have the same probability $\frac{1}{2}$ for success. (This assumption will be unreasonable if the glasses are too large.) We have then an independent trials process with $p = \frac{1}{2}$ to describe the entire experiment. The probability that Jones will win the bet is the probability that Smith gets fewer than eight correct. From the table in Figure 14 we compute that this probability is approximately .945. Thus Jones sees that, if he is right, it is very likely that he will win the bet.

Table of Values of $f(10, x; p)$

x \ p	0.1	0.25	0.50	0.75	0.90
0	.349	.056	.001	.000	.000
1	.387	.188	.010	.000	.000
2	.194	.282	.044	.000	.000
3	.057	.250	.117	.003	.000
4	.011	.146	.205	.016	.000
5	.001	.058	.246	.058	.001
6	.000	.016	.205	.146	.011
7	.000	.003	.117	.250	.057
8	.000	.000	.044	.282	.194
9	.000	.000	.010	.188	.387
10	.000	.000	.001	.056	.349

Figure 14

Smith, on the other hand, believes that p is significantly greater than $\frac{1}{2}$. If he believes that p is as high as .9, we see from Figure 14 that the probability of his getting eight or more correct is .930. Then both men will be satisfied by the bet.

Suppose, however, that Smith thinks the value of p is only about .75. Then the probability that he will get eight or more correct and thus win the bet is .526. There is then only an approximately even chance that the experiment will discover his abilities, and he probably will not be satisfied with this. If Smith really thinks his ability is represented by a p value of about $\frac{3}{4}$, we would have to devise a different method of awarding the dollar. We might, for example, propose that Smith win the bet if he gets seven or more correct. Then, if he has probability $\frac{3}{4}$ of being correct on a single trial, the probability that he will win the bet is approximately .776. If $p = \frac{1}{2}$, the probability that Jones will win the bet is about .828 under this new arrangement. Jones' chances of winning are thus decreased, but Smith may be able to convince him that it is a fairer arrangement than the first procedure.

In the above example, it was possible to make two kinds of errors. The probability of making these errors depended on the way we designed the experiment and the method we used for the required decision. In some cases we are not too worried about the errors and can make a relatively simple experiment. In other cases, errors are very important, and the experiment must be designed with that fact in mind. For example, the possibility of error is certainly important in the case that a vaccine for a given disease is proposed, and the statistician is asked to help in deciding whether or not it should be used. In this case it might be assumed that there is a certain probability p that a person will get the disease if not vaccinated, and a probability r that he will get it if he is vaccinated. If we have some knowledge of the approximate value of p, we are then led to construct an experiment to decide whether r is greater than p, equal to p, or less than p. The first case would be interpreted to mean that the vaccine actually tends to produce the disease, the second that it has no effect, and the third that it prevents the disease; so that we can make three kinds of errors. We could recommend acceptance when it is actually harmful, we could recommend acceptance when it has no effect, or finally we could reject it when it actually is effective. The first and third might result in the loss of lives, the second in the loss of time and money of those administering the test. Here it would certainly be important that the probability of the first and third kinds of errors be made small. To see how it is possible to make the probability of both errors small, we return to the case of Smith and Jones.

Suppose that, instead of demanding that Smith make at least eight correct identifications out of ten trials, we insist that he make at least 60 correct identifications out of 100 trials. (The glasses must now be very small.) Then, if $p = \frac{1}{2}$, the probability that Jones wins the bet is about .98; so that we are extremely unlikely to give the dollar to Smith when in fact it should go to Jones. (If $p < \frac{1}{2}$, it is even more likely that Jones will win.) If $p > \frac{1}{2}$, we can also calculate the probability that

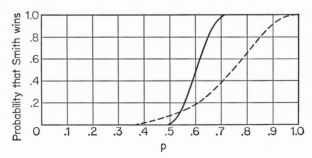

Figure 15

Smith will win the bet. These probabilities are shown in the graph in Figure 15. The dashed curve gives for comparison the corresponding probabilities for the test requiring eight out of ten correct. Note that with 100 trials, if p is $\frac{3}{4}$, the probability that Smith wins the bet is nearly 1, while in the case of eight out of ten, it was only about $\frac{1}{2}$. Thus in the case of 100 trials, it would be easy to convince both Smith and Jones that whichever one is correct is very likely to win the bet.

Thus we see that the probability of both types of errors can be made small at the expense of having a large number of experiments.

EXERCISES

1. Assume that in the beer and ale experiment Jones agrees to pay Smith if Smith gets at least nine out of ten correct.
   (a) What is the probability of Jones paying Smith even though Smith cannot distinguish beer and ale, and guesses?   [*Ans.* .011.]
   (b) Suppose that Smith can distinguish with probability .9. What is the probability of his not collecting from Jones?   [*Ans.* .264.]

2. Suppose that in the beer and ale experiment Jones wishes the probability to be less than .1 that Smith will be paid if, in fact, he guesses. How many of ten trials must he insist that Smith get correct to achieve this?

3. In the analysis of the beer and ale experiment, we assume that the various trials were independent. Discuss several ways that error can enter, because of the nonindependence of the trials, and how this error can be eliminated. (For example, the glasses in which the beer and ale were served might be distinguishable.)

4. Consider the following two procedures for testing Smith's ability to distinguish beer from ale.
   (a) Four glasses are given at each trial, three containing beer and one ale, and he is asked to pick out the one containing ale. This procedure is repeated ten times. He must guess correctly seven or more times.
   (b) Ten glasses are given him, and he is told that five contain beer and five ale, and he is asked to name the five which he believes contain ale. He must choose all five correctly.
In each case, find the probability that Smith establishes his claim by guessing. Is there any reason to prefer one test over the other?
                                        [*Ans.* (a) .003; (b) .004.]

5. A testing service claims to have a method for predicting the order in which a group of freshmen will finish in their scholastic record at the end of college. The college agrees to try the method on a group of five students, and says that it will adopt the method if, for these five students, the prediction is either exactly correct or can be changed into the correct order by interchanging one pair of *adjacent* men in the predicted order. If the method is equivalent to simply guessing, what is the probability that it will be accepted?   [*Ans.* $\frac{1}{24}$.]

6. The standard treatment for a certain disease leads to a cure in $\frac{1}{4}$ of the cases. It is claimed that a new treatment will result in a cure in $\frac{3}{4}$ of the cases. The new treatment is to be tested on ten people having the disease. If seven or more are cured, the new treatment will be adopted. If three or fewer people are cured, the treatment will not be considered further. If the number cured is four, five, or six, the results will be called inconclusive, and a further study will be made. Find the probabilities for each of these three alternatives under the assumption first, that the new treatment has the same effectiveness as the old, and second, under the assumption that the claim made for the treatment is correct.

7. Three students debate the intelligence of blonde dates. One claims that blondes are mostly (say 90 per cent of them) intelligent. A second claims that very few (say 10 per cent) blondes are intelligent, while a third one claims that a blonde is just as likely to be intelligent as not. They administer an intelligence test to ten blondes, classifying them as intelligent or not. They agree that the first man wins the bet if eight or more are intelligent, the second if two or fewer, the third in all other cases. For each man, calculate the probability that he wins the bet, if he is right.   [*Ans.* .930, .930, .890.]

8. Ten men take a test with ten problems. Each man on each question has probability $\frac{1}{2}$ of being right, if he does not cheat. The instructor determines the number of students who get each problem correct. If he finds on four or more problems there are fewer than three or more than seven correct, he considers this convincing evidence of communication between the students. Give a justification for the procedure. [*Hint:* The table in Figure 14 must be used twice, once for the probability of fewer than three or more than seven correct answers on a given problem, and the second time to find the probability of this happening on four or more problems.]

10.   THE LAW OF LARGE NUMBERS

In this section we shall study some further properties of the independent trials process with two outcomes. In Section 8 we saw that the probability for x successes in n trials is given by

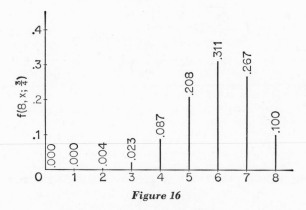

Figure 16

$$f(n, x; p) = \binom{n}{x} p^x q^{n-x}.$$

In Figure 16 we show these probabilities graphically for $n = 8$ and $p = \frac{3}{4}$. In Figure 17 we have done similarly for the case of $n = 7$ and $p = \frac{3}{4}$.

We see in the first case that the values increase up to a maximum value at $x = 6$ and then decrease. In the second case the values increase up to a maximum value at $x = 5$, have the same value for $x = 6$, and then decrease. These two cases are typical of what can happen in general.

Consider the ratio of the probability of $x + 1$ successes in n trials to the probability of x successes in n trials, which is

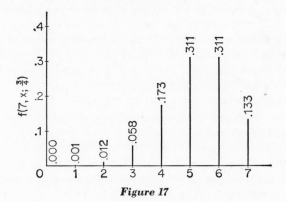

Figure 17

$$\frac{\binom{n}{x+1} p^{x+1} q^{n-x-1}}{\binom{n}{x} p^x q^{n-x}} = \frac{n-x}{x+1} \cdot \frac{p}{q}.$$

This ratio will be greater than one as long as $(n - x)p > (x + 1)q$ or as long as $x < np - q$. If $np - q$ is not an integer, the values $\binom{n}{x} p^x q^{n-x}$ increase up to a maximum value, which occurs at the first integer greater than $np - q$, and then decrease. In case $np - q$ is an integer, the values $\binom{n}{x} p^x q^{n-x}$ increase up to $x = np - q$, are the same for $x = np - q$ and $x = np - q + 1$, and then decrease.

Thus we see that, in general, values near np will occur with the largest probability. It is not true that one particular value near np is highly likely to occur, but only that it is relatively more likely than a value further from np. For example, in 100 throws of a coin, $np = 100 \cdot \frac{1}{2} = 50$. The probability of exactly 50 heads is approximately .08. The probability of exactly 30 is approximately .00002.

More information is obtained by studying the probability of a given deviation of the proportion of successes x/n from the number p; that is, by studying for $\epsilon > 0$,

$$\Pr\left[\left|\frac{x}{n} - p\right| < \epsilon\right].$$

For any fixed n, p, and ϵ, the latter probability can be found by adding all the values of $f(n, x; p)$ for values of x for which the inequality $p - \epsilon < x/n < p + \epsilon$ is true. In Figure 18 we have given these probabilities for the case $p = .3$ with various values for ϵ and n. In the first column we have the case $\epsilon = .1$. We observe that as n increases, the probability that the fraction of successes deviates from .3 by less than .1 tends to the value 1. In fact to four decimal places the answer is 1 after $n = 400$. In column two we have the same probabilities for the smaller value of $\epsilon = .05$. Again the probabilities are tending to 1 but not so fast. In the third column we have given these probabilities for the case $\epsilon = .02$. We see now that even after 1000 trials there is still a reasonable chance that the fraction x/n is not within .02 of the value of $p = .3$. It is natural to ask if we can expect these probabilities also to tend to 1 if we increase n sufficiently. The answer is yes and this is assured by one

$$\Pr\left[\left|\frac{x}{n} - p\right| < \epsilon\right] \text{ for } p = .3 \text{ and } \epsilon = .1, .05, .01.$$

n	$\Pr\left[\left|\frac{x}{n} - .3\right| < .10\right]$	$\Pr\left[\left|\frac{x}{n} - .3\right| < .05\right]$	$\Pr\left[\left|\frac{x}{n} - .3\right| < .02\right]$
20	.5348	.1916	.1916
40	.7738	.3945	.1366
60	.8800	.5184	.3269
80	.9337	.6068	.2853
100	.9626	.6740	.2563
200	.9974	.8577	.4107
300	.9998	.9326	.5116
400	1.0000	.9668	.5868
500	1.0000	.9833	.6461
600	1.0000	.9915	.6944
700	1.0000	.9956	.7345
800	1.0000	.9977	.7683
900	1.0000	.9988	.7970
1000	1.0000	.9994	.8216

Figure 18

of the fundamental theorems of probability called the *law of large numbers*. This theorem asserts that, for any $\epsilon > 0$,

$$\Pr\left[\left|\frac{x}{n} - p\right| < \epsilon\right]$$

tends to 1 as n increases indefinitely.

It is important to understand what this theorem says and what it does not say. Let us illustrate its meaning in the case of coin tossing.

We are going to toss a coin n times and we want the probability to be very high, say greater than .99, that the fraction of heads which turn up will be very close, say within .001 of the value .5. The law of large numbers assures us that we can have this if we simply choose n large enough. The theorem itself gives us no information about how large n must be. Let us however consider this question.

To say that the fraction of the times success results is near p is the same as saying that the actual number of successes x does not deviate too much from the expected number np. To see the kind of deviations which might be expected we can study the value of $\Pr\left[|x - np| \geq d\right]$.

A table of these values for $p = .3$ and various values of n and d are given in Figure 19. Let us ask how large d must be before a deviation as large as d could be considered surprising. For example, let us see for each n the value of d which makes Pr $[|x - np| \geq d]$ about .04. From the table, we see that d should be 7 for $n = 50$, 9 for $n = 80$, 10 for $n = 100$, etc. To see deviations which might be considered more typical we look for the values of d which make Pr $[|x - np| \geq d]$ approximately $\frac{1}{3}$. Again from the table, we see that d should be 3 or 4 for $n = 50$, 4 or 5 for $n = 80$, 5 for $n = 100$, etc. The answers to these two questions are given in the last two columns of the table. An examination of these numbers shows us that deviations which we would consider surprising are approximately $\sqrt{n}$ while those which are more typical are about one half as large or $\sqrt{n}/2$.

This suggests that $\sqrt{n}$, or a suitable multiple of it, might be taken as a unit of measurement for deviations. Of course, we would also have to study how Pr $\left[\left| \dfrac{x}{n} - p \right| \geq d \right]$ depends on p. When this is done, one finds that $\sqrt{npq}$ is a natural unit; it is called a *standard deviation*. It can be shown that for large n the following approximations hold.

$$\text{Pr } [|x - np| \geq \sqrt{npq}] \approx .3174$$
$$\text{Pr } [|x - np| \geq 2\sqrt{npq}] \approx .0455$$
$$\text{Pr } [|x - np| \geq 3\sqrt{npq}] \approx .0027$$

That is, a deviation from the expected value of one standard deviation is rather typical, while a deviation of as much as two standard deviations is quite surprising and three very surprising. For values of p not too near 0 or 1, the value of $\sqrt{pq}$ is approximately $\frac{1}{2}$. Thus these approximations are consistent with the results we observed from our table.

For large n, Pr $[x - np \geq k\sqrt{npq}]$ or Pr $[x - np \leq -k\sqrt{npq}]$ can be shown to be approximately the same. Hence these probabilities can be estimated for $k = 1, 2$, and 3 by taking $\frac{1}{2}$ the values given above.

Example 1. In throwing an ordinary coin 10,000 times, the expected number of heads is 5000, and the standard deviation for the number of heads is $\sqrt{10,000(\frac{1}{2})(\frac{1}{2})} = 50$. Thus the probability that the number of heads which turn up deviates from 5000 by as much as one standard deviation, or 50, is approximately .317. The probability of a deviation

$$p = .3; \quad \Pr[|x - np| \geq d].$$

n	1	2	3	4	5	6	7	8	9	10	11	12	13	14	15	16	17	Pr near to .04	Pr near to $\frac{1}{3}$
50	.878	.644	.441	.280	.164	.088	.043	.020	.008									7	3–4
80	.903	.715	.542	.393	.272	.179	.112	.066	.037	.020	.010							9	4–5
100	.913	.744	.586	.445	.326	.230	.155	.101	.063	.037	.021	.012						10	5
120	.921	.765	.619	.486	.370	.273	.195	.135	.090	.058	.036	.022	.012					11	5–6
140	.927	.782	.645	.519	.407	.310	.230	.166	.116	.079	.052	.033	.021	.012				12	6
170	.933	.802	.676	.558	.451	.357	.276	.209	.154	.111	.078	.054	.036	.024	.015	.009		13	6
200	.939	.817	.700	.589	.488	.396	.316	.247	.189	.142	.105	.076	.053	.037	.025	.017	.011	14	7

Figure 19

180

of as much as two standard deviations, or 100, is approximately .046. The probability of a deviation of as much as three standard deviations, or 150, is approximately .003.

Example 2. Assume that in a certain large city, 900 people are chosen at random and asked if they favor a certain proposal. Of the 900 asked, 550 say they favor the proposal and 350 are opposed. If, in fact, the people in the city are equally divided on the issue, would it be unlikely that such a large majority would be obtained in a sample of 900 of the citizens? If the people were equally divided, we would assume that the 900 people asked would form an independent trials process with probability $\frac{1}{2}$ for a "yes" answer and $\frac{1}{2}$ for a "no" answer. Then the standard deviation for the number of "yes" answers in 900 trials is $\sqrt{900(\frac{1}{2})(\frac{1}{2})} = 15$. Then it would be very unlikely that we would obtain a deviation of more than 45 from the expected number of 450. The fact that the deviation in the sample from the expected number was 100, then, is evidence that the hypothesis that the voters were equally divided is incorrect. The assumption that the true proportion is any value less than $\frac{1}{2}$ would also lead to the fact that a number as large as 550 favoring in a sample of 900 is very unlikely. Thus we are led to suspect that the true proportion is greater than $\frac{1}{2}$. On the other hand, if the number who favored the proposal in the sample of 900 were 465, we would have only a deviation of one standard deviation, under the assumption of an equal division of opinion. Since such a deviation is not unlikely, we could not rule out this possibility on the evidence of the sample.

Example 3. A certain Ivy League college would like to admit 800 students in their freshman class. Experience has shown that if they accept 1250 students they will have acceptances from approximately 800. If they admit as many as 50 too many students they will have to provide additional dormitory space. Let us find the probability that this will happen assuming that the acceptances of the students can be considered to be an independent trials process. We take as our estimate for the probability of an acceptance $p = \frac{800}{1250} = .64$. Then the expected number of acceptances is 800 and the standard deviation for the number of acceptances is $\sqrt{1250 \times .64 \times .36} \approx 17$. The probability that the number accepted is three standard deviations or 51 from the mean is approximately .0027. This probability takes into account a deviation above the mean or below the mean. Since in this case we are only interested in a deviation above the mean, the probability we desire is half of this or approximately .0013. Thus we see that it is highly unlikely that the college will have to have new dormitory space under the assumptions we have made.

We finish this discussion of the law of large numbers with some final remarks about the interpretation of this important theorem.

Of course no matter how large n is we cannot prevent the coin from coming up heads every time. If this were the case we would observe a fraction of heads equal to 1. However, this is not inconsistent with the theorem, since the probability of this happening is $(\frac{1}{2})^n$ which tends to 0 as n increases. Thus a fraction of 1 is always possible, but becomes increasingly unlikely.

The law of large numbers is often misinterpreted in the following manner. Suppose that we plan to toss the coin 1000 times and after 500 tosses we have already obtained 400 heads. Then we must obtain less than one half heads in the remaining 500 tosses to have the fraction come out near $\frac{1}{2}$. It is tempting to argue that the coin therefore owes us some tails and it is more likely that tails will occur in the last 500 tosses. Of course this is nonsense, since the coin has no memory. The point is that something very unlikely has already happened in the first 500 tosses. The final result can therefore also be expected to be a result not predicted before the tossing began.

We could also argue that perhaps the coin is a biased coin but this would make us predict more heads than tails in the future. Thus the law of averages, or the law of large numbers, should not give you great comfort if you have had a series of very bad hands dealt you in your last 100 poker hands. If the dealing is fair, you have the same chance as ever of getting a good hand.

Early attempts to define the probability p that success occurs on a single experiment sounded like this. If the experiment is repeated indefinitely, the fraction of successes obtained will tend to a number p, and this number p is called the probability of success on a single experiment. While this fails to be satisfactory as a definition of probability, the law of large numbers captures the spirit of this frequency concept of probability.

EXERCISES

1. If an ordinary die is thrown 20 times, what is the expected number of times that a six will turn up? What is the standard deviation for the number of sixes that turn up? [*Ans.* $\frac{10}{3}$; $\frac{5}{3}$.]

2. Suppose that an ordinary die is thrown 450 times. What is the expected number of throws that result in either a three or a four? What is the standard deviation for the number of such throws?

3. In 16 tosses of an ordinary coin, what is the expected number of heads that turn up? What is the standard deviation for the number of heads that occur? [*Ans.* 8; 2.]

4. In 16 tosses of a coin, find the exact probability that the number of heads that turn up differs from the expected number by (a) as much as one standard deviation, and (b) by more than one standard deviation. Do the same for the case of two standard deviations, and for the case of three standard deviations. Show that the approximations given for large n lie between the values obtained, but are not very accurate for so small an n.
[*Ans.* .454; .210; .077; .021; .004; .001.]

5. Consider n independent trials with probability p for success. Let r and s be numbers such that $p < r < s$. What does the law of large numbers say about

$$\Pr\left[r < \frac{x}{n} < s\right]$$

as we increase n indefinitely? Answer the same question in the case that $r < p < s$.

6. A drug is known to be effective in 20 per cent of the cases where it is used. A new agent is introduced, and in the next 900 times the drug is used it is effective 250 times. What can be said about the effectiveness of the drug?

7. In a large number of independent trials with probability p for success, what is the approximate probability that the number of successes will deviate from the expected number by more than one standard deviation but less than two standard deviations? [*Ans.* .272.]

8. What is the approximate probability that, in 10,000 throws of an ordinary coin, the number of heads which turn up lies between 4850 and 5150? What is the probability that the number of heads lies in the same interval, given that in the first 1900 throws there were 1600 heads?

9. Suppose that it is desired that the probability be approximately .95 that the fraction of sixes that turn up when a die is thrown n times does not deviate by more than .01 from the value $\frac{1}{6}$. How large should n be?

[*Ans.* Approximately 5555.]

10. Suppose that for each roll of a fair die you lose \$1 when an odd number comes up and win \$1 when an even number comes up. Then after 10,000 rolls you can, with approximately 84 per cent confidence, expect to have lost not more than \$_____.

11. Assume that 10 per cent of the people in a certain city have cancer. If 900 people are selected at random from the city, what is the expected number which will have cancer? What is the standard deviation? What is the approximate probability that more than 108 of the 900 chosen have cancer?

[*Ans.* 90; 9; .023.]

12. Suppose that in Exercise 11, the 900 people are chosen at random from those people in the city who smoke. Under the hypothesis that smoking has no effect on the incidence of cancer, what is the expected number in the 900 chosen that have cancer? Suppose that more than 120 of the 900 chosen have cancer, what might be said concerning the hypothesis that smoking has no effect on the incidence of cancer?

13. In Example 2, we made the assumption in our calculations that, if the true proportion of voters in favor of the proposal were p, then the 900 people chosen at random represented an independent trials process with probability p for a "yes" answer, and $1 - p$ for a "no" answer. Give a method for choosing the 900 people which would make this a reasonable assumption. Criticize the following methods.

(a) Choose the first 900 people in the list of registered Republicans.

(b) Choose 900 names at random from the telephone book.

(c) Choose 900 houses at random and ask one person from each house, the houses being visited in the mid-morning.

14. For n throws of an ordinary coin, let t_n be such that

$$\Pr\left[-t_n < \frac{x}{n} - \frac{1}{2} < t_n\right] = .997,$$

where x is the number of heads that turn up. Find t_n for $n = 10^4$, $n = 10^6$, and $n = 10^{20}$.

[*Ans.* .015; .0015; .000,000,000,15.]

15. Assume that a calculating machine carries out a million operations to solve a certain problem. In each operation the machine gives the answer 10^{-5} too small, with probability $\frac{1}{2}$, and 10^{-5} too large, with probability $\frac{1}{2}$. Assume that the errors are independent of one another. What is a reasonable accuracy to attach to the answer? What if the machine carries out 10^{10} operations?

[*Ans.* ±.01; ±1.]

16. The Dartmouth Computer tossed a coin 1 million times (see Chapter VII, Section 10). It obtained 499,588 heads. Is this number reasonable?

*11. INDEPENDENT TRIALS WITH MORE THAN TWO OUTCOMES

By extending the results of Section 8, we shall study the case of independent trials in which we allow more than two outcomes. We assume that we have an independent trials process where the possible outcomes are $a_1, a_2, \ldots, a_k$, occurring with probabilities $p_1, p_2, \ldots, p_k$, respectively. We denote by

$$f(r_1, r_2, \ldots, r_k; p_1, p_2, \ldots, p_k)$$

the probability that, in

$$n = r_1 + r_2 + \ldots + r_k$$

such trials, there will be r_1 occurrences of a_1, r_2 of a_2, etc. In the case of two outcomes this notation would be $f(r_1, r_2; p_1, p_2)$. In Section 8 we wrote this as $f(n, r_1; p_1)$ since r_2 and p_2 are determined from n, r_1, and p_1. We shall indicate how this probability is found in general, but carry out the details only for a special case. We choose $k = 3$, and $n = 5$ for purposes of illustration. We shall find $f(1, 2, 2; p_1, p_2, p_3)$.

We show in Figure 20 enough of the tree for this process to indicate the branch probabilities for a path (heavy lined) corresponding to the outcomes a_2, a_3, a_1, a_2, a_3. The tree measure assigns weight $p_2 \cdot p_3 \cdot p_1 \cdot p_2 \cdot p_3 = p_1 \cdot p_2^2 \cdot p_3^2$ to this path.

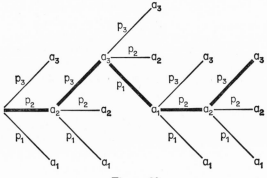

Figure 20

There are, of course, other paths through the tree corresponding to one occurrence of a_1, two of a_2, and two of a_3. However, they would all be assigned the same weight, $p_1 \cdot p_2^2 \cdot p_3^2$, by the tree measure. Hence to find $f(1, 2, 2; p_1, p_2, p_3)$, we must multiply this weight by the number of paths having the specified number of occurrences of each outcome.

We note that the path a_2, a_3, a_1, a_2, a_3 can be specified by the three-cell partition $[\{3\}, \{1, 4\}, \{2, 5\}]$ of the numbers from 1 to 5. Here the first cell shows the experiment which resulted in a_1, the second cell shows the two that resulted in a_2, and the third shows the two that resulted in a_3. Conversely, any such partition of the numbers from 1 to 5 with one element in the first cell, two in the second, and two in the third corresponds to a unique path of the desired kind. Hence the number of paths is the number of such partitions. But this is

$$\binom{5}{1, 2, 2} = \frac{5!}{1!\ 2!\ 2!}$$

(see Chapter III, Section 4), so that the probability of one occurrence of a_1, two of a_2, and two of a_3 is

$$\binom{5}{1, 2, 2} \cdot p_1 \cdot p_2^2 \cdot p_3^2.$$

The above argument carried out in general leads, for the case of independent trials with outcomes $a_1, a_2, \ldots, a_k$ occurring with probabilities $p_1, p_2, \ldots, p_k$, to the following.

The probability for r_1 occurrences of a_1, r_2 occurrences of a_2, etc., is given by

$$f(r_1, r_2, \ldots, r_k; p_1, p_2, \ldots, p_k) = \binom{n}{r_1, r_2, \ldots, r_k} p_1^{r_1} \cdot p_2^{r_2} \ldots p_k^{r_k}.$$

Example 1. A die is thrown 12 times. What is the probability that each number will come up twice? Here there are six outcomes, 1, 2, 3, 4, 5, 6 corresponding to the six sides of the die. We assign each outcome probability $\frac{1}{6}$. We are then asked for

$$f(2, 2, 2, 2, 2, 2; \tfrac{1}{6}, \tfrac{1}{6}, \tfrac{1}{6}, \tfrac{1}{6}, \tfrac{1}{6}, \tfrac{1}{6}),$$

which is

$$\binom{12}{2, 2, 2, 2, 2, 2} \left(\frac{1}{6}\right)^2 \left(\frac{1}{6}\right)^2 \left(\frac{1}{6}\right)^2 \left(\frac{1}{6}\right)^2 \left(\frac{1}{6}\right)^2 \left(\frac{1}{6}\right)^2 = .0034 \ldots.$$

Example 2. Suppose that we have an independent trials process with four outcomes a_1, a_2, a_3, a_4 occurring with probability p_1, p_2, p_3, p_4, respectively. It might be that we are interested only in the probability that r_1 occurrences of a_1 and r_2 occurrences of a_2 will take place with no specification about the number of each of the other possible outcomes. To answer this question we simply consider a new experiment where the outcomes are a_1, a_2, $\bar{a}_3$. Here $\bar{a}_3$ corresponds to an occurrence of either a_3 or a_4 in our original experiment. The corresponding probabilities would be p_1, p_2, and $\bar{p}_3$ with $\bar{p}_3 = p_3 + p_4$. Let $\bar{r}_3 = n - (r_1 + r_2)$. Then our question is answered by finding the probability in our new experiment for r_1 occurrences of a_1, r_2 of a_2, and $\bar{r}_3$ of $\bar{a}_3$, which is

$$\binom{n}{r_1,\, r_2,\, \bar{r}_3} p_1^{r_1} \cdot p_2^{r_2} \cdot \bar{p}_3^{\bar{r}_3}.$$

The same procedure can be carried out for experiments with any number of outcomes where we specify the number of occurrences of such particular outcomes. For example, if a die is thrown ten times the probability that a one will occur exactly twice and a three exactly three times is given by

$$\binom{10}{2,\, 3,\, 5} \left(\frac{1}{6}\right)^2 \left(\frac{1}{6}\right)^3 \left(\frac{4}{6}\right)^5 = .043 \ldots .$$

EXERCISES

1. Suppose that in a city 60 per cent of the population are Democrats, 30 per cent are Republicans, and 10 per cent are Independents. What is the probability that if three people are chosen at random there will be one Republican, one Democrat, and one Independent voter?   [*Ans.* .108.]

2. Three horses, A, B, and C, compete in four races. Assuming that each horse has an equal chance in each race, what is the probability that A wins two races and B and C win one each? What is the probability that the same horse wins all four races?   [*Ans.* $\frac{4}{27}$; $\frac{1}{27}$.]

3. Assume that in a certain large college 40 per cent of the students are freshmen, 30 per cent are sophomores, 20 per cent are juniors, and 10 per cent are seniors. A committee of eight is chosen at random from the student body. What is the probability that there are equal numbers from each class on the committee?

4. Let us assume that when a batter comes to bat, he has probability .6 of being put out, .1 of getting a walk, .2 of getting a single, .1 of getting an extra base hit. If he comes to bat five times in a game, what is the probability that

      (a) He get two walks and three singles?   [*Ans.* .0008.]

      (b) He gets a walk, a single, an extra base hit (and is out twice)?

                                                     [*Ans.* .043.]

      (c) He has a perfect day (i.e., never out)?   [*Ans.* .010.]

5. Assume that a single torpedo has a probability $\frac{1}{2}$ of sinking a ship, probability $\frac{1}{4}$ of damaging it, and probability $\frac{1}{4}$ of missing. Assume further that two damaging shots sink the ship. What is the probability that four torpedoes will succeed in sinking the ship?   [*Ans.* $\frac{251}{256}$.]

6. Jones, Smith, and Green live in the same house. The mailman has observed that Jones and Smith receive the same amount of mail on the average, but that Green receives twice as much as Jones (and hence also twice as much as Smith). If he has four letters for this house, what is the probability that each man receives at least one letter?

7. If three dice are thrown, find the probability that there is one six and two fives, given that all the outcomes are greater than three.   [*Ans.* $\frac{1}{9}$.]

8. A man plays a tournament consisting of three games. In each game he has probability $\frac{1}{2}$ for a win, $\frac{1}{4}$ for a loss, and $\frac{1}{4}$ for a draw, independently of the outcomes of other games. To win the tournament he must win more games than he loses. What is the probability that he wins the tournament?

9. Assume that in a certain course the probability that a student chosen at random will get an A is .1, that he will get a B is .2, that he will get a C is .4, that he will get a D is .2, and that he will get an E is .1. What distribution of grades is most likely in the case of four students?

                                      [*Ans.* One B, two C's, one D.]

10. Let us assume that in a World Series game a batter has probability $\frac{1}{4}$ of getting no hits, $\frac{1}{2}$ for getting one hit, $\frac{1}{4}$ for getting two hits, assuming that the probability of getting more than two hits is negligible. In a four-game World Series, find the probability that the batter gets

      (a) Exactly two hits.

      (b) Exactly three hits.

      (c) Exactly four hits.

      (d) Exactly five hits.

      (e) Fewer than two hits or more than five.

                [*Ans.* $\frac{7}{64}$; $\frac{7}{32}$; $\frac{35}{128}$; $\frac{7}{32}$; $\frac{23}{128}$.]

11. Gypsies sometimes toss a thick coin for which heads and tails are equally likely, but which also has probability $\frac{1}{5}$ of standing on edge (i.e.,

neither heads nor tails). What is the probability of exactly one head and four tails in five tosses of a gypsy coin?

12. A family car is driven by the father, two sons, and the mother. The fenders have been dented four times, three times while the mother was driving. Is it fair to say that the mother is a worse driver than the men?

12. EXPECTED VALUE

In this section we shall discuss the concept of expected value. Although it originated in the study of gambling games, it enters into almost any detailed probabilistic discussion.

DEFINITION. If in an experiment the possible outcomes are numbers, $a_1, a_2, \ldots, a_k$, occurring with probability $p_1, p_2, \ldots, p_k$, then the *expected value* is defined to be

$$E = a_1 p_1 + a_2 p_2 + \ldots + a_k p_k.$$

The term "expected value" is not to be interpreted as the value that will necessarily occur on a single experiment. For example, if a person bets $1 that a head will turn up when a coin is thrown, he may either win $1 or lose $1. His expected value is $(1)(\frac{1}{2}) + (-1)(\frac{1}{2}) = 0$, which is not one of the possible outcomes. The term, expected value, had its origin in the following consideration. If we repeat an experiment with expected value E a large number of times, and if we expect a_1 a fraction p_1 of the time, a_2 a fraction p_2 of the time, etc., then the average that we expect per experiment is E. In particular, in a gambling game E is interpreted as the average winning expected in a large number of plays. Here the expected value is often taken as the value of the game to the player. If the game has a positive expected value, the game is said to be favorable; if the game has expected value zero it is said to be fair; and if it has negative expected value it is described as unfavorable. These terms are not to be taken too literally, since many people are quite happy to play games that, in terms of expected value, are unfavorable. For instance, the buying of life insurance may be considered an unfavorable game which most people choose to play.

Example 1. For the first example of the application of expected value we consider the game of roulette as played at Monte Carlo. There are several types of bets which the gambler can make, and we consider two of these.

The wheel has the number 0 and the numbers from 1 to 36 marked on equally spaced slots. The wheel is spun and a ball comes to rest in one of these slots. If the player puts a stake, say of $1, on a given number, and the ball comes to rest in this slot, then he receives from the croupier 36 times his stake, or $36. The player wins $35 with probability $\frac{1}{37}$ and loses $1 with probability $\frac{36}{37}$. Hence his expected winnings are

$$\tfrac{35}{37} - 1 \cdot \tfrac{36}{37} = -\tfrac{1}{37} = -.027.$$

This can be interpreted to mean that in the long run he can expect to lose about 2.7 per cent of his stakes.

A second way to play is the following. A player may bet on "red" or "black." The numbers from 1 to 36 are evenly divided between the two colors. If a player bets on "red," and a red number turns up, he receives twice his stake. If a black number turns up, he loses his stake. If 0 turns up, then the wheel is spun until it stops on a number different from 0. If this is black, the player loses; but if it is red, he receives only his original stake, not twice it. For this type of play, the gambler wins $1 with probability $\frac{18}{37}$, breaks even with probability $\frac{1}{2} \cdot \frac{1}{37} = \frac{1}{74}$, and loses $1 with probability $\frac{18}{37} + \frac{1}{2} \cdot \frac{1}{37} = \frac{37}{74}$. Hence his expected winning is

$$1 \cdot \tfrac{18}{37} + 0 \cdot \tfrac{1}{74} - 1 \cdot \tfrac{37}{74} = -.0135.$$

In this case the player can expect to lose about 1.35 per cent of his stakes in the long run. Thus the expected loss in this case is only half as great as in the previous case.

Example 2. A player rolls a die and receives a number of dollars corresponding to the number of dots on the face which turns up. What should the player pay for playing, to make this a fair game? To answer this question, we note that the player wins 1, 2, 3, 4, 5 or 6 dollars, each with probability $\frac{1}{6}$. Hence, his expected winning is

$$1(\tfrac{1}{6}) + 2(\tfrac{1}{6}) + 3(\tfrac{1}{6}) + 4(\tfrac{1}{6}) + 5(\tfrac{1}{6}) + 6(\tfrac{1}{6}) = 3\tfrac{1}{2}.$$

Thus if he pays $3.50, his expected winnings will be zero.

Example 3. What is the expected number of successes in the case of four independent trials with probability $\frac{1}{3}$ for success? We know that the probability of x successes is $\binom{4}{x} \left(\frac{1}{3}\right)^x \left(\frac{2}{3}\right)^{4-x}$. Thus

$$E = 0 \cdot \binom{4}{0}\left(\frac{1}{3}\right)^0\left(\frac{2}{3}\right)^4 + 1 \cdot \binom{4}{1}\left(\frac{1}{3}\right)^1\left(\frac{2}{3}\right)^3 + 2 \cdot \binom{4}{2}\left(\frac{1}{3}\right)^2\left(\frac{2}{3}\right)^2$$

$$+ 3 \cdot \binom{4}{3}\left(\frac{1}{3}\right)^3\left(\frac{2}{3}\right)^1 + 4 \cdot \binom{4}{4}\left(\frac{1}{3}\right)^4\left(\frac{2}{3}\right)^0$$

$$= 0 + \frac{32}{81} + \frac{48}{81} + \frac{24}{81} + \frac{4}{81} = \frac{108}{81} = \frac{4}{3}.$$

In general, it can be shown that in n trials with probability p for success, the expected number of successes is np.

Example 4. In the game of craps a pair of dice is rolled by one of the players. If the sum of the spots shown is 7 or 11, he wins. If it is 2, 3, or 12, he loses. If it is another sum, he must continue rolling the dice until he either repeats the same sum or rolls a 7. In the former case he wins, in the latter he loses. Let us suppose that he wins or loses $1. Then the two possible outcomes are $+1$ and -1. We will compute the expected value of the game. First we must find the probability that he will win.

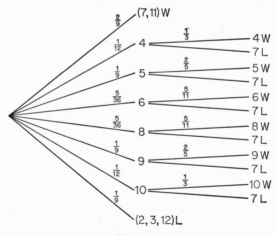

Figure 21

We represent the possibilities by a two-stage tree shown in Figure 21. While it is theoretically possible for the game to go on indefinitely, we do not consider this possibility. This means that our analysis applies only to games which actually stop at some time.

The branch probabilities at the first stage are determined by thinking of the 36 possibilities for the throw of the two dice as being equally likely and taking in each case the fraction of the possibilities which correspond to the branch as the branch probability. The probabilities for the branches at the second level are obtained as follows. If, for example, the first outcome was a 4, then when the game ends, a 4 or 7 must have occurred. The possible outcomes for the dice were

$$\{(3, 1), (1, 3), (2, 2), (4, 3), (3, 4), (2, 5), (5, 2), (1, 6), (6, 1)\}.$$

Again we consider these possibilities to be equally likely and assign to the branch considered the fraction of the outcomes which correspond to this branch. Thus to the 4 branch we assign a probability $\frac{3}{9} = \frac{1}{3}$. The other branch probabilities are determined in a similar way. Having the tree measure assigned, to find the probability of a win we must simply add the weights of all paths leading to a win. If this is done, we obtain $\frac{244}{495}$. Thus the player's expected value is

$$1 \cdot \left(\tfrac{244}{495}\right) + (-1) \cdot \left(\tfrac{251}{495}\right) = -\tfrac{7}{495} = -.0141.$$

Hence he can expect to lose 1.41 per cent of his stakes in the long run. It is interesting to note that this is just slightly less favorable than his losses in betting on "red" in roulette.

EXERCISES

1. Suppose that A tosses two coins and receives $2 if two heads appear, $1 if one head appears, and nothing if no heads appear. What is the expected value of the game to him?   [*Ans.* $1.]

2. Smith and Jones are matching coins. If the coins match, Smith gets $1, and if they do not, Jones get $1.
   (a) If the game consists of matching twice, what is the expected value of the game for Smith?
   (b) Suppose that if Smith wins the first round he quits, and if he loses the first he plays the second. Jones is not allowed to quit. What is the expected value of the game for Smith?

3. If five coins are thrown, what is the expected number of heads that will turn up?   [*Ans.* $\frac{5}{2}$.]

4. A coin is thrown until the first time a head comes up or until three tails in a row occur. Find the expected number of times the coin is thrown.

5. A man wishes to purchase a five cent newspaper. He has in his pocket one dime and five pennies. The newsman offers to let him have the paper in exchange for one coin drawn at random from the customer's pocket.

(a) Is this a fair proposition and, if not, to whom is it favorable?

[*Ans.* Favorable to man.]

(b) Answer the same questions as in (a) assuming that the newsman demands two coins drawn at random from the customer's pocket.

[*Ans.* Fair proposition.]

6. A bets 50 cents against B's x cents that, if two cards are dealt from a shuffled pack of ordinary playing cards, both cards will be of the same color. What value of x will make this bet fair?

7. Prove that if the expected value of a given experiment is E, and if a constant c is added to each of the outcomes, the expected value of the new experiment is $E + c$.

8. Prove that, if the expected value of a given experiment is E, and if each of the possible outcomes is multiplied by a constant k, the expected value of the new experiment is $k \cdot E$.

9. A man plays the following game: He draws a card from a bridge deck; if it is an ace he wins $5; if it is a jack, a queen or a king, he wins $2; for any other card he loses $1. What is his expected winning per play?

10. An urn contains two black and three white balls. Balls are successively drawn from the urn without replacement until a black ball is obtained. Find the expected number of draws required.

11. Using the result of Exercises 13 and 14 of Section 6, find the expected number of games in the World Series (a) under the assumption that each team has probability $\frac{1}{2}$ of winning each game and (b) under the assumption that the stronger team has probability .6 of winning each game.

[*Ans.* 5.81; 5.75.]

12. Suppose that we modify the game of craps as follows: On a 7 or 11 the player wins $2, on a 2, 3, or 12 he loses $3; otherwise the game is as usual. Find the expected value of the new game, and compare it with the old value.

13. Suppose that in roulette at Monte Carlo we place 50 cents on "red" and 50 cents on "black." What is the expected value on the game? Is this better or worse than placing $1 on "red"?

14. Betting on "red" in roulette can be described roughly as follows. We win with probability .49, get our money back with probability .01, and lose with probability .50. Draw the tree for three plays of the game, and compute (to three decimals) the probability of each path. What is the probability that we are ahead at the end of three bets? [*Ans.* .485.]

15. Assume that the odds are $r:s$ that a certain statement will be true. If a man receives s dollars if the statement turns out to be true, and gives r dollars if not, what is his expected winning?

16. Referring to Exercise 9 of Section 3, find the expected number of languages that a student chosen at random reads.

17. Referring to Exercise 5 of Section 4, find the expected number of men who get their own hats.   [*Ans.* 1.]

18. A pair of dice is rolled. Each die has the number 1 on two opposite faces, the number 2 on two opposite faces, and the number 3 on two opposite faces. The "roller" wins a dollar if

    (i) the sum of four occurs on the first roll; *or*

    (ii) the sum of three or five occurs on the first roll and the same sum occurs on a subsequent roll before the sum of four occurs.

Otherwise he loses a dollar.

    (a) What is the probability that the person rolling the dice wins?

    (b) What is the expected value of the game?   [*Ans.* (a) $\frac{23}{45}$; (b) $\frac{1}{45}$.]

13. MARKOV CHAINS

In this section we shall study a more general kind of process than the ones considered in the last three sections.

We assume that we have a sequence of experiments with the following properties. The outcome of each experiment is one of a finite number of possible outcomes $a_1, a_2, \ldots, a_r$. It is assumed that the probability of outcome a_j on any given experiment is not necessarily independent of the outcomes of previous experiments but depends at most upon the outcome of the immediately preceding experiment. We assume that there are given numbers p_{ij} which represent the probability of outcome a_j on any given experiment, given that outcome a_i occurred on the preceding experiment. The outcomes $a_1, a_2, \ldots, a_r$ are called *states*, and the numbers p_{ij} are called *transition probabilities*. If we assume that the process begins in some particular state, then we have enough information to determine the tree measure for the process and can calculate probabilities of statements relating to the over-all sequence of experiments. A process of the above kind is called a *Markov chain process*.

The transition probabilities can be exhibited in two different ways. The first way is that of a square array. For a Markov chain with states a_1, a_2, and a_3, this array is written as

$$P = \begin{pmatrix} p_{11} & p_{12} & p_{13} \\ p_{21} & p_{22} & p_{23} \\ p_{31} & p_{32} & p_{33} \end{pmatrix}.$$

Such an array is a special case of a *matrix*. Matrices are of fundamental importance to the study of Markov chains as well as being important in the study of other branches of mathematics. They will be studied in detail in the next chapter.

A second way to show the transition probabilities is by a *transition diagram*. Such a diagram is illustrated for a special case in Figure 22. The arrows from each state indicate the possible states to which a process can move from the given state.

The matrix of transition probabilities which corresponds to this diagram is the matrix

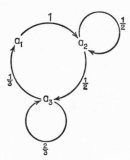

Figure 22

$$P = \begin{array}{c} \\ a_1 \\ a_2 \\ a_3 \end{array} \begin{array}{ccc} a_1 & a_2 & a_3 \\ \begin{pmatrix} 0 & 1 & 0 \\ 0 & \frac{1}{2} & \frac{1}{2} \\ \frac{1}{3} & 0 & \frac{2}{3} \end{pmatrix}. \end{array}$$

An entry of 0 indicates that the transition is impossible.

Notice that in the matrix P the sum of the elements of each row is 1. This must be true in any matrix of transition probabilities, since the elements of the ith row represent the probabilities for all possibilities when the process is in state a_i.

The kind of problem in which we are most interested in the study of Markov chains is the following. Suppose that the process starts in state i. What is the probability that after n steps it will be in state j? We denote this probability by $p_{ij}^{(n)}$. Notice that we do *not* mean by this the nth power of the number p_{ij}. We are actually interested in this probability for all possible starting positions i and all possible terminal positions j. We can represent these numbers conveniently again by a matrix. For example, for n steps in a three-state Markov chain we write these probabilities as the matrix

$$P^{(n)} = \begin{pmatrix} p_{11}^{(n)} & p_{12}^{(n)} & p_{13}^{(n)} \\ p_{21}^{(n)} & p_{22}^{(n)} & p_{23}^{(n)} \\ p_{31}^{(n)} & p_{32}^{(n)} & p_{33}^{(n)} \end{pmatrix}.$$

Example 1. Let us find for a Markov chain with transition probabilities indicated in Figure 22 the probability of being at the various possible states after three steps, assuming that the process starts at state a_1. We find these probabilities by constructing a tree and a tree measure as in Figure 23.

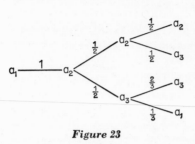

Figure 23

The probability $p_{13}^{(3)}$, for example, is the sum of the weights assigned by the tree measure to all paths through our tree which end at state a_3. That is,

$$1 \cdot \tfrac{1}{2} \cdot \tfrac{1}{2} + 1 \cdot \tfrac{1}{2} \cdot \tfrac{2}{3} = \tfrac{7}{12}.$$

Similarly

$$p_{12}^{(3)} = 1 \cdot \tfrac{1}{2} \cdot \tfrac{1}{2} = \tfrac{1}{4} \quad \text{and} \quad p_{11}^{(3)} = 1 \cdot \tfrac{1}{2} \cdot \tfrac{1}{3} = \tfrac{1}{6}.$$

By constructing a similar tree measure, assuming that we start at state a_2, we could find $p_{21}^{(3)}, p_{22}^{(3)}$, and $p_{23}^{(3)}$. The same is true for $p_{31}^{(3)}, p_{32}^{(3)}$, and $p_{33}^{(3)}$. If this is carried out (see Exercise 7) we can write the results in matrix form as follows:

$$P^{(3)} = \begin{array}{c} \\ a_1 \\ a_2 \\ a_3 \end{array} \begin{array}{ccc} a_1 & a_2 & a_3 \\ \begin{pmatrix} \tfrac{1}{6} & \tfrac{1}{4} & \tfrac{7}{12} \\ \tfrac{7}{36} & \tfrac{7}{24} & \tfrac{37}{72} \\ \tfrac{4}{27} & \tfrac{7}{18} & \tfrac{25}{54} \end{pmatrix} \end{array}.$$

Again the rows add up to 1, corresponding to the fact that if we start at a given state we must reach some state after three steps. Notice now that all the elements of this matrix are positive, showing that it is possible to reach any state from any state in three steps. In the next chapter we will develop a simple method of computing $P^{(n)}$.

Example 2. Suppose that we are interested in studying the way in which a given state votes in a series of national elections. We wish to make long-term predictions and so will not consider conditions peculiar to a particular election year. We shall base our predictions only on past history of the outcomes of the elections, Republican or Democratic. It is clear that a knowledge of these past results would influence our predictions for the future. As a first approximation, we assume that the knowledge of the past beyond the last election would not cause us to change the probabilities for the outcomes on the next election. With this assumption we obtain a Markov chain with two states R and D and matrix of transition probabilities

$$
\begin{array}{cc}
 & \begin{array}{cc} R & D \end{array} \\
\begin{array}{c} R \\ D \end{array} & \begin{pmatrix} 1 - a & a \\ b & 1 - b \end{pmatrix}.
\end{array}
$$

The numbers a and b could be estimated from past results as follows. We could take for a the fraction of the previous years in which the outcome has changed from Republican in one year to Democratic in the next year, and for b the fraction of reverse changes.

We can obtain a better approximation by taking into account the previous two elections. In this case our states are RR, RD, DR, and DD, indicating the outcome of two successive elections. Being in state RR means that the last two elections were Republican victories. If the next election is a Democratic victory, we will be in state RD. If the election outcomes for a series of years is $DDDRDRR$, then our process has moved from state DD to DD to DR to RD to DR, and finally to RR. Notice that the first letter of the state to which we move must agree with the second letter of the state from which we came, since these refer to the same election year. Our matrix of transition probabilities will then have the form,

$$
\begin{array}{c}
\begin{array}{cccc} RR & DR & RD & DD \end{array} \\
\begin{array}{c} RR \\ DR \\ RD \\ DD \end{array} \begin{pmatrix} 1 - a & 0 & a & 0 \\ b & 0 & 1 - b & 0 \\ 0 & 1 - c & 0 & c \\ 0 & d & 0 & 1 - d \end{pmatrix}.
\end{array}
$$

Again the numbers a, b, c, and d would have to be estimated. The study of this example is continued in Chapter V, Section 7.

Example 3. The following example of a Markov chain has been used in physics as a simple model for diffusion of gases. We shall see later that a similar model applies to an idealized problem in changing populations.

We imagine n black balls and n white balls which are put into two urns so that there are n balls in each urn. A single experiment consists in choosing a ball from each urn at random and putting the ball obtained from the first urn into the second urn, and the ball obtained from the second urn into the first. We take as state the number of black balls in the first urn. If at any time we know this number, then we know the exact composition of each urn. That is, if there are j black balls in urn 1, there must be $n - j$ black balls in urn 2, $n - j$ white balls in urn 1, and j white balls in urn 2. If the process is in state j, then after the next exchange it will be in state $j - 1$, if a black ball is chosen from urn 1 and a white ball from urn 2. It will be in state j if a ball of the same color is drawn from each urn. It will be in state $j + 1$ if a white ball is drawn from urn 1 and a black ball from urn 2. The transition probabilities are then given by (see Exercise 12)

$$p_{jj-1} = \left(\frac{j}{n}\right)^2 \qquad j > 0$$

$$p_{jj} = \frac{2j(n - j)}{n^2}$$

$$p_{jj+1} = \left(\frac{n - j}{n}\right)^2 \qquad j < n$$

$$p_{jk} = 0 \qquad \text{otherwise.}$$

A physicist would be interested, for example, in predicting the composition of the urns after a certain number of exchanges have taken place. Certainly any predictions about the early stages of the process would depend upon the initial composition of the urns. For example, if we started with all black balls in urn 1, we would expect that for some time there would be more black balls in urn 1 than in urn 2. On the other hand, it might be expected that the effect of this initial distribution would wear off after a large number of exchanges. We shall see later, in Chapter V, Section 7, that this is indeed the case.

EXERCISES

1. Draw a state diagram for the Markov chain with transition probabilities given by the following matrices.

$$\begin{pmatrix} \frac{1}{2} & \frac{1}{2} & 0 \\ 0 & 1 & 0 \\ \frac{1}{2} & 0 & \frac{1}{2} \end{pmatrix}, \qquad \begin{pmatrix} \frac{1}{3} & \frac{1}{3} & \frac{1}{3} \\ \frac{1}{3} & \frac{1}{3} & \frac{1}{3} \\ \frac{1}{3} & \frac{1}{3} & \frac{1}{3} \end{pmatrix},$$

$$\begin{pmatrix} 0 & 1 \\ 1 & 0 \end{pmatrix}, \qquad \begin{pmatrix} 0 & 1 & 0 & 0 \\ 1 & 0 & 0 & 0 \\ 0 & 0 & \frac{1}{2} & \frac{1}{2} \\ 0 & 0 & \frac{1}{2} & \frac{1}{2} \end{pmatrix}.$$

2. Give the matrix of transition probabilities corresponding to the following transition diagrams.

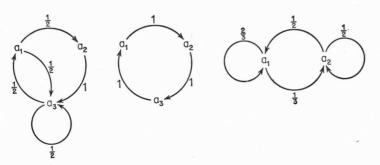

3. Find the matrix $P^{(2)}$ for the Markov chain determined by the matrix of transition probabilities

$$P = \begin{pmatrix} \frac{1}{2} & \frac{1}{2} \\ \frac{1}{3} & \frac{2}{3} \end{pmatrix}. \qquad [Ans. \ \begin{pmatrix} \frac{5}{12} & \frac{7}{12} \\ \frac{7}{18} & \frac{11}{18} \end{pmatrix}.]$$

4. What is the matrix of transition probabilities for the Markov chain in Example 3, for the case of two white balls and two black balls?

5. Find the matrices $P^{(2)}$, $P^{(3)}$, $P^{(4)}$ for the Markov chain determined by the transition probabilities

$$\begin{pmatrix} 1 & 0 \\ 0 & 1 \end{pmatrix}.$$

Find the same for the Markov chain determined by the matrix

$$\begin{pmatrix} 0 & 1 \\ 1 & 0 \end{pmatrix}.$$

6. Suppose that a Markov chain has two states, a_1 and a_2, and transition probabilities given by the matrix

$$\begin{pmatrix} \frac{1}{3} & \frac{2}{3} \\ \frac{1}{2} & \frac{1}{2} \end{pmatrix}.$$

By means of a separate chance device we choose a state in which to start the process. This device chooses a_1 with probability $\frac{1}{2}$ and a_2 with probability $\frac{1}{2}$. Find the probability that the process is in state a_1 after the first step. Answer the same question in the case that the device chooses a_1 with probability $\frac{1}{3}$ and a_2 with probability $\frac{2}{3}$. $[Ans. \ \frac{5}{12}; \frac{4}{9}.]$

7. Referring to the Markov chain with transition probabilities indicated in Figure 22, construct the tree measures and determine the values of

$$p_{21}^{(3)}, p_{22}^{(3)}, p_{23}^{(3)}, \quad \text{and} \quad p_{31}^{(3)}, p_{32}^{(3)}, p_{33}^{(3)}.$$

8. A certain calculating machine uses only the digits 0 and 1. It is supposed to transmit one of these digits through several stages. However, at every stage there is a probability p that the digit which enters this stage will be changed when it leaves. We form a Markov chain to represent the process of transmission by taking as states the digits 0 and 1. What is the matrix of transition probabilities?

9. For the Markov chain in Exercise 8, draw a tree and assign a tree measure, assuming that the process begins in state 0 and moves through three stages of transmission. What is the probability that the machine after three stages produces the digit 0, i.e., the correct digit? What is the probability that the machine never changed the digit from 0?

10. Assume that a man's profession can be classified as professional, skilled laborer, or unskilled laborer. Assume that of the sons of professional men 80 per cent are professional, 10 per cent are skilled laborers, and 10 per cent are unskilled laborers. In the case of sons of skilled laborers, 60 per cent are skilled laborers, 20 per cent are professional, and 20 per cent are unskilled laborers. Finally, in the case of unskilled laborers, 50 per cent of the sons are unskilled laborers, and 25 per cent each are in the other two categories. Assume that every man has a son, and form a Markov chain by following a given family through several generations. Set up the matrix of transition probabilities. Find the probability that the grandson of an unskilled laborer is a professional man. [*Ans.* .375.]

11. In Exercise 10 we assumed that every man has a son. Assume instead that the probability a man has a son is .8. Form a Markov chain with four states. The first three states are as in Exercise 10, and the fourth state is such that the process enters it if a man has no son, and that the state cannot be left. This state represents families whose male line has died out. Find the matrix of transition probabilities and find the probability that an unskilled laborer has a grandson who is a professional man. [*Ans.* .24.]

12. Explain why the transition probabilities given in Example 3 are correct.

SUPPLEMENTARY EXERCISES

13. Five points are marked on a circle. A process moves clockwise from a given point to its neighbor with probability $\frac{2}{3}$, or counterclockwise to its neighbor with probability $\frac{1}{3}$.

    (a) Considering the process to be a Markov chain process, find the matrix of transition probabilities.

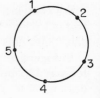

(b) Given that the process starts in a state 3, what is the probability that it returns to the same state in two steps?

14. In northern New England, years for apples can be described as good, average, or poor. Suppose that following a good year the probabilities of good, average, or poor years are respectively .4, .4, and .2. Following a poor year the probabilities of good, average, or poor years are .2, .4, and .4 respectively. Following an average year the probabilities that the next year will be good or poor are each .2, and of an average year, .6.

(a) Set up the transition matrix of this Markov chain.

(b) 1965 was a good year. Compute the probabilities for 1966, 1967, and 1968.   [*Partial Ans. For* 1967: .28, .48, .24.]

15. In Exercise 14 suppose that there is probability $\frac{1}{4}$ for a good year, $\frac{1}{2}$ for an average year, and $\frac{1}{4}$ for a poor year. What are the probabilities for the following year?

16. A teacher in an oversized mathematics class finds, after grading all homework papers for the first two assignments, that it is necessary to reduce the amount of time spent in such grading. He therefore designs the following system: Papers will be marked satisfactory or unsatisfactory. All papers of students receiving a mark of unsatisfactory on any assignment will be read on each of the two succeeding days. Of the remaining papers, the teacher will read one-fifth, chosen at random. Assuming that each paper has a probability of one-fifth of being classified "unsatisfactory."

(a) Set up a three-state Markov chain to describe the process.

(b) Suppose that a student has just handed in an unsatisfactory paper. What are the probabilities for the next two assignments?

17. In another model for diffusion, it is assumed that there are two urns which together contain N balls numbered from 1 to N. Each second a number from 1 to N is chosen at random, and the ball with the corresponding number is moved to the other urn. Set up a Markov chain by taking as state the number of balls in urn 1. Find the transition matrix.

*14. THE CENTRAL LIMIT THEOREM

We continue our discussion of the independent trials process with two outcomes. As usual, let p be the probability of success on a trial, and $f(n, p; x)$ be the probability of exactly x successes in n trials.

In Figure 24 we have plotted bar graphs which represent $f(n, .3; x)$ for $n = 10, 50, 100$, and 200. We note first of all that the graphs are drifting off to the right. This is not surprising, since their peaks occur

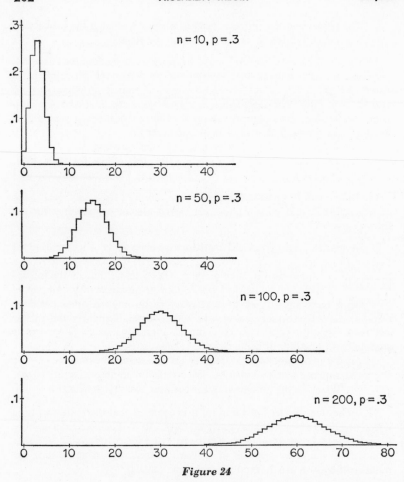

Figure 24

at np, which is steadily increasing. We also note that while the total area is always 1, this area becomes more and more spread out.

We want to redraw these graphs in a manner that prevents the drifting and the spreading out. First of all, we replace x by $x - np$, assuring that our peak always occurs at 0. Next we introduce a new unit for measuring the deviation, which depends on n, and which gives comparable scales. As we saw in Section 10, the standard deviation $\sqrt{npq}$ is such a unit.

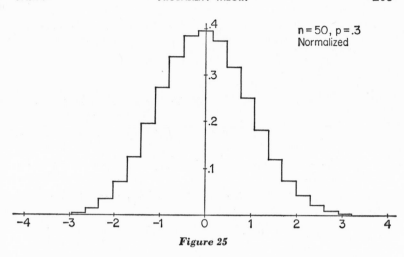

Figure 25

We must still insure that probabilities are represented by areas in the graph. In Figure 24 this is achieved by having a unit base for each rectangle, and having the probability $f(n, p; x)$ as height. Since we are now representing a standard deviation as a single unit on the horizontal axis, we must take $f(n, p; x)\sqrt{npq}$ as the heights of our rectangles. The resulting curves for $n = 50$ and 200 are shown in Figures 25 and 26, respectively.

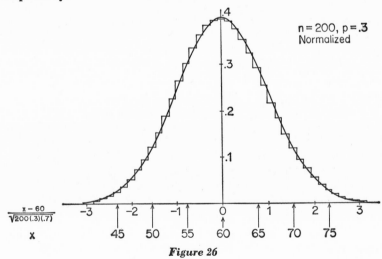

Figure 26

We note that the two figures look very much alike. We have also shown in Figure 26 that it can be approximated by a bell-shaped curve. This curve represents the function

$$f(x) = \frac{1}{\sqrt{2\pi}} e^{-x^2/2},$$

and is known as the *normal curve*. It is a fundamental theorem of probability theory that as n increases, the appropriately rescaled bargraphs more and more closely approach the normal curve. The theorem is known as the *Central Limit Theorem*, and we have illustrated it graphically.

More precisely, the theorem states that for any two numbers a and b, with $a < b$,

$$\Pr \left[a < \frac{x - np}{\sqrt{npq}} < b \right]$$

approaches the area under the normal curve between a and b, as n increases. This theorem is particularly interesting in that the normal curve is symmetric about 0, while $f(n, p; x)$ is symmetric about the expected value np only for the case $p = \frac{1}{2}$. It should also be noted that we always arrive at the same normal curve, no matter what the value of p is.

In Figure 27 we give a table for the area under the normal curve between 0 and d. Since the total area is 1, and since it is symmetric about the origin, we can compute arbitrary areas from this table. For example, suppose that we wish the area between -1 and $+2$. The area between 0 and 2 is given in the table as .477. The area between -1 and 0 is the same as between 0 and 1, and hence is given as .341. Thus the total area is .818. The area outside the interval $(-1, 2)$ is then $1 - .818 = .182$.

Example 1. Let us find the probability that x differs from the expected value np by as much as d standard deviations.

$$\Pr \left[|x - np| \geq d\sqrt{npq} \right] = \Pr \left[\left| \frac{x - np}{\sqrt{npq}} \right| \geq d \right],$$

and hence the approximate answer should be the area outside the interval $(-d, d)$ under the normal curve. For $d = 1, 2, 3$ we obtain

$$1 - (2 \times .341) = .318, \ 1 - (2 \times .477) = .046$$

and

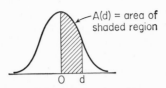

A(d) = area of shaded region

d	A(d)	d	A(d)	d	A(d)	d	A(d)
.0	.000	1.1	.364	2.1	.482	3.1	.4990
.1	.040	1.2	.385	2.2	.486	3.2	.4993
.2	.079	1.3	.403	2.3	.489	3.3	.4995
.3	.118	1.4	.419	2.4	.492	3.4	.4997
.4	.155	1.5	.433	2.5	.494	3.5	.4998
.5	.191	1.6	.445	2.6	.495	3.6	.4998
.6	.226	1.7	.455	2.7	.497	3.7	.4999
.7	.258	1.8	.464	2.8	.497	3.8	.49993
.8	.288	1.9	.471	2.9	.498	3.9	.49995
.9	.316	2.0	.477	3.0	.4987	4.0	.49997
1.0	.341					5.0	.49999997

Figure 27

$$1 - (2 \times .4987) = .0026,$$

respectively. These agree with the values given in Section 10, to within rounding errors. In fact, the Central Limit Theorem is the basis of those estimates.

Example 2. In Section 10 we considered the example of throwing a coin 10,000 times. The expected number of heads that turn up is 5000, and the standard deviation is $\sqrt{10,000, \frac{1}{2} \cdot \frac{1}{2}} = 50$. We observed that the probability of a deviation of more than two standard deviations (or 100) was very unlikely. On the other hand, consider the probability of a deviation of less than .1 standard deviation. That is, of a deviation of less than five. The area from 0 to .1 under the normal curve is .040 and hence the probability of a deviation from 5000 of less than five is approximately .08. Thus, while a deviation of 100 is very unlikely, it is also very unlikely that a deviation of less than five will occur.

Example 3. The normal approximation can be used to estimate the individual probabilities $f(n, x; p)$ for large n. For example, let us estimate $f(200, 65; .3)$. The graph of the probabilities $f(200, x; .3)$ was given in Figure 26 together with the normal approximation. The desired probability is the area of the bar corresponding to $x = 65$. An inspection of the graph suggests that we should take the area under the normal curve between 64.5 and 65.5 as an estimate for this probability. In normalized units this is the area between

$$\frac{4.5}{\sqrt{200(.3)(.7)}} \quad \text{and} \quad \frac{5.5}{\sqrt{200(.3)(.7)}},$$

or between .6944 and .8487. Our table is not fine enough to find this area, but from more complete tables, or by machine computation, this area may be found to be .046 to three decimal places. The exact value to three decimal places is .045. This procedure gives us a good estimate.

If we check all of the values of $f(200, x; .3)$ we find in each case that we would make an error of at most .001 by using the normal approximation. There is unfortunately no simple way to estimate the error caused by the use of the Central Limit Theorem. The error will clearly depend upon how large n is, but it also depends upon how near p is to 0 or 1. The greatest accuracy occurs when p is near $\frac{1}{2}$.

Example 4. Suppose that a drug has been administered to a number of patients and found to be effective a fraction $\bar{p}$ of the time. Assuming an independent trials process, it is natural to take $\bar{p}$ as an estimate for the unknown probability p for success on any one trial. It is useful to have a method of estimating the reliability of this estimate. One method is the following. Let x be the number of successes for the drug given to n patients. Then by the Central Limit Theorem

$$\Pr\left[\left|\frac{x - np}{\sqrt{npq}}\right| \leq 2\right] \approx .95.$$

This is the same as saying

$$\Pr\left[\left|\frac{x/n - p}{\sqrt{pq/n}}\right| \leq 2\right] \approx .95.$$

Putting $\bar{p} = x/n$, we have

$$\Pr\left[|\bar{p} - p| \leq 2\sqrt{\frac{pq}{n}}\right] \approx .95.$$

Using the fact that $pq \leq \frac{1}{4}$ (see Exercise 12) we have

$$\Pr\left[|\bar{p} - p| \le \frac{1}{\sqrt{n}}\right] \ge .95.$$

This says that no matter what p is, with probability $\ge .95$, the true value will not deviate from the estimate $\bar{p}$ by more than $1/\sqrt{n}$. It is customary then to say that

$$\bar{p} - \frac{1}{\sqrt{n}} \le p \le \bar{p} + \frac{1}{\sqrt{n}}$$

with confidence .95. The interval $\left[\bar{p} - \frac{1}{\sqrt{n}}, \bar{p} + \frac{1}{\sqrt{n}}\right]$ is called a 95 per cent *confidence interval*. Had we started with

$$\Pr\left[\left|\frac{x - np}{\sqrt{npq}}\right| \le 3\right] \approx .99,$$

we would have obtained the 99 per cent confidence interval

$$\left[\bar{p} - \frac{3}{2\sqrt{n}}, \bar{p} + \frac{3}{2\sqrt{n}}\right].$$

For example, if in 400 trials the drug is found effective 124 times, or .31 of the times, the 95 per cent confidence interval for p is

$$[.31 - \tfrac{1}{20}, .31 + \tfrac{1}{20}] \quad \text{or} \quad [.26, .36]$$

and the 99 per cent confidence interval is

$$[.31 - \tfrac{3}{40}, .31 + \tfrac{3}{40}] \quad \text{or} \quad [.235, .385].$$

EXERCISES

1. Let x be the number of successes in n trials of an independent trials process with probability p for success. Let $x^* = \dfrac{x - np}{\sqrt{npq}}$. For large n estimate the following probabilities.

    (a) $\Pr[x^* < -2.5]$.   [*Ans.* .006.]
    (b) $\Pr[x^* < 2.5]$.
    (c) $\Pr[x^* \ge -.5]$.
    (d) $\Pr[-1.5 < x^* < 1]$.   [*Ans.* .774.]

2. A coin is biased in such a way that a head comes up with probability .8 on a single toss. Use the normal approximation to estimate the probability that in a million tosses there are more than 800,400 heads.

3. Plot a graph of the probabilities $f(10, x; .5)$. Plot a graph also of the normalized probabilities as in Figures 25 and 26.

4. An ordinary coin is tossed one million times. Let x be the number of heads which turn up. Estimate the following probabilities.

(a) Pr $[499,500 \leq x \leq 500,500]$.

(b) Pr $[499,000 \leq x \leq 501,000]$.

(c) Pr $[498,500 \leq x \leq 501,500]$.

[*Ans.* .682; .954; .997 (Approximate answers.).]

5. Assume that a baseball player has probability .37 of getting a hit each time he comes to bat. Find the probability of getting an average of .388 or better if he comes to bat 300 times during the season. (In 1957 Ted Williams had a batting average of .388 and Mickey Mantle had an average of .353. If we assume this difference is due to chance, we may estimate the probability of a hit as the combined average, which is about .37.)   [*Ans.* .242.]

6. A true-false examination has 48 questions. Assume that the probability that a given student knows the answer to any one question is $\frac{3}{4}$. A passing score is 30 or better. Estimate the probability that the student will fail the exam.

7. In Example 3 of Section 10, assume that the school decides to admit 1296 students. Estimate the probability that they will have to have additional dormitory space.   [*Ans.* Approximately .115.]

8. Peter and Paul each have 20 pennies. They agree to match pennies 400 times, keeping score but not paying until the 400 matches are over. What is the probability that one of the players will not be able to pay? Answer the same question for the case that Peter has 10 pennies and Paul has 30.

9. In tossing a coin 100 times, the probability of getting 50 heads is, to three decimal places, .080. Estimate this same probability using the Central Limit Theorem.   [*Ans.* .080.]

10. A standard medicine has been found to be effective in 80 per cent of the cases where it is used. A new medicine for the same purpose is found to be effective in 90 of the first 100 patients on which the medicine is used. Could this be taken as good evidence that the new medication is better than the old?

11. In the Weldon dice experiment, 12 dice were thrown 26,306 times and the appearance of a 5 or a 6 was considered to be a success. The mean number of successes observed was, to four decimal places, 4.0524. Is this result significantly different from the expected average number of 4?   [*Ans.* Yes.]

12. Prove that $pq \leq \frac{1}{4}$.   [*Hint:* write $p = \frac{1}{2} + x$.]

13. Suppose that out of 1000 persons interviewed 650 said that they would vote for Mr. Big for mayor. Construct the 99 per cent confidence interval for p, the proportion in the city that would vote for Mr. Big.

14. Opinion pollsters in election years usually poll about 3000 voters. Suppose that in an election year 51 per cent favor candidate A and 49 per cent favor candidate B. Construct 95 per cent confidence limits for candidate A winning.   [*Ans.* .492, .528.]

15. In an experiment with independent trials we are going to estimate p by the fraction $\bar{p}$ of successes. We wish our estimate to be within .02 of the correct value with probability .95. Show that 2500 observations will always suffice. Show that if it is known that p is approximately .1, then 900 observations would be sufficient.

16. An experimenter has an independent trials process and he has a hypothesis that the true value of p is p_0. He decides to carry out a number of trials, and from the observed $\bar{p}$ calculate the 95 per cent confidence interval for p. He will reject p_0 if it does not fall within these limits. What is the probability that he will reject p_0 when in fact it is correct? Should he accept p_0 if it does fall within the confidence interval?

17. A coin is tossed 100 times and turns up heads 61 times. Using the method of Exercise 16 test the hypothesis that the coin is a fair coin.
                                                        [*Ans.* Reject.]

18. Two railroads are competing for the passenger traffic of 1000 passengers by operating similar trains at the same hour. If a given passenger is equally likely to choose one train as the other, how many seats should the railroad provide if it wants to be sure that its seating capacity is sufficient in 99 out of 100 cases?   [*Ans.* 537.]

*15.   GAMBLER'S RUIN

In this section we will study a particular Markov chain, which is interesting in itself and has far-reaching applications. Its name, "gambler's ruin," derives from one of its many applications. In the text we will describe the chain from the gambling point of view, but in the exercises we will present several other applications.

Let us suppose that you are gambling against a professional gambler, or gambling house. You have selected a specific game to play, on which you have probability p of winning. The gambler has made sure that the game is favorable to him, so that $p < \frac{1}{2}$. However, in most situations p will be close to $\frac{1}{2}$. (The cases $p = \frac{1}{2}$ and $p > \frac{1}{2}$ are considered in the exercises.)

At the start of the game you have A dollars, and the gambler has B dollars. You bet \$1 on each game, and play until one of you is ruined.

What is the probability that you will be ruined? Of course, the answer depends on the exact values of p, A, and B. We will develop a formula for the ruin-probability in terms of these three given numbers.

First we will set the problem up as a Markov chain. Let $N = A + B$, the total amount of money in the game. As states for the chain we choose the numbers $0, 1, 2, \ldots, N$. At any one moment the position of the chain is the amount of money *you* have. The initial position is shown in Figure 28.

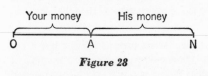

Your money   His money

0   A   N

Figure 28

If you win a game, your money increases by $1, and the gambler's fortune decreases by $1. Thus the new position is one state to the right of the previous one. If you lose a game, the chain moves one step to the left. Thus at any step there is probability p of moving one step to the right, and probability $q = 1 - p$ of one step to the left. Since the probabilities for the next position are determined by the present position, it is a Markov chain.

If the chain reaches 0 or N, we stop. When 0 is reached, you are ruined. When N is reached, you have all the money, and you have ruined the gambler. We will be interested in the probability of *your* ruin, i.e., the probability of reaching 0.

Let us suppose that p and N are fixed. We actually want the probability of ruin when we start at A. However, it turns out to be easier to solve a problem that appears much harder: Find the ruin-probability for every possible starting position. For this reason we introduce the notation x_i, to stand for the probability of your ruin if you start in position i (that is, if you have i dollars).

Let us first solve the problem for the case $N = 5$. We have the unknowns x_0, x_1, x_2, x_3, x_4, and x_5. Suppose that we start at position 2. The chain moves to 3, with probability p, or to 1, with probability q. Thus

$$\Pr[\text{ruin}|\text{start at } 2] = \Pr[\text{ruin}|\text{start at } 3] \cdot p + \Pr[\text{ruin}|\text{start at } 1] \cdot q,$$

using the conditional probability formula, with a set of two alternatives. But once it has reached state 3, a Markov chain behaves just as if it had been started there. Thus

$$\Pr[\text{ruin}|\text{start at } 3] = x_3.$$

And, similarly;

$$\Pr[\text{ruin}|\text{start at } 1] = x_1.$$

We obtain the key relation

$$x_2 = px_3 + qx_1.$$

We can modify this as follows:

$$(p + q)x_2 = px_3 + qx_1,$$
$$p(x_2 - x_3) = q(x_1 - x_2),$$
$$x_1 - x_2 = r(x_2 - x_3),$$

where $r = p/q$, and hence $r < 1$. When we write such an equation for each of the four "ordinary" positions, we obtain

(1)
$$\begin{aligned}
x_0 - x_1 &= r(x_1 - x_2) \\
x_1 - x_2 &= r(x_2 - x_3) \\
x_2 - x_3 &= r(x_3 - x_4) \\
x_3 - x_4 &= r(x_4 - x_5).
\end{aligned}$$

We must still consider the two extreme positions. Suppose that the chain reaches 0. Then you are ruined, hence the probability of your ruin is 1. While if the chain reaches $N = 5$, the gambler drops out of the game, and you can't be ruined. Thus

(2)
$$x_0 = 1, \qquad x_5 = 0.$$

If we substitute the value of x_5 in the last equation of (1), we have $x_3 - x_4 = rx_4$. This in turn may be substituted in the previous equation, etc. We thus have the simpler equations

(3)
$$\begin{aligned}
x_4 &= 1 \cdot x_4 \\
x_3 - x_4 &= rx_4 \\
x_2 - x_3 &= r^2 x_4 \\
x_1 - x_2 &= r^3 x_4 \\
x_0 - x_1 &= r^4 x_4.
\end{aligned}$$

Let us add all the equations. We obtain

$$x_0 = (1 + r + r^2 + r^3 + r^4)x_4.$$

From (2) we have that $x_0 = 1$. We also use the simple identity

$$(1 - r)(1 + r + r^2 + r^3 + r^4) = 1 - r^5.$$

And then we solve for x_4:

$$x_4 = \frac{1 - r}{1 - r^5}.$$

If we add the first two equations in (3), we have that $x_3 = (1 + r)x_4$. Similarly, adding the first three equations, we solve for x_2, and adding the first four equations we obtain x_1. We now have our entire solution,

$$(4) \quad x_1 = \frac{1 - r^4}{1 - r^5}, \quad x_2 = \frac{1 - r^3}{1 - r^5}, \quad x_3 = \frac{1 - r^2}{1 - r^5}, \quad x_4 = \frac{1 - r}{1 - r^5}.$$

The same method will work for any value of N. And it is easy to guess from (4) what the general solution looks like. If we want x_A, the answer is a fraction like those in (4). In the denominator the exponent of r is always N. In the numerator the exponent is $N - A$, or B. Thus the ruin-probability is

$$(5) \quad x_A = \frac{1 - r^B}{1 - r^N}.$$

We recall that A is the amount of money you have, B is the gambler's stake, $N = A + B$, p is your probability of winning a game, and $r = p/(1 - p)$.

In Figure 29 we show some typical values of the ruin-probability. Some of these are quite startling. If the probability of p is as low as .45 (odds against you on each game 11:9) and the gambler has 20 dollars to put up, you are almost sure to be ruined. Even in a nearly fair game, say $p = .495$, with each of you having \$50 to start with, there is a .731 chance for your ruin.

It is worth examining the ruin-probability formula, (5), more closely. Since the denominator is always less than 1, your probability of ruin is at least $1 - r^B$. This estimate does not depend on how much money you have, only on p and B. Since r is less than 1, by making B large enough, we can make r^B practically 0, and hence make it almost certain that you will be ruined.

Suppose, for example, that a gambler wants to have probability .999 of ruining you. (You can hardly call him a gambler under those circumstances!) He must make sure that $r^B < .001$. For example, if $p = .495$, the gambler needs \$346 to have probability .999 of ruining you, even if you are a millionaire. If $p = .48$, he needs only \$87. And even for the almost fair game with $p = .499$, \$1727 will suffice.

There are two ways that gamblers achieve this goal. Small gambling houses will fix the odds quite a bit in their favor, making r much less than 1. Then even a relatively small bank of B dollars suffices to assure them of winning. Larger houses, with B quite sizable, can afford to let you play nearly fair games.

Ruin-probabilities for $p = .45, .48, .49, .495.$

$p = .45$

A＼B	1	5	10	20	50
1	.550	.905	.973	.997	1
5	.260	.732	.910	.988	1
10	.204	.666	.881	.984	1
20	.185	.638	.868	.982	1
50	.182	.633	.866	.982	1

$p = .48$

A＼B	1	5	10	20	50
1	.520	.865	.941	.981	.999
5	.202	.599	.788	.923	.994
10	.131	.472	.690	.878	.990
20	.095	.381	.606	.832	.985
50	.078	.334	.555	.801	.982

$p = .49$

A＼B	1	5	10	20	50
1	.510	.850	.926	.969	.994
5	.184	.550	.731	.871	.972
10	.110	.402	.599	.788	.951
20	.069	.287	.472	.690	.921
50	.045	.204	.363	.586	.881

$p = .495$

A＼B	1	5	10	20	50
1	.505	.842	.918	.961	.989
5	.175	.525	.699	.838	.948
10	.100	.367	.550	.731	.905
20	.058	.242	.402	.599	.839
50	.031	.143	.259	.438	.731

Figure 29

EXERCISES

1. An urn has nine white balls and 11 black balls. A ball is drawn, and replaced. If it is white, you win five cents, if black, you lose five cents. You have a dollar to gamble with, and your opponent has fifty cents. If you keep on playing till one of you loses all his money, what is the probability that you will lose your dollar?   [*Ans*. .868.]

2. Suppose that you are shooting craps, and you always hold the dice. You have $20, your opponent has $10, and $1 is bet on each game; estimate your probability of ruin.

3. Two government agencies, A and B, are competing for the same task. A has 50 positions, and B has 20. Each year one position is taken away from one of the agencies, and given to the other. If 52 per cent of the time the shift is from A to B, what do you predict for the future of the two agencies?
          [*Ans*. One agency will be abolished. B survives with probability .8,
          A with probability .2.]

4. What is the approximate value of x_A if you are rich, and the gambler starts with $1?

5. Consider a simple model for evolution. On a small island there is room for 1000 members of a certain species. One year a favorable mutant appears. We assume that in each subsequent generation either the mutants take one place from the regular members of the species, with probability .6, or the reverse happens. Thus, for example, the mutation disappears in the very first generation with probability .4. What is the probability that the mutants eventually take over? [*Hint:* See Exercise 4.]   [*Ans*. $\frac{1}{3}$.]

6. Verify that the proof of the text is still correct when $p > \frac{1}{2}$. Interpret formula (5) for this case.

7. Show that if $p > \frac{1}{2}$, and both parties have a substantial amount of money, your probability of ruin is approximately $1/r^4$.

8. Modify the proof in the text to apply to the case $p = \frac{1}{2}$. What is the probability of your ruin?   [*Ans*. B/N.]

9. You are matching pennies. You have 25 pennies to start with, and your opponent has 35. What is the probability that you will win all his pennies?

10. Mr. Jones lives on a short street, about 100 steps long. At one end of the street is his home, at the other a lake, and in the middle a bar. One evening he leaves the bar in a state of intoxication, and starts to walk at random. What is the probability that he will fall into the lake if

(a) He is just as likely to take a step to the right as to the left?
[*Ans.* $\frac{1}{2}$.]

(b) If he has probability .51 of taking a step towards his home?
[*Ans.* .119.]

11. You are in the following hopeless situation: You are playing a game in which you have only $\frac{1}{3}$ chance of winning. You have $1, and your opponent has $7. What is the probability of your winning all his money if

(a) You bet $1 each time?   [*Ans.* $\frac{1}{255}$.]

(b) You bet all your money each time?   [*Ans.* $\frac{1}{27}$.]

12. Repeat Exercise 11 for the case of a fair game, where you have probability $\frac{1}{2}$ of winning.

13. Modify the proof in the text to compute y_i, the probability of reaching state $N = 5$.

14. Verify, in Exercise 13, that $x_i + y_i = 1$ for every state. Interpret.

Note: Exercises 15–18 deal with the following ruin problem: A and B play a game in which A has probability $\frac{2}{3}$ of winning. They keep playing until either A has won six times or B has won three times.

15. Set up the process as a Markov chain whose states are (a, b), where a is the number of times A won, and b the number of B wins.

16. For each state compute the probability of A winning from that position. [*Hint:* Work from higher a- and b-values to lower ones.]

17. What is the probability that A reaches his goal first?   [*Ans.* $\frac{1024}{2187}$.]

18. Suppose that payments are made as follows: If A wins six games, he receives $1, if B wins three games then A pays $1. What is the expected value of the payment, to the nearest penny?

SUGGESTED READING

Cramer, Harold, *The Elements of Probability Theory*, Wiley, New York, 1955, Part I.

Feller, W., *An Introduction to Probability Theory and its Applications*, Wiley, New York, 1950.

Goldberg, S., *Probability: An Introduction*, Prentice-Hall, Inc., Englewood Cliffs, N. J., 1960.

Mosteller, F., *Fifty Challenging Problems in Probability with Solutions,* Addison-Wesley, Reading, Mass., 1965, 88 pp.

Neyman, J., *First Course in Probability and Statistics,* Holt, New York, 1950.

Parzen, E., *Modern Probability Theory and Its Applications,* Wiley, New York, 1960.

Whitworth, W. A., *Choice and Chance, with 1000 Exercises,* Stechert, New York, 1934.

Vectors and matrices

1. COLUMN AND ROW VECTORS

A *column vector* is an ordered collection of numbers written in a column. Examples of such vectors are

$$\begin{pmatrix} 1 \\ -2 \end{pmatrix}, \quad \begin{pmatrix} 0.6 \\ 0.4 \end{pmatrix}, \quad \begin{pmatrix} 0 \\ 0 \\ 0 \end{pmatrix}, \quad \begin{pmatrix} 3 \\ -4 \\ 0 \end{pmatrix}, \quad \begin{pmatrix} 1 \\ -1 \\ 2 \\ 4 \end{pmatrix}.$$

The individual numbers in these vectors are called *components*, and the number of components a vector has is one of its distinguishing characteristics. Thus the first two vectors above have two components, the next two have three components, and the last has four components. When talking more generally about n-component column vectors we shall write

$$u = \begin{pmatrix} u_1 \\ u_2 \\ \cdot \\ \cdot \\ \cdot \\ u_n \end{pmatrix}.$$

217

Analogously, a *row vector* is an ordered collection of numbers written in a row. Examples of row vectors are

$$(1, 0), \quad (-2, 1), \quad (2, -3, 4, 0), \quad (-1, 2, -3, 4, -5).$$

Each number appearing in the vector is again called a *component* of the vector, and the number of components a row vector has is again one of its important characteristics. Thus, the first two examples are two-component, the third a four-component, and the fourth a five-component vector. The vector $v = (v_1, v_2, \ldots, v_n)$ is an n-component row vector.

Two row vectors, or two column vectors, are said to be *equal* if and and only if corresponding components of the vector are equal. Thus for the vectors

$$u = (1, 2), \quad v = \begin{pmatrix} 1 \\ 2 \end{pmatrix}, \quad w = (1, 2), \quad x = (2, 1),$$

we see that $u = w$ but $u \neq v$, and $u \neq x$.

If u and v are three-component column vectors, we shall define their sum $u + v$ by component-wise addition as follows:

$$u + v = \begin{pmatrix} u_1 \\ u_2 \\ u_3 \end{pmatrix} + \begin{pmatrix} v_1 \\ v_2 \\ v_3 \end{pmatrix} = \begin{pmatrix} u_1 + v_1 \\ u_2 + v_2 \\ u_3 + v_3 \end{pmatrix}.$$

Similarly, if u and v are three-component row vectors, their sum is defined to be

$$u + v = (u_1, u_2, u_3) + (v_1, v_2, v_3)$$
$$= (u_1 + v_1, u_2 + v_2, u_3 + v_3).$$

Note that the sum of two three-component vectors yields another three-component vector. For example,

$$\begin{pmatrix} 1 \\ -1 \\ 2 \end{pmatrix} + \begin{pmatrix} 2 \\ 3 \\ -1 \end{pmatrix} = \begin{pmatrix} 3 \\ 2 \\ 1 \end{pmatrix},$$

and

$$(4, -7, 12) + (3, 14, -14) = (7, 7, -2).$$

The sum of two n-component vectors (either row or column) is defined by component-wise addition in an analogous manner, and yields another n-component vector. Observe that we do not define the addition of vectors unless they are both row or both column vectors, having the same number of components.

Because the order in which two numbers are added is immaterial as far as the answer goes, it is also true that the order in which vectors are added does not matter; that is,

$$u + v = v + u,$$

where u and v are both row or both column vectors. This is the so-called *commutative law of addition*. A numerical example is

$$\begin{pmatrix} 1 \\ -1 \\ 2 \end{pmatrix} + \begin{pmatrix} 2 \\ 3 \\ -1 \end{pmatrix} = \begin{pmatrix} 3 \\ 2 \\ 1 \end{pmatrix} = \begin{pmatrix} 2 \\ 3 \\ -1 \end{pmatrix} + \begin{pmatrix} 1 \\ -1 \\ 2 \end{pmatrix}.$$

Once we have the definition of the addition of two vectors we can easily see how to add three or more vectors by grouping them in pairs as in the addition of numbers. For example,

$$\begin{pmatrix} 1 \\ 0 \\ 0 \end{pmatrix} + \begin{pmatrix} 0 \\ 2 \\ 0 \end{pmatrix} + \begin{pmatrix} 0 \\ 0 \\ 3 \end{pmatrix} = \begin{pmatrix} 1 \\ 0 \\ 0 \end{pmatrix} + \begin{pmatrix} 0 \\ 2 \\ 3 \end{pmatrix} = \begin{pmatrix} 1 \\ 2 \\ 3 \end{pmatrix} = \begin{pmatrix} 1 \\ 2 \\ 0 \end{pmatrix} + \begin{pmatrix} 0 \\ 0 \\ 3 \end{pmatrix} = \begin{pmatrix} 1 \\ 2 \\ 3 \end{pmatrix},$$

and

$$(1, 0, 0) + (0, 2, 0) + (0, 0, 3) = (1, 2, 0) + (0, 0, 3) = (1, 2, 3)$$
$$= (1, 0, 0) + (0, 2, 3) = (1, 2, 3).$$

In general, the sum of any number of vectors (row or column), each having the same number of components, is the vector whose first component is the sum of the first components of the vectors, whose second component is the sum of the second components, etc.

The multiplication of a number a times a vector v is defined by component-wise multiplication of a times the components of v. For the three-component case we have

$$au = a \begin{pmatrix} u_1 \\ u_2 \\ u_3 \end{pmatrix} = \begin{pmatrix} au_1 \\ au_2 \\ au_3 \end{pmatrix}$$

for column vectors and

$$av = a(v_1, v_2, v_3) = (av_1, av_2, av_3)$$

for row vectors. If u is an n-component vector (row or column), then au is defined similarly by component-wise multiplication.

If u is any vector we define its negative $-u$ to be the vector $-u = (-1)u$. Thus in the three-component case for row vectors we have

$$-u = (-1)(u_1, u_2, u_3) = (-u_1, -u_2, -u_3).$$

Once we have the negative of a vector it is easy to see how to subtract vectors, i.e., we simply add "algebraically." For the three-component column vector case we have

$$u - v = \begin{pmatrix} u_1 \\ u_2 \\ u_3 \end{pmatrix} - \begin{pmatrix} v_1 \\ v_2 \\ v_3 \end{pmatrix} = \begin{pmatrix} u_1 - v_1 \\ u_2 - v_2 \\ u_3 - v_3 \end{pmatrix}.$$

Specific examples of subtraction of vectors occur in the exercises at the end of this section.

An important vector is the zero vector all of whose components are zero. For example, three-component zero vectors are

$$0 = \begin{pmatrix} 0 \\ 0 \\ 0 \end{pmatrix} \quad \text{and} \quad 0 = (0, 0, 0).$$

When there is no danger of confusion we shall use the symbol 0, as above, to denote the zero (row or column) vector. The meaning will be clear from the context. The zero vector has the important property that, if u is any vector, then $u + 0 = u$. A proof for the three-component column vector case is as follows:

$$u + 0 = \begin{pmatrix} u_1 \\ u_2 \\ u_3 \end{pmatrix} + \begin{pmatrix} 0 \\ 0 \\ 0 \end{pmatrix} = \begin{pmatrix} u_1 + 0 \\ u_2 + 0 \\ u_3 + 0 \end{pmatrix} = \begin{pmatrix} u_1 \\ u_2 \\ u_3 \end{pmatrix} = u.$$

One of the chief advantages of the vector notation is that one can denote a whole collection of numbers by a single letter such as u, $v, \ldots,$ and treat such a collection as if it were a single quantity. By using the vector notation it is possible to state very complicated relationships in a simple manner. The student will see many examples of this in the remainder of the present chapter and the two succeeding chapters.

EXERCISES

1. Compute the quantities below for the vectors

$$u = \begin{pmatrix} 3 \\ 1 \\ 2 \end{pmatrix}, \quad v = \begin{pmatrix} -2 \\ 3 \\ 0 \end{pmatrix}, \quad w = \begin{pmatrix} -1 \\ -1 \\ 1 \end{pmatrix}.$$

(a) $2u$. $\left[\textit{Ans.} \begin{pmatrix} 6 \\ 2 \\ 4 \end{pmatrix} . \right]$

(b) $-v$.

(c) $2u - v$.

(d) $v + w$. [*Ans.* $\begin{pmatrix} -3 \\ 2 \\ 1 \end{pmatrix}$.]

(e) $u + v - w$.

(f) $2u - 3v - w$.

(g) $3u - v + 2w$. [*Ans.* $\begin{pmatrix} 9 \\ -2 \\ 8 \end{pmatrix}$.]

2. Compute (a) through (g) of Exercise 1 if the vectors u, v, and w are

$$u = (7, 0, -3), \quad v = (2, 1, -5), \quad w = (1, -1, 0).$$

3. (a) Show that the zero vector is not changed when multiplied by any number.

(b) If u is any vector, show that $0 + u = u$.

4. If u and v are two row or two column vectors having the same number of components, prove that $u + 0v = u$ and $0u + v = v$.

5. If $2u - v = 0$, what is the relationship between the components of u and those of v? [*Ans.* $v_i = 2u_i$.]

6. Answer the question in Exercise 5 for the equation $-3u + 5v + u - 7v = 0$. Do the same for the equation $20v - 3u + 5v + 8u = 0$.

7. When possible, compute the following sums; when not possible, give reasons.

(a) $\begin{pmatrix} -1 \\ 3 \end{pmatrix} + \begin{pmatrix} 6 \\ -2 \\ 5 \\ -4 \end{pmatrix} = $?

(b) $(2, -1, -1) + 0(4, 7, -2) = $?

(c) $(5, 6) + 7 - 21 + \begin{pmatrix} 0 \\ 1 \end{pmatrix} = $?

(d) $1 \begin{pmatrix} 1 \\ 0 \\ 1 \end{pmatrix} + 2 \begin{pmatrix} 1 \\ 1 \\ 0 \end{pmatrix} + 3 \begin{pmatrix} 0 \\ 1 \\ 1 \end{pmatrix} = $?

8. If $\begin{pmatrix} 1 \\ 1 \\ 2 \end{pmatrix} + \begin{pmatrix} u_1 \\ u_2 \\ u_3 \end{pmatrix} = \begin{pmatrix} 1 \\ -1 \\ 0 \end{pmatrix}$, find u_1, u_2, and u_3. [*Ans.* 0; -2; -2.]

9. If $2 \begin{pmatrix} v_1 \\ v_2 \\ v_3 \end{pmatrix} = \begin{pmatrix} 0 \\ 1 \\ 3 \end{pmatrix}$, find the components of v.

10. If $\begin{pmatrix} 0 \\ 0 \\ 0 \end{pmatrix} + \begin{pmatrix} u_1 \\ u_2 \\ u_3 \end{pmatrix} = \begin{pmatrix} 0 \\ 0 \\ 0 \end{pmatrix}$, what can be said concerning the components u_1, u_2, u_3?

11. If $0 \cdot \begin{pmatrix} u_1 \\ u_2 \\ u_3 \end{pmatrix} = \begin{pmatrix} 0 \\ 0 \\ 0 \end{pmatrix}$, what can be said concerning the components u_1, u_2, u_3?

12. Suppose that we associate with each person a three-component row vector having the following entries: age, height, and weight. Would it make sense to add together the vectors associated with two different persons? Would it make sense to multiply one of these vectors by a constant?

13. Suppose that we associate with each person leaving a supermarket a row vector whose components give the quantities of each available item that he has purchased. Answer the same questions as those in Exercise 12.

14. Let us associate with each supermarket a column vector whose entries give the prices of each item in the store. Would it make sense to add together the vectors associated with two different supermarkets? Would it make sense to multiply one of these vectors by a constant? Discuss the differences in the situations given in Exercises 12, 13, and 14.

SUPPLEMENTARY EXERCISES

15. In a certain school students take four courses each semester. At the end of the semester the registrar records the grades of each student as a row vector. He then gives the student 4 points for each A, 3 points for each B, 2 points for each C, 1 point for each D, and 0 for each F. The sum of these numbers, divided by 4 is the student's grade point average.

    (a) If a student has a 4.0 average, what are the logical possibilities for his grade vector?

    (b) What are the possibilities if he has a 3.0 average?

    (c) What are the possibilities if he has a 2.0 average?

16. Consider the vectors

$$x = \begin{pmatrix} x_1 \\ x_2 \end{pmatrix}, \qquad y = \begin{pmatrix} y_1 \\ y_2 \end{pmatrix}$$

Show that the vector

$$\tfrac{1}{2}(x + y)$$

has components that are the *averages* of the components of x and y. Generalize this result to the case of n vectors.

17. (a) Show that the vector equation

$$x \begin{pmatrix} 3 \\ -4 \end{pmatrix} + y \begin{pmatrix} -4 \\ 5 \end{pmatrix} = \begin{pmatrix} 2 \\ -3 \end{pmatrix}$$

represents two simultaneous linear equations for the two variables x and y.

(b) Solve these equations for x and y and substitute into the above vector equation to check your work.

18. Write the following simultaneous linear equations in vector form

$$ax + by = e$$
$$cx + dy = f.$$

[*Hint:* Follow the form given in Exercise 17.]

19. Let $x = \begin{pmatrix} x_1 \\ x_2 \end{pmatrix}$. Define $x \geq 0$ to be the conjunction of the statements $x_1 \geq 0$ *and* $x_2 \geq 0$. Define $x \leq 0$ analogously. Now prove that if $x \geq 0$, then $-x \leq 0$.

20. Using the definition in Exercise 19, define $x \geq y$ to mean $x - y \geq 0$, where x and y are vectors of the same shape. Consider the following four vectors:

$$x = \begin{pmatrix} -1 \\ 2 \\ 0 \end{pmatrix}, \quad y = \begin{pmatrix} -4 \\ 0 \\ -1 \end{pmatrix}, \quad u = \begin{pmatrix} 1 \\ 1 \\ 1 \end{pmatrix}, \quad v = \begin{pmatrix} 4 \\ 5 \\ 6 \end{pmatrix}.$$

(a) Show that $x \geq y$.
(b) Show that $u \geq y$.
(c) Is there any relationship between x and u?
(d) Show that $v \geq x$, $v \geq y$, and $v \geq u$.

21. If $x \geq y$ and $y \geq u$, prove that $x \geq u$.

22. If $x^{(1)}, x^{(2)}, \ldots, x^{(n)}$ is a set of n vectors, show how to find a vector u such that $u \geq x^{(i)}$ for all i. Also show how to find a vector v such that $v \leq x^{(i)}$ for all i.

2. THE PRODUCT OF VECTORS

The reader may have wondered why it was necessary to introduce both column and row vectors when their properties are so similar. This question can be answered in several different ways. In the first place, in many applications there are two kinds of quantities which are studied simultaneously, and it is convenient to represent one of them as a row vector and the other as a column vector. Second, there is a way of combining row and column vectors that is very useful for certain types of calculations. To bring out these points let us look at the following simple economic example.

Example 1. Suppose a man named Smith goes into a grocery store to buy a dozen each of eggs and oranges, a half dozen each of apples and pears, and three lemons. Let us represent his purchases by means of the following row vector:

$$x = [6 \text{ (apples)}, 12 \text{ (eggs)}, 3 \text{ (lemons)}, 12 \text{ (oranges)}, 6 \text{ (pears)}]$$
$$= (6, 12, 3, 12, 6).$$

Suppose that apples are 4 cents each, eggs are 6 cents each, lemons are 9 cents each, oranges are 5 cents each, and pears are 7 cents each. We can then represent the prices of these items as a column vector,

$$y = \begin{pmatrix} 4 \\ 6 \\ 9 \\ 5 \\ 7 \end{pmatrix} \begin{array}{l} \text{cents per apple} \\ \text{cents per egg} \\ \text{cents per lemon} \\ \text{cents per orange} \\ \text{cents per pear.} \end{array}$$

The obvious question to ask now is, what is the total amount that Smith must pay for his purchases? What we would like to do is to multiply the quantity vector x by the price vector y, and we would like the result to be Smith's bill. We see that our multiplication should have the following form:

$$x \cdot y = (6, 12, 3, 12, 6) \begin{pmatrix} 4 \\ 6 \\ 9 \\ 5 \\ 7 \end{pmatrix}$$

$$= 6 \cdot 4 + 12 \cdot 6 + 3 \cdot 9 + 12 \cdot 5 + 6 \cdot 7$$
$$= 24 + 72 + 27 + 60 + 42$$
$$= 225 \text{ cents or } \$2.25.$$

This is, of course, the computation that the cashier performs in figuring Smith's bill.

We shall adopt in general the above definition of multiplication of row times column vectors.

DEFINITION. Let u be a row vector and v a column vector each having the same number n of components; then we shall define the product $u \cdot v$ to be

$$u \cdot v = u_1 v_1 + u_2 v_2 + \ldots + u_n v_n.$$

Notice that we always write the row vector first and the column vector second, and this is the only kind of vector multiplication that we consider. Some examples of vector multiplication are given below.

$$(2, 1, -1) \cdot \begin{pmatrix} 3 \\ -1 \\ 4 \end{pmatrix} = 2 \cdot 3 + 1 \cdot (-1) + (-1) \cdot 4 = 1.$$

$$(1, 0) \cdot \begin{pmatrix} 0 \\ 1 \end{pmatrix} = 1 \cdot 0 + 0 \cdot 1 = 0 + 0 = 0.$$

Note that the result of vector multiplication is always a *number*.

Example 2. Consider an oversimplified economy which has three industries, which we call coal, electricity, and steel, and three consumers 1, 2, and 3. Suppose that each consumer uses some of the output of each industry and also that each industry uses some of the output of each other industry. We assume that the amounts used are positive or zero, since using a negative quantity has no immediate interpretation. We can represent the needs of each consumer and industry by a three-component demand (row) vector, the first component measuring the amount of coal needed by the consumer or industry, the second component the amount of electricity needed, and the third component the amount of steel needed, in some convenient units. For example, the demand vectors of the three consumers might be

$$d_1 = (3, 2, 5), \qquad d_2 = (0, 17, 1), \qquad d_3 = (4, 6, 12);$$

and the demand vectors of each of the industries might be

$$d_C = (0, 1, 4), \qquad d_E = (20, 0, 8), \qquad d_S = (30, 5, 0),$$

where the subscript C stands for coal, the subscript E, for electricity, and the subscript S, for steel. Then the total demand for these goods by the consumers is given by the sum

$$d_1 + d_2 + d_3 = (3, 2, 5) + (0, 17, 1) + (4, 6, 12) = (7, 25, 18).$$

Also, the total industrial demand for these goods is given by the sum

$$d_C + d_E + d_S = (0, 1, 4) + (20, 0, 8) + (30, 5, 0) = (50, 6, 12).$$

Therefore the total overall demand is given by the sum

$$(7, 25, 18) + (50, 6, 12) = (57, 31, 30).$$

Suppose now that the price of coal is \$1 per unit, the price of electricity is \$2 per unit, and the price of steel is \$4 per unit. Then these prices can be represented by the column vector

$$p = \begin{pmatrix} 1 \\ 2 \\ 4 \end{pmatrix}.$$

Consider the steel industry: It sells a total of 30 units of steel at \$4 per unit so that its total income is \$120. Its bill for the various goods is given by the vector product

$$d_S \cdot p = (30, 5, 0) \cdot \begin{pmatrix} 1 \\ 2 \\ 4 \end{pmatrix} = 30 + 10 = \$40.$$

Hence the profit of the steel industry is \$120 − \$40 = \$80. In the exercises below the profits of the other industries will be found.

This model of an economy is unrealistic in two senses. First, we have not chosen realistic numbers for the various quantities involved. Second, and more important, we have neglected the fact that the more an industry produces the more inputs it requires. The latter complication will be introduced in Chapter VII.

Example 3. Consider the rectangular coordinate system in the plane shown in Figure 1. A two-component row vector $x = (a, b)$ can be regarded as a point in the plane located by means of the coordinate axes as shown. The point x can be found by starting at the origin of coordinates O and moving a distance a along the x_1 axis, then moving a distance b along a line parallel to the x_2 axis. If we have two such points, say $x = (a, b)$ and $y = (c, d)$, then the points $x + y$, $-x, -y, x - y, y - x, -x - y$ have the geometric significance shown in Figure 2.

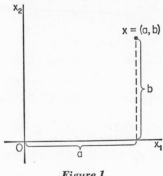

Figure 1

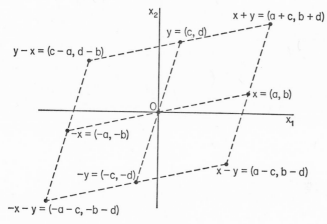

Figure 2

The idea of multiplying a row vector by a number can also be given a geometric meaning, see Figure 3. There we have plotted the points corresponding to the vector $x = (1, 2)$ and $2x$, $\frac{1}{2}x$, $-x$, and $-2x$. Observe that all these points lie on a line through the origin of coordinates. Another vector quantity which has geometrical significance is the vector $z = ax + (1 - a)y$, where a is any number between 0 and 1. Observe in Figure 4 that the points z all lie on the line segment between

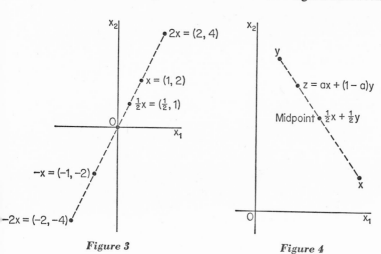

Figure 3   **Figure 4**

the points x and y. If $a = \frac{1}{2}$, the corresponding point on the line segment is the mid-point of the segment. Thus, if $x = (a, b)$ and $y = (c, d)$, then the point

$$\tfrac{1}{2}x + \tfrac{1}{2}y = \tfrac{1}{2}(a, b) + \tfrac{1}{2}(c, d)$$
$$= \left(\frac{a + c}{2}, \frac{b + d}{2}\right)$$

is the mid-point of the line segment between x and y.

EXERCISES

1. Compute the quantities below for the following vectors:

$$u = (1, -1, 4), \qquad x = (0, 1, 2),$$

$$v = \begin{pmatrix} 5 \\ 0 \\ 1 \end{pmatrix}, \qquad y = \begin{pmatrix} -1 \\ -1 \\ 2 \end{pmatrix}.$$

(a) $u \cdot v + x \cdot y = $?   [*Ans.* 12.]

(b) $(-u + 5x) \cdot (3v - 2y) = $?

(c) $5u \cdot v + 10[x \cdot (2v - y)] = $?   [*Ans.* 55.]

(d) $2[(u - x) \cdot (v + y)] = $?

2. Plot the points corresponding to the row vectors $x = (3, 4)$ and $y = (-2, 7)$. Then compute and plot the following vectors.

(a) $\tfrac{1}{2}x + \tfrac{1}{2}y$.

(b) $x + y$.

(c) $x - 2y$.

(d) $\tfrac{7}{8}x + \tfrac{1}{8}y$.

(e) $3x - 2y$.

(f) $4y - 3x$.

3. If $x = (1, -1, 2)$ and $y = (0, 1, 3)$ are points in space, what is the midpoint of the line segment joining x to y?   [*Ans.* $(\tfrac{1}{2}, 0, \tfrac{5}{2})$.]

4. If u is a three-component row vector and v is a three-component column vector, and a is a number, prove that $a(u \cdot v) = (au) \cdot v = u \cdot (av)$.

5. Suppose that Brown, Jones, and Smith go to the grocery store and purchase the following items:

Brown: two apples, six lemons, and five pears;

Jones: two dozen eggs, two lemons, and two dozen oranges;

Smith: ten apples, one dozen eggs, two dozen oranges, and a half dozen pears.

(a) How many different kinds of items did they purchase? [*Ans.* 5.]
(b) Write each of their purchases as row vectors with as many components as the answer found in (a).
(c) Using the price vector given in Example 1, compute each man's grocery bill. [*Ans.* $0.97, $2.82, $2.74.]
(d) By means of vector addition, find the total amount of their purchases as a row vector.
(e) Compute in two different ways the total amount spent by the three men at the grocery store. [*Ans.* $6.53.]

6. Prove that vector multiplication satisfies the following property:

$$u \cdot (v + w) = u \cdot v + u \cdot w,$$

where u is a three-component row vector, v and w are three-component column vectors.

7. The production of a book involves several steps: first it must be set in type, then it must be printed, and finally it must be supplied with covers and bound. Suppose that the typesetter charges $6 an hour, paper costs $\frac{1}{4}$ cent per sheet, that the printer charges 11 cents for each minute that his press runs, that the cover costs 28 cents, and that the binder charges 15 cents to bind each book. Suppose now that a publisher wishes to print a book that requires 300 hours of work by the typesetter, 220 sheets of paper per book, and five minutes of press time per book.

(a) Write a five-component row vector which gives the requirements for the first book. Write another row vector which gives the requirements for the second, third, . . . copies of the book. Write a five-component column vector whose components give the prices of the various requirements for each book, in the same order as they are listed in the requirement vectors above.
(b) Using vector multiplication, find the cost of publishing one copy of a book. [*Ans.* $1,801.53.]
(c) Using vector addition and multiplication, find the cost of printing a first edition run of 5000 copies. [*Ans.* $9,450.]
(d) Assuming that the type plates from the first edition are used again, find the cost of printing a second edition of 5000 copies.
[*Ans.* $7,650.]

8. Perform the following calculations for Example 2.
(a) Compute the amount that each industry and each consumer has to pay for the goods it receives.
(b) Compute the profit made by each of the industries.
(c) Find the total amount of money that is paid out by all the industries and consumers.

(d) Find the proportion of the total amount of money found in (c) paid out by the industries. Find the proportion of the total money that is paid out by the consumers.

9. A building contractor has accepted orders for five ranch style houses, seven Cape Cod houses, and twelve Colonial style houses. Write a three-component row vector x whose components give the numbers of each type of house to be built. Suppose that he knows that a ranch style house requires 20 units of wood, a Cape Cod 18 units, and a Colonial style 25 units of wood. Write a column vector u whose components give the various quantities of wood needed for each type of house. Find the total amount of wood needed by computing the matrix product xu.   [*Ans.* 526.]

10. Let $x = (x_1, x_2)$ and let a and b be the vectors

$$a = \begin{pmatrix} 3 \\ 4 \end{pmatrix}, \qquad b = \begin{pmatrix} 2 \\ 3 \end{pmatrix}.$$

If $x \cdot a = -1$ and $x \cdot b = 7$, determine x_1 and x_2.   [*Ans.* $x_1 = -31$; $x_2 = 23$.]

11. Let $x = (x_1, x_2)$ and let a and b be the vectors

$$a = \begin{pmatrix} 4 \\ 8 \end{pmatrix}, \qquad b = \begin{pmatrix} 1 \\ 2 \end{pmatrix}.$$

If $x \cdot a = x_1$ and $x \cdot b = x_2$, determine x_1 and x_2.

SUPPLEMENTARY EXERCISES

12. Consider the vectors

$$x = (5, 8), \qquad y = (3, 7), \qquad f = \begin{pmatrix} 1 \\ 1 \end{pmatrix}.$$

(a) Compute $\frac{1}{2}xf$ and $\frac{1}{2}yf$, and show that these numbers are the averages of the components of x and y, respectively.   [*Ans.* 6.5, 5.]

(b) Compute $\frac{1}{4}(x + y)f$ and give an interpretation for this number.
[*Partial Ans.* 5.75.]

13. Let x and y be two n-component row vectors, and let f be an n-component column vector all of whose entries are 1's.

(a) Compute $\frac{1}{n} xf$ and $\frac{1}{n} yf$ and interpret the result.

(b) Compute $\frac{1}{2n} (x + y)f$ and interpret the result.

[*Hint:* Exercise 12 is a special case.]

14. Consider an experiment in which there are two outcomes; we get \$2 with probability $\frac{1}{3}$ and \$3 with probability $\frac{2}{3}$. Let

$$a = (2, 3) \quad \text{and} \quad p = \begin{pmatrix} \frac{1}{3} \\ \frac{2}{3} \end{pmatrix}.$$

Show that the expected outcome of the experiment is ap.

15. If an experiment has outcomes $a_1, a_2, \ldots, a_n$ occurring with probabilities $p_1, p_2, \ldots, p_n$, define the vectors

$$a = (a_1, \ldots, a_n) \quad \text{and} \quad p = \begin{pmatrix} p_1 \\ p_2 \\ \vdots \\ p_n \end{pmatrix}.$$

Show that the expected outcome is ap.

16. Consider the vectors

$$a = (a_1, a_2), \qquad x = \begin{pmatrix} x_1 \\ x_2 \end{pmatrix}$$

and a number c. Show that the equation $ax = c$ is a single equation in two variables.

17. Consider the vectors

$$a = (a_1, a_2), \qquad b = (b_1, b_2), \qquad x = \begin{pmatrix} x_1 \\ x_2 \end{pmatrix}$$

and two numbers c_1 and c_2. Show that the equations

$$ax = c_1$$
$$bx = c_2$$

represent two simultaneous equations in two unknowns.

18. Show that every set of two simultaneous equations in two unknowns can be written as in Exercise 17.

3. MATRICES AND THEIR COMBINATION WITH VECTORS

A matrix is a rectangular array of numbers written in the form

$$A = \begin{pmatrix} a_{11} & a_{12} & \ldots & a_{1n} \\ a_{21} & a_{22} & \ldots & a_{2n} \\ \cdot & \cdot & \ldots & \cdot \\ a_{m1} & a_{m2} & \ldots & a_{mn} \end{pmatrix}.$$

Here the letters a_{ij} stand for real numbers and m and n are integers.

Observe that m is the number of rows and n is the number of columns of the matrix. For this reason we call it an $m \times n$ matrix. If $m = n$, the matrix is *square*. The following are examples of matrices.

$$(1, 2, 3), \quad \begin{pmatrix} 1 \\ 2 \\ 3 \end{pmatrix}, \quad \begin{pmatrix} 1 & -1 \\ -2 & 2 \end{pmatrix},$$

$$\begin{pmatrix} 1 & 0 & 0 & 0 \\ 0 & 1 & 0 & 0 \\ 0 & 0 & 1 & 0 \\ 0 & 0 & 0 & 1 \end{pmatrix}, \quad \begin{pmatrix} 1 & 7 & -8 & 9 & 10 \\ 3 & -1 & 14 & 2 & -6 \\ 0 & 3 & -5 & 7 & 0 \end{pmatrix}.$$

The first example is a row vector which is a 1×3 matrix; the second is a column vector which is a 3×1 matrix; the third example is a 2×2 square matrix; the fourth is a 4×4 square matrix; and the last is a 3×5 matrix.

Two matrices having the same shape (i.e., having the same number of rows and columns) are said to be equal if and only if the corresponding entries are equal.

Recall that in Chapter IV, Section 13, we found that a matrix arose naturally in the consideration of a Markov chain process. To give another example of how matrices occur in practice and are used in connection with vectors, we consider the following example.

Example 1. Suppose that a building contractor has accepted orders for five ranch style houses, seven Cape Cod houses, and twelve Colonial style houses. We can represent his orders by means of a row vector $x = (5, 7, 12)$. The contractor is familiar, of course, with the kinds of "raw materials" that go into each type of house. Let us suppose that these raw materials are steel, wood, glass, paint, and labor. The numbers in the matrix below give the amounts of each raw material going into each type of house, expressed in convenient units. (The numbers are put in arbitrarily, and are not meant to be realistic.)

	Steel	Wood	Glass	Paint	Labor	
Ranch:	5	20	16	7	17	
Cape Cod:	7	18	12	9	21	$= R$
Colonial:	6	25	8	5	13	

Observe that each row of the matrix is a five-component row vector which gives the amounts of each raw material needed for a given kind of house. Similarly, each column of the matrix is a three-component column vector which gives the amounts of a given raw material needed for each kind of house. Clearly, a matrix is a very succinct way of summarizing this information.

Suppose now that the contractor wishes to compute how much of each raw material to obtain in order to fulfill his contracts. Let us denote the matrix above by R; then he would like to obtain something like the product xR, and he would like the product to tell him what orders to make out. The product should have the following form:

$$xR = (5, 7, 12) \begin{pmatrix} 5 & 20 & 16 & 7 & 17 \\ 7 & 18 & 12 & 9 & 21 \\ 6 & 25 & 8 & 5 & 13 \end{pmatrix}$$

$$= (5 \cdot 5 + 7 \cdot 7 + 12 \cdot 6, \quad 5 \cdot 20 + 7 \cdot 18 + 12 \cdot 25,$$

$$5 \cdot 16 + 7 \cdot 12 + 12 \cdot 8, \quad 5 \cdot 7 + 7 \cdot 9 + 12 \cdot 5,$$

$$5 \cdot 17 + 7 \cdot 21 + 12 \cdot 13)$$

$$= (146, 526, 260, 158, 388).$$

Thus we see that the contractor should order 146 units of steel, 526 units of wood, 260 units of glass, 158 units of paint, and 388 units of labor. Observe that the answer we get is a five-component row vector and that each entry in this vector is obtained by taking the vector product of x times the corresponding column of the matrix R.

The contractor is also interested in the prices that he will have to pay for these materials. Suppose that steel costs $15 per unit, wood costs $8 per unit, glass costs $5 per unit, paint costs $1 per unit, and labor costs $10 per unit. Then we can write the cost as a column vector as follows:

$$y = \begin{pmatrix} 15 \\ 8 \\ 5 \\ 1 \\ 10 \end{pmatrix}.$$

Here the product Ry should give the costs of each type of house, so that the multiplication should have the form

$$Ry = \begin{pmatrix} 5 & 20 & 16 & 7 & 17 \\ 7 & 18 & 12 & 9 & 21 \\ 6 & 25 & 8 & 5 & 13 \end{pmatrix} \begin{pmatrix} 15 \\ 8 \\ 5 \\ 1 \\ 10 \end{pmatrix}$$

$$= \begin{pmatrix} 5 \cdot 15 + 20 \cdot 8 + 16 \cdot 5 + 7 \cdot 1 + 17 \cdot 10 \\ 7 \cdot 15 + 18 \cdot 8 + 12 \cdot 5 + 9 \cdot 1 + 21 \cdot 10 \\ 6 \cdot 15 + 25 \cdot 8 + 8 \cdot 5 + 5 \cdot 1 + 13 \cdot 10 \end{pmatrix}$$

$$= \begin{pmatrix} 492 \\ 528 \\ 465 \end{pmatrix}.$$

Thus the cost of materials for the ranch style house is \$492, for the Cape Cod house is \$528, and for the Colonial house \$465.

The final question which the contractor might ask is what is the total cost of raw materials for all the houses he will build. It is easy to see that this is given by the vector xRy. We can find it in two ways as shown below.

$$xRy = (xR)y = (146, 526, 260, 158, 388) \cdot \begin{pmatrix} 15 \\ 8 \\ 5 \\ 1 \\ 10 \end{pmatrix} = 11{,}736$$

$$xRy = x(Ry) = (5, 7, 12) \cdot \begin{pmatrix} 492 \\ 528 \\ 465 \end{pmatrix} = 11{,}736.$$

The total cost is then \$11,736.

We shall adopt, in general, the above definitions for the multiplication of a matrix times a row or a column vector.

DEFINITION. Let A be an $m \times n$ matrix, let x be an m-component row vector, and let u be an n-component column vector; then we define the products xA and Au as follows:

$$xA = (x_1, x_2, \ldots, x_m) \begin{pmatrix} a_{11} & a_{12} & \ldots & a_{1n} \\ a_{21} & a_{22} & \ldots & a_{2n} \\ & & \ldots & \\ a_{m1} & a_{m2} & \ldots & a_{mn} \end{pmatrix}$$

$$= (x_1 a_{11} + x_2 a_{21} + \ldots + x_m a_{m1}, \quad x_1 a_{12} + x_2 a_{22} + \ldots + x_m a_{m2},$$
$$\ldots, \quad x_1 a_{1n} + x_2 a_{2n} + \ldots + x_m a_{mn});$$

$$Au = \begin{pmatrix} a_{11} & a_{12} & \cdots & a_{1n} \\ a_{21} & a_{22} & \cdots & a_{2n} \\ & & \cdots & \\ a_{m1} & a_{m2} & \cdots & a_{mn} \end{pmatrix} \begin{pmatrix} u_1 \\ u_2 \\ \cdot \\ \cdot \\ \cdot \\ u_n \end{pmatrix} = \begin{pmatrix} a_{11}u_1 + a_{12}u_2 + \ldots + a_{1n}u_n \\ a_{21}u_1 + a_{22}u_2 + \ldots + a_{2n}u_n \\ \cdots \\ a_{m1}u_1 + a_{m2}u_2 + \ldots + a_{mn}u_n \end{pmatrix}.$$

The reader will find these formulas easy to work with if he observes that each entry in the products xA or Au is obtained by vector multiplication of x or u by a column or row of the matrix A. Notice that in order to multiply a row vector times a matrix, the number of rows of the matrix must equal the number of components of the vector, and the result is another row vector; similarly, to multiply a matrix times a column vector, the number of columns of the matrix must equal the number of components of the vector, and the result of such a multiplication is another column vector.

Some numerical examples of the multiplication of vectors and matrices are:

$$(1, 0, -1) \begin{pmatrix} 3 & 1 \\ 2 & 3 \\ 2 & 8 \end{pmatrix} = (1 \cdot 3 + 0 \cdot 2 - 1 \cdot 2, \ 1 \cdot 1 + 0 \cdot 3 - 1 \cdot 8)$$

$$= (1, -7);$$

$$\begin{pmatrix} 3 & 1 & 2 \\ 2 & 3 & 8 \end{pmatrix} \begin{pmatrix} 1 \\ -1 \\ 2 \end{pmatrix} = \begin{pmatrix} 3 - 1 + 4 \\ 2 - 3 + 16 \end{pmatrix} = \begin{pmatrix} 6 \\ 15 \end{pmatrix};$$

$$\begin{pmatrix} 3 & 2 & -1 \\ 1 & 0 & 2 \\ 0 & 3 & 1 \\ 5 & -4 & 7 \\ -3 & 2 & -1 \end{pmatrix} \begin{pmatrix} 1 \\ 0 \\ -2 \end{pmatrix} = \begin{pmatrix} 5 \\ -3 \\ -2 \\ -9 \\ -1 \end{pmatrix}.$$

Observe that if x is an m-component row vector and A is $m \times n$, then xA is an n-component row vector; similarly, if u is an n-component column vector, then Au is an m-component column vector. These facts can be observed in the examples above.

Example 2. In Exercise 6 of Chapter IV, Section 13, we considered a Markov chain with transition matrix

$$P = \begin{pmatrix} \frac{1}{3} & \frac{2}{3} \\ \frac{1}{2} & \frac{1}{2} \end{pmatrix}.$$

The initial state was chosen by a random device that selected states a_1 and a_2 each with probability $\frac{1}{2}$. Let us indicate the choice of initial state by the vector $p^{(0)} = (\frac{1}{2}, \frac{1}{2})$ where the first component gives the probability of choosing state a_1 and the second the probability of choosing state a_2. Let us compute the product $p^{(0)}P$. We have

$$p^{(0)}P = (\tfrac{1}{2}, \tfrac{1}{2}) \begin{pmatrix} \frac{1}{3} & \frac{2}{3} \\ \frac{1}{2} & \frac{1}{2} \end{pmatrix} = (\tfrac{1}{6} + \tfrac{1}{4}, \tfrac{1}{3} + \tfrac{1}{4}) = (\tfrac{5}{12}, \tfrac{7}{12}).$$

Using the methods of Chapter IV, one can show that after one step there is probability $\frac{5}{12}$ that the process will be in state a_1 and probability $\frac{7}{12}$ that it will be in state a_2. Let $p^{(1)}$ be the vector whose first component gives the probability of the process being in state a_1 after one step and whose second component gives the probability of it being in state a_2 after one step. In our example we have $p^{(1)} = (\frac{5}{12}, \frac{7}{12}) = p^{(0)}P$.

In general, the formula $p^{(1)} = p^{(0)}P$ holds for any Markov process with transition matrix P and initial probability vector $p^{(0)}$.

Example 3. In Example 1 of Section 2 assume that Smith has two stores at which he can make his purchases, and let us assume that the prices charged at these two stores are slightly different. Let the price vector at the second store be

$$y = \begin{pmatrix} 5 \\ 5 \\ 10 \\ 4 \\ 6 \end{pmatrix} \quad \begin{matrix} \text{cents per apple} \\ \text{cents per egg} \\ \text{cents per lemon} \\ \text{cents per orange} \\ \text{cents per pear.} \end{matrix}$$

Smith now has the option of buying all his purchases at store 1, all at store 2, or buying just the lower-priced items at the store charging the lower price. To help him decide, we form a price matrix as follows:

	Prices, Store 1	Prices, Store 2	Minimum Price
	4	5	4
	6	5	5
$P =$	9	10	9
	5	4	4
	7	6	6

The first column lists the prices of store 1, the second column lists the prices of store 2, and the third column lists the lesser of these two prices. To compute Smith's bill under the three possible ways he can make his purchases, we compute the produce xP, as follows:

$$xP = (6, 12, 3, 12, 6) \begin{pmatrix} 4 & 5 & 4 \\ 6 & 5 & 5 \\ 9 & 10 & 9 \\ 5 & 4 & 4 \\ 7 & 6 & 6 \end{pmatrix} = (225, 204, 195).$$

We thus see that if Smith buys only in store 1, his bill will be \$2.25; if he buys only in store 2, his bill will be \$2.04; but if he buys each item in the cheaper of the two stores (apples and lemons in store 1, and the rest in store 2), his bill will be \$1.95.

Exactly what Smith will, or should, do depends upon circumstances. If both stores are equally close to him, he will probably split his purchases and obtain the smallest bill. If store 1 is close and store 2 is very far away, he may buy everything at store 1. If store 2 is closer and store 1 is far enough away so that the 9 cents he would save by splitting his purchases is not worth the travel effort, he may buy everything at store 2.

The problem just cited is an example of a *decision problem*. In such problems it is necessary to choose one of several courses of action, or *strategies*. For each such course of action or strategy, it is possible to compute the cost or *worth* of such a strategy. The decision-maker will choose a strategy with maximum worth.

Sometimes the worth of an outcome must be measured in psychological units and we then say that we measure the *utility* of an outcome. For the purposes of this book we shall always assume that the utility of an outcome is measured in monetary units, so that we can compare the worths of two different outcomes to the decision maker.

Example 4. As a second example of a decision problem, consider the following. An urn contains five red, three green, and one white ball. One ball will be drawn at random, and then payments will be made to holders of three kinds of lottery tickets, A, B, and C, according to the following schedule:

$$M = \begin{array}{c} \\ \text{Red} \\ \text{Green} \\ \text{White} \end{array} \begin{array}{ccc} \text{Ticket A} & \text{Ticket B} & \text{Ticket C} \\ \left(\begin{array}{ccc} 1 & 3 & 0 \\ 4 & 1 & 0 \\ 0 & 0 & 16 \end{array} \right) \end{array}.$$

Thus, if a red ball is selected, holders of ticket A will get \$1, holders of ticket B will get \$3, and holders of ticket C will get nothing. If green is chosen, the payments are 4, 1, and 0, respectively. If white is chosen, holders of ticket C get \$16, and the others nothing. Which ticket would we prefer to have?

Our decision will depend upon the concept of expected value discussed in the preceding chapter. The statements "draw a red ball," "draw a green ball," and "draw a white ball" have probabilities $\frac{5}{9}$, $\frac{3}{9}$, and $\frac{1}{9}$, respectively. From these probabilities we can calculate the expected value of holding each of the lottery tickets as described in the last chapter. However, a compact way of performing all these calculations is to compute the product pM, where p is the probability vector

$$p = (\tfrac{5}{9}, \quad \tfrac{3}{9}, \quad \tfrac{1}{9}).$$

From this we have

$$pM = (\tfrac{5}{9}, \tfrac{3}{9}, \tfrac{1}{9}) \begin{pmatrix} 1 & 3 & 0 \\ 4 & 1 & 0 \\ 0 & 0 & 16 \end{pmatrix}$$

$$= (1 \cdot \tfrac{5}{9} + 4 \cdot \tfrac{3}{9} + 0 \cdot \tfrac{1}{9}, \quad 3 \cdot \tfrac{5}{9} + 1 \cdot \tfrac{3}{9} + 0 \cdot \tfrac{1}{9}, \quad 0 \cdot \tfrac{5}{9} + 0 \cdot \tfrac{3}{9} + 16 \cdot \tfrac{1}{9})$$

$$= (\tfrac{17}{9}, \quad \tfrac{18}{9}, \quad \tfrac{16}{9}).$$

It is easy to see that the three components of pM give the expected values of holding lottery tickets A, B, and C, respectively. From these numbers we can see that ticket B is the best, A is the next best, and C is third best.

If we have to pay for the tickets, then the cost of the tickets will determine which is the best buy. If each ticket costs \$3 we would be better off by not buying any ticket, since we would then expect to lose money. If each ticket costs \$1 then we should buy ticket B, since it would give us a net expected gain of \$2 − \$1 = \$1. If the first two tickets cost \$2.10, and the third cost \$1.50, we should buy ticket C since it is the only one for which we would have a positive net expectation.

EXERCISES

1. Perform the following multiplications.

(a) $\begin{pmatrix} 1 & -1 \\ -2 & 2 \end{pmatrix} \begin{pmatrix} 7 \\ 2 \end{pmatrix} = ?$

(b) $(3, -4) \begin{pmatrix} 1 & -1 \\ -2 & 2 \end{pmatrix} = ?$ [*Ans.* (11, −11).]

(c) $\begin{pmatrix} 1 & 3 & 0 \\ 7 & -1 & 3 \\ -8 & 14 & -5 \\ 9 & 2 & 7 \\ 10 & -6 & 0 \end{pmatrix} \cdot \begin{pmatrix} 3 \\ -1 \\ 1 \end{pmatrix} = ?$

(d) $(2, 2) \begin{pmatrix} 1 & -1 \\ -1 & 1 \end{pmatrix} = ?$ [*Ans.* (0, 0).]

(e) $\begin{pmatrix} 1 & -1 \\ -1 & 1 \end{pmatrix} \begin{pmatrix} 5 \\ 5 \end{pmatrix} = ?$

(f) $(0, 2, -3) \begin{pmatrix} 1 & 7 & -8 & 9 & 10 \\ 3 & -1 & 14 & 2 & -6 \\ 0 & 3 & -5 & 7 & 0 \end{pmatrix} = ?$

(g) $(x_1, x_2) \begin{pmatrix} a & b \\ c & d \end{pmatrix} = ?$ [*Ans.* $(ax_1 + cx_2, bx_1 + dx_2)$.]

(h) $\begin{pmatrix} a & b \\ c & d \end{pmatrix} \begin{pmatrix} u_1 \\ u_2 \end{pmatrix} = ?$

(i) $\begin{pmatrix} 1 & 0 & 0 \\ 0 & 1 & 0 \\ 0 & 0 & 1 \end{pmatrix} \begin{pmatrix} u_1 \\ u_2 \\ u_3 \end{pmatrix} = ?$

(j) $(x_1, x_2, x_3) \begin{pmatrix} 1 & 0 & 0 \\ 0 & 1 & 0 \\ 0 & 0 & 1 \end{pmatrix} = ?$

2. What number does the matrix in parts (i) and (j) above resemble?

3. Notice that in Exercise 1(d) above the product of a row vector, none of whose components is zero, times a matrix, none of whose components is zero, yields the zero row vector. Find another example which is similar to this one. Answer the analogous question for Exercise 1(e).

4. When possible, solve for the indicated quantities.

(a) $(x_1, x_2) \begin{pmatrix} 0 & -1 \\ 7 & 3 \end{pmatrix} = (7, 0)$. Find the vector x.   [*Ans.* (3, 1).]

(b) $(2, -1) \begin{pmatrix} a & b \\ c & d \end{pmatrix} = (6, 3)$. Find the matrix $\begin{pmatrix} a & b \\ c & d \end{pmatrix}$. In this case can you find more than one solution?

(c) $\begin{pmatrix} 1 & -1 \\ -1 & 1 \end{pmatrix} \begin{pmatrix} u_1 \\ u_2 \end{pmatrix} = \begin{pmatrix} 3 \\ 4 \end{pmatrix}$. Find the vector u.

(d) $\begin{pmatrix} -1 & 4 \\ 2 & -8 \end{pmatrix} \begin{pmatrix} u_1 \\ u_2 \end{pmatrix} = \begin{pmatrix} 3 \\ -6 \end{pmatrix}$. Find u.

How many solutions can you find?

[*Ans.* $u = \begin{pmatrix} 4k - 3 \\ k \end{pmatrix}$, for any number k.]

5. Solve for the indicated quantities below and give an interpretation for each.

(a) $(1, -1) \begin{pmatrix} 0 & 2 \\ -2 & 4 \end{pmatrix} = a(1, -1)$; find a.   [*Ans.* $a = 2$.]

(b) $\begin{pmatrix} 1 & 2 \\ 2 & 4 \end{pmatrix} \begin{pmatrix} u_1 \\ u_2 \end{pmatrix} = 5 \begin{pmatrix} u_1 \\ u_2 \end{pmatrix}$; find u. How many answers can you find?

[*Ans.* $u = \begin{pmatrix} k \\ 2k \end{pmatrix}$ for any number k.]

(c) $\begin{pmatrix} \frac{5}{8} & \frac{1}{8} \\ \frac{3}{8} & \frac{7}{8} \end{pmatrix} \begin{pmatrix} u_1 \\ u_2 \end{pmatrix} = \begin{pmatrix} u_1 \\ u_2 \end{pmatrix}$; find u. How many answers are there?

6. In Exercise 5 of the preceding section construct the 3×5 matrix whose rows give the various purchases of Brown, Jones, and Smith. Multiply on the right by the five-component price (column) vector to find the three-component column vector whose entries give each person's grocery bill. Multiply on the left by the row vector $x = (1, 1, 1)$ and on the right by the price vector to find the total amount that they spent in the store.

7. In Example 1 of this section, assume that the contractor is to build seven ranch style, three Cape Cod, and five Colonial type houses. Recompute, using matrix multiplication, the total cost of raw materials, in two different ways as in the example.

8. In Example 2 of this section, assume that the initial probability vector is $p^{(0)} = (\frac{1}{3}, \frac{2}{3})$. Find the vector $p^{(1)}$.   [*Ans.* $(\frac{4}{9}, \frac{5}{9})$.]

9. For the Markov chain whose transition matrix is

$$P = \begin{pmatrix} 0 & 1 & 0 \\ 0 & \frac{1}{2} & \frac{1}{2} \\ \frac{1}{3} & 0 & \frac{2}{3} \end{pmatrix}$$

assume the initial probability vector is $p^{(0)} = (\frac{1}{2}, \frac{1}{6}, \frac{1}{3})$. Draw the tree of the process and find the tree measures. Compute $p^{(1)}$ by means of the tree measure and also from the formula $p^{(1)} = p^{(0)}P$ and show that the two answers agree.

10. Consider the Markov chain with two states whose transition matrix is

$$P = \begin{pmatrix} a & 1 - a \\ 1 - b & b \end{pmatrix}$$

where a and b are nonnegative numbers. Suppose the initial probability vector for the process is

$$p^{(0)} = (p_1^{(0)}, p_2^{(0)})$$

where $p_1^{(0)}$ is the initial probability of choosing state 1 and $p_2^{(0)}$ is the initial probability of choosing state 2. Derive the formulas for the components of the vector $p^{(1)}$.   [*Ans.* $p^{(1)} = \{ap_1^{(0)} + (1 - b)p_2^{(0)}, (1 - a)p_1^{(0)} + bp_2^{(0)}\}$.]

11. In Example 2 use tree measures to show that $p^{(2)} = p^{(1)}P$.

12. The following matrix gives the vitamin contents of three food items, in conveniently chosen units.

	Vitamin: A	B	C	D
Food I:	.5	.5	0	0
Food II:	.3	0	.2	.1
Food III:	.1	.1	.2	.5

If we eat five units of food I, ten units of food II, and eight units of food III, how much of each type of vitamin have we consumed? If we pay only for the vitamin content of each food, paying 10 cents, 20 cents, 25 cents, and 50 cents, respectively, for units of the four vitamins, how much does a unit of each type of food cost? Compute in two ways the total cost of the food eaten.

$$\left[\textit{Ans. } (6.3, 3.3, 3.6, 5.0), \begin{pmatrix} 15 \\ 13 \\ 33 \end{pmatrix}, \$4.69.\right]$$

13. In Example 3, by how much would store 1 have to reduce the price of oranges in order to make Smith's purchases less expensive at store 1 than at store 2?

14. In Example 3, find the store at which the total cost to Smith is less when he wishes to purchase

(a) $x = (4, 1, 2, 0, 1)$.   [*Ans.* Store 1, cost 47 cents.]
(b) $x = (2, 1, 3, 1, 0)$.
(c) $x = (2, 1, 1, 2, 0)$.

15. In Example 4, let us assume that an individual chooses ticket A with probability r_1, ticket B with probability r_2, and ticket C with probability r_3.

Let $r = \begin{pmatrix} r_1 \\ r_2 \\ r_3 \end{pmatrix}$. Give an interpretation for pMr. Compute this for the case

that $r_1 = r_2 = r_3$.   [*Ans.* $pMr = \frac{17}{9}$, which is the expected return.]

SUPPLEMENTARY EXERCISES

16. A company is considering which of three methods of production it should use in producing three goods, A, B, and C. The amount of each good produced by each method is shown in the matrix

$$
\begin{array}{cc}
& \text{A B C} \\
R = & \begin{pmatrix} 2 & 3 & 1 \\ 1 & 2 & 3 \\ 2 & 4 & 1 \end{pmatrix}
\end{array}
\begin{array}{l}
\text{Method 1} \\
\text{Method 2} \\
\text{Method 3.}
\end{array}
$$

Let p be a vector whose components represent the profit per unit for each of the goods. What does the vector Rp represent? Find three different vectors p such that under each of these profit vectors a different method would be most profitable. [*Partial Ans.* For $p = \begin{pmatrix} 10 \\ 8 \\ 7 \end{pmatrix}$ method 3 is most profitable.]

17. Consider the matrices

$$
A = \begin{pmatrix} a_{11} & a_{12} \\ a_{21} & a_{22} \end{pmatrix}, \qquad x = \begin{pmatrix} x_1 \\ x_2 \end{pmatrix}, \qquad b = \begin{pmatrix} b_1 \\ b_2 \end{pmatrix}.
$$

(a) Show that the equation $Ax = b$ represents two simultaneous equations in two unknowns.

(b) Show that every set of two simultaneous equations in two unknowns can be written in this form for the proper choice of A and b.

18. Consider the matrices

$$
P = \begin{pmatrix} \frac{1}{2} & \frac{1}{2} \\ \frac{3}{4} & \frac{1}{4} \end{pmatrix} \quad \text{and} \quad f = \begin{pmatrix} 1 \\ 1 \end{pmatrix}.
$$

Show that $Pf = f$.

19. Let P be the matrix of transition probabilities for a Markov chain having n states, and let f be a column matrix all of whose entries are 1's. Show that $Pf = f$. [*Hint:* Exercise 18 provides a special case.]

20. If $Ax = 0$ and $Ay = 0$, show that $A(x + y) = 0$.

21. If $Ax = b$ and $Ay = 0$, show that $A(x + y) = b$.

4.   THE ADDITION AND MULTIPLICATION OF MATRICES

Two matrices of the same shape, that is, having the same numbers of rows and columns, can be added together by adding corresponding components. For example, if A and B are two 2×3 matrices, we have

$$A + B = \begin{pmatrix} a_{11} & a_{12} & a_{13} \\ a_{21} & a_{22} & a_{23} \end{pmatrix} + \begin{pmatrix} b_{11} & b_{12} & b_{13} \\ b_{21} & b_{22} & b_{23} \end{pmatrix}$$

$$= \begin{pmatrix} a_{11} + b_{11} & a_{12} + b_{12} & a_{13} + b_{13} \\ a_{21} + b_{21} & a_{22} + b_{22} & a_{23} + b_{23} \end{pmatrix}.$$

Observe that the addition of vectors (row or column) is simply a special case of the addition of matrices. Numerical examples of the addition of matrices are the following:

$$(1, 0, -2) + (0, 5, 0) = (1, 5, -2);$$

$$\begin{pmatrix} 1 & 0 \\ 0 & 1 \end{pmatrix} + \begin{pmatrix} -1 & 0 \\ 0 & -1 \end{pmatrix} = \begin{pmatrix} 0 & 0 \\ 0 & 0 \end{pmatrix};$$

$$\begin{pmatrix} 7 & 0 & 0 \\ -3 & 1 & -6 \\ 4 & 0 & 7 \\ 0 & -2 & -2 \\ 1 & 1 & 1 \end{pmatrix} + \begin{pmatrix} -8 & 0 & 1 \\ 4 & 5 & -1 \\ 0 & 3 & 0 \\ -1 & 1 & -1 \\ 0 & -4 & 2 \end{pmatrix} = \begin{pmatrix} -1 & 0 & 1 \\ 1 & 6 & -7 \\ 4 & 3 & 7 \\ -1 & -1 & -3 \\ 1 & -3 & 3 \end{pmatrix}.$$

Other examples occur in the exercises. The reader should observe that we do *not* add matrices of different shapes.

If A is a matrix and k is any number, we define the matrix kA as

$$kA = k \begin{pmatrix} a_{11} & a_{12} & \ldots & a_{1n} \\ a_{21} & a_{22} & \ldots & a_{2n} \\ \cdot & \cdot & \ldots & \cdot \\ a_{m1} & a_{m2} & \ldots & a_{mn} \end{pmatrix} = \begin{pmatrix} ka_{11} & ka_{12} & \ldots & ka_{1n} \\ ka_{21} & ka_{22} & \ldots & ka_{2n} \\ \cdot & \cdot & \ldots & \cdot \\ ka_{m1} & ka_{m2} & \ldots & ka_{mn} \end{pmatrix}.$$

Observe that this is merely component-wise multiplication, as was the analogous concept for vectors. Some examples of multiplication of matrices by constants are

$$-2 \begin{pmatrix} 7 & -2 & 8 \\ 0 & 5 & -1 \end{pmatrix} = \begin{pmatrix} -14 & 4 & -16 \\ 0 & -10 & 2 \end{pmatrix};$$

$$6 \begin{pmatrix} 1 & 0 \\ 0 & 1 \\ 3 & -4 \end{pmatrix} = \begin{pmatrix} 6 & 0 \\ 0 & 6 \\ 18 & -24 \end{pmatrix}.$$

The multiplication of a vector by a number is, of course, a special case of the multiplication of a matrix by a number.

Under certain conditions two matrices can be multiplied together to give a new matrix. As an example, let A be a 2×3 matrix and B be a 3×2 matrix. Then the product AB is found as

$$AB = \begin{pmatrix} a_{11} & a_{12} & a_{13} \\ a_{21} & a_{22} & a_{23} \end{pmatrix} \begin{pmatrix} b_{11} & b_{12} \\ b_{21} & b_{22} \\ b_{31} & b_{32} \end{pmatrix}$$

$$= \begin{pmatrix} a_{11}b_{11} + a_{12}b_{21} + a_{13}b_{31} & a_{11}b_{12} + a_{12}b_{22} + a_{13}b_{32} \\ a_{21}b_{11} + a_{22}b_{21} + a_{23}b_{31} & a_{21}b_{12} + a_{22}b_{22} + a_{23}b_{32} \end{pmatrix}.$$

Observe that the product is a 2×2 matrix. Also notice that each entry in the new matrix is the product of one of the rows of A times one of the columns of B; for example, the entry in the second row and first column is found as the product

$$(a_{21} \quad a_{22} \quad a_{23}) \begin{pmatrix} b_{11} \\ b_{21} \\ b_{31} \end{pmatrix} = a_{21}b_{11} + a_{22}b_{21} + a_{23}b_{31}.$$

The following definition holds for the general case of matrix multiplication.

DEFINITION. Let A be an $m \times k$ matrix and B be a $k \times n$ matrix; then the product matrix $C = AB$ is an $m \times n$ matrix whose components are

$$c_{ij} = (a_{i1} \quad a_{i2} \quad \dots \quad a_{ik}) \begin{pmatrix} b_{1j} \\ b_{2j} \\ \cdot \\ \cdot \\ \cdot \\ b_{kj} \end{pmatrix} = a_{i1}b_{1j} + a_{i2}b_{2j} + \dots + a_{ik}b_{kj}.$$

The important things to remember about this definition are: first, in order to be able to multiply matrix A times matrix B, the number of columns of A must be equal to the number of rows of B; second, the product matrix $C = AB$ has the same number of rows as A and the same number of columns as B; finally, to get the entry in the ith row and jth column of AB we multiply the ith row of A times the jth column of B. Notice that the product of a vector times a matrix is a special case of matrix multiplication.

Below are several examples of matrix multiplication.

$$\begin{pmatrix} 2 & -1 \\ 0 & 3 \end{pmatrix} \begin{pmatrix} 7 & 0 \\ -2 & -3 \end{pmatrix} = \begin{pmatrix} 16 & 3 \\ -6 & -9 \end{pmatrix};$$

$$\begin{pmatrix} 3 & 0 & 1 \\ -1 & 2 & 0 \\ 0 & 0 & 2 \end{pmatrix} \begin{pmatrix} 1 & 0 & 0 \\ 0 & -1 & 0 \\ 1 & 1 & 1 \end{pmatrix} = \begin{pmatrix} 4 & 1 & 1 \\ -1 & -2 & 0 \\ 2 & 2 & 2 \end{pmatrix};$$

$$\begin{pmatrix} 3 & 1 & 4 \\ 2 & 0 & 5 \end{pmatrix} \begin{pmatrix} 1 & 3 & 0 & 0 \\ 1 & 1 & 0 & 0 \\ 0 & 0 & 1 & 1 \end{pmatrix} = \begin{pmatrix} 4 & 10 & 4 & 4 \\ 2 & 6 & 5 & 5 \end{pmatrix}.$$

One obvious question that now arises is that of multiplying more than two matrices together. Let A be an $m \times h$ matrix, let B be an $h \times k$ matrix, and let C be a $k \times n$ matrix. Then we can certainly define the products $(AB)C$ and $A(BC)$. It turns out that these two products are equal, and we define the product ABC to be their common value, i.e.,

$$ABC = A(BC) = (AB)C.$$

The rule expressed in the above equation is called the *associative law* for multiplication. We shall not prove the associative law here, although the student will be asked to check an example of it in Exercise 5.

If A and B are square matrices of the same size, then they can be multiplied in either order. It is not true, however, that the product AB is necessarily equal to the product BA. For example, if

$$A = \begin{pmatrix} 1 & 1 \\ 0 & 0 \end{pmatrix} \quad \text{and} \quad B = \begin{pmatrix} 1 & 0 \\ 1 & 0 \end{pmatrix},$$

then we have

$$AB = \begin{pmatrix} 1 & 1 \\ 0 & 0 \end{pmatrix} \begin{pmatrix} 1 & 0 \\ 1 & 0 \end{pmatrix} = \begin{pmatrix} 2 & 0 \\ 0 & 0 \end{pmatrix}$$

whereas

$$BA = \begin{pmatrix} 1 & 0 \\ 1 & 0 \end{pmatrix} \begin{pmatrix} 1 & 1 \\ 0 & 0 \end{pmatrix} = \begin{pmatrix} 1 & 1 \\ 1 & 1 \end{pmatrix},$$

and it is clear that $AB \neq BA$.

EXERCISES

1. Perform the following operations.

(a) $2 \begin{pmatrix} 6 & 1 \\ 0 & -3 \\ -1 & 2 \end{pmatrix} - 3 \begin{pmatrix} 4 & 2 \\ 0 & 1 \\ -5 & -1 \end{pmatrix} = ?$ [*Ans.* $\begin{pmatrix} 0 & -4 \\ 0 & -9 \\ 13 & 7 \end{pmatrix}$.]

(b) $\begin{pmatrix} 6 & 1 & -1 \\ 1 & -3 & 2 \end{pmatrix} - 5 \begin{pmatrix} 4 & 0 & -5 \\ 2 & 1 & -1 \end{pmatrix} = ?$

(c) $\begin{pmatrix} 6 & 1 \\ 0 & -3 \end{pmatrix} \begin{pmatrix} 4 & 0 & -4 \\ 2 & 1 & -1 \end{pmatrix} = ?$

(d) $\begin{pmatrix} 6 & 0 & -1 \\ 1 & -3 & 2 \end{pmatrix} \begin{pmatrix} 4 & 2 \\ 0 & 1 \\ -5 & -1 \end{pmatrix} = ?$ [Ans. $\begin{pmatrix} 29 & 13 \\ -6 & -3 \end{pmatrix}$.]

(e) $\begin{pmatrix} 1 & -1 \\ -1 & 1 \end{pmatrix} \begin{pmatrix} 1 & -1 \\ -1 & 1 \end{pmatrix} = ?$

(f) $\begin{pmatrix} 4 & 1 & 4 \\ -1 & -2 & -1 \\ 2 & -1 & -2 \end{pmatrix} \begin{pmatrix} 3 & 0 & 1 \\ -1 & 2 & 0 \\ 0 & 0 & 2 \end{pmatrix} = ?$ [Ans. $\begin{pmatrix} 11 & 2 & 12 \\ -1 & -4 & -3 \\ 7 & -2 & -2 \end{pmatrix}$.]

(g) $\begin{pmatrix} 1 & -2 \\ 0 & 0 \\ 7 & 5 \\ -4 & 8 \\ 0 & -2 \end{pmatrix} \begin{pmatrix} -7 & 9 & -5 & 6 & 0 \\ -1 & 0 & 3 & -4 & 1 \end{pmatrix} = ?$

2. Let A be any 3×3 matrix and let I be the matrix

$$I = \begin{pmatrix} 1 & 0 & 0 \\ 0 & 1 & 0 \\ 0 & 0 & 1 \end{pmatrix}.$$

Show that $AI = IA = A$. The matrix I acts for the products of matrices in the same way that the number 1 acts for products of numbers. For this reason it is called the *identity* matrix.

3. Let A be any 3×3 matrix and let 0 be the matrix

$$0 = \begin{pmatrix} 0 & 0 & 0 \\ 0 & 0 & 0 \\ 0 & 0 & 0 \end{pmatrix}.$$

Show that $A0 = 0A = 0$ for any A. Also show that $A + 0 = 0 + A = A$ for any A. The matrix 0 acts for matrices in the same way that the number 0 acts for numbers. For this reason it is called the *zero* matrix.

4. If $A = \begin{pmatrix} 0 & 0 \\ 0 & 1 \end{pmatrix}$ and $B = \begin{pmatrix} 1 & 0 \\ 0 & 0 \end{pmatrix}$, show that $AB = \begin{pmatrix} 0 & 0 \\ 0 & 0 \end{pmatrix}$. Thus the product of two matrices can be the zero matrix even though neither of the matrices is itself zero. Find another example that illustrates this point.

5. Verify the associative law for the special case when

$$A = \begin{pmatrix} -1 & 0 & 5 \\ 7 & -2 & 0 \end{pmatrix}, \quad B = \begin{pmatrix} 1 & 7 & 0 \\ -3 & -1 & 0 \\ 1 & 0 & 5 \end{pmatrix}, \quad C = \begin{pmatrix} -1 & -1 \\ 2 & 0 \\ 0 & 4 \end{pmatrix}.$$

6. Consider the matrices

$$A = \begin{pmatrix} 1 & 0 & 1 \\ -1 & 17 & 57 \end{pmatrix}, \quad B = \begin{pmatrix} 1 & 1 & 1 \\ 2 & 2 & 2 \\ 3 & 3 & 3 \\ 0 & 0 & 0 \end{pmatrix}, \quad C = \begin{pmatrix} 1 & 0 & -1 \\ 0 & -1 & 1 \\ -1 & 1 & 0 \end{pmatrix},$$

$$D = \begin{pmatrix} -1 & -1 \\ 2 & 2 \\ 1 & 1 \end{pmatrix}.$$

The shapes of these are 2×3, 4×3, 3×3, and 3×2, respectively. What is the shape of

(a) AC.

(b) DA.

(c) AD.

(d) BC.

(e) CB.

(f) DAC.

(g) $BCDA$.   [*Ans.* 4×3.]

7. In Exercise 6 find

(a) The component in the second row and second column of AC.

                                                 [*Ans.* 40.]

(b) The component in the fourth row and first column of BC.

(c) The component in the last row and last column of DA.   [*Ans.* 58.]

(d) The component in the first row and first column of CB.

8. If A is a square matrix, it can be multiplied by itself; hence we can define (using the associative law)

$$A^2 = A \cdot A$$
$$A^3 = A^2 \cdot A = A \cdot A \cdot A$$
$$\cdots$$
$$A^n = A^{n-1} \cdot A = A \cdot A \cdot \ldots A \quad (n \text{ factors}).$$

These are naturally called "powers" of a matrix—the first one being called the square, the second, the cube, etc. Compute the indicated powers of the following matrices.

(a) If $A = \begin{pmatrix} 1 & 0 \\ 3 & 4 \end{pmatrix}$, find A^2, A^3, and A^4.

            [*Ans.* $\begin{pmatrix} 1 & 0 \\ 15 & 16 \end{pmatrix}$; $\begin{pmatrix} 1 & 0 \\ 63 & 64 \end{pmatrix}$; $\begin{pmatrix} 1 & 0 \\ 255 & 256 \end{pmatrix}$.]

(b) If I and 0 are the matrices defined in Exercises 2 and 3, find I^2, I^3, I^n, 0^2, 0^3, and 0^n.

(c) If $A = \begin{pmatrix} 0 & 0 & 0 \\ 1 & 0 & 0 \\ 2 & -1 & 0 \end{pmatrix}$, find A^2, A^3, and A^n.

(d) If $A = \begin{pmatrix} 1 & 1 \\ 1 & 1 \end{pmatrix}$, find A^n.

9. Cube the matrix

$$\begin{pmatrix} 0 & 1 & 0 \\ 0 & \frac{1}{2} & \frac{1}{2} \\ \frac{1}{3} & 0 & \frac{2}{3} \end{pmatrix}.$$

Compare your answer with the matrix $P^{(3)}$ in Example 1, Chapter IV, Section 13, and comment on the result.

10. Consider a two-stage Markov process whose transition matrix is

$$P = \begin{pmatrix} p_{11} & p_{12} \\ p_{21} & p_{22} \end{pmatrix}.$$

(a) Assuming that the process starts in state 1, draw the tree and set up tree measures for three stages of the process. Do the same, assuming that the process starts in state 2.

(b) Using the trees drawn in (a), compute the quantities $p_{11}^{(3)}$, $p_{12}^{(3)}$, $p_{21}^{(3)}$, $p_{22}^{(3)}$. Write the matrix $P^{(3)}$.

(c) Compute the cube P^3 of the matrix P.

(d) Compare the answers you found in parts (b) and (c) and show that $P^{(3)} = P^3$.

11. Show that the fifth and all higher powers of the matrix

$$\begin{pmatrix} 0 & 1 & 0 \\ 0 & 0 & 1 \\ 1 & 1 & 0 \end{pmatrix}$$

have all entries positive. Show that no smaller power has this property.

12. In Example 1 of Section 3 assume that the contractor wishes to take into account the cost of transporting raw materials to the building site as well as the purchasing cost. Suppose the costs are as given in the matrix below.

$$Q = \begin{pmatrix} \text{Purchase} & \text{Transport} & \\ 15 & 4.5 & \text{Steel} \\ 8 & 2 & \text{Wood} \\ 5 & 3 & \text{Glass} \\ 1 & 0.5 & \text{Paint} \\ 10 & 0 & \text{Labor} \end{pmatrix}$$

Referring to the example:

(a) By computing the product RQ find a 3×2 matrix whose entries give the purchase and transportation costs of the materials for each kind of house.

(b) Find the product xRQ, which is a two-component row vector whose first component gives the total purchase price and second component gives the total transportation cost.

(c) Let $z = \begin{pmatrix} 1 \\ 1 \end{pmatrix}$ and then compute $xRQz$, which is a number giving the total cost of materials and transportation for all the houses being built.   [*Ans.* $14,304.]

13. A college survey at an all-male school shows that dates of students are distributed as follows: a freshman dates one blonde and one brunette during the year; each sophomore dates one blonde, three brunettes, and one redhead; each junior dates three blondes, two brunettes, and two redheads; each senior dates three redheads. It is further known that each blonde brings three dresses with her, two skirts, two blouses, and one sweater; each brunette brings five dresses, four skirts, one blouse, and three sweaters; each redhead brings one dress, four skirts, and four sweaters. If each dress costs $50, each skirt $15, each blouse $10, and each sweater $5; and if there are 500 freshmen, 400 sophomores, 300 juniors, and 200 seniors,

(a) What is the total number of blondes, brunettes, and redheads dated?

(b) What is the total number of each type of clothing item in the dates' wardrobes?

(c) What is the cost of the wardrobe of a blonde? A brunette? A redhead?

(d) What is the total cost of all the wardrobes of all the dates? Calculate two ways.   [*Ans.* $1,347,500.]

SUPPLEMENTARY EXERCISES

14. Find three different 2×2 matrices A such that $A^2 = I$.

15. The *commutative law for addition* is

$$A + B = B + A$$

for any two matrices A and B of the same shape. Prove that the commutative law for addition is true from the definition of matrix addition and the fact that it is true for ordinary numbers.

16. The *distributive law for numbers and matrices* is

$$k(A + B) = kA + kB$$

for any number k and any two matrices A and B of the same shape. Prove that this law holds from the definitions of numerical multiplication of matrices, addition of matrices and the ordinary rules for numbers.

17. The *distributive laws for matrices* are

$$(A + B)C = AC + BC$$
$$C(A + B) = CA + CB,$$

where A, B, and C are matrices of suitable shapes. Show that these laws hold from the definitions of matrix multiplication and addition, and the ordinary rules for numbers.

18. A *diagonal matrix* is square and its only nonzero entries are on the main diagonal. For instance, the matrices

$$A = \begin{pmatrix} 1 & 0 \\ 0 & 4 \end{pmatrix}, \qquad B = \begin{pmatrix} 3 & 0 \\ 0 & 2 \end{pmatrix}$$

are 2×2 diagonal matrices.

(a) Show that A and B commute, i.e., $AB = BA$.

(b) Show that any pair of diagonal matrices of the same size commute when multiplied together.

19. Consider the matrices

$$A = \begin{pmatrix} 0 & 1 & 0 \\ 0 & 0 & 1 \\ 1 & 0 & 0 \end{pmatrix} \quad \text{and} \quad B = \begin{pmatrix} 0 & 0 & 1 \\ 1 & 0 & 0 \\ 0 & 1 & 0 \end{pmatrix}.$$

(a) Show that $A^2 = B$ and $A^3 = I$. What is A^4?

(b) Show that $B^2 = A$ and $B^3 = I$.

(c) Show that $A^3 = BA = AB = B^3 = I$, hence A and B commute.

20. For the matrix

$$A = \begin{pmatrix} 0 & 1 & 0 & 0 \\ 0 & 0 & 1 & 0 \\ 0 & 0 & 0 & 1 \\ 1 & 0 & 0 & 0 \end{pmatrix},$$

what is the smallest k such that $A^k = I$?

21. Let $A = \begin{pmatrix} 1 & 1 \\ 0 & 1 \end{pmatrix}$.

(a) Find a matrix B such that $AB = \begin{pmatrix} 1 & 0 \\ 0 & 1 \end{pmatrix}$.

(b) Find a matrix D such that $AD = \begin{pmatrix} 2 & 0 \\ 4 & 3 \end{pmatrix}$.

[*Ans.* (a) $\begin{pmatrix} 1 & -1 \\ 0 & 1 \end{pmatrix}$; (b) $\begin{pmatrix} -2 & -3 \\ 4 & 3 \end{pmatrix}$.]

5. THE SOLUTION OF LINEAR EQUATIONS

There are many occasions when the simultaneous solutions of linear equations is important. In this section we shall develop methods for finding out whether a set of linear equations has solutions, and for finding all such solutions.

Example 1. Consider the following example of three linear equations in three unknowns.

(1) $$x_1 + 4x_2 + 3x_3 = 1$$
(2) $$2x_1 + 5x_2 + 4x_3 = 4$$
(3) $$x_1 - 3x_2 - 2x_3 = 5.$$

Equations such as these, that contain one or more variables, are called *open statements*. Statement (1) is true for some values of the variables (for instance, when $x_1 = 1$, $x_2 = 0$, and $x_3 = 0$), and false for other values of the variables (for instance, when $x_1 = 0$, $x_2 = 1$, and $x_3 = 0$). The truth set of (1) is the set of all vectors $\begin{pmatrix} x_1 \\ x_2 \\ x_3 \end{pmatrix}$ for which (1) is true.

Similarly, the truth set of the three simultaneous equations (1), (2), and (3) is the set of all vectors $\begin{pmatrix} x_1 \\ x_2 \\ x_3 \end{pmatrix}$ which make their conjunction

$$(x_1 + 4x_2 + 3x_3 = 1) \wedge (2x_1 + 5x_2 + 4x_3 = 4)$$
$$\wedge (x_1 - 3x_2 - 2x_3 = 5)$$

true. When we say that we solve a set of simultaneous equations, we mean that we determine the truth set of their conjunction.

Before we discuss the solution of these equations we note that they can be written as a single equation in matrix form as follows:

$$\begin{pmatrix} 1 & 4 & 3 \\ 2 & 5 & 4 \\ 1 & -3 & -2 \end{pmatrix} \begin{pmatrix} x_1 \\ x_2 \\ x_3 \end{pmatrix} = \begin{pmatrix} 1 \\ 4 \\ 5 \end{pmatrix}.$$

One of the uses of vector and matrix notation is in writing a large number of linear equations in a single simple matrix equation such as the one above. It also leads to the detached coefficient form of solving simultaneous equations that we shall discuss at the end of the present section and in the next section.

The method of solving the linear equations above is the following. First we use equation (1) to eliminate the variable x_1 from equations (2) and (3); i.e., we subtract 2 times (1) from (2) and then subtract (1) from (3), giving

(1') $$x_1 + 4x_2 + 3x_3 = 1$$

(2') $$-3x_2 - 2x_3 = 2$$

(3') $$-7x_2 - 5x_3 = 4.$$

Next we divide equation (2') through by the coefficient of x_2, namely, -3, obtaining $x_2 + \frac{2}{3}x_3 = -\frac{2}{3}$. We use this equation to eliminate x_2 from each of the other two equations. In order to do this we subtract 4 times this equation from (1') and add 7 times this equation to (3'), obtaining

(1'') $$x_1 + 0 + \frac{1}{3}x_3 = \frac{11}{3}$$

(2'') $$x_2 + \frac{2}{3}x_3 = -\frac{2}{3}$$

(3'') $$-\frac{1}{3}x_3 = -\frac{2}{3}.$$

The last step is to divide through (3'') by $-\frac{1}{3}$, which is the coefficient of x_3, obtaining the equation $x_3 = 2$; we use this equation to eliminate x_3 from the first two equations as follows:

(1''') $$x_1 + 0 + 0 = 3$$

(2''') $$x_2 + 0 = -2$$

(3''') $$x_3 = 2.$$

The solution can now be read from these equations as $x_1 = 3$, $x_2 = -2$, and $x_3 = 2$. The reader should substitute these values into the original equations (1), (2), and (3) above to see that the solution has actually been obtained.

In the example just discussed we saw that there was only one solution to the set of three simultaneous equations in three variables. Example 2 will be one in which there is *more* than one solution, and Example 3 will be one in which there are *no* solutions to a set of three simultaneous equations in three variables.

Example 2. Consider the following linear equations.

(4)	$x_1 - 2x_2 - 3x_3 = 2$
(5)	$x_1 - 4x_2 - 13x_3 = 14$
(6)	$-3x_1 + 5x_2 + 4x_3 = 0.$

Let us proceed as before and use equation (4) to eliminate the variable x_1 from the other two equations. We have

(4')	$x_1 - 2x_2 - 3x_3 = 2$
(5')	$-2x_2 - 10x_3 = 12$
(6')	$-x_2 - 5x_3 = 6.$

Proceeding as before, we divide equation (5') by -2, obtaining the equation $x_2 + 5x_3 = -6$. We use this equation to eliminate the variable x_2 from each of the other equations—namely, we add twice this equation to (4') and then add the equation to (6').

(4'')	$x_1 + 0 + 7x_3 = -10$
(5'')	$x_2 + 5x_3 = -6$
(6'')	$0 = 0.$

Observe that we have eliminated the last equation completely! We also see that the variable x_3 can be chosen completely arbitrarily in these equations. To emphasize this, we move the terms involving x_3 to the right-hand side, giving

| (4''') | $x_1 = -10 - 7x_3$ |
| (5''') | $x_2 = -6 - 5x_3.$ |

The reader should check, by substituting these values of x_1 and x_2 into equations (4), (5), and (6), that they are solutions regardless of the value of x_3. Let us also substitute particular values for x_3 to obtain numerical solutions. Thus, if we let $x_3 = 1, 0, -2$, respectively, and compute the resulting numbers, using (4''') and (5'''), we obtain the following numerical solutions.

$$x_1 = -17, \quad x_2 = -11, \quad x_3 = 1$$
$$x_1 = -10, \quad x_2 = -6, \quad x_3 = 0$$
$$x_1 = 4, \quad x_2 = 4, \quad x_3 = -2.$$

The reader should also substitute these numbers into (4), (5), and (6) to show that they are solutions. To summarize, our second example has an infinite number of solutions, one for each numerical value of x_3 which is substituted into equations $(4''')$ and $(5''')$.

Example 3. Suppose that we modify equation (6) by changing the number on the right-hand side to 2. Then we have

$$(7) \qquad x_1 - 2x_2 - 3x_3 = 2$$
$$(8) \qquad x_1 - 4x_2 - 13x_3 = 14$$
$$(9) \qquad -3x_1 + 5x_2 + 4x_3 = 2.$$

If we carry out the same procedure as before and use (7) to eliminate x_1 from (8) and (9), we obtain

$$(7') \qquad x_1 - 2x_2 - 3x_3 = 2$$
$$(8') \qquad -2x_2 - 10x_3 = 12$$
$$(9') \qquad -x_2 - 5x_3 = 8.$$

We divide $(8')$ by -2, the coefficient of x_2, obtaining, as before, $x_2 + 5x_3 = -6$. Using this equation to eliminate x_2 from the other two equations, we have

$$(7'') \qquad x_1 + 0 + 7x_3 = -10$$
$$(8'') \qquad x_2 + 5x_3 = -6$$
$$(9'') \qquad 0 = 2.$$

Observe that the last equation is *logically false*, that is, false for all values of x_1, x_2, x_3. Because our elimination procedure has led to a false result we conclude that the equations (7), (8), and (9) have *no* solution. The student should always keep in mind that this possibility exists when considering simultaneous equations.

In the examples above the equations we considered had the same number of variables as equations. The next example has more variables than equations and the last has more equations than variables.

Example 4. Consider the following two equations in three variables.

$$(10) \qquad -4x_1 + 3x_2 + 2x_3 = -2$$
$$(11) \qquad 5x_1 - 4x_2 + x_3 = 3.$$

Using the elimination method outlined above, we divide (10) by -4, and then subtract 5 times the result from (11), obtaining

$$(10') \qquad x_1 - \tfrac{3}{4}x_2 - \tfrac{1}{2}x_3 = \tfrac{1}{2}$$
$$(11') \qquad -\tfrac{1}{4}x_2 + \tfrac{7}{2}x_3 = \tfrac{1}{2}.$$

Multiplying $(11')$ by -4 and using it to eliminate x_2 from $(10')$, we have

$$(10'') \qquad x_1 + 0 - 11x_3 = -1$$
$$(11'') \qquad x_2 - 14x_3 = -2.$$

We can now let x_3 take on any value whatsoever and solve these equations for x_1 and x_2. We emphasize this fact by rewriting them as in Example 2 as

$$(10''') \qquad x_1 = 11x_3 - 1$$
$$(11''') \qquad x_2 = 14x_3 - 2.$$

The reader should check that these are solutions and also, by choosing specific values for x_3, find numerical solutions to these equations.

Example 5. Let us consider the other possibility suggested by Example 4, namely, the case in which we have more equations than variables. Consider the following equations.

$$(12) \qquad -4x_1 + 3x_2 = 2$$
$$(13) \qquad 5x_1 - 4x_2 = 0$$
$$(14) \qquad 2x_1 - x_2 = a,$$

where a is an arbitrary number. Using equation (12) to eliminate x_1 from the other two we obtain

$$(12') \qquad x_1 - \tfrac{3}{4}x_2 = -\tfrac{1}{2}$$
$$(13') \qquad -\tfrac{1}{4}x_2 = \tfrac{5}{2}$$
$$(14') \qquad \tfrac{1}{2}x_2 = a + 1.$$

Next we use $(13')$ to eliminate x_2 from the other equations, obtaining

$$(12'') \qquad x_1 + 0 = -8$$
$$(13'') \qquad x_2 = -10$$
$$(14'') \qquad 0 = a + 6.$$

These equations remind us of the situation in Example 3, since we will be led to a false result unless $a = -6$. We see that equations (12), (13), and (14) have the solution $x_1 = -8$ and $x_2 = -10$ only if $a = -6$. If $a \neq -6$, then there is *no* solution to these equations.

The examples above illustrate all the possibilities that can occur in the general case. There may be no solutions, exactly one solution, or an infinite number of solutions to a set of simultaneous equations.

The procedure that we have illustrated above is one that turns any

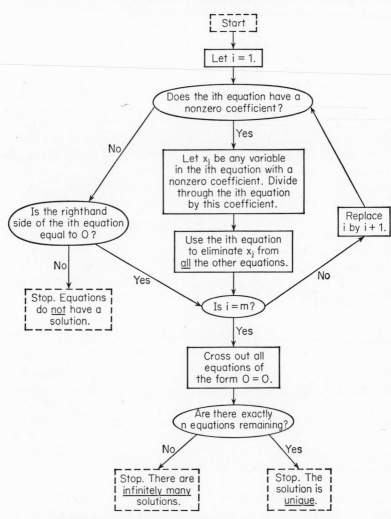

Figure 5   *Flow diagram for solving m equations in n variables.*

set of linear equations into an equivalent set of equations from which the existence of solutions and the solutions can be easily read. A student who learned other ways of solving linear equations may wonder why we use the above procedure—one which is not always the quickest way of solving equations. The answer is that we use it because it always works, that is, it is a *canonical* procedure to apply to *any* set of linear equations. The faster methods usually work only for equations that have solutions, and even then may not find all solutions.

The computational process illustrated above is summarized in the flow diagram of Figure 5. In that diagram the instructions encircled by dotted lines are either beginning or ending instructions; those enclosed in rectangles are intermediate computational steps; and those enclosed in ovals ask questions, the answers to which determine which of two paths the computational process will follow.

The direction of the process is always indicated by arrows. The flow diagram of Figure 5 can easily be turned into a computer program for solving m linear equations in n variables. Students having access to a computer will find it a useful exercise to write such a program.

Let us return again to the equations of Example 1. Note that the variables, coefficients, and equals signs are in columns at the beginning of the solution and are always kept in the same column. It is obvious that the *location* of the coefficient is sufficient identification for it and that it is unnecessary to keep writing the variables. We can start with the format or *tableau*

$$
(15) \qquad \begin{pmatrix} 1 & 4 & 3 & | & 1 \\ 2 & 5 & 4 & | & 4 \\ 1 & -3 & -2 & | & 5 \end{pmatrix}.
$$

Note that the coefficients of x_1 are found in the first column, the coefficients of x_2 in the second column, of x_3 in the third column, and the constants on the right-hand side of the equation all occur in the fourth column. The vertical line represents the equals signs in the equations.

The tableau of (15) will be called the *detached coefficient tableau* for simultaneous linear equations. We now show how to solve simultaneous equations using the detached coefficient tableau.

Example 6. Starting with the tableau of (15) we carry out exactly the same calculations as in Example 1, which lead to the following series of tableaus.

$$(16) \qquad \begin{pmatrix} 1 & 4 & 3 & | & 1 \\ 0 & -3 & -2 & | & 2 \\ 0 & -7 & -5 & | & 4 \end{pmatrix}$$

$$(17) \qquad \begin{pmatrix} 1 & 0 & \frac{1}{3} & | & \frac{11}{3} \\ 0 & 1 & \frac{2}{3} & | & -\frac{2}{3} \\ 0 & 0 & -\frac{1}{3} & | & -\frac{2}{3} \end{pmatrix}$$

$$(18) \qquad \begin{pmatrix} 1 & 0 & 0 & | & 3 \\ 0 & 1 & 0 & | & -2 \\ 0 & 0 & 1 & | & 2 \end{pmatrix}.$$

From the tableau of (18) we can easily read the answer $x_1 = 3$, $x_2 = -2$, and $x_3 = 2$, which is the same as before.

The correspondence between the calculations of Example 1 and of the present example is as follows:

(1), (2), and (3)	correspond to	(15)
(1′), (2′), and (3′)	correspond to	(16)
(1″), (2″), and (3″)	correspond to	(17)
(1‴), (2‴), and (3‴)	correspond to	(18)

Note that in the tableau form we are always careful to keep zero coefficients in each column when necessary.

Example 7. Suppose that we have two sets of simultaneous equations to solve and that they differ only in their right-hand sides. For instance, suppose we want to solve

$$(19) \qquad \begin{pmatrix} 1 & 4 & 3 \\ 2 & 5 & 4 \\ 1 & -3 & -2 \end{pmatrix} \begin{pmatrix} x_1 \\ x_2 \\ x_3 \end{pmatrix} = \begin{pmatrix} 1 \\ 4 \\ 5 \end{pmatrix} \quad \text{and} \quad = \begin{pmatrix} -1 \\ 0 \\ 2 \end{pmatrix}.$$

It is obvious that the calculations on the left-hand side will be the same regardless of the numbers appearing on the right-hand side. Therefore, it is possible to solve both sets of simultaneous equations at once. We shall illustrate this in the following series of tableaus.

$$(20) \qquad \begin{pmatrix} 1 & 4 & 3 & | & 1 & -1 \\ 2 & 5 & 4 & | & 4 & 0 \\ 1 & -3 & -2 & | & 5 & 2 \end{pmatrix}$$

$$(21) \qquad \begin{pmatrix} 1 & 4 & 3 & | & 1 & -1 \\ 0 & -3 & -2 & | & 2 & 2 \\ 0 & -7 & -5 & | & 4 & 3 \end{pmatrix}$$

$$(22) \quad \begin{pmatrix} 1 & 0 & \frac{1}{3} & \frac{11}{3} & \frac{5}{3} \\ 0 & 1 & \frac{2}{3} & -\frac{2}{3} & -\frac{2}{3} \\ 0 & 0 & -\frac{1}{3} & -\frac{2}{3} & -\frac{5}{3} \end{pmatrix}$$

$$(23) \quad \begin{pmatrix} 1 & 0 & 0 & 3 & 0 \\ 0 & 1 & 0 & -2 & -4 \\ 0 & 0 & 1 & 2 & 5 \end{pmatrix}.$$

We find the answers

$$x_1 = 3, \qquad x_2 = -2, \qquad x_3 = 2$$

to the first set of equations and the answers

$$x_1 = 0, \qquad x_2 = -4, \qquad x_3 = 5$$

to the second set of equations. The reader should check these answers by substituting into the original equations.

EXERCISES

1. Work again Examples 2–4 using the detached coefficient tableau.

2. Find all the solutions of the following simultaneous equations.
   (a) $4x_1 \quad + 5x_0 = \quad 6$
   $\quad\quad x_2 - 6x_3 = -2$
   $\quad 3x_1 \quad + 4x_3 = \quad 3.$ [*Ans.* $x_1 = 9, x_2 = -38, x_3 = -6.$]
   (b) $3x_1 - \quad x_2 - 2x_3 = \quad 2$
   $\quad\quad\quad 2x_2 - \quad x_3 = -1$
   $\quad 3x_1 - 5x_2 \quad = \quad 3.$ [*Ans.* No solution.]
   (c) $\quad -x_1 + 2x_2 + \quad 3x_3 = 0$
   $\quad\quad x_1 - 4x_2 - 13x_3 = 0$
   $\quad -3x_1 + 5x_2 + \quad 4x_3 = 0.$ [*Ans.* $x_1 = -7x_3, x_2 = -5x_3.$]

3. Find all the solutions of the following simultaneous equations.
   (a) $\quad x_1 + \quad x_2 + \quad x_3 = 0$
   $\quad 2x_1 + 4x_2 + 3x_3 = 0$
   $\quad\quad\quad 4x_2 + 4x_3 = 0.$
   (b) $\quad x_1 + \quad x_2 + \quad x_3 = -2$
   $\quad 2x_1 + 4x_2 + 3x_3 = \quad 3$
   $\quad\quad\quad 4x_2 + 2x_3 = \quad 2.$
   (c) $4x_1 \quad\quad + 4x_3 = \quad 8$
   $\quad\quad x_2 - 6x_3 = -3$
   $\quad 3x_1 + \quad x_2 - 3x_3 = \quad 3.$

4. Find all solutions of the following equations using the detached coefficient tableau.

(a) $5x_1 - 3x_2 = -7$
      $-2x_1 + 9x_2 = 4$
      $2x_1 + 4x_2 = -2.$ [*Ans.* $x_1 = -\frac{17}{13}$; $x_2 = \frac{2}{13}$.]

(b) $x_1 + 2x_2 = 1$
      $-3x_1 + 2x_2 = -2$
      $2x_1 + 3x_2 = 1.$ [*Ans.* No solution.]

(e) $5x_1 - 3x_2 - 7x_3 + x_4 = 10$
      $-x_1 + 2x_2 + 6x_3 - 3x_4 = -3$
      $x_1 + x_2 + 4x_3 - 5x_4 = 0.$

5. Find all solutions of:

$$x_1 + 2x_2 + 3x_3 + 4x_4 = 10$$
$$2x_1 - x_2 + x_3 - x_4 = 1$$
$$3x_1 + x_2 + 4x_3 + 3x_4 = 11$$
$$-2x_1 + 6x_2 + 4x_3 + 10x_4 = 18$$

[*Ans.* $x_1 = \frac{12}{5} - x_3 - \frac{2}{5}x_4$; $x_2 = \frac{19}{5} - x_3 - \frac{8}{5}x_4$, x_3 and x_4 arbitrary.]

6. We consider buying three kinds of food. Food I has one unit of vitamin A, three units of vitamin B, and four units of vitamin C. Food II has two, three, and five units, respectively. Food III has three units each of vitamin A and vitamin C, none of vitamin B. We need to have 11 units of vitamin A, nine of vitamin B, and 20 of vitamin C.

(a) Find all possible amounts of the three foods that will provide precisely these amounts of the vitamins.

(b) If food I costs 60 cents and the others cost 10 cents each per unit, is there a solution costing exactly $1?   [*Ans.* (b) Yes; 1, 2, 2.]

7. Solve the following four simultaneous sets whose right-hand sides are listed under (a), (b), (c), and (d) below. Use the detached coefficient tableau.

	(a)	(b)	(c)	(d)
$4x_1 + 5x_3 =$	1	1	0	0
$x_2 - 6x_3 =$	2	0	0	1
$3x_1 + 4x_3 =$	3	0	1	0.

[*Ans.* (a) $x_1 = -11$, $x_2 = 56$, $x_3 = 9$.]

8. Solve the following four sets of simultaneous equations, which differ only in their right-hand sides.

	(a)	(b)	(c)	(d)
$x_1 + x_2 + x_3 =$	3	0	12	0
$x_1 - x_2 + 2x_3 =$	2	-1	7	0
$2x_1 + x_2 - x_3 =$	2	3	11	0.

9. Solve the following three sets of simultaneous equations.

$$\begin{array}{cccc} & \text{(a)} & \text{(b)} & \text{(c)} \\ x_1 + x_2 + x_3 = & 1 & 2 & 0 \\ x_1 - x_2 + 2x_3 = & -2 & 2 & 0 \\ 3x_1 - x_2 + 5x_3 = & -3 & 2 & 0. \end{array}$$

10. Show that the equations

$$\begin{aligned} -4x_1 + 3x_2 + ax_3 &= c \\ 5x_1 - 4x_2 + bx_3 &= d \end{aligned}$$

always have a solution for all values of a, b, c, and d.

11. Find conditions on a, b, and c in order that the equations

$$\begin{aligned} -4x_1 + 3x_2 &= a \\ 5x_1 - 4x_2 &= b \\ -3x_1 + 2x_2 &= c \end{aligned}$$

have a solution.   [*Ans.* $2a + b = c$.]

12. (a) Let $x = (x_1, x_2)$ and let A be the matrix

$$A = \begin{pmatrix} 3 & -4 \\ 2 & -6 \end{pmatrix}.$$

Find all solutions of the equation $xA = x$.   [*Ans.* $x = (0, 0)$.]

(b) Let $x = (x_1, x_2)$ and let A be the matrix

$$A = \begin{pmatrix} 3 & 6 \\ -2 & -5 \end{pmatrix}.$$

Find all solutions of the equation $xA = x$.

[*Ans.* $x = (k, k)$ for any number k.]

13. Let $x = (x_1, x_2)$ and let P be the matrix

$$P = \begin{pmatrix} \frac{1}{3} & \frac{2}{3} \\ \frac{4}{5} & \frac{1}{5} \end{pmatrix}.$$

(a) Find all solutions of the equation $xP = x$.

(b) Choose the solution for which $x_1 + x_2 = 1$.

14. If $x = (x_1, x_2, x_3)$ and A is the matrix

$$A = \begin{pmatrix} 1 & -2 & 0 \\ 0 & 5 & 4 \\ 0 & -6 & -4 \end{pmatrix},$$

find all solutions of the equation $xA = x$.

[*Ans.* $x = (-k/2, 5k/4, k)$ for any number k.]

15. If $x = (x_1, x_2, x_3)$ and P is the matrix

$$P = \begin{pmatrix} 0 & \frac{1}{2} & \frac{1}{2} \\ \frac{1}{3} & \frac{1}{3} & \frac{1}{3} \\ \frac{1}{5} & 0 & \frac{4}{5} \end{pmatrix},$$

find all solutions of the equation $xP = x$. Select the unique solution for which $x_1 + x_2 + x_3 = 1$.

16. (a) Show that the simultaneous linear equations

$$\begin{aligned} x_1 + x_2 + x_3 &= 1 \\ x_1 + 2x_2 + 3x_3 &= 0 \end{aligned}$$

can be interpreted as a single matrix-times-column-vector equation of the form

$$\begin{pmatrix} 1 & 1 & 1 \\ 1 & 2 & 3 \end{pmatrix} \begin{pmatrix} x_1 \\ x_2 \\ x_3 \end{pmatrix} = \begin{pmatrix} 1 \\ 0 \end{pmatrix}.$$

(b) Show that *any* set of simultaneous linear equations may be interpreted as a matrix equation of the form $Ax = b$, where A is an $m \times n$ matrix, x is an n-component column vector, and b is an m-component column vector.

17. (a) Show that the equations of Exercise 16(a) can be interpreted as a row-vector-times-matrix equation of the form

$$(x_1 \quad x_2 \quad x_3) \begin{pmatrix} 1 & 1 \\ 1 & 2 \\ 1 & 3 \end{pmatrix} = (1 \quad 0).$$

(b) Show that *any* set of simultaneous linear equations may be interpreted as a matrix equation of the form $xA = b$, where A is an $m \times n$ matrix, x is an m-component row vector, and b is an n-component row vector.

18. (a) Show that the simultaneous linear equations of Exercise 16(a) can be interpreted as asking for all possible ways of expressing the column vector $\begin{pmatrix} 1 \\ 0 \end{pmatrix}$ in terms of the column vectors $\begin{pmatrix} 1 \\ 1 \end{pmatrix}$, $\begin{pmatrix} 1 \\ 2 \end{pmatrix}$, and $\begin{pmatrix} 1 \\ 3 \end{pmatrix}$.

(b) Show that *any* set of linear equations may be interpreted as asking for all possible ways of expressing a column vector in terms of given column vectors.

SUPPLEMENTARY EXERCISES

19. For what value of the constant k does the following system have a unique solution? Find the solution in this case. What is the case if k does not take on this value?

$$\begin{align}
2x \phantom{{}+y} + 4z &= 6 \\
3x + y + z &= -1 \\
2y - z &= -2 \\
x - y + kz &= -5.
\end{align}$$

[*Ans.* $k = -2$; $x = -1$, $y = 0$, $z = 2$; no solution.]

20. Consider the following set of simultaneous equations.

$$\begin{align}
x_1 \phantom{{}+x_2} + y_1 &= a \\
x_1 \phantom{{}+x_2} + y_2 &= b \\
x_2 + y_1 \phantom{{}+y_2} &= c \\
x_2 \phantom{{}+y_1} + y_2 &= d.
\end{align}$$

(a) For what conditions on a, b, c, and d will these equations have a solution?

(b) Give a set of values for a, b, c, and d for which the equations do *not* have a solution.

(c) Show that if there is *one* solution to these equations, then there are *infinitely many* solutions.

21. Which of the following statements are true and which false concerning the solution of m simultaneous linear equations in n unknowns written in the form $Ax = b$?

(a) If there are infinitely many solutions, then $n > m$.

(b) If the solution is unique, then $n = m$.

(c) If $m = n$, then the solution is unique.

(d) If $n > m$, then there cannot be a unique solution.

(e) If $b = 0$, then there is always at least one solution.

(f) If $b = 0$, then there are always infinitely many solutions.

(g) If $b = 0$ and $x^{(1)}$ and $x^{(2)}$ are solutions, then $x^{(1)} + x^{(2)}$ is also a solution.   [*Ans.* (d), (e), and (g) are true.]

22. Let

$$A = (a, b, c), \qquad x = \begin{pmatrix} x_1 \\ x_2 \\ x_3 \end{pmatrix}$$

and let d be any number. Consider the open statement $Ax = d$.

(a) If $A \neq 0$, show that the truth set of $Ax = d$ is not empty.

(b) If $A = 0$ and $d = 0$, show that $Ax = d$ is logically true.

(c) If $A = 0$ and $d \neq 0$, show that $Ax = d$ is logically false.

(d) Use (a), (b), and (c) to prove the following theorem: A single open statement $Ax = d$ is logically false if and only if $A = 0$ and $d \neq 0$.

6. THE INVERSE OF A SQUARE MATRIX

If A is a square matrix and B is another square matrix of the same size having the property that $BA = I$ (where I is the identity matrix), then we say that B is the *inverse* of A. When it exists, we shall denote the inverse of A by the symbol A^{-1}. To give a numerical example, let A and A^{-1} be the following.

$$(1) \qquad A = \begin{pmatrix} 4 & 0 & 5 \\ 0 & 1 & -6 \\ 3 & 0 & 4 \end{pmatrix}$$

$$(2) \qquad A^{-1} = \begin{pmatrix} 4 & 0 & -5 \\ -18 & 1 & 24 \\ -3 & 0 & 4 \end{pmatrix}.$$

Then we have

$$A^{-1}A = \begin{pmatrix} 4 & 0 & -5 \\ -18 & 1 & 24 \\ -3 & 0 & 4 \end{pmatrix} \cdot \begin{pmatrix} 4 & 0 & 5 \\ 0 & 1 & -6 \\ 3 & 0 & 4 \end{pmatrix} = \begin{pmatrix} 1 & 0 & 0 \\ 0 & 1 & 0 \\ 0 & 0 & 1 \end{pmatrix} = I.$$

If we multiply these matrices in the other order, we also get the identity matrix; thus

$$AA^{-1} = \begin{pmatrix} 4 & 0 & 5 \\ 0 & 1 & -6 \\ 3 & 0 & 4 \end{pmatrix} \cdot \begin{pmatrix} 4 & 0 & -5 \\ -18 & 1 & 24 \\ -3 & 0 & 4 \end{pmatrix} = \begin{pmatrix} 1 & 0 & 0 \\ 0 & 1 & 0 \\ 0 & 0 & 1 \end{pmatrix} = I.$$

In general it can be shown that if A is a square matrix with inverse A^{-1}, then the inverse satisfies the equation

$$A^{-1}A = AA^{-1} = I.$$

It is easy to see that a square matrix can have only one inverse. Suppose that in addition to A^{-1} we also have a B such that

$$BA = I.$$

Then we see that

$$B = BI = B(AA^{-1}) = (BA)A^{-1} = IA^{-1} = A^{-1}.$$

Finding the inverse of a matrix is analogous to finding the reciprocal of an ordinary number, but the analogy is not complete. Every non-zero number has a reciprocal, but there are matrices, not the zero matrix, which have no inverse. For example, if

$$A = \begin{pmatrix} 1 & -1 \\ -1 & 1 \end{pmatrix} \quad \text{and} \quad B = \begin{pmatrix} 1 & 1 \\ 1 & 1 \end{pmatrix},$$

then

$$AB = \begin{pmatrix} 1 & -1 \\ -1 & 1 \end{pmatrix} \cdot \begin{pmatrix} 1 & 1 \\ 1 & 1 \end{pmatrix} = \begin{pmatrix} 0 & 0 \\ 0 & 0 \end{pmatrix} = 0.$$

From this it follows that neither A nor B can have an inverse. To show that A does not have an inverse, let us assume that A had an inverse A^{-1}. Then

$$B = (A^{-1}A)B = A^{-1}(AB) = A^{-1}0 = 0,$$

contradicting the fact that $B \neq 0$. The proof that B cannot have an inverse is similar.

Let us now try to calculate the inverse of the matrix A in (1). Specifically, let's try to calculate the first column of A^{-1}. Let

$$x = \begin{pmatrix} x_1 \\ x_2 \\ x_3 \end{pmatrix}$$

be the desired entries of the first column. Then from the equation $AA^{-1} = I$ we see that we must solve

$$\begin{pmatrix} 4 & 0 & 5 \\ 0 & 1 & -6 \\ 3 & 0 & 4 \end{pmatrix} \begin{pmatrix} x_1 \\ x_2 \\ x_3 \end{pmatrix} = \begin{pmatrix} 1 \\ 0 \\ 0 \end{pmatrix}.$$

Similarly, to find the second and third columns of A^{-1} we want to solve the additional sets of equations,

$$\begin{pmatrix} 4 & 0 & 5 \\ 0 & 1 & -6 \\ 3 & 0 & 4 \end{pmatrix} \begin{pmatrix} x_1 \\ x_2 \\ x_3 \end{pmatrix} = \begin{pmatrix} 0 \\ 1 \\ 0 \end{pmatrix} \quad \text{and} \quad = \begin{pmatrix} 0 \\ 0 \\ 1 \end{pmatrix},$$

respectively. We thus have three sets of simultaneous equations that differ only in their right-hand sides. This is exactly the situation described in Example 7 of the previous section.

To solve them, we start with the tableau

(3)
$$\begin{pmatrix} 4 & 0 & 5 & | & 1 & 0 & 0 \\ 0 & 1 & -6 & | & 0 & 1 & 0 \\ 3 & 0 & 4 & | & 0 & 0 & 1 \end{pmatrix}$$

and carry out the calculations as described in the last section. This gives rise to the following series of tableaus. In (3) divide the first row by 4, copy the second row, and subtract 3 times the new first row from the old third row, which yields the tableau

$$
(4) \qquad \begin{pmatrix} 1 & 0 & \frac{5}{4} & \frac{1}{4} & 0 & 0 \\ 0 & 1 & -6 & 0 & 1 & 0 \\ 0 & 0 & \frac{1}{4} & -\frac{3}{4} & 0 & 1 \end{pmatrix}.
$$

Next we multiply the third row of (4) by 4, multiply the new third row by 6 and add to the old second row, and multiply the new third row by $\frac{5}{4}$ and subtract from the old first row. We have the final tableau

$$
(5) \qquad \begin{pmatrix} 1 & 0 & 0 & 4 & 0 & -5 \\ 0 & 1 & 0 & -18 & 1 & 24 \\ 0 & 0 & 1 & -3 & 0 & 4 \end{pmatrix}.
$$

We see that the inverse A^{-1} which is given in (2) appears to the right of the vertical line in the tableau of (5).

The procedure just illustrated will find the inverse of any square matrix A, *providing A has an inverse.* We summarize it as follows:

RULE FOR INVERTING A MATRIX. Let A be a matrix that has an inverse. To find the inverse of A start with the tableau

$$
(A \mid I)
$$

and change it by row transformations (as described in Section 5) into the tableau

$$
(I \mid B).
$$

The resulting matrix B is the inverse A^{-1} of A.

Even if A has no inverse, the procedure just outlined can be started. At some point in the procedure a tableau will be found that is not of the desired final form and from which it is impossible to change by row transformations of the kind described.

Example 1. Show that the matrix

$$
A = \begin{pmatrix} 4 & 0 & 8 \\ 0 & 1 & -6 \\ 2 & 0 & 4 \end{pmatrix}
$$

has no inverse.

We set up the initial tableau as follows:

(6)
$$\begin{pmatrix} 4 & 0 & 8 & | & 1 & 0 & 0 \\ 0 & 1 & -6 & | & 0 & 1 & 0 \\ 2 & 0 & 4 & | & 0 & 0 & 1 \end{pmatrix}.$$

Carrying out one set of row transformations, we obtain the second tableau as follows:

(7)
$$\begin{pmatrix} 1 & 0 & 2 & | & \frac{1}{4} & 0 & 0 \\ 0 & 1 & -6 & | & 0 & 1 & 0 \\ 0 & 0 & 0 & | & -\frac{1}{2} & 0 & 1 \end{pmatrix}.$$

It is clear that we cannot proceed further since there is a row of zeros to the left of the equals sign on the third set of equations. Hence we conclude that A has no inverse.

Because of the form of the final tableau in (7), we see that it is impossible to solve the equations

$$\begin{pmatrix} 4 & 0 & 8 \\ 0 & 1 & -6 \\ 2 & 0 & 4 \end{pmatrix} \begin{pmatrix} x_1 \\ x_2 \\ x_3 \end{pmatrix} = \begin{pmatrix} 0 \\ 0 \\ 1 \end{pmatrix},$$

since these equations are inconsistent as is shown by the tests developed in Section 5. In other words, it is not possible to solve for the third column of the inverse matrix.

It is clear that an $n \times n$ matrix A has an inverse if and only if the following sets of simultaneous equations,

$$Ax = \begin{pmatrix} 1 \\ 0 \\ \cdot \\ \cdot \\ \cdot \\ 0 \end{pmatrix}, \quad Ax = \begin{pmatrix} 0 \\ 1 \\ \cdot \\ \cdot \\ \cdot \\ 0 \end{pmatrix}, \quad \ldots; \quad Ax = \begin{pmatrix} 0 \\ 0 \\ \cdot \\ \cdot \\ \cdot \\ 1 \end{pmatrix}$$

can all be uniquely solved. And these sets of simultaneous equations, since they all share the same left-hand sides, can be solved uniquely if and only if the transformation of the rule for inverting a matrix can be carried out. Hence we have proved the following theorem.

Theorem. A square matrix A has an inverse if and only if the tableau

$$(A \mid I)$$

can be transformed by row transformations into the tableau

$$(I \mid A^{-1}).$$

Example 2. Let us find the inverse of the matrix

$$A = \begin{pmatrix} 1 & 4 & 3 \\ 2 & 5 & 4 \\ 1 & -3 & -2 \end{pmatrix}.$$

The initial tableau is

$$\begin{pmatrix} 1 & 4 & 3 & | & 1 & 0 & 0 \\ 2 & 5 & 4 & | & 0 & 1 & 0 \\ 1 & -3 & -2 & | & 0 & 0 & 1 \end{pmatrix}.$$

Transforming it by row transformations, we obtain the following series of tableaus.

$$\begin{pmatrix} 1 & 4 & 3 & | & 1 & 0 & 0 \\ 0 & -3 & -2 & | & -2 & 1 & 0 \\ 0 & -7 & -5 & | & -1 & 0 & 1 \end{pmatrix}$$

$$\begin{pmatrix} 1 & 0 & \frac{1}{3} & | & -\frac{5}{3} & \frac{4}{3} & 0 \\ 0 & 1 & \frac{2}{3} & | & \frac{2}{3} & -\frac{1}{3} & 0 \\ 0 & 0 & -\frac{1}{3} & | & \frac{11}{3} & -\frac{7}{3} & 1 \end{pmatrix}$$

$$\begin{pmatrix} 1 & 0 & 0 & | & 2 & -1 & 1 \\ 0 & 1 & 0 & | & 8 & -5 & 2 \\ 0 & 0 & 1 & | & -11 & 7 & -3 \end{pmatrix}.$$

The inverse of A is then

$$A^{-1} = \begin{pmatrix} 2 & -1 & 1 \\ 8 & -5 & 2 \\ -11 & 7 & -3 \end{pmatrix}.$$

The reader should check that $A^{-1}A = AA^{-1} = I$.

EXERCISES

1. Compute the inverse of each of the following matrices.

$$A = \begin{pmatrix} 1 & 0 & 0 \\ 3 & 1 & 5 \\ -2 & 0 & 1 \end{pmatrix}, \qquad B = \begin{pmatrix} 4 & 3 & 2 \\ 0 & 1 & -1 \\ 0 & 0 & 7 \end{pmatrix},$$

$$C = \begin{pmatrix} 9 & -1 & 0 & 0 \\ 0 & 8 & -2 & 0 \\ 0 & 0 & 7 & -3 \\ 0 & 0 & 0 & 6 \end{pmatrix}, \qquad D = \begin{pmatrix} 1 & 0 & 0 \\ \frac{1}{3} & 4 & 0 \\ \frac{1}{2} & 3 & 2 \end{pmatrix}.$$

$$[\textit{Partial Ans. } A^{-1} = \begin{pmatrix} 1 & 0 & 0 \\ -13 & 1 & -5 \\ 2 & 0 & 1 \end{pmatrix}; \qquad D^{-1} = \begin{pmatrix} 1 & 0 & 0 \\ -\frac{1}{12} & \frac{1}{4} & 0 \\ -\frac{1}{8} & -\frac{3}{8} & \frac{1}{2} \end{pmatrix}.]$$

2. Show that each of the following matrices fails to have an inverse.

$$A = \begin{pmatrix} 1 & 2 & 3 \\ -1 & 1 & 0 \\ 0 & 3 & 3 \end{pmatrix}, \qquad B = \begin{pmatrix} 1 & 1 & 0 \\ 2 & 0 & 5 \\ -1 & 1 & -5 \end{pmatrix},$$

$$C = \begin{pmatrix} 1 & 1 & 2 & 3 \\ 0 & 5 & 4 & 2 \\ -1 & -3 & 1 & 0 \\ 0 & 3 & 7 & 5 \end{pmatrix}, \qquad D = \begin{pmatrix} 1 & 1 & 1 \\ 1 & 1 & 1 \\ 1 & 1 & 1 \end{pmatrix}.$$

3. Let A, B, and D be the matrices of Exercise 1; let

$$x = \begin{pmatrix} x_1 \\ x_2 \\ x_3 \end{pmatrix} \quad \text{and} \quad w = (w_1, w_2, w_3);$$

let b, c, d, e, and f be the following vectors.

$$b = \begin{pmatrix} 3 \\ -1 \\ 0 \end{pmatrix}, \quad c = \begin{pmatrix} -1 \\ 2 \\ -3 \end{pmatrix}, \quad d = (3, 7, -2), \quad e = (1, 1, 1), \quad f = \begin{pmatrix} 1 \\ 1 \\ 1 \end{pmatrix}.$$

Use the inverses you computed in Exercise 1 to solve the following equations.

(a) $Ax = b$.	(b) $Bx = c$.	(c) $wD = e$.
(d) $wB = d$.	(e) $wA = e$.	(f) $Dx = f$.

[*Partial Ans.* (a) $x = \begin{pmatrix} 3 \\ -40 \\ 6 \end{pmatrix}$; (e) $w = (-10, 1, -4)$; (f) $x = \begin{pmatrix} 1 \\ \frac{1}{6} \\ 0 \end{pmatrix}$.]

4. Rework Exercise 7 of Section 5 by first writing the equations in the form $Ax = b$, and finding the inverse of A.

5. Solve the following problem by first inverting the matrix. (Assume $ad \neq bc$.) If a grinding machine is supplied with x pounds of meat and y pounds of scraps (meat scraps and fat) per day, then it will produce $ax + by$ pounds of ground meat and $cx + dy$ pounds of hamburger per day. In other words, its production vector is

$$\begin{pmatrix} a & b \\ c & d \end{pmatrix} \begin{pmatrix} x \\ y \end{pmatrix}.$$

What inputs are necessary in order to get 25 pounds of ground meat and 70 pounds of hamburger? In order to get 20 pounds of ground meat and 100 pounds of hamburger?

6. For each of the matrices A and D in Exercise 2 find a nonzero vector whose product with the given matrix is 0.

7. Show that if A has no inverse, then neither does any of its positive powers A^k.

8. The formula $(A^{-1})^{-1} = A$ states that if A has an inverse A^{-1}, then A^{-1} itself has an inverse, and this inverse is A. Prove both parts of this statement.

9. Expand the formula $(AB)^{-1} = B^{-1}A^{-1}$ into a two-part statement analogous to the one in the exercise above. Then prove both parts of your statement.

10. (a) Show that $(AB)^{-1} \neq A^{-1}B^{-1}$ for the matrices $A = \begin{pmatrix} 1 & 1 \\ 0 & 1 \end{pmatrix}$ and $B = \begin{pmatrix} 1 & 0 \\ 2 & 1 \end{pmatrix}$.

(b) Find $(AB)^{-1}$ in two different ways. [*Hint:* Use Exercise 9.]

11. Give a criterion for deciding whether the 2×2 matrix $\begin{pmatrix} a & b \\ c & d \end{pmatrix}$ has an inverse.   [*Ans. $ad \neq bc$.*]

12. Give a formula for $\begin{pmatrix} a & b \\ c & d \end{pmatrix}^{-1}$, when it exists.

13. If $\begin{pmatrix} a & b \\ c & d \end{pmatrix}$ has an inverse and has integer components, what condition must it fulfill in order that $\begin{pmatrix} a & b \\ c & d \end{pmatrix}^{-1}$ have integer components?

SUPPLEMENTARY EXERCISES

14. Let A be the matrix $\begin{pmatrix} 2 & -5 \\ -1 & 3 \end{pmatrix}$.

(a) Find A^{-1}.

(b) Use the result of (a) to solve the matrix equation $A^2x = b$, where

$$x = \begin{pmatrix} x_1 \\ x_2 \end{pmatrix} \quad \text{and} \quad b = \begin{pmatrix} -1 \\ 2 \end{pmatrix}$$

[*Ans. $x = \begin{pmatrix} 36 \\ 13 \end{pmatrix}$.*]

15. Let A be a square matrix that has an inverse. Show that the inverse of A^2 is $(A^{-1})^2$. What is the inverse of A^n?

Note: The remaining exercises refer to the problem of computing $(I - Q)^{-1}$ where Q is a lower triangular matrix.

16. A matrix is *lower triangular* if it has zeros on and above its main diagonal. For instance,

$$Q = \begin{pmatrix} 0 & 0 & 0 \\ 4 & 0 & 0 \\ 10 & 5 & 0 \end{pmatrix}$$

is lower triangular.

(a) Compute Q^2, saving the result for later exercises.

(b) Show that $Q^3 = 0$, and also that $Q^k = 0$ for $k \geq 3$.

17. Consider the equation $w = wQ + d$ where Q is as in Exercise 16, and

$$w = (w_1, w_2, w_3), \qquad d = (20, 5, 3).$$

Solve symbolically for w.   [*Ans.* $w = d(I - Q)^{-1}$.]

18. (a) Establish the identity

$$(I - Q)(I + Q + Q^2) = I - Q^3 = I$$

where Q is as in Exercise 16.

(b) Show from (a) that $(I - Q)^{-1} = I + Q + Q^2$.

(c) Use (b) to compute $(I - Q)^{-1}$.

$$\left[\text{Ans.}\ (I - Q)^{-1} = \begin{pmatrix} 1 & 0 & 0 \\ 4 & 1 & 0 \\ 30 & 5 & 1 \end{pmatrix} . \right]$$

(d) Use (c) to solve for the w of Exercise 17.   [*Ans.* $w = (130, 20, 3)$.]

19. Let Q be any $n \times n$ lower triangular matrix.

(a) Show that $Q^k = 0$ for $k \geq n$.

(b) Show that $(I - Q)(I + Q + \ldots + Q^{n-1}) = I - Q^n = I$.

(c) Show that $(I - Q)^{-1} = I + Q + \ldots + Q^{n-1}$.

20. Find $(I - Q)^{-1}$ for Q being each of the following.

(a) $\begin{pmatrix} 0 & 0 & 0 & 0 \\ 7 & 0 & 0 & 0 \\ 2 & 0 & 0 & 0 \\ 3 & 4 & 5 & 0 \end{pmatrix}.$ (b) $\begin{pmatrix} 0 & 0 & 0 & 0 & 0 \\ 2 & 0 & 0 & 0 & 0 \\ 5 & 3 & 0 & 0 & 0 \\ 0 & 1 & 8 & 0 & 0 \\ 10 & 5 & 0 & 3 & 0 \end{pmatrix}.$

$$\left[\text{Ans. (a)} \begin{pmatrix} 1 & 0 & 0 & 0 \\ 7 & 1 & 0 & 0 \\ 2 & 0 & 1 & 0 \\ 41 & 4 & 5 & 1 \end{pmatrix} . \right]$$

21. Use Exercise 19 to show that if Q is lower triangular and has non-negative *integer* entries, then so does the matrix $(I - Q)^{-1}$.

7.   APPLICATIONS OF MATRIX THEORY TO MARKOV CHAINS

In this section we shall show applications of matrix theory to Markov chains. For simplicity we shall confine our discussion to two-state and three-state Markov chains, but a similar procedure will work for any other Markov chain.

In Section 13 of Chapter IV, we noted that to each Markov chain there was a matrix of transition probabilities. For instance, if there are three states, a_1, a_2, and a_3, then

$$P = \begin{array}{c} \\ a_1 \\ a_2 \\ a_3 \end{array} \begin{array}{ccc} a_1 & a_2 & a_3 \\ \begin{pmatrix} p_{11} & p_{12} & p_{13} \\ p_{21} & p_{22} & p_{23} \\ p_{31} & p_{32} & p_{33} \end{pmatrix} \end{array}$$

is the transition matrix for the chain. Recall that the *row sums* of P are all equal to 1. Such a matrix is called a transition matrix.

DEFINITION. A *transition matrix* is a square matrix with nonnegative entries such that the sum of the entries in each row is 1.

In order to obtain a Markov chain we must specify how the process starts. Suppose that the initial state is chosen by a chance device that selects state a_j with probability $p_j^{(0)}$. We can represent these initial probabilities by means of the vector $p^{(0)} = (p_1^{(0)}, p_2^{(0)}, p_3^{(0)})$. As in Exercise 10 of Section 4, we can construct a tree measure for as many steps of the process as we wish to consider. Let $p_j^{(n)}$ be the probability that the process will be in state a_j after n steps. Let the vector of these probabilities be $p^{(n)} = (p_1^{(n)}, p_2^{(n)}, p_3^{(n)})$.

DEFINITION. A row vector p is called a *probability vector* if it has nonnegative components whose sum is 1.

Obviously the vectors $p^{(0)}$ and $p^{(n)}$ are probability vectors. Also each row of a transition matrix is a probability vector.

By means of the tree measure it can be shown that these probabilities satisfy the following equations.

$$p_1^{(n)} = p_1^{(n-1)}p_{11} + p_2^{(n-1)}p_{21} + p_3^{(n-1)}p_{31}$$
$$p_2^{(n)} = p_1^{(n-1)}p_{12} + p_2^{(n-1)}p_{22} + p_3^{(n-1)}p_{32}$$
$$p_3^{(n)} = p_1^{(n-1)}p_{13} + p_2^{(n-1)}p_{23} + p_3^{(n-1)}p_{33}.$$

It is not hard to give intuitive meanings to these equations. The first one, for example, expresses the fact that the probability of being in state a_1 after n steps is the sum of the probabilities of being at each of the three possible states after $n - 1$ steps and then moving to state a_1 on the nth step. The interpretation of the other equations is similar.

If we recall the definition of the product of a vector times a matrix we can write the above equations as

$$p^{(n)} = p^{(n-1)}P.$$

If we substitute values of n we get the equations $p^{(1)} = p^{(0)}P$, $p^{(2)} = p^{(1)}P = p^{(0)}P^2$, $p^{(3)} = p^{(2)}P = p^{(0)}P^3$, etc. In general, it can be seen that

$$p^{(n)} = p^{(0)}P^n.$$

Thus we see that, if we multiply the vector $p^{(0)}$ of initial probabilities by the nth power of the transition matrix P, we obtain the vector $p^{(n)}$, whose components give the probabilities of being in each of the states after n steps.

In particular, let us choose $p^{(0)} = (1, 0, 0)$ which is equivalent to letting the process start in state a_1. From the equation above we see that then $p^{(n)}$ is the first row of the matrix P^n. Thus the elements of the first row of the matrix P^n give us the probabilities that after n steps the process will be in a given one of the states, under the assumption that it started in state a_1. In the same way, if we choose $p^{(0)} = (0, 1, 0)$, we see that the second row of P^n gives the probabilities that the process will be in one of the various states after n steps, given that it started in state a_2. Similarly, the third row gives these probabilities, assuming that the process started in state a_3.

In Section 13 of Chapter IV, we considered special Markov chains that started in given fixed states. There we arrived at a matrix $P^{(n)}$ whose ith row gave the probabilities of the process ending in the various states, given that it started at state a_j. By comparing the work that we did there with what we have just done, we see that the matrix $P^{(n)}$ is merely the nth power of P, that is, $P^{(n)} = P^n$. (Compare Exercise 10 of Section 4.) Matrix multiplication thus gives a convenient way of computing the desired probabilities.

DEFINITION. The probability vector w is a *fixed point* of the matrix P, if $w = wP$.

Example 1. Consider the transition matrix

$$P = \begin{pmatrix} \frac{2}{3} & \frac{1}{3} \\ \frac{1}{2} & \frac{1}{2} \end{pmatrix} = \begin{pmatrix} .667 & .333 \\ .500 & .500 \end{pmatrix}.$$

If $w = (.6, .4)$, then we see that

$$wP = (.6, .4) \begin{pmatrix} \frac{2}{3} & \frac{1}{3} \\ \frac{1}{2} & \frac{1}{2} \end{pmatrix} = (.6, .4) = w,$$

so that w is a fixed point of the matrix P.

If we had happened to choose the vector w as our initial probability vector $p^{(0)}$, we would have had $p^{(n)} = p^{(0)}P^n = wP^n = w = p^{(0)}$. In this case the probability of being at any particular state is the same at all steps of the process. Such a process is in *equilibrium*.

As seen above, in the study of Markov chains we are interested in the powers of the matrix P. To see what happens to these powers, let us further consider the example.

Example 1 (continued). Suppose that we compute powers of the matrix P in the example above. We have

$$P^2 = \begin{pmatrix} .611 & .389 \\ .583 & .417 \end{pmatrix}, \qquad P^3 = \begin{pmatrix} .602 & .398 \\ .597 & .403 \end{pmatrix}, \qquad \text{etc.}$$

It looks as if the matrix P^n is approaching the matrix

$$W = \begin{pmatrix} .6 & .4 \\ .6 & .4 \end{pmatrix}$$

and, in fact, it can be shown that this is the case. (When we say that P^n approaches W, we mean that each entry in the matrix P^n gets close to the corresponding entry in W.) Note that each row of W is a fixed point w of the matrix P.

DEFINITION. A transition matrix is said to be *regular* if some power of the matrix has only positive components.

Thus the matrix in the example is regular, since every entry in it is positive, so that the first power of the matrix has all positive entries. Other examples occur in the exercises.

Theorem. If P is a regular transition matrix, then
(a)   The powers P^n approach a matrix W.
(b)   Each row of W is the same probability vector w.
(c)   The components of w are positive.

We omit the proof of this theorem;* however, we can prove the next theorem.

Theorem. If P is a regular transition matrix, and W and w are given by the previous theorem, then

(a)   If p is any probability vector, pP^n approaches w.

(b)   The vector w is the unique fixed point probability vector of P.

Proof. First let us consider the vector pW. The first column of W has a w_1 in each row. Hence in the first component of pW each component of p is multiplied by w_1, and therefore we have w_1 times the sum of the components of p, which is w_1. Doing the same for the other components, we note that pW is simply w. But pP^n approaches pW; hence it approaches w. Thus if any probability vector is multiplied repeatedly by P, it approaches the vector w. This proves part (a).

Since the powers of P approach W, $P^{n+1} = P^nP$ approaches W, but it also approaches WP; hence $WP = W$. Any one row of this matrix equation states that $wP = w$; hence w is a fixed point (and by the previous theorem, a probability vector). We must still show that it is unique. Let u be any probability vector fixed point of P. By part (a) we know that uP^n approaches w. But since u is a fixed point, $uP^n = u$. Hence u remains fixed but "approaches" w. This is possible only if $u = w$. Hence w is the only probability vector fixed point. This completes the proof of part (b).

The following is an important consequence of this theorem. If we take as p the vector $p^{(0)}$ of initial probabilities, then the vector $pP^n = p^{(n)}$ gives the probabilities after n steps, and this vector approaches w. Therefore, no matter what the initial probabilities are, if P is regular, then after a large number of steps the probability that the process is in state a_j will be very nearly w_j. Hence the Markov chain approaches equilibrium.

We noted for an independent trials process that if p is the probability of a given outcome d, then this may be given an alternate interpretation by means of the law of large numbers: In a long series of experiments the fraction of outcomes in which a occurs is approximately p, and the

---

* For an elementary proof see Kemeny, Mirkil, Snell, and Thompson, *Finite Mathematical Structures* (Englewood Cliffs, N.J.: Prentice-Hall, Inc., 1959) Chapter 6, Section 3.

approximation gets better and better as the number of experiments increases. For a regular Markov chain it is the components of the vector w that play the analogous role. That is, the fraction of times that the chain is in state a_i approaches w_i, no matter how the process is started.

Example 1 (continued). Let us take $p^{(0)} = (.1, .9)$ and see how $p^{(n)}$ changes. Using P as in the example above, we have that $p^{(1)} = (.5167, .4833)$, $p^{(2)} = (.5861, .4139)$, and $p^{(3)} = (.5977, .4023)$. Recalling that $w = (.6, .4)$, we see that these vectors do approach w.

Example 2. As an example, let us derive the formulas for the fixed point of a 2×2 transition matrix with positive components. Such a matrix is of the form

$$S = \begin{pmatrix} 1 - a & a \\ b & 1 - b \end{pmatrix},$$

where $0 < a < 1$ and $0 < b < 1$. Since S is regular, it has a unique probability vector fixed point $w = (w_1, w_2)$. Its components must satisfy the equations

$$w_1(1 - a) + w_2 b = w_1$$
$$w_1 a + w_2(1 - b) = w_2.$$

Each of these equations reduces to the single equation $w_1 a = w_2 b$. This single equation has an infinite number of solutions. However, since w is a probability vector, we must also have $w_1 + w_2 = 1$, and the new equation gives the point $[b/(a + b), a/(a + b)]$ as the unique fixed-point probability vector of S.

Example 3. Suppose that the President of the United States tells person A his intention either to run or not to run in the next election. Then A relays the news to B, who in turn relays the message to C, etc., always to some new person. Assume that there is a probability $p > 0$ that any one person, when he gets the message, will reverse it before passing it on to the next person. What is the probability that the nth man to hear the message will be told that the President will run? We can consider this as a two-state Markov chain, with states indicated by "yes" and "no." The process is in state "yes" at time n if the nth person to receive the message was told that the President would run. It is in state "no" if he was told that the President would not run. The matrix P of transition probabilities is then

$$\begin{array}{c} \phantom{\text{yes}} \quad \text{yes} \quad\ \text{no} \\ \begin{array}{c} \text{yes} \\ \text{no} \end{array} \begin{pmatrix} 1 - p & p \\ p & 1 - p \end{pmatrix}. \end{array}$$

Then the matrix P^n gives the probabilities that the nth man is given a certain answer, assuming that the President said "yes" (first row) or assuming that the President said "no" (second row). We know that these rows approach w. From the formulas of the last section, we find that $w = (\frac{1}{2}, \frac{1}{2})$. Hence the probabilities for the nth man being told "yes" or "no" approach $\frac{1}{2}$ independently of the initial decision of the President. For a large number of people, we can expect that approximately one-half will be told that the President will run and the other half that he will not, independently of the actual decision of the President.

Suppose now that the probability a that a person will change the news from "yes" to "no" when transmitting it to the next person is different from the probability b that he will change it from "no" to "yes." Then the matrix of transition probabilities becomes

$$\begin{array}{c} \phantom{\text{yes}} \quad \text{yes} \quad\ \text{no} \\ \begin{array}{c} \text{yes} \\ \text{no} \end{array} \begin{pmatrix} 1 - a & a \\ b & 1 - b \end{pmatrix}. \end{array}$$

In this case $w = [b/(a + b), a/(a + b)]$. Thus there is a probability of approximately $b/(a + b)$ that the nth person will be told that the President will run. Assuming that n is large, this probability is independent of the actual decision of the President. For n large we can expect, in this case, that a proportion approximately equal to $b/(a + b)$ will have been told that the President will run, and a proportion $a/(a + b)$ will have been told that he will not run. The important thing to note is that, from the assumptions we have made, it follows that it is not the President but the people themselves who determine the probability that a person will be told "yes" or "no," and the proportion of people in the long run that are given one of these predictions.

Example 4. For this example, we continue the study of Example 2 in Chapter IV, Section 13. The first approximation treated in that example leads to a two-state Markov chain, and the results are similar to those obtained in Example 1 above. The second approximation led to a four-state Markov chain with transition probabilities given by the matrix

$$
\begin{array}{c}
 \begin{array}{cccc} RR & DR & RD & DD \end{array} \\
\begin{array}{c} RR \\ DR \\ RD \\ DD \end{array}
\begin{pmatrix}
1-a & 0 & a & 0 \\
b & 0 & 1-b & 0 \\
0 & 1-c & 0 & c \\
0 & d & 0 & 1-d
\end{pmatrix}.
\end{array}
$$

If a, b, c, and d are all different from 0 or 1, then the square of the matrix has no zeros, and hence the matrix is regular. The fixed probability vector is found in the usual way (see Exercise 18) and is

$$
\left(\frac{bd}{bd + 2ad + ca}, \frac{ad}{bd + 2ad + ca}, \frac{ad}{bd + 2ad + ca}, \frac{ca}{bd + 2ad + ca} \right).
$$

Note that the probability of being in state DR after a large number of steps is equal to the probability of being in state RD. This shows that in equilibrium a change from R to D must have the same probability as a change from D to R.

From the fixed vector we can find the probability of being in state R in the far future. This is found by adding the probability of being in state RR and DR, giving

$$
\frac{bd + ad}{bd + 2ad + ca}.
$$

Notice that, to find the probability of being in state R on the election preceding some election far in the future, we should add the probabilities of being in states RR and RD. That we get the same result corresponds to the fact that predictions far in the future are essentially independent of the particular period being predicted. In other words, the process is acting as if it were in equilibrium.

EXERCISES

1. Which of the following matrices are regular?

(a) $\begin{pmatrix} \frac{1}{2} & \frac{1}{2} \\ \frac{1}{2} & \frac{1}{2} \end{pmatrix}$.

(b) $\begin{pmatrix} 0 & 1 \\ \frac{1}{4} & \frac{3}{4} \end{pmatrix}$.   [*Ans.* Regular.]

(c) $\begin{pmatrix} 1 & 0 \\ \frac{1}{3} & \frac{2}{3} \end{pmatrix}$.

(d) $\begin{pmatrix} \frac{1}{5} & \frac{4}{5} \\ 1 & 0 \end{pmatrix}$.   [*Ans.* Regular.]

(e) $\begin{pmatrix} \frac{1}{2} & \frac{1}{2} \\ 0 & 1 \end{pmatrix}$.

(f) $\begin{pmatrix} 0 & 1 \\ 1 & 0 \end{pmatrix}$.   [*Ans.* Not regular.]

(g) $\begin{pmatrix} \frac{1}{2} & \frac{1}{2} & 0 \\ 0 & \frac{1}{2} & \frac{1}{2} \\ \frac{1}{3} & \frac{1}{3} & \frac{1}{3} \end{pmatrix}$.

(h) $\begin{pmatrix} \frac{1}{3} & 0 & \frac{2}{3} \\ 0 & 1 & 0 \\ 0 & \frac{1}{5} & \frac{4}{5} \end{pmatrix}$.   [*Ans.* Not regular.]

2. Show that the 2×2 matrix

$$S = \begin{pmatrix} 1 - a & a \\ b & 1 - b \end{pmatrix}$$

is a regular transition matrix if and only if either
 (i) $0 < a \leq 1$ and $0 < b < 1$; or
 (ii) $0 < a < 1$ and $0 < b \leq 1$.

3. Find the fixed point for the matrix in Exercise 2 for each of the cases listed there. [*Hint:* Most of the cases were covered in the text above.]

4. Find the fixed point w for each of the following regular matrices.

 (a) $\begin{pmatrix} \frac{3}{4} & \frac{1}{4} \\ \frac{1}{2} & \frac{1}{2} \end{pmatrix}$.   [*Ans.* $w = (\frac{2}{3}, \frac{1}{3})$.]

 (b) $\begin{pmatrix} .9 & .1 \\ .1 & .9 \end{pmatrix}$.

 (c) $\begin{pmatrix} \frac{3}{4} & \frac{1}{4} & 0 \\ 0 & \frac{2}{3} & \frac{1}{3} \\ \frac{1}{4} & \frac{1}{4} & \frac{1}{2} \end{pmatrix}$.   [*Ans.* $w = (\frac{2}{7}, \frac{3}{7}, \frac{2}{7})$.]

5. Let $p^0 = (\frac{1}{2}, \frac{1}{2})$ and compute $p^{(1)}$, $p^{(2)}$, and $p^{(3)}$ for the matrices in Exercises 4(a) and 4(b). Do they approach the fixed points of these matrices?

6. Give a probability theory interpretation to the condition of regularity.

7. Consider the two-state Markov chain with transition matrix

$$P = \begin{matrix} & \begin{matrix} a_1 & a_2 \end{matrix} \\ \begin{matrix} a_1 \\ a_2 \end{matrix} & \begin{pmatrix} 0 & 1 \\ 1 & 0 \end{pmatrix} \end{matrix}.$$

What is the probability that after n steps the process is in state a_1, if it started in state a_2? Does this probability become independent of the initial position for large n? If not, the theorem of this section must not apply. Why? Does the matrix have a unique fixed point probability vector?

8. Prove that, if a regular 3×3 transition matrix has the property that its column sums are 1, its fixed point probability vector is $(\frac{1}{3}, \frac{1}{3}, \frac{1}{3})$. State a similar result for $n \times n$ transition matrices having column sums equal to 1.

9. Compute the first five powers of the matrix

$$P = \begin{pmatrix} .8 & .2 \\ .2 & .8 \end{pmatrix}.$$

From these, guess the fixed point vector w. Check by computing what w is.

10. Show that all transition matrices of the form

$$\begin{pmatrix} 1 - a & a \\ a & 1 - a \end{pmatrix},$$

where $0 < a < 1$, have the same unique fixed point.   [*Ans.* $w = (\frac{1}{2}, \frac{1}{2})$.]

11. A professor has three pet questions, one of which occurs on every test he gives. The students know his habits well. He never uses the same question twice in a row. If he used question one last time, he tosses a coin, and uses question two if a head comes up. If he used question two, he tosses two coins and switches to question three if both come up heads. If he used question three, he tosses three coins and switches to question one if all three come up heads. In the long run, which question does he use most often, and how frequently is it used?   [*Ans.* Question two, 40 per cent of the time.]

12. A professor tries not to be late for class too often. If he is late one day, he is 90 per cent sure to be on time next time. If he is on time, then the next day there is a 30 per cent chance of his being late. In the long run, how often is he late for class?

13. The Land of Oz is blessed by many things, but not good weather. They *never* have two nice days in a row. If they have a nice day they are just as likely to have snow as rain the next day. If they have snow (or rain), they have an even chance of having the same the next day. If there is a change from snow or rain, only half of the time is this a change to a nice day. Set up a three-state Markov chain to describe this situation. Find the long-range probability for rain, for snow, and for a nice day. What fraction of the days does it rain in the Land of Oz?

    [*Ans.* The probabilities are: nice, $\frac{1}{5}$; rain, $\frac{2}{5}$; snow, $\frac{2}{5}$.]

14. Let S be the matrix

$$S = \begin{pmatrix} 1 & 0 \\ \frac{1}{2} & \frac{1}{2} \end{pmatrix}.$$

Compute the unique probability vector fixed point of S, and use your result to prove that S is not regular.

15. Show that the matrix

$$S = \begin{pmatrix} 1 & 0 & 0 \\ \frac{1}{2} & 0 & \frac{1}{2} \\ 0 & 0 & 1 \end{pmatrix}$$

has more than one probability vector fixed point. Find the matrix that S^n approaches, and show that it is not a matrix all of whose rows are the same.

16. Let P be a transition matrix in which all the entries that are not zero have been replaced by x's. Devise a method of raising such a matrix to powers in order to check for regularity. Illustrate your method by showing that

$$P = \begin{pmatrix} 0 & 1 & 0 \\ 0 & 0 & 1 \\ \frac{1}{2} & \frac{1}{2} & 0 \end{pmatrix}$$

is regular.

17. Consider a Markov chain such that it is possible to go from any state a_i to any state a_j and such that p_{kk} is not 0 for at least one state a_k. Prove that the chain is regular. [*Hint:* Consider the times that it is possible to go from a_i to a_j via a_k.]

18. Show that the vector given in Example 4 is the fixed vector of the transition matrix.

SUPPLEMENTARY EXERCISES

19. Determine whether each of the following matrices is regular.

(a) $\begin{pmatrix} 0 & 1 \\ \frac{3}{4} & \frac{1}{4} \end{pmatrix}$.

(b) $\begin{pmatrix} \frac{1}{2} & 0 & \frac{1}{2} \\ 0 & 1 & 0 \\ \frac{1}{3} & \frac{1}{2} & \frac{1}{6} \end{pmatrix}$.

(c) $\begin{pmatrix} 0 & 0 & 1 \\ 0 & 1 & 0 \\ 1 & 0 & 0 \end{pmatrix}$.

(d) $\begin{pmatrix} 0 & 0 & 1 \\ \frac{1}{2} & 0 & \frac{1}{2} \\ \frac{1}{2} & \frac{1}{2} & 0 \end{pmatrix}$.

(e) $\begin{pmatrix} \frac{1}{2} & \frac{1}{2} & 0 & 0 \\ \frac{3}{4} & \frac{1}{2} & 0 & 0 \\ 0 & 0 & \frac{1}{3} & \frac{2}{3} \\ \frac{1}{4} & 0 & \frac{1}{4} & \frac{1}{2} \end{pmatrix}$.

(f) $\begin{pmatrix} 0 & \frac{1}{2} & \frac{1}{2} \\ 1 & 0 & 0 \\ 1 & 0 & 0 \end{pmatrix}$.

[*Ans.* (a) and (d) are regular.]

20. Consider the three-state Markov chain with transition matrix

$$P = \begin{pmatrix} \frac{1}{2} & \frac{1}{3} & \frac{1}{6} \\ \frac{1}{2} & \frac{1}{2} & 0 \\ \frac{1}{2} & \frac{1}{2} & 0 \end{pmatrix}.$$

(a) Show that the matrix has a unique fixed probability vector.

[*Ans.* $(\frac{1}{2}, \frac{5}{12}, \frac{1}{12})$.]

(b) Approximately what is the entry in the third column of the first row of P^{100}?

(c) What is the interpretation of the entry estimated in (b)?

21. Assume that it is known that of the sons of Harvard alumni, 80 per cent go to Harvard and all the rest go to Yale; of the sons of Yale men, 40 per cent go to Yale, the remainder split evenly between Harvard and Dartmouth; and of the sons of Dartmouth men, 70 per cent go to Dartmouth, 20 per cent to Harvard, and 10 per cent to Yale.

(a) Set up this process as a Markov chain.

(b) What is the probability that the grandson of a Harvard man goes to Harvard?

(c) What is the long run fraction expected in each school?

[*Ans.* (b) .7; (c) (Harvard, $\frac{5}{9}$; Yale, $\frac{2}{9}$; Dartmouth, $\frac{2}{9}$.)]

22. A carnival man moves a pea among three shells, A, B, and C. Whenever the pea is under A, he moves it with equal probability to A or B. When it is under B, he is sure to move it to C. When it is under C, he is sure to put it next time under C or B, but is twice as likely to put it under C as B.

Set up a Markov chain taking as states the letters of the shells under which the pea appears after a move. Give the matrix of transition probabilities. Assume that the pea is initially under shell A. Which of the following statements are logically true?

    (a) After the first move, the pea is under A or B.

    (b) After the second move, the pea is under shell B or C.

    (c) If the pea appears under B, it will eventually appear under A again if the process goes on long enough.

    (d) If the pea appears under C, it will not appear under A again.

                         [*Ans.* (a) and (d) are logically true.]

23. A certain company decides each year to add a new workers to its payroll, to remove b workers from its payroll, or to leave its workforce unchanged. There is probability $\frac{3}{4}$ that the action taken in the given year will be the *same* as the action taken in the previous year. The president of the company has ruled that they should never fire workers the year after they added some, and that they should never hire workers the year after they fired some. Moreover, if no workers were added or fired in the previous year, the company is twice as likely to add workers as to fire them.

    (a) Set up the problem as a Markov chain with three states.

    (b) Show that it is regular.

    (c) Find the long run probability of each type of action.

    (d) For what values of a and b will the company tend to increase in size? To decrease? To stay the same?

    [*Ans.* (c) Increase, $\frac{1}{3}$; decrease, $\frac{1}{6}$; same, $\frac{1}{2}$. (d) $a > b/2$; $a < b/2$; $a = b/2$.]

8. ABSORBING MARKOV CHAINS

In this section we shall consider a kind of Markov chain quite different from regular chains.

DEFINITION. A state in a Markov chain is an *absorbing state* if it is impossible to leave it. A Markov chain is *absorbing* if (1) it has at least one absorbing state, and (2) from every state it is possible to go to an absorbing state (not necessarily in one step).

Example 1. A particle moves on a line; each time it moves one unit to the right with probability $\frac{1}{2}$, or one unit to the left. We introduce barriers so that if it ever reaches one of these barriers it stays there. As a simple example, let the states be 0, 1, 2, 3, 4. States 0 and 4 are absorbing states. The transition matrix is, then,

$$P = \begin{array}{c} \\ 0 \\ 1 \\ 2 \\ 3 \\ 4 \end{array} \begin{array}{c} \begin{array}{ccccc} 0 & 1 & 2 & 3 & 4 \end{array} \\ \begin{pmatrix} 1 & 0 & 0 & 0 & 0 \\ \frac{1}{2} & 0 & \frac{1}{2} & 0 & 0 \\ 0 & \frac{1}{2} & 0 & \frac{1}{2} & 0 \\ 0 & 0 & \frac{1}{2} & 0 & \frac{1}{2} \\ 0 & 0 & 0 & 0 & 1 \end{pmatrix} \end{array}.$$

The states 1, 2, 3 are all nonabsorbing states, and from any of these it is possible to reach the absorbing states 0 and 4. Hence the chain is an absorbing chain. Such a process is usually called a *random walk*.

When a process reaches an absorbing state we shall say that it is *absorbed*.

Theorem. In an absorbing Markov chain the probability that the process will be absorbed is 1.

We shall indicate only the basic idea of the proof of the theorem. From each nonabsorbing state, a_j, it is possible to reach an absorbing state. Let n_j be the minimum number of steps required to reach an absorbing state, starting from state a_j. Let p_j be the probability that, starting from state a_j, the process will *not* reach an absorbing state in n_j steps. Then $p_j < 1$. Let n be the largest of the n_j and let p be the largest of the p_j. The probability of not being absorbed in n steps is less than p, in $2n$ steps is less than p^2, etc. Since $p < 1$, these probabilities tend to zero.

For an absorbing Markov chain we consider three interesting questions: (a) What is the probability that the process will end up in a given absorbing state? (b) On the average, how long will it take for the process to be absorbed? (c) On the average, how many times will the process be in each nonabsorbing state? The answer to all these questions depends, in general, on the state from which the process starts.

Consider then an arbitrary absorbing Markov chain. Let us renumber the states so that the absorbing states come first. If there are

r absorbing states and s nonabsorbing states, the transition matrix will have the following *canonical* (or standard) *form.*

$$r \text{ states} \qquad s \text{ states}$$

(1)
$$P = \begin{array}{c} r \\ s \end{array} \left(\begin{array}{c|c} I & O \\ \hline R & Q \end{array} \right).$$

Here I is an r-by-r identity matrix, O is an r-by-s zero matrix, R is an s-by-r matrix, and Q is an s-by-s matrix. The first r states are absorbing and the last s states are nonabsorbing.

In Section 7 we saw that the entries of the matrix P^n gave the probabilities of being in the various states starting from the various states. It is easy to show that P^n is of the form

(2)
$$P^n = \begin{pmatrix} I & O \\ * & Q^n \end{pmatrix},$$

where the asterisk * stands for the s-by-r matrix in the lower left-hand corner of P^n, which we do not compute here. The form of P^n shows that the entries of Q^n give the probabilities for being in each of the nonabsorbing states after n steps for each possible nonabsorbing starting state. (After zero steps the process must be in the same nonabsorbing state in which it started. Hence $Q^0 = I$.) By our first theorem, the probability of being in the nonabsorbing states after n steps approaches zero. Thus every entry of Q^n must approach zero as n approaches infinity, i.e., $Q^n \to 0$.

From the fact that $Q^n \to 0$ it can be shown that the matrix $(I - Q)^{-1}$ exists.* The matrix $(I - Q)^{-1}$ will be called the *fundamental matrix* of the absorbing chain. It has the following important interpretation.

Let n_{ij} be the expected number of times that the chain is in state a_j if it starts in state a_i, for two nonabsorbing states a_i and a_j. Let N be the matrix whose components are n_{ij}. If we take into account the contribution of the original state (which is 1 if $i = j$ and 0 otherwise), we may write the equation

$$n_{ij} = d_{ij} + (p_{i,r+1}n_{r+1,j} + p_{i,r+2}n_{r+2,j} + \ldots + p_{i,r+s}n_{r+s,j}),$$

where d_{ij} is 1 if $i = j$ and 0 otherwise. (Note that the sum in parentheses is merely the sum of the products $p_{ik}n_{kj}$ for k running over the

---

* For a proof see Kemeny, Mirkil, Snell, and Thompson, *Finite Mathematical Structures* (Englewood Cliffs, N.J.: Prentice-Hall, Inc., 1959) Chapter 6, Section 3.

nonabsorbing states.) This equation may be written in matrix form:

$$N = I + QN.$$

Thus $(I - Q)N = I$, and hence $N = (I - Q)^{-1}$, as was to be shown. Thus we have found a probabilistic interpretation for our fundamental matrix: its i,jth entry is the expected number of times that the chain is in state a_j if it starts at a_i. We have answered question (c) as follows.

Theorem. Let $N = (I - Q)^{-1}$ be the fundamental matrix for an absorbing chain. Then the entries of N give the expected number of times in each nonabsorbing state for each possible nonabsorbing starting state.

Example 1 (continued). In Example 1 the transition matrix in canonical form is

$$\begin{array}{c c}
 & \begin{array}{ccccc} 0 & 4 & 1 & 2 & 3 \end{array} \\
\begin{array}{c} 0 \\ 4 \\ \\ 1 \\ 2 \\ 3 \end{array} &
\left(\begin{array}{cc|ccc}
1 & 0 & 0 & 0 & 0 \\
0 & 1 & 0 & 0 & 0 \\
\hline
\frac{1}{2} & 0 & 0 & \frac{1}{2} & 0 \\
0 & 0 & \frac{1}{2} & 0 & \frac{1}{2} \\
0 & \frac{1}{2} & 0 & \frac{1}{2} & 0
\end{array}\right).
\end{array}$$

From this we see that the matrix Q is

$$Q = \begin{pmatrix} 0 & \frac{1}{2} & 0 \\ \frac{1}{2} & 0 & \frac{1}{2} \\ 0 & \frac{1}{2} & 0 \end{pmatrix}$$

and

$$I - Q = \begin{pmatrix} 1 & -\frac{1}{2} & 0 \\ -\frac{1}{2} & 1 & -\frac{1}{2} \\ 0 & -\frac{1}{2} & 1 \end{pmatrix}.$$

Computing $(I - Q)^{-1}$, we find

$$N = (I - Q)^{-1} = \begin{array}{c} 1 \\ 2 \\ 3 \end{array}
\begin{pmatrix} \frac{3}{2} & 1 & \frac{1}{2} \\ 1 & 2 & 1 \\ \frac{1}{2} & 1 & \frac{3}{2} \end{pmatrix}.$$

Thus, starting at state 2, the expected number of times in state 1 before absorption is 1, in state 2 it is 2, and in state 3 it is 1.

We next answer question (b). If we add all the entries in a row, we will have the expected number of times in any of the nonabsorbing states for a given starting state, that is, the expected time required before being absorbed. This may be described as follows:

Theorem. Consider an absorbing Markov chain with s nonabsorbing states. Let c be an s-component column vector with all entries 1. Then the vector $t = Nc$ has as components the expected number of steps before being absorbed, for each possible nonabsorbing starting state.

Example 1 (continued). For Example 1 we have

$$
t = Nc = \begin{matrix} 1 \\ 2 \\ 3 \end{matrix} \begin{pmatrix} \frac{3}{2} & 1 & \frac{1}{2} \\ 1 & 2 & 1 \\ \frac{1}{2} & 1 & \frac{3}{2} \end{pmatrix} \begin{pmatrix} 1 \\ 1 \\ 1 \end{pmatrix}
$$

$$
= \begin{matrix} 1 \\ 2 \\ 3 \end{matrix} \begin{pmatrix} 3 \\ 4 \\ 3 \end{pmatrix}.
$$

Thus the expected number of steps to absorption starting at state 1 is 3, starting at state 2 it is 4, and starting at state 3 it is again 3. Since the process necessarily moves to 1 or 3 from 2 it is clear that it requires one more step starting from 2 than from 1 or 3.

We now consider question (a). That is, what is the probability that an absorbing chain will end up in a particular absorbing state? It is clear that this probability will depend upon the starting state and be interesting only for the case of a nonabsorbing starting state. We write, as usual, our matrix in the canonical form

$$
P = \left(\begin{array}{c|c} I & O \\ \hline R & Q \end{array} \right).
$$

Theorem. Let b_{ij} be the probability that an absorbing chain will be absorbed in state a_j if it starts in the nonabsorbing state a_i. Let B be the matrix with entries b_{ij}. Then

$$
B = NR,
$$

where N is the fundamental matrix and R is as in the canonical form.

Proof. Let a_i be a nonabsorbing state and a_j be an absorbing state. State a_j can be reached either by stepping into it on the first step, or by going to a nonabsorbing state a_k and from there eventually reaching a_j. Hence, if we compute b_{ij} in terms of the possibilities on the outcome of the first step, we have the equation

$$b_{ij} = p_{ij} + \sum_k p_{ik}b_{kj},$$

where the summation is carried out over all nonabsorbing states a_k. Writing this in matrix form gives

$$B = R + QB$$

$$(I - Q)B = R$$

and hence $\qquad B = (I - Q)^{-1}R = NR.$

Example 1 (continued). In the random walk example we found that

$$N = \begin{pmatrix} \frac{3}{2} & 1 & \frac{1}{2} \\ 1 & 2 & 1 \\ \frac{1}{2} & 1 & \frac{3}{2} \end{pmatrix}.$$

From the canonical form we find that

$$R = \begin{pmatrix} \frac{1}{2} & 0 \\ 0 & 0 \\ 0 & \frac{1}{2} \end{pmatrix}.$$

Hence

$$B = NR = \begin{pmatrix} \frac{3}{2} & 1 & \frac{1}{2} \\ 1 & 2 & 1 \\ \frac{1}{2} & 1 & \frac{3}{2} \end{pmatrix} \begin{pmatrix} \frac{1}{2} & 0 \\ 0 & 0 \\ 0 & \frac{1}{2} \end{pmatrix} = \begin{matrix} 1 \\ 2 \\ 3 \end{matrix} \begin{pmatrix} \frac{3}{4} & \frac{1}{4} \\ \frac{1}{2} & \frac{1}{2} \\ \frac{1}{4} & \frac{3}{4} \end{pmatrix}.$$

Thus, for instance, starting from a_1, there is probability $\frac{3}{4}$ of absorption in a_0 and $\frac{1}{4}$ for absorption in a_4.

Let us summarize our results. We have shown that the answers to questions (a), (b), and (c) can all be given in terms of the fundamental matrix $N = (I - Q)^{-1}$ The matrix N itself gives us the expected number of times in each state before absorption, depending upon the starting state. The column vector $t = Nc$ gives us the expected number of steps before absorption, depending upon the starting state. The matrix $B = NR$ gives us the probability of absorption in each of the absorbing states, depending upon the starting state.

EXERCISES

1. Which of the following transition matrices are from absorbing chains?

(a) $P = \begin{pmatrix} 1 & 0 \\ \frac{1}{2} & \frac{1}{2} \end{pmatrix}$.

(b) $P = \begin{pmatrix} 1 & 0 & 0 \\ 0 & \frac{1}{2} & \frac{1}{2} \\ 0 & \frac{1}{3} & \frac{2}{3} \end{pmatrix}$.

(c) $P = \begin{pmatrix} 1 & 0 & 0 & 0 & 0 \\ 0 & \frac{1}{2} & 0 & \frac{1}{2} & 0 \\ \frac{1}{5} & \frac{1}{5} & \frac{1}{5} & \frac{1}{5} & \frac{1}{5} \\ 0 & \frac{1}{3} & 0 & \frac{2}{3} & 0 \\ 0 & 0 & 0 & 0 & 1 \end{pmatrix}$.

(d) $P = \begin{pmatrix} 1 & 0 & 0 & 0 \\ \frac{1}{2} & 0 & 0 & \frac{1}{2} \\ \frac{1}{4} & \frac{1}{4} & \frac{1}{4} & \frac{1}{4} \\ 0 & 0 & 0 & 1 \end{pmatrix}$.

[*Ans.* (a) and (d).]

2. Consider the two-state transition matrix

$$P = \begin{pmatrix} 1 - a & a \\ b & 1 - b \end{pmatrix}.$$

For what choices of a and b do we obtain an absorbing chain?

3. In the random walk example (Example 1) of the present section, assume that the probability of a step to the right is $\frac{2}{3}$ and a step to the left is $\frac{1}{3}$. Find N, t, and B. Compare these with the results for probability $\frac{1}{2}$ for a step to the right and $\frac{1}{2}$ for a step to the left.

4. In the Land of Oz example (see Exercise 13, Section 7) let us change the transition matrix by making R an absorbing state. This gives

$$\begin{array}{c} \\ R \\ N \\ S \end{array} \begin{array}{ccc} R & N & S \\ \begin{pmatrix} 1 & 0 & 0 \\ \frac{1}{2} & 0 & \frac{1}{2} \\ \frac{1}{4} & \frac{1}{4} & \frac{1}{2} \end{pmatrix} \end{array}.$$

Find the fundamental matrix N, and also t and B. What is the interpretation of these quantities?

5. An analysis of a recent hockey game between Dartmouth and Princeton showed the following facts: If the puck was in the center (C) the probabilities that it next entered Princeton territory (P) or Dartmouth territory (D) were .4 and .6, respectively. From D it went back to C with probability .95 or into the Dartmouth goal ($\bar{D}$) with probability .05 (Princeton scores one point). From P it next went to C with probability .9 and to Princeton's goal ($\bar{P}$) with probability .1 (Dartmouth scores one point). Assuming that the puck begins in C after each point, find the transition matrix of this five-state Markov chain. Calculate the probability that Dartmouth will score.

[*Ans.* $\frac{4}{7}$.]

6. A number is chosen at random from the integers 1, 2, 3, 4, 5. If x is chosen, then another number is chosen from the set of integers less than or equal to x. This process is continued until the number 1 is chosen. Form a Markov chain by taking as states the largest number that can be chosen. Show that

$$N = \begin{array}{c} \\ 2 \\ 3 \\ 4 \\ 5 \end{array} \begin{array}{cccc} 2 & 3 & 4 & 5 \\ \left(\begin{array}{cccc} 1 & 0 & 0 & 0 \\ 1 & \frac{1}{2} & 0 & 0 \\ 1 & \frac{1}{2} & \frac{1}{3} & 0 \\ 1 & \frac{1}{2} & \frac{1}{3} & \frac{1}{4} \end{array} \right) \end{array} + I,$$

where I is the 4×4 identity matrix. What is the expected number of draws? [*Ans.* $\frac{37}{12}$.]

7. Using the result of Exercise 6, make a conjecture for the form of the fundamental matrix if we start with integers from 1 to n. What would the expected number of draws be if we started with numbers from 1 to 10?

8. Three tanks fight a three-way duel. Tank A has probability $\frac{1}{2}$ of destroying the tank it fires at. Tank B has probability $\frac{1}{3}$ of destroying its target tank, and Tank C has probability $\frac{1}{6}$ of destroying its target tank. The tanks fire together and each tank fires at the strongest opponent not yet destroyed. Form a Markov chain by taking as state the tanks which survive any one round. Find N, t, B, and interpret your results.

9. The following is an alternative method of finding the probability of absorption in a particular absorbing state, say a_j. Find the column vector d such that the jth component of d is 1, all other components corresponding to absorbing states are 0, and $Pd = d$. There is only one such vector. Component d_i is the probability of absorption in a_j if the process starts in a_i. Use this method to find the probability of absorption in state 1 in the random walk example given in this section.

10. The following is an alternative method for finding the expected number of steps to absorption. Let t_i be the expected number of steps to absorption starting at state a_i. This must be the same as taking one more step and then adding $p_{ij}t_j$ for every nonabsorbing state a_j.

(a) Give reasons for the above claim that

$$t_i = 1 + \sum_j p_{ij}t_j,$$

where the summation is over the nonabsorbing states.

(b) Solve for t for the random walk example.

(c) Verify that the solution agrees with that found in the text.

SUPPLEMENTARY EXERCISES

11. Peter and Paul are matching pennies, and each player flips his (fair) coin before revealing it. They initially have three pennies between them and the game ends whenever one of them has all the pennies. Let the states be labelled with the number of pennies that Peter has.
    (a) Write the transition matrix.
    (b) What kind of a Markov chain is it?
    (c) If Peter initially has two pennies, what is the probability that he will win the game?

12. Peter and Paul are matching pennies as in Exercise 11, except that whenever one of the players gets all three pennies, he returns one to his opponent, and the game continues.
    (a) Set up the transition matrix.
    (b) Identify the kind of Markov chain that results. [*Ans.* Not regular.]
    (c) Find the long run probabilities of being in each of the states.

13. Peter and Paul are matching pennies as in Exercise 11, except that if Peter gets all the pennies, the game is over, while if Paul gets all the pennies, he gives one back to Peter, and the game continues.
    (a) Set up the transition matrix.
    (b) Identify the resulting Markov chain. [*Ans.* Absorbing.]
    (c) If Peter initially has one penny, what is the probability of his winning the game? If he has two pennies?

14. A rat is put into the maze of the figure below. Each time period, it chooses at random one of the doors in the compartment it is in and moves into another compartment.

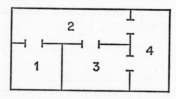

    (a) Set up the process as a Markov chain (with states being the compartments) and identify it. [*Ans.* Regular.]
    (b) In the long run, what fraction of his time will the rat spend in compartment 2? [*Ans.* $\frac{3}{8}$.]
    (c) Make compartment 4 into an absorbing state by assuming the rat will stay in it once it reaches it. Set up the new process and identify it as a kind of Markov chain. [*Ans.* Absorbing.]

(d) In part (c), if the rat starts in compartment 1, how many steps will it take him, on the average, to reach compartment 4?

[*Ans.* $4\frac{1}{3}$ steps.]

15. Consider the following model. A man buys a store. The profits of the store vary from month to month. For simplicity we assume that he earns either $5000 or $2000 a month ("high" or "low"). The man may sell his store at any time, and there is a 10 per cent chance of his selling during a high-profit month, and a 40 per cent chance during a low-profit month. If he does not sell, with probability $\frac{2}{3}$ the profits will be the same the next month, and with probability $\frac{1}{3}$ they will change.

(a) Set up the transition matrix.

$$[Ans. \quad \begin{array}{c} \text{Sell} \\ \text{High} \\ \text{Low} \end{array} \begin{pmatrix} 1 & 0 & 0 \\ \frac{1}{10} & \frac{3}{5} & \frac{3}{10} \\ \frac{2}{5} & \frac{1}{5} & \frac{2}{5} \end{pmatrix}.]$$

(b) Compute N, Nc, and NR and interpret each.

(c) Let $f = \begin{pmatrix} 5000 \\ 2000 \end{pmatrix}$ and compute the vector $g = Nf$.

$$[Ans. \quad g = \begin{pmatrix} 20,000 \\ 10,000 \end{pmatrix}.]$$

(d) Show that the components of g have the following interpretation. g_i is the expected amount that he will gain before selling, given that he started in state i.

16. Suppose that P is the transition matrix of an absorbing Markov chain. Assume that each time the process is in a nonabsorbing state i, a reward f_i is received (including the starting state). Let f be the vector with components f_i and let $g = Nf$. Show that g_i is the expected winnings before absorption if the process starts in state i. [*Hint:* Exercise 15 is a specific example of this process.]

*9. LINEAR FUNCTIONS AND TRANSFORMATIONS

The primary use of vectors and matrices in science is the representation of several different quantities as a single one. For example, the demands on all the industries in the United States may be represented by a row vector x. We have seen examples where such a vector is multiplied by a column vector y, giving the number $x \cdot y$. The components of y could be the values of unit outputs of the various industries. Then $x \cdot y$ is the total monetary value of the demand on industries.

This illustration is typical of much that we meet in the sciences. It has two fundamental properties. If the demand increases by a given factor k, then $(kx) \cdot y = k(x \cdot y)$, and hence the value increases by the same factor. And if we have two demand vectors x and x', then $(x + x') \cdot y = (x \cdot y) + (x' \cdot y)$, and hence their values are also added.

Thus we see that y has the effect of assigning to each row vector x a number $f(x)$, and has the two very simple properties,

(i) $$f(kx) = kf(x)$$
(ii) $$f(x + x') = f(x) + f(x').$$

Such an assignment of a number to each row vector x we call a *linear function*. We have seen that each column vector with n components defines a linear function for row vectors with n components.

Linear functions represent the simplest type of dependence. Fortunately, very many problems can be represented at least approximately by linear functions. While it is not strictly true that manufacturing 100 tons of steel costs ten times as much as manufacturing ten tons, this is at least a reasonable approximation. And the same holds for necessary raw materials, for labor needed, transportation costs, etc. Linear functions are so simple to handle that we try to use them whenever this is reasonable.

Not only is it true that every column vector represents a linear function, but every linear function of row vectors can be so represented. We will prove this for linear functions of three-component row vectors.

Let us suppose that f assigns a number $f(x)$ to each three-component vector x, and that it has the properties (i) and (ii). Consider the three special vectors,

$$e_1 = (1, 0, 0), \qquad e_2 = (0, 1, 0), \qquad e_3 = (0, 0, 1).$$

Let us call $f(e_1) = y_1$; let $y_2 = f(e_2)$, $y_3 = f(e_3)$ and let $y = \begin{pmatrix} y_1 \\ y_2 \\ y_3 \end{pmatrix}$. If $x = (x_1, x_2, x_3)$, we can write $x = x_1 e_1 + x_2 e_2 + x_3 e_3$. Hence, using properties (i) and (ii), we see that

$$\begin{aligned} f(x) &= f(x_1 e_1 + x_2 e_2 + x_3 e_3) \\ &= f(x_1 e_1) + f(x_2 e_2) + f(x_3 e_3) \\ &= x_1 f(e_1) + x_2 f(e_2) + x_3 f(e_3) \\ &= x_1 y_1 + x_2 y_2 + x_3 y_3 = x \cdot y. \end{aligned}$$

Hence the column vector y represents the linear function f.

Example 1. An office buys three kinds of paper, heavy bond, light ond, and a cheaper quality for intra-office use. The amounts bought in reams) are given by the row vector $x = (20, 50, 70)$. The prices per eam of these types of paper are given (in cents) by the column vector

$$= \begin{pmatrix} 160 \\ 140 \\ 120 \end{pmatrix}.$$ Then $f(x) = x \cdot y = \$186$ is the cost of the order. So far,

defines a linear function of x. It is customary to give a discount if 00 or more reams are ordered of one item. The new rules for comput-ıg the bill define a new function of x, different from f. Let us call the ew function by the letter g. Then $g(2x) < 2g(x)$, since the office gets discount on the light bond and on the cheaper paper. Now we have function that is not linear. It often happens that a function in science ı nearly linear for restricted values of the components, but not even oughly linear outside this range.

Sometimes we assign, not a single number to a row vector, but several umbers. Then we say that the vector is transformed into another vec-ır. We say further that the transformation is a *linear transformation* f the vector if each component in the resulting vector is a linear func-on of the given vector, that is, it satisfies (i) and (ii).

Example 2. In Example 1 of Section 3 we considered a vector $x =$, 7, 12), giving the number of each of three styles of houses to be ıilt by a contractor, and a matrix

$$R = \begin{pmatrix} 5 & 20 & 16 & 7 & 17 \\ 7 & 18 & 12 & 9 & 21 \\ 6 & 25 & 8 & 5 & 13 \end{pmatrix},$$

hich gives the raw material requirements for each type of house. ıppose that $x' = (8, 2, 3)$ is another vector of house orders that are ı be built in another location. Then it is easy to check that

$$\begin{aligned} (x + x')R &= (13, 9, 15)R = (218, 797, 436, 247, 605) \\ &= (146, 526, 260, 158, 388) + (72, 271, 176, 89, 217) \\ &= xR + x'R \end{aligned}$$

.milarly, if the contractor is going to produce $2x$ houses,

$$\begin{aligned} (2x)R &= (10, 14, 24)R = (292, 1052, 520, 316, 776) \\ &= 2(146, 526, 260, 158, 388). \end{aligned}$$

It can be shown in the same way that (i) and (ii) hold true in genera and $f(x) = xR$ is a linear transformation of vectors x.

In the same manner (see Exercise 10) one can show that R is a linea transformation of five-component y (price) vectors.

Theorem. Let M be any $m \times n$ matrix; then M defines a linea transformation of m-component row vectors x, and it also defines linear transformation of n-component column vectors y.

To prove this theorem we define $f(x) = xM$ and show, using th properties of ordinary numbers, that (i) and (ii) hold. This was don for a specific numerical example in Example 2 above. Similarly, w define $g(y) = My$ and show that (i) and (ii) hold.

It can be shown that the effect of any linear transformation can b described by a suitable matrix. This is illustrated in Example 3.

Example 3. Let us suppose that the population of the Unite States is divided into five groups according to income. The compo nents of the row vector x are the number of people in each bracke Say x_1 people have an income of \$100,000 or above, x_2 have income between \$40,000 and \$100,000, etc. If we know the average numbe of cars owned by men in a given income bracket, we can represen these five numbers as a column vector, and we get the number c privately owned cars as a linear function of x. Similarly, we could ge the number of yachts, privately owned houses, or television sets. Eac of these four quantities is a linear function of x (at least approximatel and each is represented by a five-component column vector whose en tries are averages. Writing the four vectors together as a rectangula array, we get a 5×4 matrix. This is a linear transformation tran forming x into a four-component row vector, whose components a the total number of cars, yachts, houses, and television sets, respectivel

EXERCISES

1. $x = (x_1, x_2, x_3)$. Test each of the following functions of x as to wheth it has properties (i) and (ii).

(a) $f(x) = 3x_1 + x_2 - 2x_3$.   [*Ans.* Linear

(b) $f(x) = x_1 x_2 x_3$.

(c) $f(x) = \sqrt{(x_1)^2 + (x_2)^2 + (x_3)^2}$.   [*Ans.* Not linear

(d) $f(x) = x_2$.

2. $x = (x_1, x_2)$. Test each of the following transformations of x into y as to whether it is a linear transformation.

(a) $y_1 = 2x_1 + 3x_2$ and $y_2 = x_1 - x_2$.   [*Ans.* Linear.]

(b) $y_1 = x_1 + 2x_2$ and $y_2 = -x_1 x_2$.   [*Ans.* Not linear.]

(c) $y_1 = x_2$ and $y_2 = -x_1$.

For the linear transformations above, write the matrix representing the transformation.

3. Prove that the function $f(x) = c$, where x is a two-component row vector and c is a constant, is a linear function if and only if $c = 0$.

4. Prove that the function $f(x) = ax_1 + bx_2 + c$, where x is a two-component row vector and a, b, and c are constants, is a linear function if and only if $c = 0$.

5. Prove that the transformation $T(x) = xA + C$, where x is a two-component row vector and A and C are 2×2 matrices, is a linear transformation if and only if $C = 0$.

6. Prove that $f(x) = $ (least component of x) is not a linear function.

7. Let x be a 12-component row vector. Its components are the enrollment figures in 12 mathematics courses. Give an example of

(a) A linear function of x.

[*An Ans.* The total enrollment in all mathematics courses.]

(b) A linear transformation of x.

(c) A nonlinear function of x.

8. Let the components of x be the number of fiction books, the number of nonfiction books, and the number of other publications in a library. For each of the following functions, state whether or not it is a linear function of x.

(a) The total number of publications.   [*Ans.* Linear.]

(b) The total number of cards in the catalogue. (Assume that each book has two cards, each other publication has one.)

9. If in (i) and (ii), x is taken as a column vector, then the conditions define a linear function of a column vector. How can we represent such a function? How can we represent a linear transformation of column vectors?

10. Show that the matrix R defined in Example 2 can be thought of as a transformation of both row vectors and column vectors.

*10. PERMUTATION MATRICES

In Chapter III we defined a permutation of n objects to be an arrangement of these objects in a definite order. Thus the set $\{a, b, c\}$ has six permutations: abc, acb, bac, bca, cab, and cba. There is a slightly different way of thinking of a permutation. We may think of our set as given originally in a definite order, say abc, and then think of a permutation as a *rearrangement* of the set. Thus one permutation changes abc into bac; i.e., the first element is put into the second spot, the second into the first spot, and the third element is left unchanged. In order to arrive at the same number, $n!$, of permutations as before, we must consider the "rearrangement" that changes nothing, i.e., the permutation that "changes" abc into abc. We shall consider our n objects as components of a row vector. A permutation changes the row vector into another having the same components, but possibly in a different order.

A convenient way to describe permutations is by means of certain special matrices. For example, the rearrangement given above can be described by the product

$$(x_1, x_2, x_3) \begin{pmatrix} 0 & 1 & 0 \\ 1 & 0 & 0 \\ 0 & 0 & 1 \end{pmatrix} = (x_2, x_1, x_3).$$

In this we do not have to think of the x_i as numbers. They are objects of any sort for which multiplication by 0 and 1 and addition is defined as for numbers. The 3×3 matrix then represents our permutation. It has only 0's and 1's as components, and there is exactly one 1 in each row and in each column.

DEFINITION 1. A *permutation matrix* is a square matrix having exactly one 1 in each row and each column, and having 0's in all other places.

$$A = \begin{pmatrix} 0 & 1 \\ 1 & 0 \end{pmatrix}, \qquad B = \begin{pmatrix} 0 & 1 & 0 \\ 0 & 0 & 1 \\ 1 & 0 & 0 \end{pmatrix}, \qquad C = \begin{pmatrix} 1 & 0 & 0 \\ 0 & 1 & 0 \\ 0 & 0 & 1 \end{pmatrix},$$

$$D = \begin{pmatrix} 0 & 1 & 0 & 0 \\ 1 & 0 & 0 & 0 \\ 0 & 0 & 1 & 0 \\ 0 & 0 & 0 & 1 \end{pmatrix}$$

Figure 6

Examples of permutation matrices are shown in Figure 6. Since these matrices are square matrices ($n \times n$), we can speak of the matrix as having *degree n*. Thus Figure 6 shows one matrix of degree 2, two of degree 3, and one of degree 4.

Theorem 1. Every permutation matrix of degree n represents a permutation of n objects, and every such permutation has a unique matrix representation.

Proof. Let us consider n objects $x_1, x_2, \ldots, x_n$ which by a permutation are rearranged to give $y_1, y_2, \ldots, y_n$. Here each of the y's is one of the x's, and every x is some y. If it happens that $y_j = x_i$, then the object in the ith position was changed to the jth position. In this case, define $p_{ij} = 1$ and $p_{ik} = 0$ for $k \neq i$. Doing this for every i, we obtain an $n \times n$ permutation matrix P such that

(1) $(x_1, x_2, \ldots, x_n)P = (y_1, y_2, \ldots, y_n).$

The fact that no two elements of a single row or a single column of P are 1 (i.e., that P is a permutation matrix) follows from the fact that in a permutation each element appears once and only once in the rearrangement.

On the other hand, if we are given a permutation matrix P, then we can define a permutation by the product (1). The fact that each column of P has exactly one 1 means that each y_j is some x_i. The fact that P has only one 1 in each row means that every x_i appears as only one y_j. Hence the vector $(y_1, y_2, \ldots, y_n)$ does represent a rearrangement of the vector $(x_1, x_2, \ldots, x_n)$, completing the proof of the theorem.

We shall restrict ourselves to the case of $n = 4$ for illustrating the following discussion, but all the results we are about to establish will hold for every n. In Figure 7 we find four examples of permutation matrices of degree 4.

We want to study the product of two permutation matrices of degree 4. If $x = (x_1, x_2, x_3, x_4)$, then $xJ = (x_4, x_1, x_3, x_2)$ and $xK = (x_2, x_1, x_4, x_3)$. The former puts the first component into second place, the second component into fourth place, and the fourth component into first place; leaving the third component unchanged. The latter interchanges the first two and the last two. What happens if we perform the two permutations, one after the other? Let us first consider x_1. In the first transformation it is changed into the second component,

$$I = \begin{pmatrix} 1 & 0 & 0 & 0 \\ 0 & 1 & 0 & 0 \\ 0 & 0 & 1 & 0 \\ 0 & 0 & 0 & 1 \end{pmatrix}, \quad J = \begin{pmatrix} 0 & 1 & 0 & 0 \\ 0 & 0 & 0 & 1 \\ 0 & 0 & 1 & 0 \\ 1 & 0 & 0 & 0 \end{pmatrix}$$

$$K = \begin{pmatrix} 0 & 1 & 0 & 0 \\ 1 & 0 & 0 & 0 \\ 0 & 0 & 0 & 1 \\ 0 & 0 & 1 & 0 \end{pmatrix}, \quad L = \begin{pmatrix} 0 & 0 & 0 & 1 \\ 1 & 0 & 0 & 0 \\ 0 & 0 & 1 & 0 \\ 0 & 1 & 0 & 0 \end{pmatrix}$$

Figure 7

while in the second transformation, the second component is changed into the first. Hence x_1 ends up where it started, in first place. The component x_2 is first sent into the number four slot, and then this is changed to number three by the second transformation. Hence x_2 ends up as the third component. Component x_3 is at first not changed, but later changed into component four. Component x_4 is first made into the first component, and in the second transformation it is changed into the second component. Hence, starting with x, after two transformations we end up with (x_1, x_4, x_2, x_3).

Let us now consider the product

$$JK = \begin{pmatrix} 1 & 0 & 0 & 0 \\ 0 & 0 & 1 & 0 \\ 0 & 0 & 0 & 1 \\ 0 & 1 & 0 & 0 \end{pmatrix}.$$

The matrix JK is again a permutation matrix, and it is easy to check that it represents precisely the permutation described above.

Theorem 2. The product JK of two permutation matrices of the same degree is again such a permutation matrix. It represents the result of first performing permutation J, then permutation K.

Proof. This theorem is very easy to prove in matrix form. We wish to know what $x(JK)$ is. By the associative law (see Section 4) this is the same as $(xJ)K$. But xJ is the result of the J permutation, and $(xJ)K$ is the result of applying the K permutation to xJ. This proves the theorem.

Example. Referring to Figure 7, let us consider the products IJ and JI. We know, of course, that $IJ = JI = J$. Hence Theorem 2 tells us that performing the I permutation followed by the J permutation (or the reverse) will result simply in the J permutation. If we note that the I permutation leaves everything unchanged, this result is obvious.

Let us now consider the product JL, where again J and L are as in Figure 7. The product is equal to I; hence $L = J^{-1}$. By Theorem 2 we know that the permutation J followed by L will result in the permutation I, i.e., in no change at all. Thus we see that $L = J^{-1}$ is a permutation that undoes all changes made by J. We also note a similarity in the structure of J and L; the latter is formed from the former by turning it over its main diagonal (the diagonal slanting from the upper left-hand corner to the lower right-hand corner). In other words, L has as its i,jth component what J has as its j,ith component.

Definition 2. The *transpose* A^* of a square matrix A is formed by turning it over its main diagonal; that is, the entries of A^* are given by $a_{ij}^* = a_{ji}$.

Theorem 3. If P is a permutation matrix, then P^* is its inverse; that is, P^* represents the permutation which undoes what the permutation P does.

Proof. We must show that P^* undoes what P does; the remainder will follow from the above discussion and Section 6. Let us suppose that $p_{ij}^* = 1$. Then $p_{ji} = 1$; hence the permutation P moves component x_j into position i. But then, because $p_{ij}^* = 1$, the component is moved from position i into position j. Hence x_j ends up in position j, where it started; and this holds for every component. Thus P^* undoes the work of P, which proves the theorem.

Definition 3. A set of objects forms a *group* (with respect to multiplication) if
- (i)   The product of two elements of the set is always an element of the set.
- (ii)   There is in the set an element I, called the identity element, such that for every A in the set, $IA = AI = A$.
- (iii)   For every A in the set there is an element A^{-1} in the set such that $AA^{-1} = A^{-1}A = I$.
- For every A, B, C in the set, $A(BC) = (AB)C$.

DEFINITION 4. A set of objects form a *commutative group* if, in addition to the above four properties, they also satisfy

(v) For every A and B in the set, $AB = BA$.

Theorem 4. The permutation matrices of degree n form a group (with respect to matrix multiplication), but this group is not commutative if $n > 2$.

Proof. Property (i) was shown in Theorem 2. Property (ii) follows from the more general fact that $IM = MI = M$, for every $n \times n$ matrix M. From Theorem 3 we know that A has an inverse, namely $A^{-1} = A^*$. It is easy to show that A^* is again a permutation matrix (see Exercise 1). Hence (iii) follows. And (iv) again follows from the more general theorem that all matrices obey this associative law. (See Section 4.) On the other hand it is easy to show examples, for any $n > 2$, where $AB \neq BA$. (See Exercises 2–3.) This completes the proof.

The group formed by the $n \times n$ permutation matrices is known as the *permutation group of degree n*. Since permutations are used in the study of symmetry, this group is also called the *symmetric group of degree n*.

EXERCISES

1. Prove that the transpose of a permutation matrix is a permutation matrix; i.e., that if A satisfies Definition 1, then so does A^*.

2. Write all permutation matrices of degree 1. Write all permutation matrices of degree 2. Show that these two groups are commutative.

3. For $n > 2$, we can form the matrix A which only interchanges x_1 and x_2, and the matrix B which only interchanges x_1 and x_3. What permutations are performed by AB and by BA? Are these two the same? Use this fact to show that the permutation group of order $n > 2$ is not commutative.

4. Write down the permutation matrices which change (x_1, x_2, x_3, x_4) into

(a) (x_2, x_3, x_4, x_1).
(b) (x_1, x_3, x_2, x_4).
(c) (x_2, x_3, x_1, x_4).
(d) (x_1, x_2, x_3, x_4).

$$[\textit{Ans.} \text{ (a) } \begin{pmatrix} 0 & 0 & 0 & 1 \\ 1 & 0 & 0 & 0 \\ 0 & 1 & 0 & 0 \\ 0 & 0 & 1 & 0 \end{pmatrix}.]$$

5. For the following pairs of matrices, find the permutations they represent. In each case show that AB represents the permutation A followed by the permutation B, and that BA represents the permutation B followed by the permutation A.

(a) $A = \begin{pmatrix} 0 & 1 & 0 \\ 0 & 0 & 1 \\ 1 & 0 & 0 \end{pmatrix}$, $\qquad B = \begin{pmatrix} 1 & 0 & 0 \\ 0 & 0 & 1 \\ 0 & 1 & 0 \end{pmatrix}$,

(b) $A = \begin{pmatrix} 0 & 1 & 0 \\ 0 & 0 & 1 \\ 1 & 0 & 0 \end{pmatrix}$, $\qquad B = \begin{pmatrix} 0 & 0 & 1 \\ 1 & 0 & 0 \\ 0 & 1 & 0 \end{pmatrix}$,

(c) $A = \begin{pmatrix} 0 & 1 & 0 & 0 \\ 0 & 0 & 0 & 1 \\ 1 & 0 & 0 & 0 \\ 0 & 0 & 1 & 0 \end{pmatrix}$, $\qquad B = \begin{pmatrix} 0 & 1 & 0 & 0 \\ 1 & 0 & 0 & 0 \\ 0 & 0 & 0 & 1 \\ 0 & 0 & 1 & 0 \end{pmatrix}$.

[*Ans.* (a) xA is (x_3, x_1, x_2); xB is (x_1, x_3, x_2); xAB is (x_3, x_2, x_1); xBA is (x_2, x_1, x_3).]

6. Prove that the set of *all* 3×3 matrices does *not* form a group (with respect to matrix multiplication).

7. Find the inverses of the six matrices in Exercise 5 by using Theorem 3. Check your answers by multiplying the matrices by their inverses.

$$[\textit{Ans. } (a) \ A^{-1} = \begin{pmatrix} 0 & 0 & 1 \\ 1 & 0 & 0 \\ 0 & 1 & 0 \end{pmatrix}; B^{-1} = \begin{pmatrix} 1 & 0 & 0 \\ 0 & 0 & 1 \\ 0 & 1 & 0 \end{pmatrix}.]$$

8. The process of division is usually introduced by saying that b/a is the solution of the equation $ax = b$ (or of $xa = b$).

(a) Prove that in a group the equation $AX = B$ always has a unique solution.

(b) Prove that in a group the equation $XA = B$ always has a unique solution.

(c) Show by means of an example that the two equations need not have the same solution.

9. For the set of numbers $\{1, 2, 3, 4\}$ we define "multiplication" by means of the following table.

x	1	2	3	4
1	1	2	3	4
2	2	4	1	3
3	3	1	4	2
4	4	3	2	1

(In this table we have neglected all multiples of 5; e.g., $2 \times 4 = 8$, but we neglected the 5 and just kept the remainder 3. Again $3 \times 4 = 12$, but we ignored the 10, which is a multiple of 5, and kept the remainder 2.) Prove that this set, with multiplication so defined, forms a commutative group.

10. For the set $\{1, 2, 3, 4, 5, 6\}$ write down a multiplication table, ignoring all multiples of 7. (See Exercise 9.) Prove that the result is a commutative group.

11. For the set $\{1, 2, 3, 4, 5\}$ write down a multiplication table, ignoring multiples of 6. (See Exercises 9 and 10.) Prove that the result is *not* a group. Why do 5 and 7 give us groups, but not 6?

12. Write down all permutation matrices of degree 3, and assign letter-names to them. Write a multiplication table for this group. How, from this table alone, can we see that properties (i), (ii), and (iii) hold? How do we see that (v) does not hold?

13. Consider a group with four elements, $G = \{a, b, c, d\}$. For each x in G let x' be the vector $x' = (xa, xb, xc, xd)$; e.g., $a' = (a^2, ab, ac, ad)$. Show that x' is a permutation of (a, b, c, d). Show that the four permutations, a', b', c', d' form a permutation group having the same multiplication table as G; i.e., show $x'y' = z'$ if and only if $xy = z$.

14. Find the permutation group associated with the group in Exercise 9 by the method of Exercise 13.

*11. SUBGROUPS OF PERMUTATION GROUPS

Within a group we sometimes can find smaller groups. Here we shall study some of the subgroups of permutation groups. It will be understood that whenever we speak of a group we have a set with a finite number of elements in mind. In particular, this will be assumed for the theorems given below, since some of the theorems are not valid for groups with an infinite number of elements. The concept of a group has important applications for infinite sets, but these do not belong in this book.

DEFINITION 1. If a given set G forms a group, and some subset H of it also forms a group, we call the subset H a *subgroup* of G. If the subset H is a proper subset of G, we speak of a *proper subgroup*.

Theorem 1. If we select any element of a group, the powers of the element form a subgroup which is commutative.

Proof. Select any element A of the given group; we must show that the powers A^n have the properties (i)–(v) given in the last section. The product of two powers is again a power, $A^j A^k = A^{j+k}$; hence (i) holds. Next we observe that the powers cannot be all different, since this would give us infinitely many elements in our group. Hence we must have an equation $A^j = A^k$, with, say, $j > k$. However, this implies that $A^{j-k} = I$. Hence I occurs among the powers of A, say $I = A^m$. Therefore (ii) holds. If $m = 1$ or 2, then A is its own inverse (see Exercise 9). On the other hand, if $m > 2$, then among the powers we find A^{m-1}, and $AA^{m-1} = A^m = I$, so that A^{m-1} is the inverse of A. This shows that property (iii) holds. The associative law (iv) follows from the fact that all matrices obey this law. Finally, we get commutativity (v) from the fact that $A^j A^k = A^{j+k} = A^{k+j} = A^k A^j$, completing the proof.

DEFINITION 2. A group which consists of the powers of one element A is known as the *cyclic* group *generated* by A.

Thus we know that we can form a cyclic subgroup of a given group by picking any one element A and taking all its powers. The number of elements in this subgroup is called the *order* of A. In the proof above, the order of A is the smallest possible m such that $A^m = I$.

Example 1. The permutation group of degree 4 has $4! = 24$ elements. Let us consider the cyclic subgroup generated by J (see Figure 7). We find that $J^2 = L = J^{-1}$, so that $J^3 = JJ^2 = I$. Thus our cyclic subgroup consists of J, $J^2 = L$, and $J^3 = I$. If we continue to take higher powers, we get $J^4 = J$, $J^5 = L$, $J^6 = I$, etc. The elements are repeated in this fixed cycle. This is the source of the name "cyclic."

Example 2. We can get a larger cyclic subgroup by choosing the matrix M and its powers (see Figure 8). M has order 4; hence $M^{-1} = M^* = M^3$, and $M^4 = I$.

$$M = \begin{pmatrix} 0 & 1 & 0 & 0 \\ 0 & 0 & 1 & 0 \\ 0 & 0 & 0 & 1 \\ 1 & 0 & 0 & 0 \end{pmatrix}, \quad M^2 = \begin{pmatrix} 0 & 0 & 1 & 0 \\ 0 & 0 & 0 & 1 \\ 1 & 0 & 0 & 0 \\ 0 & 1 & 0 & 0 \end{pmatrix}$$

$$M^3 = \begin{pmatrix} 0 & 0 & 0 & 1 \\ 1 & 0 & 0 & 0 \\ 0 & 1 & 0 & 0 \\ 0 & 0 & 1 & 0 \end{pmatrix}, \quad M^4 = \begin{pmatrix} 1 & 0 & 0 & 0 \\ 0 & 1 & 0 & 0 \\ 0 & 0 & 1 & 0 \\ 0 & 0 & 0 & 1 \end{pmatrix}$$

Figure 8

Theorem 2. If in a group we select any subset having property (i), then this subset is a subgroup.

Proof. We must show that the subset also has properties (ii)–(iv). Let A be any element of the subset. By (i), $AA = A^2$ is also in the subset, and then $AA^2 = A^3$ is in the subset, etc. Hence all powers of A are in the subset. One of these powers is I and one is A^{-1}. Hence we have properties (ii) and (iii). Property (iv) again follows from the fact that all matrices have this property, completing the proof of the theorem.

We now have a practical way of finding subgroups. We select one or more elements of the group, and form all possible products of these, using each one as many times as necessary. If we form all possible products, then the product of any two products will also be on our list, and hence property (i) holds. Then, by Theorem 2, we have a subgroup, which is called the subgroup *generated* by the elements. If we start with a single element, we obtain a cyclic subgroup. Some very interesting subgroups can be generated by two elements.

Example 3. Let us start with J (see Figure 7), and D (see Figure 6), and form the subgroup they generate. First of all we get the powers of J, namely, J and $J^2 = L$ and $J^3 = I$, as was shown in Example 1. Then we have D, and D^2, which is again I. In products formed using both J and D we need consider only J and J^2 and D, since the next higher power is I, and then the powers are repeated. Theoretically, we should consider products like $DJDJ^2$ and $JDJDJDJ$, but we can show, as follows, that such long products give nothing new. First we observe that $DJ = J^2D$, so that in a long product we may always replace DJ by J^2D, and thus put all the J's in front and all the D's at the end. (See Exercise 14.) Therefore the only new products that we need consider are of the form J^aD^b; and since J can occur only to the first or second power and D only to the first power, we arrive at JD and J^2D as the only additional products. Hence our subgroup has six elements: J, J^2, D, I, JD, and J^2D. Since $JD \neq DJ$, the subgroup is *not* commutative.

So far we have found subgroups of 3, 4, and 6 elements. Each of these numbers is a divisor of 24, the total number of elements in the group. It can be shown that the number of elements in a subgroup is always a divisor of the number of elements in the group, but we will not prove that fact here.

Example 4. Let us now form the subgroup generated by D and K. Since $D^2 = I = K^2$, both D and K will occur only to the first power in a product. Furthermore $DK = KD$; hence the subgroup will have only four elements: I, D, K, DK. This subgroup is commutative. The fact that the subgroup happens to be commutative is a consequence of the following theorem.

Theorem 3. If A and B commute (i.e., $AB = BA$), then any two products formed from A and B also commute. Hence the subgroup generated by A and B is a commutative subgroup.

Proof. Given any product formed from A and B, say $AABBBABAB$, we can make use of the fact that $AB = BA$ to move all the A's up front and all the B's to the end. Hence the product can be written A^iB^j. A second such product can be written A^kB^m. The product of these, $A^iB^jA^kB^m$, can again be rearranged so that all the A's come at the beginning. Hence $(A^iB^j)(A^kB^m) = A^{i+k}B^{j+m} = A^{k+i}B^{m+j} = (A^kB^m)(A^iB^j)$, completing the proof.

We have now found two types of commutative subgroups: (1) cyclic subgroups and (2) subgroups generated by two elements that commute. For the latter it is convenient to have a technique for finding two commuting elements. We will develop one method for finding such pairs.

DEFINITION 3. The *effective set* of a permutation matrix is the set of all those components of the row vector which are changed by the matrix.

For example, D has $\{x_1, x_2\}$ as its effective set, J has $\{x_1, x_2, x_4\}$, K has the set of all four components, and I has the empty set as its effective set. K suggests the definition:

DEFINITION 4. A permutation matrix having all the components in its effective set is called a *complete* permutation matrix.

Theorem 4. Two permutation matrices, whose effective sets are disjoint, commute.

Proof. Let A_1 have X_1 as its effective set, and A_2 have X_2, so that $X_1 \cap X_2 = \varepsilon$. Then A_1A_2 will make some changes on X_1 and then on X_2. The latter are not affected by the former, since X_1 and X_2 have nothing in common. Thus we get the same result if we perform A_2 followed by A_1.

We now have a simple way of getting a commutative subgroup, other than a cyclic one. Just select any two matrices (other than I) with disjoint effective sets, and form the subgroup that they generate.

EXERCISES

1. Write down the six permutation matrices of degree 3.

2. Form the cyclic subgroup for each of the six matrices in Exercise 1. Are these subgroups all different? What is the order of each matrix?
   [*Ans.* Five distinct groups; one of order 1, three of order 2, two of order 3.]

3. Prove that there are no proper subgroups of the permutation group of degree 3, other than those found in Exercise 2.

4. Write the 24 permutation matrices of degree 4.

5. Form the cyclic subgroup for each of the matrices in Exercise 4. How many different ones do you get? What is the order of each matrix?
   [*Ans.* 17 distinct groups; one of order 1, nine of order 2, eight of order 3, six of order 4.]

6. Show by an example that the subgroups found in Exercise 5 are not the only proper subgroups of the permutation group of degree 4.

7. Prove the following facts about orders of permutations.
   (a) I has order 1.
   (b) A permutation which does nothing but interchange one or more pairs of elements has order 2.
   (c) Every other permutation has an order greater than 2.

8. Prove that the subgroup generated by A and B is cyclic if and only if one generator is a power of the other.

9. Prove that if a matrix has order 1 or 2, then it is its own inverse.

10. A matrix M is said to be *symmetric* if $m_{ij} = m_{ji}$ for all i and j. Prove that a permutation matrix is symmetric if and only if it has order 1 or 2.

11. Form the subgroup generated by J and K.
    [*Ans.* There are 12 elements.]

12. Prove the following facts about effective sets.
    (a) I has an effective set of zero elements.
    (b) A matrix which simply interchanges two elements has as its effective set a set of two elements.
    (c) All other matrices have an effective set of at least three elements.

(d) A matrix is complete if and only if the number of elements in its effective set equals its degree.

13. We wish to form a commutative subgroup of the permutation group of degree 4, by means of the method described above. We want to choose two matrices (other than I) with disjoint effective sets, and form the subgroup they generate.

    (a) Using the results of Exercise 12, what must the number of elements be in the two effective sets?   [*Ans.* 2, 2.]

    (b) Choose such a pair of matrices.

    (c) Form the subgroup.

14. Prove the following facts about Example 3 above.

    (a) $DJ = J^2D$.

    (b) From this it follows that $DJ^2 = JD$.

    (c) In any product of D's and J's we can put all the J's up front.

15. If A has order m, and m is an even number, then $A^{m/2}$ is its own inverse. Prove this fact. What does this say about an element of order 2?

16. Prove that the cyclic group generated by A^2 is a subgroup of that generated by A. When will this be a proper subgroup?

SUGGESTED READING

Birkhoff, G., and S. MacLane, *A Survey of Modern Algebra*, Macmillan, third ed., 1965.

Weiss, M. J., *Higher Algebra for the Undergraduate*, Wiley, New York, 1949, Chaps. 3, 6, 7.

Johnson, R. E., *First Course in Abstract Algebra*, Prentice-Hall, Englewood Cliffs, N.J., 1953.

Beaumont, R. A., and R. W. Ball, *Introduction to Modern Algebra and Matrix Theory*, Holt, Rinehart and Winston, New York, 1954, Chaps. I–IV.

Thrall, R. M., and L. Tornheim, *Vector Spaces and Matrices*, Wiley, New York, 1957, Chaps. 1–3.

Hohn, F. E., *Elementary Matrix Algebra*, Macmillan, New York, 1958, Chaps. 1, 3, 5.

Hadley, G., *Linear Algebra*, Addison-Wesley, Reading, Mass., 1961, Chaps. 1–5.

*Linear programming

and the theory of games

1. CONVEX SETS

An equation containing one or more variables will be called an *open statement*. For instance,

(a) $$-2x_1 + 3x_2 = 6$$

is an example of an open statement. If we let $A = (-2, 3)$, $x = \begin{pmatrix} x_1 \\ x_2 \end{pmatrix}$, and $b = 6$, we can write (a) in matrix form as

$$Ax = (-2, 3) \begin{pmatrix} x_1 \\ x_2 \end{pmatrix} = -2x_1 + 3x_2 = 6 = b.$$

For some two-component vectors x the statement $Ax = b$ is true and for others it is false. For instance, if $x = \begin{pmatrix} 3 \\ 4 \end{pmatrix}$ it is true since $-2 \cdot 3 + 3 \cdot 4 = 6$, and if $x = \begin{pmatrix} 2 \\ 4 \end{pmatrix}$ it is false since $-2 \cdot 2 + 3 \cdot 4 = 8$. The set of all two-component vectors x that make the open statement $Ax = b$ true is defined to be the *truth set* of the open statement.

Example 1. In plane geometry it is usual to picture in the plane the truth sets of open statements such as (a). Thus we can regard each two-component vector x as being the components of a point in the plane in the usual way. Then the truth set or *locus* (which is the geometric term for truth set) of (a) is the straight line plotted in Figure 1. Points on this line may be obtained by assuming values for one of the variables

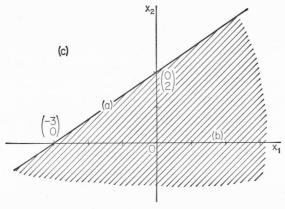

Figure 1

and computing the corresponding values for the other variable. Thus, setting $x_1 = 0$, we find $x_2 = 2$, so that the point $x = \begin{pmatrix} 0 \\ 2 \end{pmatrix}$ lies on the locus; similarly, setting $x_2 = 0$, we find $x_1 = -3$, so that the point $\begin{pmatrix} -3 \\ 0 \end{pmatrix}$ lies on the locus, etc.

In the same way, inequalities of the form $Ax \leq b$ or $Ax < b$ or $Ax \geq b$ or $Ax > b$ are open statements and possess truth sets. And in the case that x is a two-component vector, these can be plotted in the plane.

Example 2. Consider the inequalities (b) $Ax < b$, (c) $Ax > b$, (d) $Ax \leq b$, and (e) $Ax \geq b$, where A, x, and b are as in Example 1. They may be written as

(b) $-2x_1 + 3x_2 < 6$
(c) $-2x_1 + 3x_2 > 6$
(d) $-2x_1 + 3x_2 \leq 6$
(e) $-2x_1 + 3x_2 \geq 6.$

Consider (b) first. What points $\begin{pmatrix} x_1 \\ x_2 \end{pmatrix}$ satisfy this inequality? By trial and error we can find many points on the locus. Thus the point $\begin{pmatrix} 1 \\ 2 \end{pmatrix}$ is on it since $-2 \cdot 1 + 3 \cdot 2 = 4 < 6$; on the other hand, the point $\begin{pmatrix} 1 \\ 3 \end{pmatrix}$ is not on the locus because $-2 \cdot 1 + 3 \cdot 3 = -2 + 9 = 7$, which is not less than 6. In between these two points we find $\begin{pmatrix} 1 \\ \frac{8}{3} \end{pmatrix}$, which lies on the boundary, i.e., on the locus of (a). We note that, starting with $\begin{pmatrix} 1 \\ \frac{8}{3} \end{pmatrix}$ on locus (a), by increasing x_2 we went outside the locus (b); by decreasing x_2 we came into the locus (b) again. This holds in general. Given a point on the locus of (a), by increasing its second coordinate we get more than 6, but by decreasing the second coordinate we get less than 6, and hence the latter gives a point in the truth set of (b). Thus we find that the locus of (b) consists of all points of the plane *below* the line (a), in other words, the shaded area in Figure 1. The area on one side of a straight line is called an *open half plane*.

We can apply exactly the same analysis to show that the locus of (c) is the open half plane above the line (a). This can also be deduced from the fact that the truth sets of statements (a), (b), and (c) are disjoint and have as union the entire plane.

Since (d) is the disjunction of (a) and (b), the truth set of (d) is the union of the truth sets of (a) and (b). Such a set, which consists of an open half plane together with the points on the line that defines the half plane, is called a *closed half plane*. Obviously, the truth set of (e) consists of the union of (a) and (c) and therefore is also a closed half plane.

Frequently we want to assert several different open statements at once, that is, we want to assert the conjunction of several such statements. The easy way to do this is to let A be an $m \times n$ matrix, x an n-component column vector, and b an m-component column vector. Then the statement $Ax \le b$ is the conjunction of the m statements $A_i x \le b_i$ where A_i is the ith row of A and b_i is the ith entry of b.

Example 3. Consider the following example: $Ax \le b$ where

$$A = \begin{pmatrix} -1 & 0 \\ 0 & -1 \\ 2 & 3 \end{pmatrix}, \qquad x = \begin{pmatrix} x_1 \\ x_2 \end{pmatrix}, \qquad b = \begin{pmatrix} 0 \\ 0 \\ 6 \end{pmatrix}.$$

If we write the components of the equations $Ax \leq b$, we obtain

(f) $-x_1 \leq 0$ which is equivalent to $x_1 \geq 0$
(g) $-x_2 \leq 0$ which is equivalent to $x_2 \geq 0$
(h) $2x_1 + 3x_2 \leq 6$.

Here we are simultaneously asserting three different statements; i.e., we assert their conjunction. Therefore the truth set of $Ax \leq b$ is the intersection of the three individual truth sets. The truth set of (f) is

the right half plane; the truth set of (g) is the upper half plane; and the truth set of (h) is the half plane below the line $2x_1 + 3x_2 = 6$. The intersection of these is the triangle (including the sides) shaded in Figure 2. The area shaded in Figure 2 contains those points which simultaneously satisfy (f), (g), and (h).

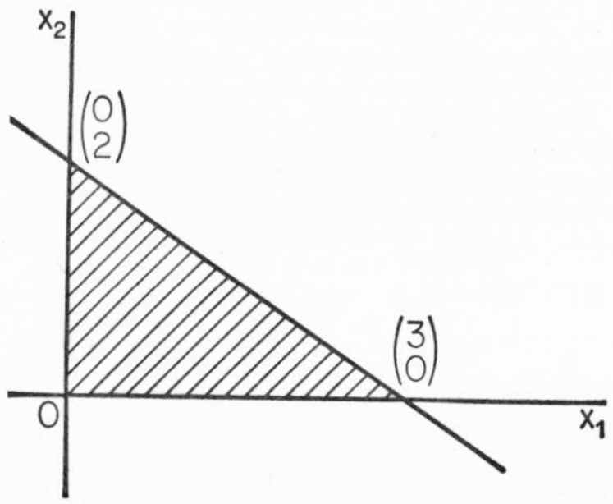

Figure 2

In the examples so far we have restricted ourselves to open statements with two variables. Such statements have truth sets that can be sketched in the plane. In the same way, open statements with three variables have truth sets that can be visualized in three-dimensional space. Open statements with four or more variables have truth sets in four or more dimensions, which we can no longer visualize. However, applied problems frequently lead to such statements. Fortunately, methods have been developed for handling them without having to visualize the truth sets geometrically. We shall illustrate these ideas in three-dimensional space, but everything that we do there can be extended without essential change to the general case of n variables.

In order to have a notation that will enable us to talk in general about conjunctions of m open statements in three dimensions, we shall consider x to be a three-component column vector, b an m-component column vector, and A an $m \times 3$ matrix. The ith row of A will be denoted by A_i for $i = 1, 2, \ldots, m$. Similarly, the ith component of b will be denoted by b_i. Of course, A_i is a three-component row vector and b_i is a number. We shall call the set of all three-component x vectors, *three-space*. Similarly, we call the set of all two-component x vectors, *two-space* or *the plane*.

We now set up some definitions for later use.

DEFINITION. The truth set of $A_i x = b_i$ is called a *plane* in three-space. The truth sets of inequalities of the form $A_i x < b_i$ or $A_i x > b_i$ are called *open half spaces*, while the truth sets of the inequalities $A_i x \leq b_i$ or $A_i x \geq b_i$ are called *closed half spaces* in three-space.

When we assert the conjunction of several open statements, the resulting truth set is the intersection of the truth sets of the individual open statements. Thus, in Example 3, we have the conjunction of $m = 3$ open statements in the plane. In Figure 2 we show this geometrically as the intersection of $m = 3$ closed half spaces (half planes) in two dimensions. Such intersections of closed half spaces are of special importance.

DEFINITION. The intersection of a finite number of closed half spaces is a *polyhedral convex set*.

The intuitive idea of polyhedral convex sets in two or three dimensions is very easy. In two dimensions they are sets, bounded by segments of straight lines that always "bulge out." For example, triangles, rectangles, pentagons, etc. are plane polyhedral (or polygonal) convex sets. In three dimensions they are sets, bounded by "pieces" of planes that always "bulge out." For instance, tetrahedra, cubes, octahedra, etc., are all such examples.

Theorem. Any polyhedral convex set is the truth set of an inequality statement of the form $Ax \leq b$.

Proof. A closed half space is the truth set of an inequality of the form $A_i x \leq b_i$. (An inequality of the form $A_i x \geq b_i$ can be converted into one of this form by multiplying by -1.) Now a polyhedral convex set is the truth set of the conjunction of several such statements. Since A is the matrix whose ith row is A_i and b is the column vector with components b_i, then the inequality statement $Ax \leq b$ is a succinct way of stating the conjunction of the inequalities $A_1 x \leq b_1, \ldots, A_m x \leq b_m$. This completes the proof.

The terminology polyhedral *convex* sets is used because these sets are special examples of convex sets. A convex set C is a set such that whenever u and v are points of C, the entire line segment between u and v also belongs to C. This is equivalent to saying that all points of the form $z = au + (1 - a)v$ for $0 \leq a \leq 1$ belong to C whenever u and v do. We shall be concerned primarily with polyhedral convex sets in this chapter.

EXERCISES

1. Draw pictures of the truth sets of $Ax \leq b$, where A and b are as given below. (Construct the truth sets of the individual statements first and then take their intersection.)

(a) $A = \begin{pmatrix} 1 & 0 \\ 0 & 1 \\ -2 & -3 \end{pmatrix}$, $b = \begin{pmatrix} 3 \\ 2 \\ 0 \end{pmatrix}$.

(b) $A = \begin{pmatrix} -2 & -3 \\ -1 & 1 \\ 1 & 1 \end{pmatrix}$, $b = \begin{pmatrix} -6 \\ 2 \\ 3 \end{pmatrix}$.

(c) $A = \begin{pmatrix} 2 & 3 \\ -1 & 1 \\ 1 & 1 \end{pmatrix}$, $b = \begin{pmatrix} 6 \\ 2 \\ 3 \end{pmatrix}$.

(d) $A = \begin{pmatrix} 0 & -1 \\ -1 & 0 \\ 1 & 0 \end{pmatrix}$, $b = \begin{pmatrix} 0 \\ 0 \\ 2 \end{pmatrix}$.

(e) $A = \begin{pmatrix} 1 & 0 \\ -1 & 0 \\ 0 & 1 \\ 0 & -1 \end{pmatrix}$, $b = \begin{pmatrix} 2 \\ 2 \\ 3 \\ 3 \end{pmatrix}$.

(f) $A = \begin{pmatrix} 3 & 2 \\ 3 & 2 \end{pmatrix}$, $b = \begin{pmatrix} -6 \\ 6 \end{pmatrix}$.

(g) $A = \begin{pmatrix} -3 & -2 \\ 3 & 2 \end{pmatrix}$, $b = \begin{pmatrix} -6 \\ 6 \end{pmatrix}$.

(h) $A = \begin{pmatrix} -1 & 1 \\ 1 & 1 \end{pmatrix}$, $b = \begin{pmatrix} 0 \\ 0 \end{pmatrix}$.

(i) $A = \begin{pmatrix} 1 & 0 \\ -1 & 0 \end{pmatrix}$, $b = \begin{pmatrix} 2 \\ -5 \end{pmatrix}$.

(j) $A = \begin{pmatrix} -3 & -2 \\ -2 & -3 \\ -1 & 0 \\ 0 & -1 \end{pmatrix}$, $b = \begin{pmatrix} -6 \\ -6 \\ 0 \\ 0 \end{pmatrix}$.

$$(k)\ A = \begin{pmatrix} -2 & -1 \\ 1 & 0 \\ 0 & 1 \end{pmatrix}, \quad b = \begin{pmatrix} -7 \\ 0 \\ 0 \end{pmatrix}.$$

2. Consider the following sets.

$\mathfrak{U}$ is the whole plane;

A is the half plane which is the locus of $-2x_1 + x_2 < 3$.

B is the half plane which is the locus of $-2x_1 + x_2 > 3$.

C is the half plane which is the locus of $-2x_1 + x_2 \leq 3$.

D is the half plane which is the locus of $-2x_1 + x_2 \geq 3$.

L is the line which is the locus of $\qquad -2x_1 + x_2 = 3$.

ε is the empty set.

Show that the following relationships hold among these sets: $\tilde{A} = D$, $\tilde{B} = C$, $\tilde{L} = A \cup B$, $C \cap D = L$, $A \cap B = \varepsilon$, $A \cap C = A$, $B \cap D = B$, $A \cup D = \mathfrak{U}$, $B \cup C = \mathfrak{U}$, $A \cup C = C$, $B \cup D = D$, $A \cup L = C$, $B \cup L = D$. Can you find other relationships?

3. Of the polyhedral convex sets constructed in Exercise 1, which have a finite area and which have infinite area?

[*Partial Ans.* (c), (d), (f), (h), and (j) are of infinite area; (g) is a line; (i) and (k) are empty.]

4. For each of the following half planes give an inequality of which it is the truth set.

(a) The open half plane above the x_1-axis.　　　　[*Ans.* $x_2 > 0$.]

(b) The closed half plane on and above the straight line making angles of 45° with the positive x_1- and x_2-axis.

Exercises 5–9 refer to a situation in which a retailer is trying to decide how many units of items A and B he should keep in stock. Let x be the number of units of A and y be the number of units of B. A costs \$4 per unit and B costs \$3 per unit.

5. One cannot stock a negative number of units of either A or B. Write these conditions as inequalities and draw their truth sets.

6. The maximum demand over the period for which the retailer is contemplating holding inventory will not exceed 600 units of A or 600 units of B. Modify the set found in Exercise 5 to take this into account.

7. The retailer is not willing to tie up more than \$2400 in inventory altogether. Modify the set found in Exercise 6.

8. The retailer decides to invest at least twice as much in inventory of item A as he does in inventory of item B. Modify the set of Exercise 7.

9. Finally, the retailer decides that he wants to invest \$900 in inventory of item B. What possibilities are left?   [*Ans.* None.]

10. Assume that the minimal nutritional requirements of human beings are given by the following table.

	Phosphorus	Calcium
Adult	.02	.01
Child	.03	.03
Infant	.01	.02

Plot the amount of phosphorus on the vertical axis and the amount of calcium on the horizontal. Then draw in the convex sets of minimal diet requirements for adults, children (noninfants), and infants. State whether or not the following assertions are true.

   (a) If a child's needs are satisfied, so are an adult's.
   (b) An infant's needs are satisfied only if a child's needs are.
   (c) An adult's needs are satisfied only if an infant's needs are.
   (d) Both an adult's and an infant's needs are satisfied only if a child's needs are.
   (e) It is possible to satisfy adult needs without satisfying the needs of an infant.

11. Prove that the following sets are convex. Which are polyhedral convex sets?

   (a) The interior plus the edges of a triangle.
   (b) The interior of a circle.
   (c) The interior of a rectangle.
   (d) A rectangle surmounted by a semicircle.

12. Consider the plane with a cartesian coordinate system. A rectangle with sides of length a_1 and a_2 ($a_1 \neq a_2$) is placed with one corner at the origin and two of its sides along the axes. Prove that the interior of the rectangle plus its edges forms a polyhedral convex set and find the statement of the form $Ax \leq b$ of which it is the truth set.

13. The following polygons are placed in a plane with a cartesian coordinate system with one corner at the origin and one side along an axis. Find the statements $Ax \leq b$ of which they are the truth sets.

   (a) A regular pentagon.
   (b) A regular hexagon.

SUPPLEMENTARY EXERCISES

14. Consider the inequalities

(i) $-x + 2y \leq 3$
(ii) $x + y \leq 6$
(iii) $x \qquad \geq 0$
(iv) $y \geq 0$

as open statements, and vectors $\begin{pmatrix} x \\ y \end{pmatrix}$ as logical possibilities for these open statements.

(a) Sketch the truth set of each open statement, and also of their conjunction. Show that the statements are consistent by finding a logical possibility making all of them true.

(b) Show that the four statements cannot all be false.

15. How many regions would four independent statements yield? How many regions did we obtain in Exercise 14?

16. Add to the statements in Exercise 14, the statement

(v) $3x + 4y \leq 22$.

(a) Show that the statement, "If (i), (ii), (iii), and (iv) are true, then (v) is true," is logically true.

(b) Show that the convex set determined by the statements (i)–(v) is the same as that determined by (i)–(iv).

(c) Show that (a) and (b) are just two different ways of saying that (v) is unnecessary or superfluous in the determination of the convex set.

17. A manufacturer has two machines M_1 and M_2 which he uses to manufacture two products P_1 and P_2. To produce one unit of P_1, three hours of time on M_1 and six hours on M_2 are needed. And to produce one unit of P_2, six hours on M_1 and five hours on M_2 are needed. Assume that each machine can run a maximum of 2100 hours per year.

(a) Let x_1 be the number of units of P_1 and x_2 the number of units of P_2 produced. Write the inequality restrictions on $x = \begin{pmatrix} x_1 \\ x_2 \end{pmatrix}$.

(b) Draw the convex set of possible production vectors x. (Save your work for later use.)

18. Two breakfast cereals, Krix and Kranch, supply varying amounts of vitamin B and iron; these are listed together with $\frac{1}{3}$ of the daily minimum requirements in the table below.

	Vitamin B	Iron
Krix	.15 mg./oz.	1.67 mg./oz.
Kranch	.10 mg./oz.	3.33 mg./oz.
$\frac{1}{3}$ Minimum requirements	.12 mg./day	2.0 mg./day

(a) Let w_1 be the amount of Krix eaten and w_2 the amount of Kranch eaten. Write the inequality restrictions on w_1 and w_2 in order that $\frac{1}{3}$ of the minimum daily requirements are met.

(b) Draw the convex set of possible amounts eaten defined by the inequalities of (a).

(c) What feasible diet requires a person to eat the fewest ounces of cereal?

[*Ans.* The diet requiring him to eat $\frac{6}{10}$ of an ounce of Krix and $\frac{3}{10}$ of an ounce of Kranch.]

19. Rework Exercise 18 under the assumption that a person wants to eat at least as much Kranch as Krix.

2.   MAXIMA AND MINIMA OF LINEAR FUNCTIONS

In the present section we first discuss the problem of finding the extreme points of a bounded polyhedral convex set. Then we find out how to compute the maximum and minimum values of a linear function defined on such a set.

As in the preceding section, we use the following notation that is adapted for three-space, but which extends easily to any number of dimensions. The polyhedral convex set C is the truth set of the statement $Ax \leq b$ where A is an $m \times 3$ matrix, x is a three-component column vector, and b is an m-component column vector. We let $A_1, A_2, \ldots, A_m$ denote the rows of A, so that each A_i is a three-component row vector and

$$A = \begin{pmatrix} A_1 \\ A_2 \\ \cdot \\ \cdot \\ \cdot \\ A_m \end{pmatrix}.$$

The statement $Ax \leq b$ is then the conjunction of the statements

$$A_1x \leq b_1, A_2x \leq b_2, \ldots, A_mx \leq b_m.$$

DEFINITION. We shall call the truth set of the statement $A_i x = b_i$ the *bounding plane* of the half space $A_i x \leq b_i$. (In the two-dimensional case it is called the bounding *line*.)

Thus, in Figure 1 of the preceding section the slanting line (a) is the bounding line of the half space (b).

Sometimes it happens that one of the inequality statements defining a polyhedral convex set is unnecessary in the sense that the conjunction of the statements defining C is the same (equivalent) with or without the given statement. For instance, in Example 3 of Section 1, if we add the statement $x_1 \geq -1$ to the statements defining the convex set, it is superfluous, since the statement $x_1 \geq 0$ implies the statement $x_1 \geq -1$. But there are less obvious examples of superfluous statements, such as the one given in Exercise 16 of the preceding section. Still other examples are given in Exercise 1. Obviously, the elimination of superfluous inequalities does not change the polyhedral convex set C, and we assume that all such superfluous inequalities have been removed.

If the inequality $A_i x \leq b_i$ is not superfluous, then its bounding plane $A_i x = b_i$ must contain a point of the polyhedral convex set C. The *bounding planes* of C are the bounding planes of the (nonsuperfluous) half spaces of which C is the intersection.

In Example 3 of Section 1 the bounding planes (lines) of the convex set given there are the three boundary lines of the triangle shaded in Figure 2. Note that these lines intersect in pairs in three points, the vertices of the triangle. Such intersections are called *extreme points* of C. And in three dimensions, if T is a point of C that is the intersection of three bounding planes of C, then it is an *extreme point* of C.

Example 1. Find the extreme points of the polyhedral convex set $Ax \leq b$ where

$$A = \begin{pmatrix} -2 & -1 \\ 1 & -3 \\ 1 & 2 \end{pmatrix}, \qquad b = \begin{pmatrix} 9 \\ 6 \\ 3 \end{pmatrix}.$$

A sketch of the three half planes, Figure 3, shows that the set is a triangle. Hence we can find the extreme points by changing the inequalities to equalities in pairs and solving three sets of simultaneous equations. We obtain in this way the points

$$\begin{pmatrix} -3 \\ -3 \end{pmatrix}, \qquad \begin{pmatrix} -7 \\ 5 \end{pmatrix}, \quad \text{and} \quad \begin{pmatrix} \frac{21}{5} \\ -\frac{3}{5} \end{pmatrix},$$

which are the extreme points of the set.

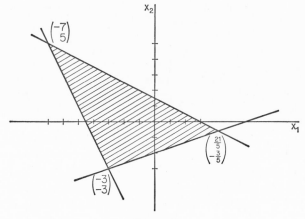

Figure 3

We can now give an interpretation for the various points of the polyhedral convex set in terms of the system of inequalities. An extreme point, in the plane, lies on two boundaries, which means that two of the inequalities are actually equalities. A point on a side, other than an extreme point, lies on one boundary and hence one inequality is an equality. An interior point of the polygon must, by a process of elimination, correspond to the case where the inequalities are all strict inequalities, i.e., not only $\leq$ but $<$ holds.

There is a mechanical (but lengthy) method for finding all the extreme points of a polyhedral convex set C in three-space defined by $Ax \leq b$. Consider the bounding hyperplanes $A_1x = b_1, \ldots, A_mx = b_m$ of the half spaces that determine C. Select a subset of three of these hyperplanes and solve their equations simultaneously. If the result is a unique point x^0 (and only then), check to see whether or not x^0 belongs to C. If it does, by the above definition, x^0 is an extreme point of C. Moreover, all extreme points of C can be found in this manner.

Example 2. Let

$$A = \begin{pmatrix} -1 & 0 \\ 0 & -1 \end{pmatrix} \quad \text{and} \quad b = \begin{pmatrix} 0 \\ 0 \end{pmatrix}.$$

Then the polyhedral convex set C defined by $Ax \leq b$ is the first quadrant of the x_1, x_2 plane, shaded in Figure 4. The only extreme point is the origin, which is the intersection of the lines $x_1 = 0$ and $x_2 = 0$. This is an example of an *unbounded* polyhedral convex set.

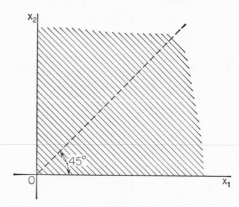

Figure 4

Notice that the set C contains the *ray* or half line that starts at the origin of coordinates and extends upward to the right making a 45° angle with the axes. This ray is dotted in Figure 4. Of course, this set also contains many other rays.

We shall say that a polyhedral convex set is *bounded* if it does not contain a ray. A set, such as the one in Figure 4, that does contain rays will be called *unbounded*. For simplicity we shall restrict our discussion to bounded convex sets in most of this chapter. In particular, this means that necessarily $m > n$, that is, the convex set must be the intersection of at least $n + 1$ half spaces. Thus we need at least three lines in the plane, and at least four planes in three-space to produce a bounded set. This is a necessary but not sufficient condition that the convex set is bounded (see Exercise 23).

Example 3. Let us suppose that in a business problem x_1 and x_2 are quantities we can control, except that there are limitations imposed which can be stated as inequalities. We shall assume that the system of inequalities given in Example 1 limits our choice of x_1 and x_2. Let us assume that a given choice of x_1 and x_2 results in a profit of $x_1 + 2x_2$ dollars. What is the most and the least profit we can make? We must find the maximum and the minimum value of $x_1 + 2x_2$ for points (x_1, x_2) in the triangle. Let us first try the extreme points. At $(-3, -3)$ we would have a profit of -9, i.e., a loss of $9. At $(-7, 5)$ we have a profit of $3, and at $(\frac{21}{5}, -\frac{3}{5})$ also a profit of $3. What can we say about the remainder of the triangle? The last inequality tells that $x_1 + 2x_2 \leq 3$, hence our profit cannot be more than \$3. If we multiply the first inequality by $\frac{5}{7}$ and the second by $\frac{3}{7}$ and add them, we find that $x_1 + 2x_2 \geq -9$; hence, we cannot lose more than \$9. We have thus shown that both the greatest profit and the greatest loss occur at an extreme point. We will show that this is true in general.

Given a polyhedral convex set C and a linear function

$$cx = c_1x_1 + c_2x_2 + \ldots + c_nx_n,$$

where $c = (c_1, c_2, \ldots, c_n)$, we want to show in general that the maximum and minimum values of the function cx always occur at extreme points of C. We shall carry out the proof for the planar case in which $n = 2$, but our results are true in general.

First, we will show that the values of the linear function $c_1x_1 + c_2x_2$ on any line segment lie *between* the values the function has at the two end points (possibly equal to the value at one end point). We represent the points as column vectors $\begin{pmatrix} x_1 \\ x_2 \end{pmatrix}$ and then we see that our linear function is represented by the row vector $c = (c_1, c_2)$. Let the end points of the segment be

$$p = \begin{pmatrix} x_1' \\ x_2' \end{pmatrix} \quad \text{and} \quad q = \begin{pmatrix} x_1'' \\ x_2'' \end{pmatrix}.$$

We have seen in Chapter V (see Figure 4) that the points in between p and q can be represented as $tp + (1 - t)q$, with $0 \leq t \leq 1$. If the values of the function at the points p and q are P and Q, respectively (assume that $P \geq Q$), then at a point in between the value will be $tP + (1 - t)Q$, since the function is linear. This value can also be written as

$$tP + (1 - t)Q = Q + (P - Q)t = P - (1 - t)(P - Q),$$

which (for $0 \leq t \leq 1$) is at least Q and at most P.

We are now in a position to prove the result illustrated in Example 3.

Theorem. A linear function cx defined over a polyhedral convex set C takes on its maximum (and minimum) value at an extreme point of C.

The proof of the theorem is illustrated in Figure 5. We shall suppose that at the extreme point p the function takes on a value P greater than or equal to the value at any other extreme point, and at the extreme point q it takes on its smallest extreme point value, Q. Let r be any

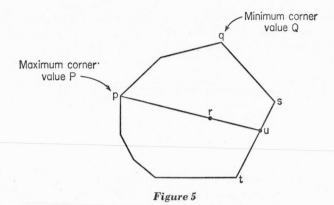

Figure 5

point of the polygon. Draw a straight line between p and r and continue it until it cuts the polygon again at a point u lying on an edge of the polygon, say the edge between the corner points s and t. (The line may even cut the edge at one of the points s and t; the analysis remains unchanged.) By hypothesis the value of the function at any corner point must lie between Q and P. By the above result the value of the function at u must lie between its values at s and t, and hence must also lie between Q and P. Again by the above result the value of the function at r must lie between its values at p and u, and hence must also lie between Q and P. Since r was any point of the polygon, our theorem is proved.

Suppose that in place of the linear function $c_1x_1 + c_2x_2$ we had considered the function $c_1x_1 + c_2x_2 + k$. The addition of the constant k merely changes every value of the function, including the maximum and minimum values of the function, by that amount. Hence the analysis of where the maximum and minimum values of the function are taken on is unchanged. Therefore, we have the following theorem.

Theorem. The function $cx + k$ defined over a polyhedral convex set C takes on its maximum (and minimum) value at an extreme point of C.

A method of finding the maximum or minimum of the function $cx + k$ defined over a convex set C is then the following: Find the extreme points of the set; there will be a finite number of them. Substitute the coordinates of each into the function. The largest of the values so obtained will be the maximum of the function and the smallest value will be the minimum of the function. The method is illustrated in Example 3 above.

EXERCISES

1. In the following sets of inequalities at least one is superfluous. In each case find the superfluous ones.

(a) $\quad x_1 + x_2 \leq 3$
$\quad\quad -x_1 - x_2 \geq 0$
$\quad\quad\quad\quad x_1 \geq -1$
$\quad\quad\quad\quad -x_2 \leq 2.$

(b) $x_1 + x_2 \geq 0$
$\quad\quad x_1 - x_2 \leq 0$
$\quad\quad\quad\quad x_1 \leq 4$
$\quad\quad\quad\quad x_2 \geq -4.$

(c) $-1 \leq x_1 \leq 1$
$\quad\quad -2 \leq x_2 \leq 2$
$\quad\quad x_1 + x_2 \geq -10$
$\quad\quad 2x_1 - x_2 \leq 2.$ $\quad\quad\quad\quad\quad$ [*Ans.* (a) $x_1 + x_2 \leq 3.$]

2. (a) Draw a picture of the convex set defined by the inequalities

$$2x_1 + \ \ x_2 + 9 \leq 0$$
$$-x_1 + 3x_2 + 6 \leq 0$$
$$x_1 + 2x_2 - 3 \leq 0.$$

(b) What is the relationship between this and Figure 3?

3. Find the corner points of the convex polygons given in parts (a), (b), and (e) of Exercise 1 of Section 1.

[*Ans.* (a) $\begin{pmatrix} 3 \\ -2 \end{pmatrix}, \begin{pmatrix} 3 \\ 2 \end{pmatrix}, \begin{pmatrix} -3 \\ 2 \end{pmatrix}$; (e) $\begin{pmatrix} 2 \\ 3 \end{pmatrix}, \begin{pmatrix} -2 \\ 3 \end{pmatrix}, \begin{pmatrix} 2 \\ -3 \end{pmatrix}, \begin{pmatrix} -2 \\ -3 \end{pmatrix}.$]

4. (a) Show that the three lines whose equations are

$$2x_1 + \ \ x_2 + 9 = 0$$
$$-x_1 + 3x_2 + 6 = 0$$
$$x_1 + 2x_2 - 3 = 0$$

divide the plane into seven convex regions. Mark these regions with Roman numerals I–VII.

(b) For each of the seven regions found in part (a), write a set of three inequalities, having the region as its locus. [*Hint:* Two of these sets of inequalities are considered in Exercise 2.]

(c) There is one more way of putting inequality signs into the three equations given in (a). What is the locus of this last set of inequalities? $\quad\quad\quad\quad\quad\quad\quad$ [*Ans.* The empty set ε.]

5. A convex polygon has the points $(-1, 0)$, $(3, 4)$, $(0, -3)$, and $(1, 6)$ as extreme points. Find a set of inequalities which defines the convex polygon having these extreme points.

6. Find the extreme points of the convex polygon given by the equations

$$2x_1 + x_2 + 9 \geq 0$$
$$-x_1 + 3x_2 + 6 \geq 0$$
$$x_1 + 2x_2 - 3 \leq 0$$
$$x_1 + x_2 \leq 0.$$

[*Hint:* Use some of the results of Example 1 in the text.]

7. Find the extreme values of the function G defined by

$$G(x) = 7x_1 + 5x_2 - 3$$

over the convex polygon of Exercise 6.

8. Find the maximum and minimum of the function

$$G(x) = -2x_1 + 5x_2 + 17$$

over each of the convex polygons given in parts (a), (b), and (e) of Exercise 1 of Section 1.   [*Ans.* (a) 33, 1; (e) 36, -2.]

9. Find the maximum and minimum, when they exist, of the function

$$G(x) = 5x_1 + 3x_2 - 6$$

over each of the polyhedral convex sets given in parts (h) and (j) of Exercise 1 of Section 1.   [*Ans.* (h) Neither maximum nor minimum; (j) minimum is 3.]

10. The owner of an oil truck with a capacity of 500 gallons hauls gasoline and oil products from city to city. On any given trip he wishes to load his truck with at least 200 gallons of regular test gasoline, at least 100 gallons of high test gasoline, and at most 150 gallons of kerosene. Assuming that he always fills his truck to capacity, find the convex set of ways that he can load his truck. Interpret the extreme points of the set. [*Hint:* There are four extreme points.]

11. An advertiser wishes to sponsor a half hour television comedy and must decide on the composition of the show. The advertiser insists that there be at least three minutes of commercials, while the television network requires that the commercial time be limited to at most 15 minutes. The comedian refuses to work more than 22 minutes each half hour show. If a band is added to the show to play during the time that neither the comedian nor the commercials are on, construct the convex set C of possible assignments of time to the comedian, the commercials, and the band that use up the 30 minutes. Find the extreme points of C.

[*Ans.* If x_1 is the comedian time, x_2 the commercial time, and $30 - x_1 - x_2$ the band time, the extreme points are

$$\binom{0}{3}, \quad \binom{22}{3}, \quad \binom{22}{8}, \quad \binom{15}{15} \quad \text{and} \quad \binom{0}{15}.]$$

12. In Exercise 10 suppose that the oil truck operator gets 3 cents per gallon for delivering regular gasoline, 2 cents per gallon for high test, and 1 cent per gallon for kerosene. Write the expression that gives the total amount he will be paid for each possible load that he carries. How should he load his truck in order to earn the maximum amount?

[*Ans.* He should carry 400 gallons of regular gasoline, 100 gallons of high test, and no kerosene.]

13. In Exercise 12, if he gets 3 cents per gallon of regular and 2 cents per gallon of high test gasoline, how high must his payment for kerosene become before he will load it on his truck in order to make a maximum profit?

[*Ans.* He must get paid at least 3 cents per gallon of kerosene.]

14. In Exercise 11 let x_1 be the number of minutes the comedian is on and x_2 be the number of minutes the commercial is on the program. Suppose the comedian costs \$200 per minute, the commercials cost \$50 per minute, and the band is free. How should the advertiser choose the composition of the show in order that its cost be a minimum?

15. Consider the polyhedral convex set P defined by the inequalities

$$-1 \leq x_1 \leq 4$$
$$0 \leq x_2 \leq 6.$$

Find four different sets of conditions on the constants a and b that the function $F(x) = ax_1 + bx_2$ should have its maximum at one and only one of the four corner points of P. Find conditions that F should have its minimum at each of these points.

[*Ans.* For example, the maximum is at $\binom{4}{6}$ if $a > 0$ and $b > 0$.]

16. Let H be the quadratic function defined by $H(x) = (x_1 - \frac{1}{4})^2 + (x_2 - \frac{1}{4})^2$ on the convex set C which is the truth set of the inequalities

$$x_1 + x_2 \leq 1, \qquad x_1 \geq 0, \qquad x_2 \geq 0.$$

Are the maximum and minimum values of H taken on at the extreme points of C? Discuss reasons why this problem is essentially harder than that of finding the extreme values of a linear function on a polyhedral convex set.

17. A set of points is said to be convex if whenever it contains two points it also contains the line segment connecting them. Show that

(a) If two points are in the truth set of an inequality, then any point on the connecting segment is also in the truth set.

(b) Every polygonal convex set is a convex set in the above-mentioned sense.

18. Give an example of a quadrilateral that is not a convex set.

19. Prove that for any three vectors, u, v, w, the set of all points $au + bv + cw$ ($a \geq 0$, $b \geq 0$, $c \geq 0$, $a + b + c = 1$) is a convex set. What geometric figure is this locus? [*Ans.* In general, the locus is a triangle.]

20. Let C be any plane polyhedral convex set. Show that if x is a point that lies on three bounding lines of C, then one of the inequalities defining C is superfluous.

21. Let x and y be two distinct points of a polyhedral convex set C, let t be a number such that $0 < t < 1$, and define $z = tx + (1 - t)y$. Show that z is not an extreme point of C.

22. Prove that the intersection of two half planes is a bounded convex set only if it is empty.

23. Construct examples that show that the intersection of three half planes either may or may not be a bounded convex set.

SUPPLEMENTARY EXERCISES

24. In Exercise 17 of Section 1 assume that the manufacturer makes a profit of $4 for each unit of P_1 and $5 for each unit of P_2. How many units of each should he produce in order to maximize his profit? What is his maximum profit?

[*Ans.* 100 units of P_1 and 300 units of P_2; his maximum profit is $1900.]

25. In Exercise 18 of Section 1 assume that Krix costs $\frac{5}{3}$ of a cent per ounce and Kranch costs $\frac{5}{2}$ of a cent per ounce. In order to satisfy $\frac{1}{3}$ of the daily minimum requirements at minimum cost, how many ounces of each cereal should a person eat? What is the cost of the minimum cost diet?

[*Partial Ans.* The cost is $\frac{7}{4}$ of a cent per day.]

26. Rework Exercise 25 under the assumption that a person wants to eat at least as much Kranch as Krix (see Exercise 19 of Section 1).

27. An automobile manufacturer has 900 tons of metal on hand from which he is to make x_1 automobiles and x_2 trucks. It takes 2 tons of metal and 200 man-hours of work to make an automobile, and it takes 4 tons of metal and 150 man-hours of work to make a truck. He has 60,000 man-hours of time available. If he makes a profit of $500 on an automobile and $800 on a truck, how many of each should he make to maximize his profit?

(a) Set up the inequality constraints on the variables.

(b) Draw the convex set of feasible vectors.

(c) Find the optimal production vector and the maximum profit.
[*Ans.* He should produce 210 automobiles and 120 trucks for a maximum profit of $201,000.]

28. Suppose in Exercise 27 that the profit on automobiles drops to $350. How will this affect the production and profits?
[*Ans.* He produces only trucks for profit of $180,000.]

29. Suppose in Exercise 27 that the profit on trucks drops to $350. How should the manufacturer now produce?

3. LINEAR PROGRAMMING PROBLEMS

An important class of practical problems are those which require the determination of the maximum or the minimum of a linear function $cx + k$ defined over a polyhedral convex set of points C. We illustrate these so-called *linear programming problems* by means of the following examples.*

Example 1. An automobile manufacturer makes automobiles and trucks in a factory that is divided into two shops. Shop 1, which performs the basic assembly operation, must work five man-days on each truck but only two man-days on each automobile. Shop 2, which performs finishing operations, must work three man-days for each automobile or truck that it produces. Because of men and machine limitations, shop 1 has 180 man-days per week available while shop 2 has 135 man-days per week. If the manufacturer makes a profit of $300 on each truck and $200 on each automobile, how many of each should he produce to maximize his profit?

To state the problem mathematically, we set up the following notation: Let x_1 be the number of trucks and x_2 the number of automobiles to be produced per week. Then these quantities must satisfy the following restrictions.

$$5x_1 + 2x_2 \leq 180$$
$$3x_1 + 3x_2 \leq 135.$$

* Readers interested in an elementary treatment of the simplex method of linear programming are referred to Kemeny, Schleifer, Snell, and Thompson, *Finite Mathematics with Business Applications* (Englewood Cliffs, N.J.: Prentice-Hall, Inc., 1962), pp. 384–401.

We want to maximize the linear function $300x_1 + 200x_2$, subject to these inequality constraints, together with the obviously necessary constraints that $x_1 \geq 0$ and $x_2 \geq 0$.

To further simplify notation, we define the quantities

$$A = \begin{pmatrix} 5 & 2 \\ 3 & 3 \end{pmatrix}, \quad b = \begin{pmatrix} 180 \\ 135 \end{pmatrix} \quad \text{and} \quad c = (300, 200).$$

Then we can state this linear programming problem as follows.

Maximum problem: Determine the vector x so that the weekly profit, given by the quantity cx, is a maximum, subject to the inequality constraints $Ax \leq b$ and $x \geq 0$. The inequality constraints insure that the weekly number of available man-hours is not exceeded and that non-negative quantities of automobiles and trucks are produced.

The graph of the convex set of possible x vectors is pictured in Figure 6. Clearly this is a problem of the kind discussed in the previous section.

The extreme points of the convex set C are

$$T_1 = \begin{pmatrix} 0 \\ 0 \end{pmatrix}, \quad T_2 = \begin{pmatrix} 36 \\ 0 \end{pmatrix}, \quad T_3 = \begin{pmatrix} 0 \\ 45 \end{pmatrix} \quad \text{and} \quad T_4 = \begin{pmatrix} 30 \\ 15 \end{pmatrix}.$$

Following the solution procedure outlined in the previous section, we

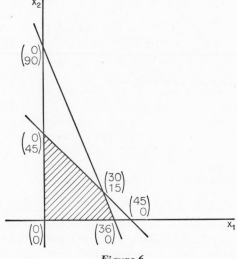

Figure 6

test the function $cx = 300x_1 + 200x_2$ at each of these extreme points. The values taken on are 0, 10,800, 9000, and 12,000. Thus the maximum weekly profit is $12,000 and is achieved by producing 30 trucks and 15 automobiles per week.

Example 2. A mining company owns two different mines that produce a given kind of ore. The mines are located in different parts of the country and hence have different production capacities. After crushing, the ore is graded into three classes: high-grade, medium-grade, and low-grade ores. There is some demand for each grade of ore. The mining company has contracted to provide a smelting plant with 12 tons of high-grade, eight tons of medium-grade, and 24 tons of low-grade ore per week. It costs the company $200 per day to run the first mine and $160 per day to run the second. However, in a day's operation the first mine produces six tons of high-grade, two tons of medium-grade, and four tons of low-grade ore, while the second mine produces daily two tons of high-grade, two tons of medium-grade, and 12 tons of low-grade ore. How many days a week should each mine be operated in order to fulfill the company's orders most economically?

Before solving the problem it is convenient to summarize the above information as in the tableau of Figure 7. The numbers in the tableau form a 2-by-3 matrix, the requirements form a row vector c, and the

	High-grade ore	Medium-grade ore	Low-grade ore	
Mine 1	6	2	4	$200
Mine 2	2	2	12	$160
	12	8	24	

b

c

Figure 7

costs form a column vector b. The entries in the matrix indicate the production of each kind of ore by the mines, the entries in the requirements vector c indicate the quantities that must be produced, and the entries in the cost vector b indicate the daily costs of running each mine.

Let $w = (w_1, w_2)$ be the two-component row vector whose component w_1 gives the number of days per week that mine 1 operates and w_2 gives the number of days per week that mine 2 operates. If we define the quantities

$$A = \begin{pmatrix} 6 & 2 & 4 \\ 2 & 2 & 12 \end{pmatrix}, \quad c = (12, 8, 24), \quad \text{and} \quad b = \begin{pmatrix} 200 \\ 160 \end{pmatrix},$$

we can state the above problem as a minimum problem.

Minimum problem: Determine the vector w so that the weekly operating cost, given by the quantity wb, is a minimum, subject to the inequality restraints $wA \geq c$ and $w \geq 0$. The inequality restraints insure that the weekly output requirements are met and the limits on the components of w are not exceeded.

It is clear that this is a minimum problem of the type discussed in detail in the preceding section. In Figure 8 we have graphed the convex

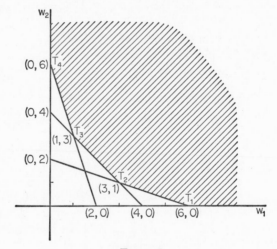

Figure 8

polyhedral set C defined by the inequalities $wA \geq c$. (We have omitted the additional obvious constraints $w_1 \leq 7$ and $w_2 \leq 7$, for simplicity. These, if added, would make the convex set bounded.)

The extreme points of the convex set C are

$$T_1 = (6, 0), \quad T_2 = (3, 1), \quad T_3 = (1, 3), \quad T_4 = (0, 6).$$

Testing the function $wb = 200w_1 + 160w_2$ at each of these extreme points, we see that it takes on the values 1200, 760, 680, and 960, respectively. We see that the minimum operating cost is $680 per week and it is achieved at T_3, i.e., by operating the first mine one day per week and the second mine three days a week.

Observe that if the mines are operated as indicated, then the combined weekly production will be 12 tons of high-grade ore, 8 tons of medium-grade ore, and 40 tons of low-grade ore. In other words, for this solution, low-grade ore is overproduced. If the company has no other demand for the low-grade ore, then it must discard 16 tons of it per week in this minimum-cost solution of its production problem.

Example 3. As a variant of Example 2, assume that the cost vector is $b = \begin{pmatrix} 160 \\ 200 \end{pmatrix}$; in other words, the first mine now has a lower daily cost than the second. By the same procedure as above we find that the minimum cost level is again $680 and is achieved by operating the first mine three days a week and the second mine one day per week. In this solution, 20 tons of high-grade ore, instead of the required 12 tons, are produced, while the requirements of medium- and low-grade ores are exactly met. Thus eight tons of high-grade ore must be discarded per week.

Example 4. As another variant of Example 2, assume that the cost vector is $b = \begin{pmatrix} 200 \\ 200 \end{pmatrix}$; in other words, both mines have the same production costs. Evaluating the cost function wb at the extreme points of the convex set, we find costs of $1200 on two of the extreme points (T_1 and T_4) and costs of $800 on the other two extreme points (T_2 and T_3). Thus the minimum cost is attained by operating either one of the mines three days a week and the other one one day a week. But there are other solutions, since if the minimum is taken on at two distinct extreme points, it is also taken on at each of the points on the line segment between. Thus any vector w where $1 \leq w_1 \leq 3$, $1 \leq w_2 \leq 3$, and $w_1 + w_2 = 4$ also gives a minimum-cost solution. For example, each mine could operate two days a week.

It can be shown (see Exercise 2) that for any solution w with $1 < w_1 < 3$, $1 < w_2 < 3$, and $w_1 + w_2 = 4$, both high-grade and low-grade ores are overproduced.

EXERCISES

1. In Example 1, assume that profits are $200 per truck and $300 per automobile. What should the factory now produce for maximum profit?

2. In Example 4, show that both high- and low-grade ores are overproduced for solution vectors w with $1 < w_1 < 3$, $1 < w_2 < 3$, and $w_1 + w_2 = 4$.

3. A well-known nursery rhyme says "Jack Sprat could eat no fat. His wife (call her Jill) could eat no lean . . . ." Suppose Jack wishes to have at least one pound of lean meat per day, while Jill needs at least .4 pound of fat per day. Assume they buy only beef having 10 per cent fat and 90 per cent lean, and pork having 40 per cent fat and 60 per cent lean. Jack and Jill want to fulfill their minimal diet requirements at the lowest possible cost.

  (a) Let x be the amount of beef and y the amount of pork which they purchase per day. Construct the convex set of points in the plane representing purchases that fulfill both persons' minimum diet requirements.

  (b) Suggest necessary restrictions on the purchases that will change this set into a convex polygon.

  (c) If beef costs $1 per pound, and pork costs 50 cents per pound, show that the diet of least cost has only pork, and find the minimum cost.
  [*Ans.* 83 cents.]

  (d) If beef costs 75 cents and pork costs 50 cents per pound, show that there is a whole line segment of solution points and find the minimum cost.
  [*Ans.* 83 cents.]

  (e) If beef and pork each cost $1 a pound, show that the unique minimal cost diet has both beef and pork. Find the minimum cost.
  [*Ans.* $1.40.]

  (f) Show that the restriction made in part (b) did not alter the answer given in (c)–(e).

4. In Exercise 3(d) show that for all but one of the minimal cost diets Jill has more than her minimum requirement of fat, while Jack always gets exactly his minimal requirement of lean. Show that all but one of the minimal cost diets contain some beef.

5. In Exercise 3(e) show that Jack and Jill each get exactly their minimal requirements.

6. In Exercise 3, if the price of pork is fixed at $1 a pound, how low must the price of beef fall before Jack and Jill will eat only beef?   [*Ans.* 25 cents.]

7. In Exercise 3, suppose that Jack decides to reduce his minimal requirement to .6 pound of lean meat per day. How does the convex set change? How do the solutions in 3(c), (d), and (e) change?

8. A poultry farmer raises chickens, ducks, and turkeys and has room for 500 birds on his farm. While he is willing to have a total of 500 birds, he does not want more than 300 ducks on his farm at any one time. Suppose that a chicken costs $1.50, a duck $1.00, and a turkey $4.00 to raise to maturity. Assume that the farmer can sell chickens for $3.00, ducks for $2.00, and turkeys for T dollars each. He wants to decide which kind of poultry to raise in order to maximize his profit.

(a) Let x be the number of chickens and y be the number of ducks he will raise. Then $500 - x - y$ is the number of turkeys he raises. What is the convex set of possible values of x and y which satisfy the above restrictions?

(b) Find the expression for the cost of raising x chickens, y ducks, and $(500 - x - y)$ turkeys. Find the expression for the total amount he gets for these birds. Compute the profit which he would make under these circumstances.

(c) If $T = \$6.00$, show that to obtain maximal profit the farmer should raise only turkeys. What is the maximum profit?   [*Ans.* $1000.]

(d) If $T = \$5.00$, show that he should raise only chickens and find his maximum profit.   [*Ans.* $750.]

(e) If $T = \$5.50$, show that he can raise any combination of chickens and turkeys and find his maximum profit.   [*Ans.* $750.]

9. Rework Exercise 8 if the price of chickens drops to $2.00 and T is (a) $6.00, (b) $5.00, (c) $4.50, and (d) $4.00.

10. In Exercise 8 show that if the price of turkeys drops below $5.50, the farmer should raise only chickens. Also show that if the price is above $5.50, he should raise only turkeys.

11. In Exercise 10 of Section 2, assume that the truck operator gets p cents a gallon for regular gasoline, q cents a gallon for high-test gasoline, and r cents a gallon for kerosene. Show that he will carry kerosene for maximum profit only if $r \geq p$ and $r \geq q$.

12. In Exercise 11 of Section 2, suppose that for each minute the comedian is on the program 70,000 more people will tune in, for each minute the band is on 10,000 more people will tune in, and for each minute the commercial is on one more person will tune in. Let N be the function that gives the number of persons that tune in for each point in C. How should the times be allotted in order that N be a maximum?

[*Ans.* There should be 3 minutes of commercials, 22 minutes of the comedian, and 5 minutes of band music.]

13. In Exercise 11 of Section 2, assume that the band and comedian each cost $200 per minute while the commercials cost $50 per minute. Write the function that gives the cost of the program. Show that there is a whole line segment of minimum cost solutions.

[*Ans.* The commercials are on for 15 minutes while the band and comedian can share the remaining 15 minutes in any manner.]

SUPPLEMENTARY EXERCISES

14. Suppose that 1 unit of hog liver contains 1 unit of carbohydrates, 3 units of vitamins, and 3 units of proteins and costs 50 cents per unit. Suppose 1 unit of castor oil contains 3, 4, and 1 units of these items, respectively, and costs 25 cents per unit. If hog liver and castor oil are the only foods available, and the minimum daily requirements are 8 units of carbohydrates, 19 units of vitamins, and 7 units of proteins, find the minimum cost diet, using the following procedure.

(a) Let w_1 be the number of units of hog liver and w_2 the number of units of castor oil purchased. Set up the inequality constraints that these variables must satisfy.

(b) Find the objective function to be minimized.

(c) Sketch the convex set of possible food purchases.

(d) Locate the extreme point giving the minimum cost diet.
[*Ans.* Buy one unit of hog liver and four units of castor oil; cost, $1.50.]

15. Suppose that the minimum cost diet found in Exercise 14 is found to be unpalatable. In order to increase its palatability, add a constraint requiring that at least three units of hog liver be purchased, and re-solve the problem. How much is the cost of the minimum cost diet increased due to this palatability requirement?   [*Ans.* $.63.]

16. A farmer owns a 100 acre farm and can plant any combination of two crops I and II. Crop I requires one man-day of labor and $10 of capital for each acre planted, while crop II requires 4 man-days of labor and $20 of capital for each acre planted. Crop I produces $40 of net revenue per acre and crop II produces $60 net revenue per acre. The farmer has $1100 of capital and 160 man-days of labor available for the year.

(a) Let x_1 be the number of acres of crop I and x_2 the number of acres of crop II planted. Set up the inequality constraints.

(b) Set up the expression that gives the net revenue from a planting scheme $\begin{pmatrix} x_1 \\ x_2 \end{pmatrix}$.

(c) Sketch the convex set of possible planting schemes.

(d) Find the extreme point that gives the maximum revenue.
[*Partial Ans.* The maximum revenue is $4200.]

17. In Exercise 16 assume that the revenue from crop II is $90 per acre.
    (a) Find the new maximum revenue scheme, and show that now the best thing for the farmer to do is to leave 15 acres unplanted.
    (b) Explain why the farmer should leave part of his land fallow in this case.

18. A manufacturer produces two types of bearings, A and B, utilizing three types of machines, lathes, grinders, and drill presses. The machinery requirements for one unit of each product, in hours, is expressed in the following table.

Bearing	Lathe	Grinder	Drill Press
A	.01	.03	.03
B	.02	.01	.015
Weekly machine capacity (hours)	400	450	480

The weekly machine capacities are also shown in the table. He makes a profit of 10 cents per type A bearing and 15 cents per type B bearing.
    (a) Let x_1 be the number of type A bearings and x_2 the number of type B bearings produced. Write the inequality restrictions on these variables.
    (b) Write the objective function to be maximized.
    (c) Draw the convex set of possible production plans.
    (d) Find the optimum production plan.
        [*Ans.* He should produce 8000 type A and 16,000 type B bearings for a profit of $3200.]

19. In Exercise 18 assume that the manufacturer has enough money to purchase one more machine of any kind, and that doing so will increase the capacity of that type of machine by 40 hours per week.
    (a) He wants to buy a new grinder. Would you advise him to do so?
                                                            [*Ans.* No.]
    (b) Which machine would you recommend that he buy?
                                                        [*Ans.* A lathe.]

4. STRICTLY DETERMINED GAMES

We turn now from linear programming to the theory of games of strategy. Ultimately these two theories can be closely connected but superficially they are different.

Game theory considers situations in which there are two (or more) persons, each of whose actions influence, but do not completely determine, the outcome of a certain event. The manner in which their actions influence the outcome of the event is spelled out in the rules of play of the game. Depending on which event actually occurs, the players receive various payments, which we shall assume to be in money. If, for each possible event, the algebraic sum of payments to all players is zero, the game is called *zero-sum;* otherwise it is *nonzero-sum.* Usually the players will not agree as to which event should occur, so that their objectives in the game are different. In the case of a matrix game, which is a two-person game in which one player loses what the other wins (i.e., a two-person zero-sum game), game theory provides a solution, based on the principle that each player tries to choose his course of action so that, regardless of what his opponent does, he can assure himself of at least a certain amount.

Most recreational games such as tick-tack-toe, checkers, backgammon, chess, poker, bridge, and other card games can be viewed as games of strategy. Moreover, they can be put in the form of matrix games; the way in which this is done will be discussed for specific examples in Sections 6 and 9. On the other hand, gambling games such as dice, roulette, etc., are *not* (as usually formulated) games of strategy, since a person playing one of these games is merely "betting against the odds."

The actual games of strategy mentioned above are nearly all too complicated, as they stand, to be analyzed completely. We shall instead construct simple examples which, although uninteresting from a player's point of view, do illustrate the theory and are amenable to computations.

In this section we shall discuss strictly determined matrix games. The general definition and discussion of matrix games is given in Section 6.

Example 1. Consider the following very simple card game. There are two players, call them R and C (the reason for the use of these two letters will be explained later); player R is given a hand consisting of a red 5 and a black 5, while player C is given a black 5, a red 3, and a red 1. The game they are to play is the following: At a given signal the players *simultaneously* expose one of their cards. If the cards *match* in color, player R wins the (positive) difference between the numbers on the cards; if the cards do *not match* in color, player C wins the (positive) difference between the numbers on the cards played. Obviously the strategic decision that each player must make is which of his cards to play.

Player C

		bk 5	rd 3	rd 1
Player R	bk 5	0	−2	−4
	rd 5	0	2	4

Figure 9

A convenient way of representing the game is by means of the matrix G shown in Figure 9. (In game theory it is customary to present matrices in this "table" form.) The rows represent the possible choices of player R, and the columns, the possible choices of player C; hence our use of R and C. The number in position g_{ij} represents the gain of R if R chooses row i and C chooses column j. A positive entry is a payment from C to R, while a negative "gain" for R is a payment from R to C. For instance, if R chooses row 1 (plays bk 5) and C chooses column 1 (plays bk 5), then R wins the difference of the two numbers, which is 0. If R chooses row 1 but C chooses column 2 (plays rd 3), then C wins the difference of 5 minus 3, which is indicated by the −2 entry in the matrix. The rest of the entries are determined similarly.

The game shown in Figure 9 is called a *matrix game*. Any matrix can be considered a two person matrix game by allowing one player to control the rows, the other the columns, and defining the payoffs of the game to be the various matrix entries. In Section 6 such games will be discussed in detail.

How should the players play the matrix game of Figure 9? Player C would like to get the −4 entry in the matrix. However, the only way he could get it would be to play the third column of the matrix, in which case player R would surely choose the second row and C would lose 4 rather than gain 4. On the other hand, if C chooses the first column (i.e., plays bk 5), he assures himself that he will break even regardless of what R does. It is clear that R has nothing to lose and may possibly gain by choosing the second row, hence he should always do so. The knowledge that he will do so reinforces C in his choice of the first column. The optimal procedure for the players is then: R should play rd 5 and C should play bk 5. If they play this way, neither player wins from the other, that is, the game is *fair*.

A command of the form: "Play rd 5," or "Play bk 3," will be called a *strategy*. If player R uses the strategy "Play rd 5" in the game of Figure 9, then, regardless of what C does, R assures himself that he will get *at least* a payoff of zero. Similarly, if C uses the strategy "Play bk 5," then, regardless of what R does, C assures himself of obtaining a payoff of *at most zero*, i.e., a loss of at most zero. Since R cannot, by his own efforts, assure himself of gaining more than zero, and C cannot, by his own efforts, assure himself of losing less than zero, and since these two numbers are the same, we call these *optimal strategies* for the game. Also we call zero the *value* of the game, since it is the outcome of the game if each player uses his optimal strategy.

DEFINITION. We shall say that a matrix game is *strictly determined* if the matrix contains an entry, call it v, which is *simultaneously* the *minimum* of the row in which it occurs and the *maximum* of the column in which it occurs. *Optimal strategies* for the players are then the following.

> For player R: "Play a row that contains v."
> For player C: "Play a column that contains v."

The *value* of the game is v. The game is *fair* if its value is zero.

In Section 6 it will be shown that the strategies here defined are optimal in the sense indicated above, and that v has the property of being the best either player can assure for himself.

Example 1 (continued). The game of Figure 9 is strictly determined, since the 0 entry in the lower left-hand corner of the matrix is the minimum of the second row and the maximum of the first column of that matrix. Observe that the optimal strategies given in the definition above agree with those found earlier. Also the value of that game is zero, according to the above definition; hence it is fair.

Example 2. Another example of a strictly determined matrix game is shown in Figure 10. Note that the two 2 entries in the second row each are the minimum of the row and maximum of the column in which they occur. Hence the value of the game is 2 and optimal strategies are: for R, choose row 2 always; for C, choose either column 2 or column 4.

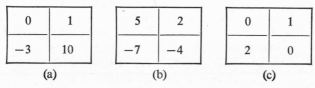

−7	0	12	−1
4	2	7	2
−3	−1	5	0

Figure 10

The solution of a strictly determined game is particularly easy to find since each player can calculate the other's optimal strategy and hence know what he will do. Not all matrix games are so easy to solve, as we shall see in the next section.

In Figure 11 we show three matrix games. The game in Figure 11a

0	1
−3	10

(a)

5	2
−7	−4

(b)

0	1
2	0

(c)

Figure 11

is strictly determined and fair, and its optimal strategies are for R to choose the first row and C to choose the first column. The game in Figure 11b is strictly determined but not fair, since its value is 2. What are its optimal strategies? Finally, the game in Figure 11c is not strictly determined, and the solution of games such as this one will be the subject of the next section.

EXERCISES

1. Determine which of the games given below are strictly determined and which are fair. When the game is strictly determined, find optimal strategies for each player.

(a)
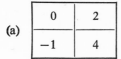

0	2
−1	4

(b)

5	0
0	2

(c)
3	1
4	0

(d)
1	−1
−1	1

(e)
3	1
−4	0

(f)
0	4
0	2

(g)
7	0
0	0

(h)
0	0
0	−7

(i)
0	0
0	0

(j)
1	1
1	1

[*Ans.* (a) Strictly determined and fair; R play row 1, C play column 1; (b) nonstrictly determined; (e) strictly determined but not fair; R play row 1, C play column 1; (j) strictly determined but not fair; both players can use any strategy.]

2. In Example 1, suppose that R is given rd 5 and bk 3, and C is given bk 3 and rd 3. Set up the matrix game corresponding to it. Is it strictly determined? Is it fair? Find optimal strategies for each player.

[*Ans.* Yes; yes; both play bk 3.]

3. Each of the two players shows one or two fingers (simultaneously) and C pays to R a sum equal to the total number of fingers shown. Write the game matrix. Show that the game is strictly determined, and find the value and optimal strategies.

4. Each of two players shows one or two fingers (simultaneously) and C pays to R an amount equal to the total number of fingers shown, while R pays to C an amount equal to the product of the numbers of fingers shown. Construct the game matrix (the entries will be the net gain of R), and find the value and the optimal strategies.

[*Ans.* $v = 1$, R must show one finger, C may show one or two.]

5. Show that a strictly determined game is fair if and only if there is a zero entry such that all entries in its row are nonnegative and all entries in its column are nonpositive.

6. Consider the game

$$G = \begin{array}{|c|c|} \hline 2 & 5 \\ \hline -1 & a \\ \hline \end{array}.$$

(a) Show that G is strictly determined regardless of the value of a.

(b) Find the value of G.   [*Ans.* 2.]

(c) Find optimal strategies for each player.

(d) If $a = 1,000,000$, obviously R would like to get it as his payoff. Is there any way he can assure himself of obtaining it? What would happen to him if he tried to obtain it?

(e) Show that the value of the game is the most that R can assure for himself.

7. Consider the matrix game

$$G = \begin{array}{|c|c|} \hline a & a \\ \hline c & d \\ \hline \end{array}.$$

show that G is strictly determined for every set of values for a, c, and d. Show that the same result is true if two entries in a given column are always equal.

8. Find necessary and sufficient conditions that the game

$$G = \begin{array}{|c|c|} \hline a & 0 \\ \hline 0 & b \\ \hline \end{array}$$

should be strictly determined. (*Hint:* These will be expressed in terms of relations among the numbers a and b and the number zero.)

9. Suppose that in Example 1, player R is given a hand consisting of bk x and rd y, and player C is given bk u and rd v, where x, y, u, and v are real numbers. Verify that the matrix game which they play is the following.

Player C

	bk u	rd v
bk x	$x - u$	$v - x$
rd y	$u - y$	$y - v$

Player R

(a) Show that if $x = u$, $v \geq x$, and $y \geq x$, the game is strictly determined and fair.

(b) Show that if $y = v$, $y \leq x$, and $y \leq u$, the game is strictly determined and fair.

10. Consider a strictly determined 2×2 matrix game G. Suppose u and v are two entries of the matrix such that each is the minimum of the row and the maximum of the column in which it occurs. Show that $u = v$.

SUPPLEMENTARY EXERCISES

11. In Example 1 assume that R has bk 5 and bk 4, and C has bk 4 and rd 2. Show that the game is favorable to C, and find optimal strategies.

[*Ans.* R choose bk 4; C choose rd 2; $v = -2$.]

12. In Example 1 assume that R has bk a and bk b, while C has bk c and rd d. If $a \geq b \geq c \geq d$, show that the game is always strictly determined. Do the same if the inequalities are reversed.

13. Solve the following games.

(a)

1	5	1	7
−2	8	0	−9
1	12	1	3

(b)

1	−12	6
0	−4	1
3	−7	2
3	−4	2
−5	−4	7

[*Ans.* R play either row 2 or 4; C play column 2; $v = -4$.]

14. Show that the following game is always strictly determined for nonnegative a and any values of the parameters b, c, d, and e.

2a	a	3a
b	-a	c
d	-2a	e

.

15. For what values of a is the following game strictly determined?

a	6	2
-1	a	-7
-2	4	a

.

[*Ans.* $-1 \leq a \leq 2$.]

5. NONSTRICTLY DETERMINED GAMES

As we saw in the numerical examples of the last section, some matrix games are nonstrictly determined, that is, they have no entry which is simultaneously a row minimum and a column maximum. We can characterize nonstrictly determined 2×2 matrix games as follows.

Theorem. The matrix game

$$G = \begin{array}{|c|c|} \hline a & b \\ \hline c & d \\ \hline \end{array}$$

is nonstrictly determined if and only if the two entries on one of the diagonals are both *larger* than the two entries on the other diagonal; that is, a and d are both larger or both smaller than b and c.

Proof. If the two entries on one of the diagonals are both larger than the two entries on the other diagonal, then it is easy to check that no entry of the matrix is simultaneously the minimum of the row and the maximum of the column in which it occurs; hence the game is not strictly determined.

To prove the other half of the theorem suppose that the game is nonstrictly determined, and suppose that the rows and columns have been arranged so that a is the largest entry in the matrix. Then, by Exercise 7 of the preceding section, no two entries in the same row or the same column are equal, since that means that the game is strictly determined. Hence, a is larger than both b and c. We must now show that d is larger than both b and c. First, d must be larger than b, for if it were less, b would be the minimum of the first row and the maximum of the second column and the game would be strictly determined. Second, d is larger than c, for if it were less, d would be the minimum of the second row and the maximum of the second column, and the game would be strictly determined. This completes the proof of the theorem.

Example 1. Consider the card game of the example in the last section and assume that player R has bk 5 and rd 3 while player C has bk 3 and rd 5. The rules of play are as before. The corresponding matrix game is

Player C

	bk 3	rd 5
bk 5	2	0
rd 3	0	2

Player R

,

which clearly is nonstrictly determined.

Example 2. Consider the following game played by two people, Jones and Smith. Jones conceals either a \$1 or a \$2 bill in his hand; Smith guesses 1 or 2, and wins the bill if he guesses its number. The matrix of this game is

Smith guesses

	1	2
\$1 bill	-1	0
\$2 bill	0	-2

Jones chooses

.

Again the game is nonstrictly determined.

How should one play a nonstrictly determined game? We must first convince ourselves that no one choice is clearly optimal for either player. In Example 1, R would like to win 2. But if he definitely chooses bk 5, and C finds this out, C can bring about a zero by playing rd 5. If R chooses rd 3, C can bring about a zero by playing bk 3. Similarly, if C's choice is found out by R, then R can win 2. So our first result is that each player must, in some way, prevent the other player from finding out which card he is going to play.

We also note that for a single play of the game there is no difference between the two strategies, as long as one's strategy is not guessed by the opponent. Let us now consider the game being played several times. What should R do? Clearly, he should not play the same card all the time, or C will be able to notice what R is doing, and profit by it. Rather, R should sometimes play one card, and sometimes the other! Our key question then is, "How often should R play each of his cards?" From the symmetry of the problem we can guess that he should play each card as often as the other, hence each one-half the time. (We will see later that this is, indeed, optimal.) In what order should he do this? For example, should he alternate bk 5 and rd 3? That is dangerous, because if C notices the pattern, he will gain by knowing just what R will do next. Thus we see that R should play bk 5 half the time, but according to some unguessable pattern. The only safe way of doing this is to play it half the time at random. He could, for example, toss a coin (without letting C see it) and play bk 5 if it comes up heads, rd 3 if it comes up tails. Then his opponent cannot guess his decision, since he himself won't know what the decision is. Thus we conclude that a rational way of playing is for each player to *mix* his strategies, selecting sometimes one, sometimes the other; and these strategies should be selected at random, according to certain fixed ratios (probabilities) of selecting each.

By a *mixed strategy* for player R we shall mean a command of the form, "Play row 1 with probability p_1 and play row 2 with probability p_2," where we assume that $p_1 \geq 0$ and $p_2 \geq 0$ and $p_1 + p_2 = 1$. Similarly, a mixed strategy for player C is a command of the form, "Play column 1 with probability q_1 and play column 2 with probability q_2," where $q_1 \geq 0$, $q_2 \geq 0$, and $q_1 + q_2 = 1$. A mixed strategy vector for player R is the probability row vector (p_1, p_2), and a mixed strategy vector for player C is the probability column vector $\begin{pmatrix} q_1 \\ q_2 \end{pmatrix}$.

Examples of mixed strategies are $(\frac{1}{2}, \frac{1}{2})$ and $\begin{pmatrix} \frac{1}{5} \\ \frac{4}{5} \end{pmatrix}$. The reader may wonder how a player could actually play one of these strategies. The mixed strategy $(\frac{1}{2}, \frac{1}{2})$ is easy to realize since it is simply the coin-flipping strategy described above. The mixed

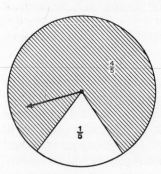

strategy $\begin{pmatrix} \frac{1}{5} \\ \frac{4}{5} \end{pmatrix}$ is more difficult to realize since there is no chance device in common use that gives these probabilities. However, suppose that a pointer is constructed with a card that is $\frac{4}{5}$ shaded and $\frac{1}{5}$ unshaded, as in Figure 12, and C simply spins the pointer (without letting R see it, of course!). Then, if the pointer stops on the unshaded part, he plays the first column, and if it stops on the shaded part, he plays the second column, and thus

Figure 12

realizes the desired strategy. By varying the proportion of shaded area on the card other mixed strategies can conveniently be realized.

Consider the nonstrictly determined game

$$G = \begin{array}{|c|c|} \hline a & b \\ \hline c & d \\ \hline \end{array}.$$

Having argued, as above, that the players should use mixed strategies in playing a nonstrictly determined game, it is still necessary to decide how to choose an optimal mixed strategy.

DEFINITION. For the nonstrictly determined game G the number v is its *value* and $p^0 = (p_1^0, p_2^0)$ and $q^0 = (q_1^0, q_2^0)$ are *optimal strategies* for R and C, respectively, if the following inequalities are satisfied.

(1) $$p^0 G = (p_1^0, p_2^0) \begin{pmatrix} a & b \\ c & d \end{pmatrix} \geq (v, v)$$

(2) $$G q^0 = \begin{pmatrix} a & b \\ c & d \end{pmatrix} \begin{pmatrix} q_1^0 \\ q_2^0 \end{pmatrix} \leq \begin{pmatrix} v \\ v \end{pmatrix}.$$

(If z and w are vectors, the inequality $z \geq w$ means that each component of z is greater than or equal to the corresponding component of w.) The game is *fair* if $v = 0$.

If R chooses a mixed strategy $p = (p_1, p_2)$ and (independently) C chooses a mixed strategy $q = \begin{pmatrix} q_1 \\ q_2 \end{pmatrix}$, then player R obtains the payoff a with probability $p_1 q_1$; he obtains the payoff b with probability $p_1 q_2$; he obtains c with probability $p_2 q_1$; and he obtains d with probability $p_2 q_2$; hence his mathematical expectation (see Chapter IV, Section 12) is then given by the expression

$$ap_1 q_1 + bp_1 q_2 + cp_2 q_1 + dp_2 q_2 = pGq.$$

By a similar computation, one can show that player C's expectation is the negative of this expression.

To justify this definition we must show that if v, p^0, q^0 exist for G, each player can guarantee himself an expectation of v. Let q be any strategy for C. Multiplying (1) on the right by q, we get $p^0 Gq \geq (v, v)q = v$, which shows that, regardless of how C plays, R can assure himself of an expectation of at least v. Similarly, let p be any strategy vector for R. Multiplying (2) on the left by p, we obtain $pGq^0 \leq p \begin{pmatrix} v \\ v \end{pmatrix} = v$, which shows that, regardless of how R plays, C can assure himself of an expectation of at most v. It is in this sense that p^0 and q^0 are optimal. It follows further that, if both players play optimally, then R's expectation is exactly v and C's expectation is exactly v. (Compare Exercise 11.)

We must now see whether there are strategies p^0 and q^0 for the game G. While in more complicated games the finding of optimal strategies is a difficult task, for a 2×2 nonstrictly determined game the following formulas provide the solution.

$$(3) \qquad p_1^0 = \frac{d - c}{a + d - b - c}$$

$$(4) \qquad p_2^0 = \frac{a - b}{a + d - b - c}$$

$$(5) \qquad q_1^0 = \frac{d - b}{a + d - b - c}$$

$$(6) \qquad q_2^0 = \frac{a - c}{a + d - b - c}$$

(7)
$$v = \frac{ad - bc}{a + d - b - c}.$$

It is an easy matter to verify (see Exercise 12) that formulas (3)–(7) satisfy conditions (1)–(2). Actually, the inequalities in (1) and (2) become equalities in this simple case, a fact that is not true in general for nonstrictly determined games of larger size.

Formulas (3)–(7) look rather complicated, but the mnemonic device of Figure 13 will make it unnecessary to remember them in detail. Observe that the numerators of (3)–(6) are the differences of the main

$$
\begin{array}{cc}
 & d-b \quad\ a-c \\
\begin{array}{r} d-c \\ \\ a-b \end{array} &
\begin{array}{|c|c|}
\hline
a & b \\
\hline
c & d \\
\hline
\end{array}
\end{array}
$$

Figure 13

diagonal and the other diagonal entries. We take the difference of the entry on the main diagonal and the other entry in the first row, and write it in the second row. Then we take the corresponding difference in the second row, and write it in the first row. For the column player we do the same, substituting "column" for "row." In order to convert these differences into strategies, simply divide by the sum of the differences, which is the denominator of each of the expressions (3)–(6). Finally, to find the value of the game, multiply one of the optimal strategy vectors into the game matrix. Let us illustrate these ideas on the two examples discussed earlier.

Example 1 (continued). Applying the rules of Figure 13, we have

$$
\begin{array}{cc}
 & d-b=2 \quad\ a-c=2 \\
\begin{array}{r} d-c=2 \\ \\ a-b=2 \end{array} &
\begin{array}{|c|c|}
\hline
2 & 0 \\
\hline
0 & 2 \\
\hline
\end{array}
\end{array}.
$$

The sum $a + d - b - c = 2 + 2 = 4$, so that the optimal strategies are $(\tfrac{1}{2}, \tfrac{1}{2})$ for R and $\left(\begin{smallmatrix} \frac{1}{2} \\ \frac{1}{2} \end{smallmatrix}\right)$ for C. Hence each player should use the coin-flipping strategy for optimal results. The value of the game is obtained by multiplying R's optimal strategy into the first column of the matrix, $v = (\frac{1}{2}, \frac{1}{2}) \begin{pmatrix} 2 \\ 0 \end{pmatrix} = 1$. Thus the game is biased in R's favor, and he has an expected gain of \$1 per game.

Example 2 (continued). Again applying the rules of Figure 13,

$$d - b = -2 \quad a - c = -1$$

	$d - b = -2$	$a - c = -1$
$d - c = -2$	-1	0
$a - b = -1$	0	-2

The sum is $a + d - b - c = -3$, so that the optimal strategies are $(\frac{2}{3}, \frac{1}{3})$ for R and $\begin{pmatrix} \frac{2}{3} \\ \frac{1}{3} \end{pmatrix}$ for C. The value of the game is $(\frac{2}{3}, \frac{1}{3}) \begin{pmatrix} -1 \\ 0 \end{pmatrix} = -\frac{2}{3}$, which means that the game is biased in Smith's favor. Smith should then pay $66\frac{2}{3}$ cents to play the game, in order to make it fair, that is, to make its value zero.

Example 3. As one final example, consider the following matrix game.

6	2
1	4

Applying the rules of Figure 13, we obtain

	2	5
3	6	2
4	1	4

which means that optimal strategies are $(\frac{3}{7}, \frac{4}{7})$ for R and $\begin{pmatrix} \frac{2}{7} \\ \frac{5}{7} \end{pmatrix}$ for C. The value of the game is $(\frac{3}{7}, \frac{4}{7}) \begin{pmatrix} 6 \\ 1 \end{pmatrix} = \frac{22}{7}$.

EXERCISES

1. Find the optimal strategies for each player and the values of the following games.

(a)

1	2
3	4

(b)

1	0
−1	2

(c)

2	3
1	4

(d)

15	3
−1	2

(e)

7	−6
5	8

(f)

3	15
−1	10

[*Ans.* (a) $v = 3; (0, 1); \binom{1}{0}$. (b) $v = \frac{1}{2}; (\frac{3}{4}, \frac{1}{4}); \binom{\frac{1}{2}}{\frac{1}{2}}$.

(d) $v = 3; (1, 0); \binom{0}{1}$. (e) $v = \frac{43}{8}; (\frac{3}{16}, \frac{13}{16}); \binom{\frac{7}{8}}{\frac{1}{8}}$.]

2. Set up the ordinary game of matching pennies as a matrix game. Find its value and optimal strategies. How are the optimal strategies realized in practice by players of this game?

3. A version of two-finger Morra is played as follows: Each player holds up either one or two fingers; if the sum of the number of fingers shown is even, player R gets the sum, and if the sum is odd, player C gets it.

(a) Show that the game matrix is

Player C

		1	2
Player R	1	2	−3
	2	−3	4

(b) Find optimal strategies for each player and the value of the game.

[*Ans.* $(\frac{7}{12}, \frac{5}{12}); v = -\frac{1}{12}$.]

4. Rework Exercise 3 if player C gets the even sum and player R gets the odd sum.

5. Consider the following "war" problem: Some attacking bombers are attempting to bomb a city that is protected by fighters. The bombers can each day attack either "high" or "low," the low attack making the bombing more accurate. Similarly, the fighters can each day look for the bombers either "high" or "low." Credit the bombers with six points if they avoid the fighters, and zero if the fighters find them. Also credit the bombers with three extra points for accurate bombing if they fly low.
   (a) Set up the game matrix.
   (b) Find optimal strategies for each player.
   (c) Give instructions to the bomber and fighter commanders so that by flipping coins they can decide what to do.
   [*Ans.* (c) The bomber commander should flip one coin to decide whether to go high or low. The fighter commander should flip two coins and then go high if both turn up heads.]

6. Generalize the problem in Exercise 5 by crediting the bombers with x points for avoiding the fighters and y points for flying low. (Assume that x and y are positive.)
   (a) Set up the matrix.
   (b) If $y \geq x$, show that the game is strictly determined and find optimal strategies.
   (c) If $y < x$, show that the game is nonstrictly determined and find optimal strategies.
   (d) Comment on these results, with special attention to the bombers' strategies.

7. If $G = \begin{array}{|c|c|} \hline a & b \\ \hline c & d \\ \hline \end{array}$ is nonstrictly determined, prove that it is fair if and only if

$$ad - bc = 0.$$

8. In formulas (3)–(7) prove that $p_1 > 0$, $p_2 > 0$, $q_1 > 0$, and $q_2 > 0$. Must v be greater than zero?

9. Utilizing the results of Exercise 7 of the last section, find necessary and sufficient conditions that the game

$$ G = \begin{array}{|c|c|} \hline a & 0 \\ \hline 0 & b \\ \hline \end{array} $$

be nonstrictly determined. Find optimal strategies for each player and the value of G, if it is nonstrictly determined.

[*Ans. a* and *b* must be both positive or both negative.

$$p_1 = \frac{b}{a+b}; \ p_2 = \frac{a}{a+b}; \ q_1 = \frac{b}{a+b}; \ q_2 = \frac{a}{a+b}; \ v = \frac{ab}{a+b}.]$$

10. Suppose that R is given bk x and rd y while C is given bk u and rd v (where x, y, u, and v stand for positive integers). Let them play the matrix game

	bk u	rd v
bk x	xu	$-xv$
rd y	$-yu$	yv

Show that the game is always nonstrictly determined and always fair.

11. If G, p^0, q^0, and v are as in the definition, show that $v = p^0 G q^0$.

12. Verify that (3)–(7) satisfy the conditions (1) and (2).

SUPPLEMENTARY EXERCISES

The remaining exercises refer to a special case of the *product payoff game* (due to A. W. Tucker, see Exercises 14–20 of Section 7). In this game, R is given two numbers x and y such that $xy < 0$, and C is given two numbers u and z such that $uz < 0$. They play the game whose matrix is

	u	z
x	xu	xz
y	yu	yz

In other words, each player chooses one of his two numbers, and they then exchange a sum of money equal to the product of these numbers. Since $xy < 0$ and $uz < 0$, each player must have one negative and one positive number.

13. Assume that $x > 0 > y$ and $u > 0 > z$. Show that the game is always nonstrictly determined.

14. Show that we can always assume that x, y, u, and z satisfy the relationships given in Exercise 13 by, if necessary, relabelling and reordering rows and columns.

15. Show that the game is always fair. [*Hint:* Use Exercise 7.]

16. For the situation in Exercise 13, find optimal strategies for both players. [*Partial Ans.* For R the optimal strategy is $(-y/(x - y), x/(x - y))$.]

17. Solve the game for $x = 3$, $y = -5$, $u = 4$, and $z = -2$. [*Partial Ans.* For R the answer is $(\frac{5}{8}, \frac{3}{8})$ and $v = 0$.]

6. MATRIX GAMES

We shall consider a large class of games in this section, and discuss them in considerable generality. Our games are played between two players, according to strictly specified rules. Each player performs certain actions, as specified by the rules of the game, and then, at the end of the play of the game, one of the players may have to pay a sum of money to the other player. The game may be repeated many times.

During such a game a player may have to make many strategic decisions. By a (pure) *strategy* for one of the players we mean a complete set of rules as to how he should make his decisions. We shall illustrate this in terms of the game of tick-tack-toe (and nearly the same remarks would apply to any game in which the players take turns moving). Let us construct a strategy for the player who moves first. His first decision concerns the opening move. He may choose any one of nine squares, and the strategy must tell him which choice to make. Let us say we tell him to move into the upper left-hand corner. His opponent may answer this in one of eight ways, and the strategy must be prepared for each alternative. It must have eight rules, such as "If he moves into the middle, move into the lower right-hand corner!" For every such move the opponent may respond with one of several alternatives, and the strategy must again have an answering move ready for each of them, etc. Hence the strategy takes into account every conceivable position of the first player, and instructs what move to make in each one.

A strategy may be thought of as a set of instructions to be given to a machine, so that the machine will play the game exactly the way we would have.

We number the strategies of the first player $1, 2, \ldots, m$, and those of the second player $1, 2, \ldots, n$. Since each of the players must play according to one of his strategies, the game may proceed in any one of mn ways, and if each player chooses a definite strategy, the outcome is determined. We may think of giving the two strategies to two machines, and let them work out what happens. Let us suppose that, when the first player chooses strategy i and the second strategy j, the former wins an amount a_{ij}. We arrange these numbers a_{ij} into an $m \times n$ matrix, the *game matrix*. We may then think of the game as consisting of a choice of a row by the first player, and a column by the second player. Hence we see that any game specified by rules may be thought of as a matrix game.

Conversely, every matrix can be considered as a game. An $m \times n$ matrix may be thought of as a game between two players, in which player R chooses one of the m rows and player C simultaneously chooses one of the n columns. The outcome of the game is that C pays to R an amount equal to the entry of the matrix in the chosen row and column. (A negative entry represents a payment from R to C, as usual.)

In an $m \times n$ matrix game, the player R has m pure strategies, and the player C has n. We have seen in the last section that, in addition, we must consider the mixed strategies of the two players. We extend this concept to $m \times n$ games.

DEFINITION. An m-component row vector p is a *mixed-strategy vector* for R if it is a probability vector; similarly, an n-component column vector q is a mixed-strategy vector for C if it is a probability vector. (Recall from Chapter V that a probability vector is one with nonnegative entries whose sum is 1.) Let V and V' be the vectors

$$V = \underbrace{(v, v, \ldots, v)}_{m \text{ components}} \quad \text{and} \quad V' = \left.\begin{pmatrix} v \\ v \\ \cdot \\ \cdot \\ \cdot \\ v \end{pmatrix}\right\} n \text{ components,}$$

where v is a number. Then v is the *value of the game* and p^0 and q^0 are *optimal strategies* for the players if and only if the following inequalities hold.

$$p^0 G \geq V$$
$$G q^0 \leq V'.$$

In Sections 4 and 5 we have given several examples of such matrix games together with their solutions. Notice that we have *not* proved that an arbitrary matrix game has a value and optimal strategies for each player; that question will be discussed later.

Theorem 1. If G is a matrix game which has a value and optimal strategies, then the value of the game is unique.

Proof. Suppose that v and w are two different values for the game G. Let $V = (v, v, \ldots, v)$ and $W = (w, w, \ldots, w)$ be m-component row vectors, and let

$$V' = \begin{pmatrix} v \\ v \\ \cdot \\ \cdot \\ \cdot \\ v \end{pmatrix} \quad \text{and} \quad W' = \begin{pmatrix} w \\ w \\ \cdot \\ \cdot \\ \cdot \\ w \end{pmatrix}$$

be n-component column vectors. Then let p^0 and q^0 be optimal mixed strategy vectors associated with the value v so that

(a) $$p^0 G \geq V,$$

(b) $$G q^0 \leq V'.$$

Similarly, let p^1 and q^1 be optimal mixed strategy vectors associated with the value w so that

(c) $$p^1 G \geq W,$$

(d) $$G q^1 \leq W'.$$

If we now multiply (a) on the right by q^1, we get $p^0 G q^1 \geq V q^1 = v$. In the same way, multiplying (d) on the left by p^0 gives $p^0 G q^1 \leq w$. The two inequalities just obtained show that $w \geq v$.

Next we multiply (b) on the left by p^1 and (c) on the right by q^0, obtaining $v \geq p^1 G q^0$ and $p^1 G q^0 \geq w$, which together imply that $v \geq w$.

Finally, we see that $v \leq w$ and $v \geq w$ imply together that $v = w$, that is, the value of the game is unique.

Theorem 2. If G is a matrix game with value v and optimal strategies p^0 and q^0, then $v = p^0 G q^0$.

Proof. By definition, v, p^0, and q^0 satisfy

$$p^0 G \geq V \quad \text{and} \quad G q^0 \leq V'.$$

Multiplying the first of these inequalities on the right by q^0, we get $p^0 G q^0 \geq v$. Similarly, multiplying the second inequality on the left by p^0, we obtain $p^0 G q^0 \leq v$. These two inequalities together imply that $v = p^0 G q^0$, concluding the proof.

Theorem 2 is important because it permits us to give an interpretation of the *value* of a game as an *expected value* in the sense of probability (see Chapter IV, Section 12). Briefly the interpretation is the following: If the game G is played repeatedly and if each time it is played player R uses the mixed strategy p^0 and player C uses the mixed strategy q^0, then the value v of G is the expected value of the game for R. The law of large numbers implies that, if the number of plays of G is sufficiently large, then the average value of R's winnings will (with high probability) be arbitrarily close to the value v of the game G.

As an example, let G be the matrix of the game of matching pennies, i.e.,

$$G = \begin{array}{|c|c|} \hline 1 & -1 \\ \hline -1 & 1 \\ \hline \end{array}.$$

As was found in Exercise 2 of the last section, optimal strategies in this game are for R to choose each row with probability $\frac{1}{2}$ and for C to choose each column with probability $\frac{1}{2}$. The value of G is zero. Notice that the only two payoffs that result from a single play of the game are $+1$ and -1, neither of which is equal to the value (zero) of the game. However, if the game is played repeatedly, the average value of R's payoffs will approach zero, which is the value of the game.

Theorem 3. If G is a game with value v and optimal strategies p^0 and q^0, then v is the largest expectation that R can assure for himself. Similarly, v is the smallest expectation that C can assure for himself.

Proof. Let p be any mixed strategy vector of R and let q^0 be an optimal strategy for C; then multiply the equation $Gq^0 \leq V'$ on the left by p, obtaining $pGq^0 \leq v$. The latter equation shows that, if C plays optimally, the most that R can assure for himself is v. Now let p^0 be optimal for R; then, for every q, $p^0Gq \geq v$, so that R can actually assure himself of an expectation of v. The proof of the other statement of the theorem is similar.

Theorem 3 gives an intuitive justification to the definition of value and optimal strategies for a game. Thus the value is the "best" that a player can do and optimal strategies are the means of achieving this "best."

Matrix game theory would not be of very great interest unless we knew under what conditions such a game has a solution. The fundamental theorem of game theory is that every matrix game has a solution. The proof of this theorem is too difficult to be included here, but we do discuss its proof for the 2 × 2 case.

Theorem 4 (Fundamental theorem). Let G be any $m \times n$ matrix game; then there exists a value v for G and optimal strategies p^0 for player R and q^0 for player C. In other words, every matrix game possesses a solution.

Proof for 2 × 2 matrices. If G is strictly determined, the value and optimal strategies were found in Section 4. If G is not strictly determined, formulas (3) through (7) of Section 5 give the optimal strategies and value for G. Since G must be either strictly determined or nonstrictly determined, we have covered all cases.

EXERCISES

1. Find the value and optimal strategies for the following games.

(a)

15	2	−3
6	5	7
−7	4	0

$$\left[\text{Ans. } v = 5; (0, 1, 0); \begin{pmatrix} 0 \\ 1 \\ 0 \end{pmatrix}.\right]$$

(b)

5	2	−1	−1
1	1	0	1
3	0	−3	7

(c)

0	5	6	−3
1	−1	2	3
1	2	3	4
−1	0	7	5

.

2. Verify that the strategies $p^0 = (\frac{1}{3}, \frac{1}{3}, \frac{1}{3})$ and

$$q^0 = \begin{pmatrix} \frac{1}{3} \\ \frac{1}{3} \\ \frac{1}{3} \end{pmatrix}$$

are optimal in the game G whose matrix is

$$G = \begin{array}{|c|c|c|} \hline 1 & 0 & 0 \\ \hline 0 & 1 & 0 \\ \hline 0 & 0 & 1 \\ \hline \end{array}.$$

What is the value of the game?

3. Generalize the result of Exercise 2 to the game G whose matrix is the $n \times n$ identity matrix.

4. Suppose that player R tries to find C in one of three towns X, Y, and Z. The distance between X and Y is five miles, the distance between Y and Z is five miles, and the distance between Z and X is ten miles. Assume that R and C can go to one and only one of the three towns and that if they both go to the same town, R "catches" C and otherwise C "escapes." Credit R with ten points if he catches C, and credit C with a number of points equal to the distance he is away from R if he escapes.

    (a) Set up the game matrix.

    (b) Show that both players have the same optimal strategy, namely, to go to towns X and Z with equal probabilities and to go to town Y with probability $\frac{1}{4}$.

    (c) Find the value of the game.

5. A version of five-finger Morra is played as follows: Each player shows from one to five fingers, and the sum is divided by three. If the sum is exactly divisible by three, there is no exchange of payoffs. If there is a remainder of one, player R wins a sum equal to the total number of fingers, while if the remainder is two, player C wins the sum.

    (a) Set up the game matrix. [*Hint:* It is 5×5.]

    (b) Verify that an optimal strategy for either player is to show one or five fingers with probability $\frac{1}{9}$, to show two or four fingers with probability $\frac{2}{9}$, and to show three fingers with probability $\frac{1}{3}$.

    (c) Is the game fair?   [*Ans.* Yes.]

6. Consider the following game:

$$G = \begin{array}{|c|c|c|} \hline a & 0 & 0 \\ \hline 0 & b & 0 \\ \hline 0 & 0 & c \\ \hline \end{array}.$$

    (a) If a, b, and c are not all of the same sign, show that the game is strictly determined with value zero.

(b) If a, b, and c are all of the same sign, show that the vector

$$\frac{bc}{ab + bc + ca}, \quad \frac{ca}{ab + bc + ca}, \quad \frac{ab}{ab + bc + ca}$$

is an optimal strategy for player R.

(c) Find player C's optimal strategy for case (b).

(d) Find the value of the game for case (b) and show that it is positive if a, b, and c are all positive, and negative if they are all negative.

7. Two players agree to play the following game. The first player will show one, two, or four fingers. The second player will show two, three, or five fingers, simultaneously. If the sum of the fingers shown is three, five, or nine, the first player receives this sum. Otherwise no payment is made.

(a) Set up the game matrix.

(b) Use the results of Exercise 6 to solve the game.

(c) How much should the first player be willing to pay to play the game? *[Ans. $\frac{45}{29}$.]*

8. Consider the (symmetric) game whose matrix is

$$G = \begin{array}{|c|c|c|}
\hline
0 & -a & -b \\
\hline
a & 0 & -c \\
\hline
b & c & 0 \\
\hline
\end{array}.$$

(a) If a and b are both positive or both negative, show that G is strictly determined.

(b) If b and c are both positive or both negative, show that G is strictly determined.

(c) If $a > 0$, $b < 0$, and $c > 0$, show that an optimal strategy for player R is given by

$$\frac{c}{a - b + c}, \quad \frac{-b}{a - b + c}, \quad \frac{a}{a - b + c}.$$

(d) In part (c) find an optimal strategy for player C.

(e) If $a < 0$, $b > 0$, and $c < 0$ show that the strategy given in (c) is optimal for R. What is an optimal strategy for player C?

(f) Prove that the value of the game is always zero.

9. In a well-known children's game each player says "stone" or "scissors" or "paper." If one says "stone" and the other "scissors," then the former wins a penny. Similarly, "scissors" beats "paper," and "paper" beats "stone." If the two players name the same item, then the game is a tie.

(a) Set up the game matrix.

(b) Use the results of Exercise 8 to solve the game.

10. In Exercise 9 let us suppose that the payments are different in different cases. Suppose that when "stone breaks scissors," the payment is one cent; when "scissors cut paper," the payment is two cents; and when "paper covers stone," the payment is three cents.

    (a) Set up the game matrix.

    (b) Use the results of Exercise 8 to solve the game.

[*Ans.* $\frac{1}{3}$ "stone," $\frac{1}{2}$ "scissors," $\frac{1}{6}$ "paper"; $v = 0$.]

SUPPLEMENTARY EXERCISES

Exercises 13–17 refer to a special case of the *exponential payoff game*. (See also Exercises 14–20 of Section 8.) To play this game we first select a number $b > 0$. Then R is given two numbers x, y such that $xy < 0$, and C is given two numbers u, z such that $uz < 0$. They play the matrix game

$$
\begin{array}{c|cc}
 & u & z \\
\hline
x & \pm b^{x+u} & \pm b^{x+z} \\
y & \pm b^{y+u} & \pm b^{y+z}
\end{array},
$$

where the plus payoff is exchanged if the two numbers chosen are of the same sign, and the minus payoff is exchanged if the two numbers chosen have opposite sign.

11. For $b = 2, x = 3, y = -2, u = 1$, and $z = -4$, show that the game is

$$
\begin{array}{|c|c|}
\hline
16 & -\frac{1}{2} \\
\hline
-\frac{1}{2} & \frac{1}{64} \\
\hline
\end{array}.
$$

12. Assume that $x > 0 > y$ and $u > 0 > z$.

    (a) Show that the game matrix is

$$
\begin{array}{c|cc}
 & u & z \\
\hline
x & b^{x+u} & -b^{x+z} \\
y & -b^{y+u} & b^{y+z}
\end{array}.
$$

    (b) Show that the game is always nonstrictly determined.

    (c) Show that the game is always fair.

13. Show that we can always assume that $x > 0 > y$ and $u > 0 > z$ by, if necessary, relabelling and reordering rows and columns.

14. For the situation in Exercise 12 find optimal strategies for each player. Show that these are also optimal for the three cases found in Exercise 13.
   [*Partial Ans.* For R the optimal strategy is $(b^y/(b^x + b^y), b^x/(b^x + b^y))$.]

15. Solve the game in Exercise 11.
   [*Partial Ans.* For R the optimal strategy is $(\frac{1}{33}, \frac{32}{33})$.]

7. MORE ON MATRIX GAMES

We recall from Section 4 that a matrix game G is *strictly determined* if there is an entry g_{ij} in G that is the minimum entry in the ith row and the maximum entry in the jth column. (By rearranging and renumbering the rows and columns of a strictly determined matrix game G we can assume that g_{11} is an entry that is the minimum of row 1 and the maximum of column 1.)

Theorem 1. If G is a strictly determined matrix game, arranged as indicated in the definition, the value of the game is $v = g_{11}$. Moreover, optimal strategies for the players are

$$p^0 = (1, 0, 0, \ldots, 0) \quad \text{and} \quad q^0 = \begin{pmatrix} 1 \\ 0 \\ 0 \\ \cdot \\ \cdot \\ \cdot \\ 0 \end{pmatrix}.$$

[These optimal strategies simply say that R should choose the row that contains the entry g_{11} (the first row) and C should choose the column that contains the entry g_{11} (the first column).]

Proof. We set $v = g_{11}$ and let p^0 and q^0 be the strategies as defined in the statement of the theorem. We have

$$p^0 G = (g_{11}, g_{12}, \ldots, g_{1n})$$
$$\geq (g_{11}, g_{11}, \ldots, g_{11}) = V,$$

where we have used the fact that g_{11} was the minimum of the first row. Similarly, using the fact that g_{11} is the maximum of the first column, we have

$$G q^0 = \begin{pmatrix} g_{11} \\ g_{21} \\ \cdot \\ \cdot \\ \cdot \\ g_{m1} \end{pmatrix} \leq \begin{pmatrix} g_{11} \\ g_{11} \\ \cdot \\ \cdot \\ \cdot \\ g_{11} \end{pmatrix} = V'.$$

From these two inequalities and the definition of a matrix game given above, we conclude that v is the value of the game and p^0 and q^0 are optimal strategies.

Theorem 2. If g_{11} and g_{ij} are two entries of G that are the minima of the rows and the maxima of the columns in which they occur, then $v = g_{11} = g_{1j} = g_{i1} = g_{ij}$.

Proof. Using the facts that g_{11} and g_{ij} are the minima of the rows and the maxima of the columns in which they occur, we see that

$$g_{ij} \geq g_{1j} \geq g_{11}, \qquad g_{ij} \leq g_{i1} \leq g_{11}.$$

(These inequalities are redundant but still true if either $i = 1$ or $j = 1$.) These two sets of inequalities imply that $g_{ij} = g_{1j} = g_{i1} = g_{11} = v$, completing the proof of the theorem.

Example 1. Although we have proved that the value of a game is unique, it may happen that a game has more than one pair of optimal strategies. For instance, let G be the game

$$G = \begin{array}{|c|c|c|c|} \hline 1 & 5 & 1 & 7 \\ \hline -2 & 8 & 0 & -9 \\ \hline 1 & 12 & 1 & 3 \\ \hline \end{array}.$$

Then we see that G is strictly determined with value 1, and optimal strategies are $(1, 0, 0)$ and $(0, 0, 1)$ for player R and

$$\begin{pmatrix} 1 \\ 0 \\ 0 \\ 0 \end{pmatrix} \quad \text{and} \quad \begin{pmatrix} 0 \\ 0 \\ 1 \\ 0 \end{pmatrix}$$

for player C. In the next theorem we shall see that there are still other optimal strategies for this game.

DEFINITION. Let r and s be two strategies for a player in a matrix game; then by a *convex combination* of the two strategies, we mean an expression of the form

$$ar + (1 - a)s,$$

where a is a number satisfying $0 \leq a \leq 1$.

Theorem 3. If p^0 and p^1 are two optimal strategies for R in a matrix game G then the convex combination

$$p = ap^0 + (1 - a)p^1, \qquad 0 \le a \le 1$$

is also an optimal strategy for R.

Similarly, if q^0 and q^1 are optimal strategies for C in G, then the convex combination

$$q = aq^0 + (1 - a)q^1, \qquad 0 \le a \le 1$$

is also an optimal strategy for C.

Proof. We shall prove the first statement only and leave the second as an exercise (see Exercise 3). It is easy to show that p is a probability vector. By hypothesis, we have $p^0G \ge V$ and $p^1G \ge V$. Hence we see that

$$\begin{aligned}
pG &= [ap^0 + (1 - a)p^1]G \\
&= ap^0G + (1 - a)p^1G \\
&\ge aV + (1 - a)V = V,
\end{aligned}$$

which shows that p is also an optimal strategy, completing the proof of the theorem.

Example 1 (continued). Theorem 3 implies that, in Example 1, convex combinations of strategies of the form $a(1, 0, 0) + (1 - a)(0, 0, 1) = (a, 0, 1 - a)$ are optimal for R. It is easy to check that $(\frac{1}{2}, 0, \frac{1}{2})$ and $(\frac{1}{4}, 0, \frac{3}{4})$ are optimal and of this form. By similar reasoning, all strategies of the form

$$a\begin{pmatrix} 1 \\ 0 \\ 0 \\ 0 \end{pmatrix} + (1 - a)\begin{pmatrix} 0 \\ 0 \\ 1 \\ 0 \end{pmatrix} = \begin{pmatrix} a \\ 0 \\ 1 - a \\ 0 \end{pmatrix},$$

for $0 \le a \le 1$, are optimal for C.

Theorem 4. If k is a nonnegative number, i.e., $k \ge 0$, and G is a matrix game with value v, then the game kG is a matrix game with value kv, and every strategy optimal in G is also optimal in kG. (Recall that the matrix kG is obtained from G by multiplying every entry of G by the number k.)

Proof. Let p^0 be an optimal strategy for R in the game G, that is, $p^0G \ge V$. Then we have

$$p^0(kG) = k(p^0G) \ge kV.$$

Similarly, if q^0 is optimal for C in the game G, then

$$(kG)q^0 = k(Gq^0) \leq kV'.$$

These two inequalities show that kv is the value of kG and also that optimal strategies in G are also optimal in the game kG.

It should be observed that it was essential for the proof of this theorem that k be nonnegative, since multiplying an inequality by a *negative* number has the effect of reversing the direction of the inequality sign. The following example shows that the above theorem is false for negative k's.

Example 2. Let $k = -1$ and let G and $(-1)G$ be the matrices

$$G = \begin{array}{|c|c|} \hline 2 & 3 \\ \hline -1 & 0 \\ \hline \end{array} \quad \text{and} \quad (-1)G = \begin{array}{|c|c|} \hline -2 & -3 \\ \hline 1 & 0 \\ \hline \end{array}.$$

Observe that each of these games is strictly determined but that the value of the first game is 2, while the value of the second is 0 [which is not equal to $(-1)2 = -2$]. Moreover, optimal strategies in G are for R to play the first row with probability 1, and for C to play the first column with probability 1, but neither of these strategies is optimal in the game $(-1)G$.

Theorem 5. Let G be an $m \times n$ matrix game with value v; let E be the $m \times n$ matrix each of whose entries is 1; and let k be *any* constant. Then the game $G + kE$ has value $v + k$, and every strategy optimal in the game G is also optimal in the game $G + kE$. (The game $G + kE$ is obtained from the game G by adding the number k to each entry in G.)

Proof. Let p^0 and q^0 be optimal strategies in G; then $p^0G \geq V$ and $Gq^0 \leq V'$. We have

$$\begin{aligned} p^0(G + kE) &= p^0G + p^0(kE) \\ &= p^0G + k(p^0E) \\ &\geq (v, v, \ldots, v) + (k, k, \ldots, k) \\ &= (v + k, v + k, \ldots, v + k). \end{aligned}$$

Similarly, we have

$$(G + kE)q^0 = Gq^0 + k(Eq^0)$$

$$\leq \begin{pmatrix} v \\ v \\ \cdot \\ \cdot \\ \cdot \\ v \end{pmatrix} + \begin{pmatrix} k \\ k \\ \cdot \\ \cdot \\ \cdot \\ k \end{pmatrix} = \begin{pmatrix} v + k \\ v + k \\ \cdot \\ \cdot \\ \cdot \\ v + k \end{pmatrix}.$$

These inequalities show that the value of the game $G + kE$ is $v + k$ and also show that each strategy optimal in G is optimal in $G + kE$.

Theorem 6. Let G be an $m \times n$ matrix game with value v; then there exist $k \geq 0$ and $M > 0$ so that the game $\frac{1}{M}(G + kE)$ has the same optimal strategies as G and has all its entries between 0 and 1.

Proof. Let k be the absolute value of the most negative entry in G, or 0 in case there are no negative entries. Then by Theorem 5 the game $G + kE$ has the same optimal strategies as G. By construction it is clear that $G + kE$ has all entries ≥ 0. Now let M be the maximum positive entry in $G + kE$, or 1 in case there are no positive entries. Hence $M > 0$. By Theorems 4 and 5 the game $\frac{1}{M}(G + kE)$ has the same optimal strategies as G, and by the choice of M all entries lie between 0 and 1.

The last three theorems show that the actual units used to measure the game payoffs are irrelevant as far as optimal strategies go. The only thing that is important for them is the relative magnitudes of the payoffs.

EXERCISES

1. Find the value of and all optimal strategies for the following games.

(a)

5	10	6	5
5	7	8	5
0	5	6	5

(b)

−2	0	−1
−5	7	8

(c)

0	0	1	0
1	0	0	0
1	0	1	0

(d)

3	2	3
6	2	7
5	1	4

.

$$[Ans. \ (a) \ v = 5, (a, 1 - a, 0), \begin{pmatrix} a \\ 0 \\ 0 \\ 1 - a \end{pmatrix}; (d) \ v = 2, (a, 1 - a, 0), \begin{pmatrix} 0 \\ 1 \\ 0 \end{pmatrix}.]$$

2. Let G be a strictly determined game with value v. Let h be the number of rows which R can choose as an optimal strategy, and let k be the number of columns which C can choose as an optimal strategy. Prove that v occurs at least $h \cdot k$ times in G. Can it occur more than this number of times?

[*Ans.* Yes.]

3. If q^0 and q^1 are optimal strategies for C in the matrix game G, show that the strategy

$$q = aq^0 + (1 - a)q^1,$$

where a is a constant with $0 \leq a \leq 1$, is also optimal in the game G.

4. Find the values of the games kG and $G + kE$ for each of the games G whose matrices are given in Exercise 1 of Section 6, if k takes on the values 3, 0, and -2.

5. If G is any matrix game and $k = 0$, find all optimal strategies for each player in the game kG. [*Ans.* Any strategy is optimal.]

6. If G is any matrix game and $k > 0$, show that every strategy optimal in kG is also optimal in G. [*Hint:* Multiply by $1/k$.]

7. If G is any matrix game and k is any constant, show that every strategy optimal in the game $G + kE$ is also optimal in the game G.

8. Suppose that before C and R play a matrix game G, player C gives to player R a payment of k dollars. In this case we shall say C has made a *side payment* of k to R. (If k is negative, then, as usual, this will be a side payment of R to C.)

(a) If C has made a side payment of k to R before playing the game G, show that the game they actually play is $G + kE$.

(b) If v is the value of the game G, find the value of the game $G - vE$.

(c) Using the results of (a) and (b), show that any matrix game G with value v can be made into a fair matrix game by requiring that C make a side payment of $-v$ to R before they play the game G.

9. Show that any matrix game G can be made into a fair matrix game, with each entry in the matrix lying between -1 and 1, by adding the same number to each entry in the matrix and by multiplying each entry by a positive number.

10. Show that the sets of optimal strategies for each player are unchanged by the transformation suggested in Exercise 9. How does the value of the game change?

11. Consider the matrix game

a	b	b
b	a	b
b	b	a

, where $a > b$.

(a) Show that this can be obtained from the identity matrix by multiplying it by a suitable number, and then adding bE.

(b) Use the results of Section 6, Exercise 2, to solve the game.

$$[\textit{Ans.} \ \ v = (a/3) + (2b/3).]$$

12. Suppose that the entries of a matrix game are rewritten in new units (e.g., dollars instead of cents). Show that the monetary value of the game has not changed.

13. Consider the game of matching pennies whose matrix is

1	-1
-1	1

.

If the entries of the matrix represent gains or losses of one penny, would you be willing to play the game at least once? If the entries represent gains or losses of one dollar, would you be willing to play the game at least once? If they represent gains or losses of one million dollars would you play the game at least once? In each of these cases show that the value is zero and optimal strategies are the same. Discuss the practical application of the theory of games in the light of this example.

SUPPLEMENTARY EXERCISES

The remaining exercises refer to the *product payoff game* (due to A. W. Tucker). Two sets, S and T, are given, each set containing at least one positive and at least one negative number (but no zeros). Player R selects a number s from set S, and player C selects a number t from set T. The payoff is st.

14. Set up the game for the sets $S = \{1, -1, 2\}$ and $T = \{1, -3, 2, -4\}$.

[*Ans.*

1	−3	2	−4
−1	3	−2	4
2	−6	4	−8

.]

15. Consider the following mixed strategy for either player: "Choose a positive number p and a negative number n with probabilities $-n/(p - n)$ and $p/(p - n)$ respectively." Assume that R uses this strategy.
   (a) If C chooses a positive number, show that the expected payoff to R is 0.
   (b) If C chooses a negative number, show that the expected payoff to R is 0.

16. Rework Exercise 15 with R and C interchanged.

17. Use the results of Exercises 15 and 16 to show that the game is fair, and that the strategy quoted in Exercise 15 is optimal for either player.

18. Find all strategies of the kind indicated in Exercise 15 for both players for the game of Exercise 14.
   [*Partial Ans.* For R they are $(\tfrac{1}{2}, \tfrac{1}{2}, 0)$ and $(0, \tfrac{2}{3}, \tfrac{1}{3})$.]

19. By subtracting ten from each entry, show that the following game is derived from a product payoff game, and find all strategies like those in Exercise 15 for both players. What is the value of the game?

11	7	12	6
9	13	8	14
12	4	14	2

[*Hint:* Use Exercises 14, 18, and Theorem 5.]

20. If a player in the product payoff game has m positive and n negative numbers in his set, show that he has mn strategies like those in Exercise 15.

8. GAMES IN WHICH ONE PLAYER HAS TWO STRATEGIES

After the 2×2 games, the simplest matrix games are the $2 \times n$ and $m \times 2$ games, i.e., where one of the players has only two strategies. Here we discuss the solution of such games.

Example 1. Suppose that Jones conceals one of the following four bills in his hand: a \$1 or a \$2 United States bill or a \$1 or a \$2 Canadian bill. Smith guesses either "United States" or "Canadian" and gets the bill if his guess is correct. The matrix of the game is the following.

Smith Guesses

		U.S.	Can.
U.S.	\$1	−1	0
	\$2	−2	0
Can.	\$1	0	−1
	\$2	0	−2

Jones Chooses

It is obvious that Jones should always choose the \$1 bill of either country rather than the \$2 bill, since by doing so he may cut his losses and will never increase them. This can be observed in the matrix above, since every entry in the second row is less than or equal to the corresponding entry in the first row, and every entry in the fourth row is less than or equal to the corresponding entry in the third row. In effect we can eliminate the second and fourth rows and reduce the game to the following 2×2 matrix game.

Smith Guesses

		U.S.	Can.
U.S. \$1		−1	0
Can. \$1		0	−1

Jones Chooses

The new matrix game is nonstrictly determined with optimal strategies $(\frac{1}{2}, \frac{1}{2})$ for Jones and $\begin{pmatrix} \frac{1}{2} \\ \frac{1}{2} \end{pmatrix}$ for Smith. The value of the game is $-\frac{1}{2}$, which means that Smith should pay 50 cents to play it.

DEFINITION. Let A be an $m \times n$ matrix game. We shall say that row i *dominates* row h if every entry in row i is as large as or larger than the corresponding entry in row h. Similarly, we shall say that column j

dominates column k if every entry in column j is as small as or smaller than the corresponding entry in column k.

Any dominated row or column can be omitted from the matrix game without affecting its solution. In the original matrix of Example 1 above, we see that row 1 dominates row 2, and also that row 3 dominates row 4.

Example 2. Consider again the card game of Section 4, this time giving R a bk 5 and rd 3, while C receives a bk 6 and a bk 5 and a rd 4 and a rd 5. The matrix of the game is

	bk 6	bk 5	rd 4	rd 5
bk 5	1	0	−1	0
rd 3	−3	−2	1	2

Observe that column 3 dominates column 4; that is, C should never play rd 5. Thus our game can be reduced to the following 2 × 3 game.

	bk 6	bk 5	rd 4
bk 5	1	0	−1
rd 3	−3	−2	1

No further rows or columns can be omitted; hence we must introduce a new technique for the solution of this game. It can be shown (though we will not attempt to do so here) that, in any 2 × n game, the column player C has an optimal mixed strategy that uses only two pure strategies. Hence he may consider the game matrix two columns at a time, and select the 2 × 2 game he likes best. That is, he solves each of the 2 × 2 games consisting of two columns of the matrix, and selects the one having the smallest value.

In the above 2 × 3 game we find three games derived in this manner,

	bk 6	bk 5
bk 5	1	0
rd 3	−3	−2

	bk 6	rd 4
bk 5	1	−1
rd 3	−3	1

	bk 5	rd 4
bk 5	0	−1
rd 3	−2	1

The first game is strictly determined and fair, the second has value $-\frac{1}{3}$, and the third value $-\frac{1}{2}$. Hence player C selects the third game, i.e., he decides to use only strategies bk 5 and rd 4. The optimal strategy for the latter game is to play each card one-half of the time, hence his optimal strategy for the 2 × 4 game is

$$\begin{pmatrix} 0 \\ \frac{1}{2} \\ \frac{1}{2} \\ 0 \end{pmatrix}.$$

Since R knows that C will select this particular 2 × 2 game, R's optimal strategy is his optimal strategy in this 2 × 2 game, which is $(\frac{3}{4}, \frac{1}{4})$.

For an $m \times 2$ game, the row player can select which two rows to use, and he does this by selecting the 2 × 2 game with largest value. Then the value of the game and the optimal strategies are found by solving this 2 × 2 game. Similarly, for the 2 × n case, C selects the two columns so that the 2 × 2 game resulting gives the smallest possible value (smallest loss), and then we need only solve this 2 × 2 game.

Example 3. A numerical example of a 3 × 2 game is

6	−1
0	2
4	3

Here the game is strictly determined, since the entry 3 is the minimum of its row and the maximum of its column. The value of the game is 3, and optimal strategies are $p^0 = (0, 0, 1)$ and $q^0 = \begin{pmatrix} 0 \\ 1 \end{pmatrix}$.

Example 4. Another numerical example is

1	−1	2	−3
−1	1	0	1

Here the fourth column dominates the second, and the first column dominates the third. The game is then reduced to

$$\begin{array}{|c|c|}
\hline
1 & -3 \\
\hline
-1 & 1 \\
\hline
\end{array},$$

whose value is $-\frac{1}{3}$, and optimal strategies are $p^0 = (\frac{1}{3}, \frac{2}{3})$ and $q^0 = \begin{pmatrix} \frac{2}{3} \\ \frac{1}{3} \end{pmatrix}$; the latter strategy extends to the strategy

$$\begin{pmatrix} \frac{2}{3} \\ 0 \\ 0 \\ \frac{1}{3} \end{pmatrix},$$

which is optimal in the original game.

Example 5. Our final example shows that there may be a multiplicity of subgames that can be chosen to give optimal strategies. Consider the 4×2 game whose matrix is

$$\begin{array}{|c|c|}
\hline
13 & -7 \\
\hline
3 & 8 \\
\hline
-1 & 14 \\
\hline
9 & -1 \\
\hline
\end{array}$$

Since there are four rows, there are $\begin{pmatrix} 4 \\ 2 \end{pmatrix} = 6$ ways that R can choose a 2×2 subgame. Of these six ways, the one that chooses the first and last row has value -1, and the one that chooses the second and third row has value 3. Each of the other four subgames has value 5. They give rise to the following four optimal strategies for R.

$$(\tfrac{1}{5}, \tfrac{4}{5}, 0, 0)$$
$$(\tfrac{3}{7}, 0, \tfrac{4}{7}, 0)$$
$$(0, 0, \tfrac{2}{5}, \tfrac{3}{5})$$
$$(0, \tfrac{2}{3}, 0, \tfrac{1}{3}).$$

Player C has a unique optimal strategy, namely, $\begin{pmatrix} \frac{3}{5} \\ \frac{2}{5} \end{pmatrix}$.

EXERCISES

1. Solve the following games.

(a)

3	0
−2	3
7	5

[*Ans.* $v = 5$; $(0, 0, 1)$; $\begin{pmatrix} 0 \\ 1 \end{pmatrix}$.]

(b)

10	5	4	6
18	3	3	4

(c)

1	0	2
0	3	2

[*Ans.* $v = \frac{3}{4}$; $(\frac{3}{4}, \frac{1}{4})$; $\begin{pmatrix} \frac{3}{4} \\ \frac{1}{4} \\ 0 \end{pmatrix}$.]

(d)

0	2
1	3
−1	0
2	0

(e)

1	2	3
4	2	1

[*An ans.* $v = 2$; $(\frac{3}{5}, \frac{2}{5})$; $\begin{pmatrix} 0 \\ 1 \\ 0 \end{pmatrix}$.]

(f)

1	0	1	1	2
0	−1	−2	−3	−10

2. Solve the following games.

(a)

0	15
8	0
−10	20
10	12

(b)

−1	−2	0	−3	−4
−2	1	0	2	5

(c)

−1	5	−1	−2	8	10
3	−6	0	8	−9	−8

$$[\textit{An ans. } v = -\tfrac{1}{2}; \ (\tfrac{1}{2}, \tfrac{1}{2}); \ \begin{pmatrix} 0 \\ \frac{1}{12} \\ \frac{11}{12} \\ 0 \\ 0 \\ 0 \end{pmatrix}.]$$

3. Solve the game

1	2	3
3	2	1

Since there is more than one optimal strategy for C, find a range of optimal strategies for him. (See Section 7, Exercise 3.)

4. In the card game of Example 2 suppose that R has bk 9, bk 5, rd 7 and rd 3, while C has bk 8 and rd 4. Set up and solve the corresponding matrix game.

[*Ans.* $v = 1$; R shows bk 5 and rd 7 each with probability $\tfrac{1}{2}$; C shows each of his cards with probability $\tfrac{1}{2}$.]

5. Suppose that Jones conceals in his hand one, two, three, or four silver dollars and Smith guesses "even" or "odd." If Smith's guess is correct, he wins the amount which Jones holds, otherwise he must pay Jones this amount.

Set up the corresponding matrix game and find an optimal strategy for each player in which he puts positive weight on all his (pure) strategies. Is the game fair?

6. Consider the following game: Player R announces "one" or "two"; then, independently of each other, both players write down one of these two numbers. If the sum of the three numbers so obtained is odd, C pays R the odd sum in dollars; if the sum of the three numbers is even, R pays C the even sum in dollars.

  (a) What are the strategies of R? [*Hint:* He has four strategies.]
  (b) What are the strategies of C? [*Hint:* We must consider what C does after "one" is announced after a "two." Hence he has four strategies.]
  (c) Write the matrix for the game.
  (d) Restrict player R to announcing "two," and allow for C only those strategies where his number does not depend on the announced number. Solve the resulting 2 × 2 game.
  (e) Extend the above mixed strategies to the original game, and show that they are optimal.
  (f) Is the game favorable to R? If so, by how much?

7. Answer the same questions as in Exercise 6, if R gets the even sum and C gets the odd sum (except that in part (d) restrict R to announce "one"). Which game is more favorable for R? Could you have predicted this without the use of game theory?

8. Rework the five-finger Morra game of Section 6, Exercise 5, with the following payoffs: If the sum of the number of fingers is even, R gets one, while if the sum is odd, C gets one. Suppose that each player shows only one or two fingers. Show that the resulting game is like matching pennies. Show that the optimal strategies for this game, when extended, are optimal in the whole game.

9. A version of three-finger Morra is played as follows: Each player shows from one to three fingers; R always pays C an amount equal to the number of fingers that C shows; if C shows exactly one more or two fewer fingers than R, then C pays R a positive amount x (where x is independent of the number of fingers shown).

  (a) Set up the game matrix for arbitrary x's.
  (b) If $x = \frac{1}{2}$, show that the game is strictly determined. Find the value.
    [*Ans.* $v = -\frac{5}{2}$.]
  (c) If $x = 2$, show that there is a pair of optimal strategies in which the first player shows one or two fingers and the second player shows two or three fingers. [*Hint:* Solve a 2 × 2 derived game.]
    Find the value.   [*Ans.* $v = -\frac{3}{2}$.]

(d) If $x = 6$, show that an optimal strategy for R is to use the mixed strategy $(\frac{1}{3}, \frac{1}{2}, \frac{1}{6})$. Show that the optimal mixed strategy for C is to choose his three strategies each with probability $\frac{1}{3}$. Find the value of the game.

10. Another version of three-finger Morra goes as follows: Each player shows from one to three fingers; if the sum of the number of fingers is even, then R gets an amount equal to the number of fingers that C shows; if the sum is odd, C gets an amount equal to the number of fingers that R shows.

(a) Set up the game matrix.

(b) Reduce the game to a 2 × 2 matrix game.

(c) Find optimal strategies for each player and show that the game is fair.

11. Two companies, one large and one small, manufacturing the same product, wish to build a new store in one of four towns located on a given highway. If we regard the total population of the four towns as 100 per cent, the distribution of population and distances between towns are as shown.

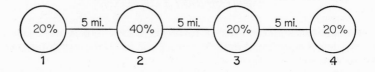

Assume that if the large company's store is nearer a town it will capture 80 per cent of the business; if both stores are equally distant, then the large company will capture 60 per cent of the business; if the small store is nearer, then the large company will capture 40 per cent of the business.

(a) Set up the matrix of the game.

(b) Test for dominated rows and columns.

(c) Find optimal strategies and value for the game and interpret your results.

[*Ans.* Both companies should locate in town 2; the large company captures 60 per cent of the business.]

12. Rework Exercise 11 if the per cent of business captured by the large company is 90, 75, and 60, respectively.

13. We have stated without proof that any 2 × n game can be solved by considering only its 2 × 2 derived games. Verify that this is the case for a game of the form $(a > 0, b > 0)$:

C

	a	0	1
R			
	0	b	1

(a) Show that if $a \leq 1$ or $b \leq 1$, then column 3 is dominated. Hence solve the game.

(b) If $a > 1$ and $b > 1$, solve the three 2×2 derived games. [*Hint:* Two of them are strictly determined.]

(c) If $a > 1$, $b > 1$, but $ab < a + b$, then show that the strategies of the nonstrictly determined derived game are optimal for both players.

(d) If $ab \geq a + b$, then show that R has as optimal strategy the same strategy as in part (c), but C has a pure strategy as optimal strategy.

(e) Using the previous results, show that the value of the game is always the smallest of the values of the three derived games.

SUPPLEMENTARY EXERCISES

Exercises 14–20 refer to the *exponential payoff game*. To play the game a number $b > 0$ is chosen. Two sets, S and T, are specified, each set containing at least one positive and at least one negative number (but no zeros). Player R selects a number s from set S, and player C selects a number t from T. If $st > 0$, the payoff is b^{s+t} and if $st < 0$, the payoff is $-b^{s+t}$.

14. Set up the game for $b = 2$ and the sets $S = \{1, -1, 2\}$ and $T = \{1, -3, 2, -4\}$.

		1	-3	2	-4
	1	4	$-\frac{1}{4}$	8	$-\frac{1}{8}$
[*Ans.*	-1	-1	$\frac{1}{16}$	-2	$\frac{1}{32}$
	2	8	$-\frac{1}{2}$	16	$-\frac{1}{4}$

.]

15. Consider the following mixed strategy for either player: "Choose a positive number p and a negative number n with probabilities $b^n/(b^p + b^n)$ and $b^p/(b^p + b^n)$, respectively." Assume that R uses this strategy.

(a) If C chooses a positive number, show that the expected payoff to R is 0.

(b) If C chooses a negative number, show that the expected payoff to R is 0.

16. Rework Exercise 15 with R and C interchanged.

17. Use the results of Exercises 15 and 16 to show that the game is fair, and that the strategy quoted in Exercise 15 is optimal for either player.

18. Find all strategies of the kind indicated in Exercise 15 for both players for the game of Exercise 14.

[*Partial Ans.* For R they are $(\frac{1}{5}, \frac{4}{5}, 0)$ and $(0, \frac{8}{9}, \frac{1}{9})$.]

19. If a player in the exponential payoff game has m positive and n negative numbers in his set, show that he has mn strategies like those in Exercise 15.

20. Find an optimal strategy for player R which is not of the kind indicated in Exercise 15.

21. Consider the product payoff game described in Exercises 14–20 of Section 7.
(a) If either player has exactly two numbers in his set, show that his optimal strategy is unique.
(b) If either player has more than two numbers in his set, show that he has more than one optimal strategy.

22. Consider the product payoff game described in Exercises 14–20 of Section 7. If player R has two numbers in his set, and C has n (> 2) in his set, show that no column in the resulting game dominates any other column. Do the same for row dominance in the case that C has exactly two numbers in his set.

23. Rework Exercises 21 and 22 for the exponential payoff game.

24. Show that, except for the addition of 5 to each matrix entry, Example 5 is the product payoff game with R choosing from the set $\{4, -1, -3, 2\}$ and C choosing from the set $\{2, -3\}$.

9. SIMPLIFIED POKER

In order to illustrate the procedure of translating a game specified by rules into a matrix game, we shall carry it out for a simplification of a well-known game. The example that we are about to discuss is a simplification (by A. W. Tucker) of the poker game discussed on pp. 211–219 in the book *The Theory of Games and Economic Behavior*, by John von Neumann and Oskar Morgenstern.

The deck that is used in simplified poker has only two types of cards, in equal numbers, which we shall call "high" and "low." For example, an ordinary bridge deck could be used with red cards high and black cards low. Each player "antes" an amount a of money and is dealt a single card which is his "hand." By a "deal" we shall mean a pair of cards, the first being given to player R and the second to player C. Thus the deal (H, H) means that each player obtains a high card. There are then four possible deals, namely,

$$(H, H), \quad (H, L), \quad (L, H), \quad (L, L).$$

Ignoring minor errors (see Exercise 1), if the number of cards in the deck is large, each of these deals is "equally likely," that is, the probability of getting a specific one of these deals is $\frac{1}{4}$.

After the deal, player R has the first move and has two alternatives, namely, to "see," or to "raise" by adding an amount b to the pot. If R elects to see, the higher hand wins the pot or equal hands split the pot equally. If R elects to raise, then C has two alternatives, to "fold," or to "call" by adding the amount b to the pot. If C folds, player R wins the pot (without revealing his hand). If C calls, then the higher hand wins the pot or equal hands split the pot equally. These are all the rules.

A pure strategy for a player is a command that tells him exactly what to do in every conceivable situation that can arise in the game. An example of a pure strategy for R is the following: "Raise if you get a high card, and see if you get a low card." We can abbreviate this strategy to simply raise-see. It is easy to see that R has four pure strategies, namely, raise-raise, raise-see, see-raise, and see-see. In the same manner, C has four pure strategies, fold-fold, fold-call, call-fold, call-call.

Given a choice of a pure strategy for each player, there are exactly four ways the play of the game can proceed, depending on which of the four deals occurs. For example, suppose that R has chosen the see-raise strategy, and C has chosen the fold-fold strategy. If the deal is (H, H), then R sees, and they split the pot, so neither wins; if the deal is (H, L), then R sees and wins the pot, giving him a; if the deal is (L, H), then R raises and C folds, so that R wins a; and if the deal is (L, L), then R raises and C folds, so that R wins a. Since the probabilities of each of these deals is $\frac{1}{4}$, the expected value of R's gain is $3a/4$. Let us compute another expected value, namely, suppose that R uses see-raise and C uses call-fold. Then, if the deal is (H, H), R sees and wins nothing; if the deal is (H, L), then R sees and wins a; if the deal is (L, H), then R raises, C calls, and C wins $a + b$; and if the deal is (L, L), then R raises, C folds, and R wins a. The expected value for R here is $(a - b)/4$.

Continuing in this manner, we can compute the expected outcome for each of the 16 possible choices of pairs of strategies. The payoff matrix so obtained is given below.

High		fold	fold	call	call
	Low	fold	call	fold	call
see	see	0	0	0	0
see	raise	$\dfrac{3a}{4}$	$\dfrac{2a}{4}$	$\dfrac{a-b}{4}$	$\dfrac{-b}{4}$
raise	see	$\dfrac{a}{4}$	$\dfrac{a+b}{4}$	0	$\dfrac{b}{4}$
raise	raise	$\dfrac{4a}{4}$	$\dfrac{3a+b}{4}$	$\dfrac{a-b}{4}$	0

The reader should observe that we have just completed the translation of a game specified by rules into a matrix game.

Since a and b are positive numbers, we see that, in the matrix above, the fourth row dominates the second, and the third row dominates the first. Similarly, the third column dominates the first and second columns. We can reduce the 4×4 matrix to the following 2×2 matrix.

			Conservative	Bluffing
High			call	call
	Low		fold	call
Conservative	raise	see	0	$\dfrac{b}{4}$
Bluffing	raise	raise	$\dfrac{a-b}{4}$	0

Notice that we have labeled the raise-see strategy as "conservative" for R, since it seems sensible to raise when he has a high card and to see when he has a low one. The strategy raise-raise which says, raise even if you have a low card, we have labeled "bluffing," since it corresponds to the ordinary notion of bluffing. In the same manner we have labeled the call-fold strategy "conservative," and the call-call strategy "bluffing," for player C.

Example 1. Suppose $a = 4$ and $b = 8$. Then the matrix becomes

	Conservative	Bluffing
Conservative	0	2
Bluffing	-1	0

Here the game is strictly determined and fair, and optimal strategies are for each player to play conservatively.

Example 2. Suppose $a = 8$ and $b = 4$. Then the matrix becomes

	Conservative	Bluffing
Conservative	0	1
Bluffing	1	0

Here the value of the game is $\frac{1}{2}$, meaning that it is biased in favor of R. Optimal strategies are for each player to bluff with probability $\frac{1}{2}$ and to play conservatively with probability $\frac{1}{2}$.

Here we have one of the most interesting results of game theory, since it turns out that, as part of an optimal strategy, one *should* actually bluff part of the time.

EXERCISES

1. Suppose that the simplified poker game is played with an ordinary bridge deck where red is "high" and black is "low." Compute to four decimal places the conditional probability of drawing a red card, given that one red card has already been drawn. From this, discuss the accuracy of the assumption that the four deals are equally likely. How could the accuracy of the assumption be improved?

2. Substitute $a = 4$ and $b = 8$ into the 4×4 matrix above, and reduce it by dominations to a 2×2 matrix game. Is it the one considered in Example 1 above? Do the same for $a = 8$ and $b = 4$ and compare with Example 2.

3. If $a \leq b$, show that the simplified poker game is strictly determined and fair. Show that both players' optimal strategy is to play conservatively.

4. If $a > b$, show that the simplified poker game is biased in favor of R. Show that, to play optimally, each player must bluff with positive probability, and find the optimal strategies.

5. If $a > b$, discuss ways of making the game fair.

6. When $b \geq a$, show that the optimal strategy of player R is not unique. Show that although he has two "optimal" strategies, the raise-see strategy is in a sense better than the other.

7. Show that in the case $a = 8$, $b = 4$, the strategy of R can be interpreted as follows: "On a high card always raise, on a low card raise with probability $\frac{1}{2}$." Reinterpret C's mixed strategy similarly.

The remaining exercises concern a variant of the simplified poker game. Real poker is characterized by the fact that there are very many poor hands, and very few good ones. We can make the above model of poker more realistic by making the draw of a low card more probable than that of a high card. Let us say that the probability of drawing a high card is only $\frac{1}{5}$. The rules of the game remain as in the text.

8. Calculate the probabilities of (H, H), (H, L), (L, H), and (L, L) deals.

9. The strategies of the two players are as in the text, hence we will get a similar 4×4 game matrix. Calculate the see-raise *vs.* fold-fold entry of the matrix, just as in the text, but using the results of Exercise 8. Do the same for the see-raise *vs.* call-fold entry.   [*Ans.* $24a/25$; $(16a - 4b)/25$.]

10. Fill in the remaining matrix entries.

11. Show that two rows are dominated, and that two columns are dominated.

12. Show that the resulting 2×2 game is strictly determined if and only if $b \geq 4a$. What is the value of the game in these cases?

13. Let $a = 4$, $b = 8$, as in the text, and solve the game. Compare your solution with that in the text.
    [*Ans.* Each player should bluff half the time; $v = \frac{16}{25}$; in the previous version there was no bluffing in this case, and the game was fair.]

14. Let $a = 8$, $b = 4$, as in the text, and solve the game. Compare your solution with that in the text.

[*Ans.* Each player plays more conservatively; game is slightly more favorable to R than in the previous version.]

15. The players have agreed that the ante will be $4. They are debating the size of the raise. What value of b should player R argue for? [*Hint:* He does not want the game to be fair. Then what are the possible values of b? Find the value of the 2×2 game for any such b, and find its maximum value by trying several values of b.]

SUGGESTED READING

Von Neumann, J., and Oskar Morgenstern, *Theory of Games and Economic Behavior*, Princeton University Press, Princeton, 1944, 3d edition, 1953, Chapter I.

Williams, J. D., *The Compleat Strategyst*, McGraw-Hill, New York, 1950.

Luce, R. Duncan, and Howard Raiffa, *Games and Decisions: Introduction and Critical Survey*, Wiley, New York, 1957.

Shubik, Martin, *Strategy and Market Structure*, Wiley, New York, 1959.

Rapoport, Anatol, *Fights, Games, and Debates*, University of Michigan Press, Ann Arbor, 1960.

Kuhn, H. W., and A. W. Tucker, "Theory of Games," *Encyclopaedia Britannica*, 1956 edition.

Morgenstern, Oskar, "The Theory of Games," *Scientific American*, 180 (1950), pp. 294–308.

Gale, David, *The Theory of Linear Economic Models*, McGraw-Hill, New York, 1960.

McKinsey, J. C. C., *Introduction to the Theory of Games*, McGraw-Hill, New York, 1952.

Bellman, R., and D. Blackwell, "Red Dog, Blackjack, Poker," *Scientific American*, 184 (1951), pp. 44–47.

MacDonald, J., *Strategy in Poker, Business and War*, Norton, New York, 1950.

Burger, Ewald, *Introduction to the Theory of Games*, Prentice-Hall, Englewood Cliffs, 1963.

Thompson, Gerald L., "Game Theory," *McGraw-Hill Encyclopedia of Science and Technology*, 1960, Volume 6, pp. 24–30.

*Applications to behavioral science problems

1. COMMUNICATION AND SOCIOMETRIC MATRICES

Matrices having only the entries 0 and 1 are useful in the analysis of graphs and networks. We shall not attempt to give a complete treatment of the subject here, but merely illustrate some of its more interesting applications.

A communication network consists of a set of people, $A_1, A_2, \ldots,$ A_n, such that between some pairs of persons there is a communication link. Such a link may be either one-way or two-way. A two-way communication link might be made by telephone or radio, and a one-way link by sending a messenger, lighting a signal light, setting off an explosion, etc. We shall use the symbol $\gg$ to indicate such a connection; $A_i \gg A_j$ shall mean that that individual A_i can communicate with A_j (in that direction). The only requirement that we put on the symbol is

(i)   It is false that $A_i \gg A_i$ for any i; that is an individual cannot (or need not) communicate with himself.

It is convenient to use directed graphs to represent communication networks. Two such graphs are drawn in Figure 1. Individuals are represented on the graph as (lettered) points and a communication relation between two individuals as a directed line segment (line segment with an arrow) connecting the two individuals.

We can also represent communication networks by means of square matrices C having only 0 and 1 entries, which we call *communication*

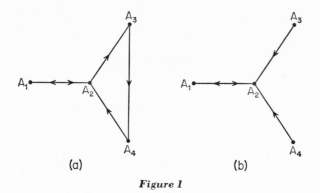

(a)   (b)

Figure 1

matrices. The entry in the ith row and jth column of C is equal to 1 if A_i can communicate with A_j (in that direction) and otherwise equal to 0. Thus the communication matrices corresponding to the com-

$$C = \begin{pmatrix} 0 & 1 & 0 & 0 \\ 1 & 0 & 1 & 0 \\ 0 & 0 & 0 & 1 \\ 0 & 1 & 0 & 0 \end{pmatrix} \qquad C = \begin{pmatrix} 0 & 1 & 0 & 0 \\ 1 & 0 & 0 & 0 \\ 0 & 1 & 0 & 0 \\ 0 & 1 & 0 & 0 \end{pmatrix}$$

(a)   (b)

Figure 2

munication networks of Figure 1 are shown in Figure 2.

Notice that the diagonal entries of the matrices in Figure 2 are all equal to 0. This is true in general for a communication matrix, since the matrix restatement of condition (i) is

(i)   For all i, $c_{ii} = 0$.

It is not hard to see that any matrix having only 0 and 1 entries, and with all zeros down the main diagonal, is the communication matrix of some network.

By a *dominance relation* we shall mean a special kind of communication relation in which, besides (i), the following condition holds.

(ii)   For each pair i, j, with $i \neq j$, either $A_i \gg A_j$ or $A_j \gg A_i$, but not both; that is, in every pair of individuals, there is exactly one who is dominant.

It has been observed that in the pecking order of chickens a dominance relation holds. Also, in the play of one round of a round robin contest among athletic teams, if ties are not allowed (as in baseball), then a dominance relation holds.

The reader may have been surprised that we did not assume that if $A_i \gg A_j$ and $A_j \gg A_k$ then $A_i \gg A_k$. This is the so-called transitive law for relations. A moment's reflection shows that the transitive law need not hold for dominance relations. Thus if team A beats team B and team B beats team C (in football, say), then we cannot assume that team A will necessarily beat team C. In every football season there are instances in which "upsets" occur.

Dominance relations may also be depicted by means of directed graphs. Two such are shown in Figure 3. The graph in Figure 3a

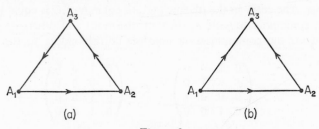

(a)   (b)

Figure 3

represents the situation: A_1 dominates A_2, A_2 dominates A_3, and A_3 dominates A_1. Similarly, the graph in Figure 3b represents the situation: A_1 dominates A_2 and A_3, and A_2 dominates A_3. These graphs represent the two essentially different dominance relations that are possible among three individuals (cf. Exercise 1).

Dominance relations may also be defined by means of matrices, called *dominance matrices*, defined as for communication matrices. In Figure 4 we have shown the two dominance matrices corresponding to the directed graphs of Figure 3.

Since a dominance matrix is derived from a dominance relation, we can investigate the effects of conditions (i) and (ii) above on the entries in the matrix. Condition (i) simply means that all entries on the main diagonal (the one which slants downward to the right) of the matrix must be zero. Condition (ii) means that, whenever an entry above the main diagonal of the matrix is 1, the corresponding entry of the matrix which is placed symmetrically to it through the main diagonal is 0, and

$$D = \begin{pmatrix} 0 & 1 & 0 \\ 0 & 0 & 1 \\ 1 & 0 & 0 \end{pmatrix}, \qquad D = \begin{pmatrix} 0 & 1 & 1 \\ 0 & 0 & 1 \\ 0 & 0 & 0 \end{pmatrix}$$

(a)   (b)

Figure 4

vice versa. To state these conditions more precisely, suppose that there are n individuals, and let D be a dominance matrix with entries d_{ij}. Then the conditions above are

(i) $d_{ii} = 0$ for $i = 1, 2, \ldots, n$.
(ii) If $i \neq j$, then $d_{ij} = 1$ if and only if $d_{ij} = 0$.

Every dominance relation is also a communication relation, hence we shall concentrate on the latter, and what we say about them will also be true for the former.

Since a communication matrix C is square, we can compute its powers, C^2, C^3, etc. Let $E = C^2$, and consider the entry in the ith row and jth column of E. It is

$$e_{ij} = c_{i1}c_{1j} + c_{i2}c_{2j} + \ldots + c_{in}c_{nj}.$$

Now a term of the form $c_{ik}c_{kj}$ can be nonzero only if both factors are nonzero, that is, only if both factors are equal to 1. But if $c_{ik} = 1$, then individual A_i communicates with A_k; and if $c_{kj} = 1$, then individual A_k communicates with A_j. In other words, $A_i \gg A_k \gg A_j$. We shall call a communication of this kind a *two-stage communication*. (To keep ideas straight, let us call $A_i \gg A_j$ a *one-stage* communication.) We can now see that the entry e_{ij} gives the total number of two-stage communication paths there are between A_i and A_j (in that direction). For example, let C be the matrix

$$C = \begin{pmatrix} 0 & 1 & 1 & 1 \\ 0 & 0 & 1 & 1 \\ 0 & 0 & 0 & 1 \\ 0 & 0 & 0 & 0 \end{pmatrix}.$$

Then C^2 is the matrix

$$C^2 = \begin{pmatrix} 0 & 0 & 1 & 2 \\ 0 & 0 & 0 & 1 \\ 0 & 0 & 0 & 0 \\ 0 & 0 & 0 & 0 \end{pmatrix}.$$

Thus we see that in this example A_1 has one two-stage communication path with A_3 and two two-stage communicat ons with A_4; similarly, A_2 has one two-stage communication with A_4. These can be written down explicitly as

$$A_1 \gg A_2 \gg A_3,$$
$$A_1 \gg A_2 \gg A_4,$$
$$A_1 \gg A_3 \gg A_4,$$
$$A_2 \gg A_3 \gg A_4.$$

The directed graph for this (dominance) situation is given in Figure 5. The reader should trace out on the graph of Figure 5 the two-stage communication paths given above.

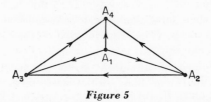

Figure 5

Theorem. Let a communication network of n individuals be such that, for every pair of individuals, at least one can communicate in one stage with the other. Then there is at least one person who can communicate with every other person in either one or two stages. Similarly, there is at least one person who can be communicated with in one or two stages by every other person.

Stated in matrix language, the above theorem is: Let C be the communication matrix for the network described above; then there is at least one row of $S = C + C^2$ which has all its elements nonzero, except possibly the entry on the main diagonal. Similarly, there is at least one column having this property.

Notice that every dominance relation satisfies the hypotheses of the theorem, but there are communication networks, not dominance relations, that also satisfy these hypotheses.

Proof. We shall prove only the first statement since the proof of the second is analogous.

First we shall prove the following statement: If A_1 cannot communicate in either one or two stages with A_i, where $i \neq 1$, then A_i can communicate in one stage with at least one more person than can A_1. We prove this in two steps. First by the hypothesis of the theorem, we see that:

(a) If it is false that $A_1 \gg A_i$, then $A_i \gg A_1$.

Second we can prove that:

(b) Suppose that for all k it is false that $A_1 \gg A_k \gg A_i$; it follows that, if $A_1 \gg A_k$, then also $A_i \gg A_k$.

For if $A_1 \gg A_k$, it is false that $A_k \gg A_i$; hence, by the hypothesis of the theorem, it is true that $A_i \gg A_k$.

Now (b) says that every one-stage communication possible for A_1 is also possible for A_i. From this and (a), it then follows that A_i can make at least one more (one-stage) communication than can A_1.

We now return to the proof of the theorem. Let $r_1, r_2, \ldots, r_n$ be the row sums of the matrix C. By renaming the individuals, if necessary, we can assume that the largest row sum is r_1, that is, $r_1 \geq r_k$ for $k = 1, 2, \ldots, n$. We shall show that A_1 can communicate with everyone else in one or two stages. (The proof is based on the indirect method.) Suppose, on the contrary, that there is an individual A_i, where $i > 1$, with whom A_1 cannot so communicate. By the statement proved above, A_i can communicate in one stage with at least one more person than A_1 can. But this implies that $r_i > r_1$, which contradicts the fact that we have named the individuals so that $r_1 \geq r_i$. This contradiction establishes the theorem.

An additional conclusion which can be made from the proof of the theorem is that the individual or individuals having the *largest* row sum in the matrix C can communicate with everyone else in one or two stages. Similarly, the individuals having the *largest* column sum can be communicated with by everyone in one or two stages.

The network shown in Figure 6 satisfies the hypothesis of the theorem, hence its conclusion. The communication matrix for this network is

$$\begin{pmatrix} 0 & 1 & 1 & 0 \\ 0 & 0 & 1 & 0 \\ 0 & 1 & 0 & 1 \\ 1 & 1 & 0 & 0 \end{pmatrix}.$$

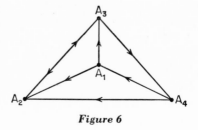

Figure 6

Here the maximum row sum of 2 occurs in rows one, three, and four, so that A_1, A_3, and A_4 can communicate with everyone else in one or two stages. (Find the necessary communication paths in Figure 6.) However, it requires three stages for A_2 to communicate with A_1. The maximum sum of 3 occurs in column two so that A_2 can be communicated with by everyone else in one or two stages (actually one stage is enough). It happens also that A_3 and A_4 can also be communicated with in one or two stages; however, as observed above, A_1 cannot be.

Neither of the networks in Figure 1 satisfies the hypothesis of the theorem. It happens that the network in Figure 1a does satisfy the conclusion of the theorem, while the network in Figure 1b does not. (See Exercise 7.)

As a final application of dominance matrices, we shall define the power of an individual. By the *power* of an individual in a dominance situation, we mean the total number of one-stage and two-stage dominances which he can exert. Since the total number of one-stage dominances exerted by A_i is the sum of the entries in row i of the matrix D, and the total number of two-stage dominances exerted by A_i is the sum of the entries in row i of the matrix D^2, we see that the power of A_i can be expressed as follows:

The power of A_i is the sum of the entries in row i of the matrix $S = D + D^2$.

In the example of Figure 7 it is easy to check that the powers of the various individuals are the following.

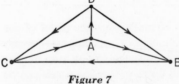

Figure 7

The power of A is 5.
The power of B is 2.
The power of C is 3.
The power of D is 4.

Example. (Athletic contest). The idea of the power of an individual can be used to judge athletic events. For example, the result of a single round of a round robin athletic event results in the following data.

Team A beats teams B and D.
Team B beats team C.
Team C beats team A.
Team D beats teams C and B.

Then it is easy to check that this is precisely the dominance situation shown in Figure 7. By the analysis given above we can rate the teams in the following order according to their respective powers: *A, D, C,* and *B.*

It should be remarked that the above definition of the power of an individual is not the only one possible. In Exercise 13 below we suggest another definition of power which gives different results. Before using one or the other of these definitions, a sociologist should examine them carefully to see which (if either) fits his needs.

EXERCISES

1. Show that there are only two essentially different pecking orders possible among three chickens, namely, those given in Figure 3. [*Hint:* Use directed graphs.]

2. Find the dominance matrices *D* corresponding to the following directed graphs.

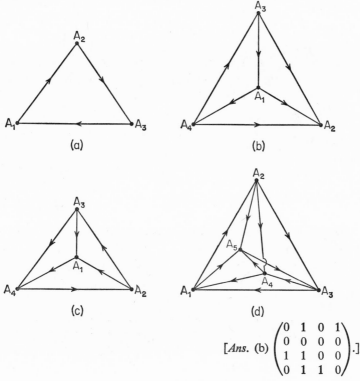

(a)   (b)

(c)   (d)

$$[Ans.\ (b)\ \begin{pmatrix} 0 & 1 & 0 & 1 \\ 0 & 0 & 0 & 0 \\ 1 & 1 & 0 & 0 \\ 0 & 1 & 1 & 0 \end{pmatrix}.]$$

3. Compute the matrices D^2 and $S = D + D^2$ and determine the powers of each of the individuals in the examples of Exercise 2.

$$[Ans. \text{ (b) } D^2 = \begin{pmatrix} 0 & 1 & 1 & 0 \\ 0 & 0 & 0 & 0 \\ 0 & 1 & 0 & 1 \\ 1 & 1 & 0 & 0 \end{pmatrix}; S = \begin{pmatrix} 0 & 2 & 1 & 1 \\ 0 & 0 & 0 & 0 \\ 1 & 2 & 0 & 1 \\ 1 & 2 & 1 & 0 \end{pmatrix}; 4, 0, 4, 4.]$$

4. Find the communication matrices for the following communication networks.

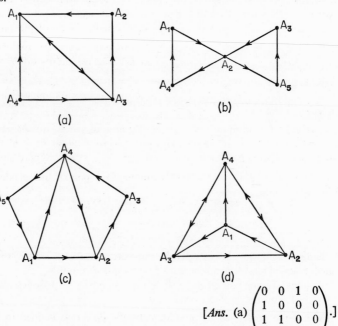

(a)

(b)

(c)

(d)

$$[Ans. \text{ (a)} \begin{pmatrix} 0 & 0 & 1 & 0 \\ 1 & 0 & 0 & 0 \\ 1 & 1 & 0 & 0 \\ 1 & 0 & 1 & 0 \end{pmatrix}.]$$

5. Draw the directed graphs corresponding to the following communication matrices.

(a) $\begin{pmatrix} 0 & 1 & 1 \\ 0 & 0 & 1 \\ 1 & 1 & 0 \end{pmatrix}.$

(b) $\begin{pmatrix} 0 & 1 & 0 & 1 \\ 1 & 0 & 0 & 1 \\ 0 & 0 & 0 & 1 \\ 1 & 1 & 1 & 0 \end{pmatrix}.$

(c) $\begin{pmatrix} 0 & 1 & 0 & 1 \\ 1 & 0 & 1 & 0 \\ 1 & 0 & 0 & 1 \\ 0 & 1 & 1 & 0 \end{pmatrix}.$

(d) $\begin{pmatrix} 0 & 0 & 0 & 0 \\ 0 & 0 & 0 & 1 \\ 1 & 0 & 0 & 0 \\ 0 & 0 & 1 & 0 \end{pmatrix}.$

6. Which of the communication networks whose matrices are given in Exercise 5 satisfy the hypothesis of the theorem of this section?

[*Ans.* (a) and (c).]

7. Show that the network in Figure 1a satisfies the conclusion of the theorem, while the network in Figure 1b does not.

8. By computing the matrix S in each case, find the persons who can communicate with everyone else in one or two stages and those who can be communicated with in one or two stages, for the communication matrices in Exercise 5. (In some cases such persons need not exist.)

[*Ans.* (a) Everyone; (b) everyone; (d) neither type of person exists.]

9. Find all the essentially different pecking orders that are possible among four chickens.   [*Ans.* There are four essentially different ones.]

10. If C is any communication matrix, give the interpretation of the entries in the columns of the matrix $S = C + C^2$. Also give the interpretation for the column sums of S.

11. Find all communication networks among three individuals which satisfy the hypothesis of the theorem of this section. How many of these are essentially different?   [*Ans.* There are seven.]

12. A round robin tennis match among four people has produced the following results.

>   Smith has beaten Brown and Jones.
>   Jones has beaten Brown.
>   Taylor has beaten Smith, Brown, and Jones.

By finding the powers of each player, rank them into first, second, third, and fourth place. Does this ranking agree with your intuition?

[*Ans.* Taylor has power $= 6$, Smith has power $= 3$, Jones has power $= 1$, and Brown has power $= 0$.]

13. Let the power$_1$ of an individual be the power as defined in the text above. Define a new power, called power$_2$, of an individual as follows: If D is the dominance matrix for a group of n individuals, then the power$_2$ of A_i is the sum of row i of the matrix

$$S' = D + \tfrac{1}{2}D^2.$$

Find the power$_2$ of each of the teams in the athletic team example in the text. Show that the power$_2$ of a team need not equal his power$_1$. Comment on the result.

14. Find the power$_2$ of the players in Exercise 12. Discuss its relation with the power$_1$ of each of the players.

[*Ans.* Taylor has power$_2 = \tfrac{9}{2}$, Smith has power$_2 = \tfrac{5}{2}$, Jones has power$_2 = 1$, Brown has power$_2 = 0$.]

15. If C is a communication matrix, give an interpretation for the entries of the matrix C^3. Do the same for the matrix C^4.

[*Ans.* The entry in row i and column j of C^3 gives the number of three-stage communications from i to j; the same entry of C^4 gives the number of four-stage communications from i to j.]

16. If C is a communication matrix, give an interpretation for the entries of the matrix $S = C + C^2 + C^3 + \ldots + C^m$.

17. Prove the second statement of the theorem of the present section.

18. Prove that the following statement is true: In a communication network involving three individuals, it is possible for a message starting from any person to get to any other person if and only if the following condition is satisfied: each individual can send a message to at least one person and can receive a message from at least one person.

19. Show that the matrix form of the condition in Exercise 18 is: Every row and column of the communication matrix must have at least one nonzero entry.

20. Is the statement in Exercise 18 true for a communication network involving two individuals? For four or more individuals? [*Ans.* Yes; no.]

2. EQUIVALENCE CLASSES IN COMMUNICATION NETWORKS

When considering communication networks, it becomes obvious that the various members of the network play different roles. Some members can only send messages, some can only receive them, and others can both send and receive. Subsets of members are also important. We shall consider subsets of members having the following two properties: (a) every member of the subset can both send and receive messages (not necessarily in one step) to and from every other member in the subset; and (b) the subset having property (a) is as large as possible. We shall show that it is possible to partition the set of all people in the network into subsets (called equivalence classes) having these two properties, and that between such equivalence classes there is at most a one-way communication link. We then apply our results to three different problems, (i) putting any nonnegative matrix into canonical form, (ii) the classification of states in a Markov chain, and (iii) the solution of an archeological problem.

As in the previous section, let $A_1, \ldots, A_n$, be the members of the communication network. We define a relation, R, between some pairs of these members as follows: let A_iRA_j mean "A_i can send a message to A_j (in that direction and not necessarily in one step) or else $i = j$." Then it is easy to show that the relation R has the following two properties:

(1) A_iRA_i for every i.   (Reflexive axiom)
(2) A_iRA_j and A_jRA_k implies A_iRA_k.   (Transitive axiom)

To see this, note that property (1) follows from the definition of R, and (2) follows since if A_i can send a message to A_j and A_j can send a message to A_k then A_i can send a message to A_k by routing it through A_j.

If S is *any* set and R is *any* relation defined for members of S that satisfies axioms (1) and (2), then R is called a *weak ordering* on S.

We next define another relation on the states of the network. Let A_iTA_j hold if and only if $(A_iRA_j) \wedge (A_jRA_i)$, that is, A_iTA_j holds if and only if "A_i has a two-way communication with A_j or else $i = j$." It is easy to show that the relation T has the following three properties:

(3) A_iTA_i.   (Reflexive axiom)
(4) A_iTA_j if and only if A_jTA_i.   (Symmetric axiom)
(5) A_iTA_j and A_jTA_k implies A_iTA_k.   (Transitive axiom)

In Exercise 1 the reader is asked to establish these three axioms.

If S is any set and T is any relation defined for members of S that satisfies axioms (3), (4), and (5), then T is called an *equivalence relation* on S. The principal result about equivalence relations defined over a set S is that they partition S into equivalence classes.

DEFINITION. We say that A_i and A_j are *equivalent* if A_iTA_j. For any A_i the *equivalence class* E_i that it determines is the truth set of the statement A_iTA_k, i.e., it is the set of all A_k such that A_iTA_k is true.

Theorem 1. The equivalence classes of T partition S, the set of members of the communication network.

Proof. We must show that every member A_i of S belongs to one and only one equivalence class. Let S' be the equivalence class of A_i. Since A_iTA_i [from (3) above], we know that A_i belongs to S', which shows that A_i belongs to some equivalence class, and also that S' is not empty.

Now let A_i and A_j be any two members of S, and let S' and S'', respectively, be their equivalence classes. We shall show that either $S' \cap S'' = \mathcal{E}$ or else $S' = S''$. If $S' \cap S'' = \mathcal{E}$ then we are done.

Hence, suppose that there is an element X of S in $S' \cap S''$. Since X is in S', we have $A_i T X$; and since X is in S'', we have $A_j T X$. Using (4) we have $X T A_j$. But, by virtue of transitivity (5), $A_i T X$ and $X T A_j$ implies $A_i T A_j$, hence A_j is in S'. Let Y be any element is S'' so that $A_j T Y$. Using transitivity again, we have $A_i T A_j$ and $A_j T Y$ so that Y is in S'. We have thus shown that every element of S'' is in S', i.e., $S'' \subset S'$. In the same manner, one can show that $S' \subset S''$. Hence $S' = S''$.

Since we have shown that every member of S belongs to an equivalence class, and that every pair of equivalence classes are either identical or else disjoint, we have shown that they partition S, completing the proof of the theorem.

We now define a relation R on the equivalence classes of S. Namely, we let $S'RS''$ mean, "either $S' = S''$ or else some member of S' can send a message to some member of S''. We leave it to the reader in Exercise 6 to show that R is a weak ordering of the set of equivalence classes of S.

Theorem 2. Let S' and S'' be two equivalence classes; then, if $S'RS''$, it is false that $S''RS'$. In other words, at most one-way communication is possible between equivalence classes.

Proof. Suppose, on the contrary, that S' and S'' are two equivalence classes such that $S'RS''$ and $S''RS'$. Then there is an element X in S' that can communicate with some element Y in S''; and there is an element Z in S'' that can communicate with some element U in S'. Since Y and Z are in S'', two-way communication is possible between them; and since X and U are in S' they also have two-way communication. Hence Y can communicate with Z, Z can communicate with U and U can communicate with X. Therefore X and Y are in the same equivalence class, contradicting the assumption that they were in different (and hence disjoint) equivalence classes. This completes the proof.

For applications it is important to be able to find the equivalence classes for a given communication network. We develop an iterative method that constructs the following sets.

(6) T_k, the set of states A_k can *send* a message *to* (not necessarily in one step),

(7) F_k, the set of states that A_k can *receive* a message *from* (not necessarily in one step),

(8) E_k, the equivalence class of A_k.

It is easily seen (see Exercise 7) that $E_k = T_k \cap F_k$, so that we develop a method for interatively (that is, step by step) constructing the sets T_k and F_k. We illustrate the method with an example.

Example 1. We wish to get in contact with five alumni of a certain college, but do not know all their addresses. However, we have information of the form, "Jones knows where Brown is," "Smith knows where Doe is," etc. We summarize this information in the communication matrix of Figure 8. In that figure for $i \neq j$ we put 1 in the i,jth

	Brown	Jones	Smith	Adams	Doe
Brown	0	0	0	0	0
Jones	1	0	0	1	0
Smith	0	0	0	0	1
Adams	0	1	1	0	0
Doe	0	0	0	0	0

Figure 8

entry if the ith person knows where the jth one is. What is the smallest number of people that we must contact in order to send a message to all of them?

In order to solve this problem we first find the "send-to" lists for each person. We start by listing all the persons a person can contact in zero or one steps; these data come directly out of the communication matrix. These people form the "first stage approximation" to the "send-to" lists. Next we go down the list of persons and add to his "send-to" list all the people who can be contacted by people already on his first-stage approximate "send-to" list. The results are the "second-stage approximation to the send-to lists." We continue this process, step by step, until for the first time we go through the list and do not add any member to any person's "send-to" list. We then have the actual "send-to" sets for each person, since going through the process again would not change any list. The computations for the example in Figure 8 are shown in Figure 9.

The first-stage approximation to the "send-to" list is shown in the second column of Figure 9. On the first pass through the list we add 3 to Jones's list, which is indicated by bold-face in the third column. We also add 1 and 5 to Adams' list, also indicated by bold-faced numerals. On the next pass through the computation we add 5 to Jones's list and make no other changes. The next pass through the computation produces no further changes so that the final lists shown in the third column of Figure 9 is the complete "send-to" list for each person.

Person	Zero- or One-Stage Communication	Send-to List
1 Brown	1	1
2 Jones	1, 2, 4	1, 2, 4, 3, 5
3 Smith	3, 5	3, 5
4 Adams	2, 3, 4	2, 3, 4, 1, 5
5 Doe	5	5

Figure 9

We see that we have solved the problem posed above, for by contacting either Jones or Adams, we can relay a message to each of the five alumni members.

Let us go further and find the "receive-from" lists and the equivalence classes for each person in the network. The "receive-from" lists are easy, for we simply go down the "send-to" list and if we find member k on the ith person's "send-to" list, we put i on the kth person's "receive-from" list. And we compute the equivalence classes from the relationship $E_k = T_k \cap F_k$. These computations are shown in Figure 10.

Person	Send-to List	Receive-from List	Equivalence Class
1 Brown	1	1, 2, 4	{1}
2 Jones	1, 2, 4, 3, 5	2, 4	{2, 4}
3 Smith	3, 5	2, 3, 4	{3}
4 Adams	2, 3, 4, 1, 5	2, 4	{2, 4}
5 Doe	5	2, 3, 4, 5	{5}

Figure 10

It is interesting to draw the graph of the weak ordering relation R on the equivalence classes. To find the graph we simply check whether one-way communication is possible between each pair of equivalence classes. Then we connect two equivalence classes in the graph if such one-way communication is possible and if there is no intermediate class in the communication path. The graph of the weak ordering relation for the matrix of Figure 8 is shown in Figure 11. Note that equivalence class $\{2, 4\}$ can communicate directly to $\{1\}$ and $\{3\}$ and to $\{5\}$ through $\{3\}$. This graph shows very clearly the fact, noted above, that in order to contact all members of the group it is sufficient to contact either member of the equivalence class $\{2, 4\}$.

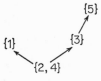

Figure 11

We can use the weak ordering of equivalence classes to put the matrix of Figure 8 in a canonical form, which is characterized by the following definition.

DEFINITION. Let C be any communication matrix, and let S', S'', ..., be the equivalence classes of its states. Then, by a *canonical form* of C, we shall mean a reordering of the rows and columns of C so that the following two properties are satisfied.

(i) Members of a given equivalence class are listed next to each other.

(ii) No equivalence class S' is listed until all classes S'' "above" it in the graph of the equivalence classes have already been listed, i.e., S' is not listed until all classes such that $S'RS''$ have already been listed.

Example 1 (continued). We illustrate this definition in terms of the matrix A of Figure 8. Using the weak ordering diagram of Figure 11, we see that the following listing of the states (row indices) of A will satisfy the definition: 1, 5, 3, 2, 4. The resulting matrix is shown in Figure 12. In that figure dotted lines appear along the main diagonal, indicating the equivalence classes. Note that above the main diagonal blocks the only entries are zeros. Matrices having this property are called *block triangular*.

The same kind of canonical form is possible for *any* nonnegative matrix A, if we let $C(A)$ be the communication matrix derived from A by putting zeros on the main diagonal, and replacing positive off-diagonal entries by ones. We discuss this for Markov chain transition matrices. When the matrix under consideration is the transition matrix of a Markov chain, the classification of the states is extremely important in the study of the behavior of the chain, as the following definition indicates.

	Brown	Doe	Smith	Jones	Adams
1 Brown	0	0	0	0	0
5 Doe	0	0	0	0	0
3 Smith	0	1	0	0	0
2 Jones	1	0	0	0	1
4 Adams	0	0	1	1	0

Figure 12

DEFINITION. Let P be the transition matrix of a Markov chain, and let $C(P)$ be the matrix obtained from P by replacing each diagonal entry by 0 and replacing each positive off-diagonal entry by 1. Let S', S'', . . . be the equivalence classes of the states of $C(P)$; then

(i) The maximal equivalence classes, that is, those classes that cannot send to other classes, are called *ergodic sets*. Members of ergodic sets are called *ergodic states*. If an ergodic set contains a single state, that state is an *absorbing state*.

(ii) All equivalence classes that can send messages to other classes are called *transient sets*. Members of transient sets are called *transient states*.

Example 2. Consider the transition matrix

$$P = \begin{pmatrix} 0 & 0 & 1 & 0 & 0 \\ 0 & \frac{1}{2} & \frac{1}{4} & \frac{1}{4} & 0 \\ 1 & 0 & 0 & 0 & 0 \\ 0 & 0 & 0 & 1 & 0 \\ 0 & 0 & \frac{1}{3} & 0 & \frac{2}{3} \end{pmatrix}.$$

Changing the diagonal entries to zeros and the positive off-diagonal entries to ones gives

$$C(P) = \begin{array}{c} 1 \\ 2 \\ 3 \\ 4 \\ 5 \end{array} \begin{array}{ccccc} 1 & 2 & 3 & 4 & 5 \\ \begin{pmatrix} 0 & 0 & 1 & 0 & 0 \\ 0 & 0 & 1 & 1 & 0 \\ 1 & 0 & 0 & 0 & 0 \\ 0 & 0 & 0 & 0 & 0 \\ 0 & 0 & 1 & 0 & 0 \end{pmatrix}. \end{array}$$

In Exercise 8 the reader will be asked to show that the equivalence classes of $C(P)$ are $\{4\}$, $\{1, 3\}$, $\{5\}$, and $\{2\}$. Moreover, the graph of the weak ordering relation on these classes is as shown in Figure 13. As before, the graph is obtained by checking whether or not one-way communication is possible between each pair of equivalence classes. From this diagram and the above definition we see that $\{4\}$ and $\{1, 3\}$ are ergodic sets and that $\{4\}$ is an absorbing state; also $\{2\}$ and $\{5\}$ are transient sets. A

Figure 13

canonical form of the matrix found by listing the states in the order 4, 1, 3, 5, 2 is

$$P = \begin{pmatrix} 1 & 0 & 0 & 0 & 0 \\ 0 & 0 & 1 & 0 & 0 \\ 0 & 1 & 0 & 0 & 0 \\ 0 & 0 & \frac{1}{3} & \frac{2}{3} & 0 \\ \frac{1}{4} & 0 & \frac{1}{4} & 0 & \frac{1}{2} \end{pmatrix}.$$

Note again that it is block triangular, as indicated by the dotted lines. There are other orders in which to list the states, which lead to slightly different canonical forms for the matrix (see Exercise 9).

We conclude this section with an application of the above theory to an archeological problem.

Example 3. Recent archeological investigations in Asia Minor, between the Mediterranean and Black Seas, have disclosed the existence of an ancient Assyrian civilization dating back to at least the nineteenth century B.C. This civilization came to light when peasants working in fields turned up clay tablets having written inscriptions. Upon being translated, these tablets turned out to be letters written between merchants located at various cities and towns of the ancient civilization. The letters contained the name of the sender, the name of the receiver, and an order to buy, sell, or transport goods, to pay money, etc. But the *date* of the letter was not included. In addition, merchants in different villages sometimes had the same name, and the location of the merchant was not always made clear in each of the letters. More than 2500 such tablets have been discovered; their contents give rise to two different problems. The first problem is to try to order the merchants according to their chronological dates. A second problem is to try to determine when the same name refers to more than one person. By studying the communication network that can be set up from the data of the tablets, we shall illustrate with small examples methods of trying to get partial answers to these questions.

To illustrate an approach to the first problem, suppose that we set up a (hypothetical) communication matrix for a group of ten merchants, as indicated in the matrix of Figure 14. In that matrix an entry of 1 is

	1	2	3	4	5	6	7	8	9	10
1	0	0	0	0	0	1	0	0	0	0
2	0	0	1	0	1	0	0	0	0	0
3	0	1	0	0	1	1	0	0	0	0
4	0	0	0	0	0	0	0	1	0	1
5	0	1	1	0	0	0	0	0	0	0
6	0	0	0	0	0	0	0	0	0	0
7	0	0	0	0	0	0	0	1	0	0
8	0	0	1	0	0	0	0	0	1	0
9	0	0	0	0	0	0	1	0	0	0
10	1	0	0	0	0	0	0	0	0	0

Figure 14

made in the i,jth entry if merchant i sent a letter to merchant j. Carrying out the same analysis as in Example 1 the equivalence classes are found to be $\{6\}$, $\{1, 10\}$, $\{2, 3, 5\}$, $\{7, 8, 9\}$, and $\{4\}$. The graph of the weak ordering relation on these classes is shown in Figure 15. It

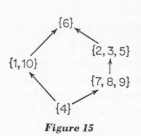

Figure 15

was determined, as before, by seeing whether there is one-way communication between each pair of equivalence classes. It is clear that members of a given equivalence class are contemporaries. But it is not clear which of the equivalence classes is earlier, merely from the one-way communication between them. However, further analysis of the content of the messages might help to establish this. For instance, if one of the messages exchanged among merchants 7, 8, and 9 were related to one of the messages exchanged among merchants 2, 3, and 5, then it would be reasonable to assume that they are all contemporaries. We see that here is a case in which mathematics cannot furnish the complete answer to the problem, but merely indicate directions in which to search for more information.

To illustrate the second problem mentioned above, we use some actual data (see p. 865 of the second reference listed at the end of the chapter) summarized in the communication matrix of Figure 16. The

	1	2	3	4	5	6	7	8	9	10
1 ASSUR-TAB	0	1	0	0	0	0	0	1	0	1
2 PUSHU-KIN	1	0	1	1	1	1	0	1	1	0
3 LAQIPUM	0	1	0	1	0	1	0	1	1	0
4 AMUR-ISHTAR	0	1	1	0	1	1	1	1	1	1
5 ASSUR-TAKLAKU	0	1	0	1	0	1	0	0	0	1
6 ASSUR-NA'DA	0	1	1	1	1	0	1	0	0	0
7 ASSUR-IMITTI	0	0	0	1	0	1	0	0	0	0
8 IM(I)D-ILUM	1	1	1	1	0	0	0	0	1	0
9 HINA	0	1	1	1	0	0	0	1	0	0
10 TARAM-KUBIM.	1	0	0	1	1	0	0	0	0	0

Figure 16

matrix is symmetric, indicating that either there is a two-way (direct) communication between two individuals or else no (direct) communication at all. All the merchants belong to the same equivalence class, so that the previous analysis does not shed any light on their relative dates, except that they are contemporaries. But is it possible that some names really stand for two different individuals? No definite answer can be provided to this question, but some indications can be provided by finding the *cliques* in the communication network.

DEFINITION. A *clique* of a communication network is a subset C of individuals containing at least three members, with the following two properties.

(i)   Every pair of members of the clique has two-way communication.

(ii) The subset C is as large as possible with every pair of members having property (i).

The problem of finding all cliques has been solved but is too lengthy to describe here. We content ourselves with listing all the maximal cliques for the data of Figure 16. They are

$\{1, 2, 8\}, \quad \{2, 3, 4, 6\}, \quad \{2, 3, 4, 8, 9\}, \quad \{2, 4, 5, 6\}, \quad \{4, 6, 7\}.$

From this list we can derive the frequency with which each merchant occurs in a clique, as shown in Figure 17. From that table it is evident that merchants 2 PUSHU-KIN and 4 AMUR-ISHTAR occur most frequently in cliques, and hence these names are most likely to be homonyms for two different people. Here again, mathematics does not completely

Merchant	1	2	3	4	5	6	7	8	9	10
Number of times in a clique	1	4	2	4	1	3	1	2	1	0

Figure 17

solve the problem, but merely indicates the direction in which to look for further evidence.

The above calculations, though oversimplified, are illustrative of the kinds of calculations that must be done n order to study the complete communication network revealed by the 2500 tablets so far found at the archeological site.

EXERCISES

1. Show that the relation T satisfies (3), (4), and (5).

2. Show that the relation " $\geq$ " is a weak ordering relation on the set of integers. [*Hint:* Show that $x \geq y$, for x and y integers, satisfies (1) and (2).]

3. Show that the relation " $=$ " is an equivalence relation on the set of all rational numbers (fractions). What are the equivalence classes it determines?

4. Let x and y be any two words and let xRy mean "Word x occurs no later than word y in the dictionary." Show that R is a weak order on the set of words.

5. Let x and y be people and let xTy mean " x is the same height as y." Show that T is an equivalence relation. What are the equivalence classes it determines? Show that the relation "at least as tall as" is a weak ordering relation on these equivalence classes.

6. Let R and T be the relations defined in the text; let S', S'', . . . be the equivalence classes determined by T; and let $S'RS''$ be as defined in the text. Show that R satisfies properties (1) and (2), that is, it is a weak ordering on the set of equivalence classes.

7. Let E_k, T_k, and F_k be as defined in the text. Show that $E_k = T_k \cap F_k$.

8. Find the equivalence classes of the communication matrix given in Example 2.

9. Show that there are ten different canonical forms for the transition matrix of Example 2.

10. Show that if A can communicate with B in a communication network having n persons, then it must be possible to do this in not more than $n - 1$ steps.

11. Suppose that there are six different individuals each of whom knows the location of certain others. This information is summarized in the following communication matrix.

$$
\begin{array}{c}
\\
1\\
2\\
3\\
4\\
5\\
6
\end{array}
\begin{array}{c}
\begin{array}{cccccc}
1 & 2 & 3 & 4 & 5 & 6
\end{array}\\
\left(\begin{array}{cccccc}
0 & 0 & 0 & 0 & 0 & 0\\
1 & 0 & 0 & 0 & 1 & 0\\
0 & 0 & 0 & 0 & 0 & 1\\
0 & 1 & 0 & 0 & 0 & 1\\
1 & 0 & 0 & 0 & 0 & 0\\
0 & 0 & 0 & 1 & 1 & 0
\end{array}\right)
\end{array}
$$

(a) Find the equivalence classes of T.

(b) Draw the graph of the weak ordering relation on the equivalence classes.

(c) Suppose you know where 3 is and you want to find out where 1 is. What is the shortest communication path from 3 to 1?

> [*Partial Ans.* It has ength 3.]

(d) What is the longest such communication path?

> [*Partial Ans.* It has length 5.]

12. Classify each of the states of the Markov chain whose transition matrix is given below, and put the matrix into a canonical form. [*Hint:* Use some of the results of Exercise 11.]

$$
\begin{pmatrix}
1 & 0 & 0 & 0 & 0 & 0\\
\frac{1}{2} & 0 & 0 & 0 & \frac{1}{2} & 0\\
0 & 0 & 0 & 0 & 0 & 1\\
0 & \frac{3}{4} & 0 & 0 & 0 & \frac{1}{4}\\
\frac{2}{5} & 0 & 0 & 0 & \frac{3}{5} & 0\\
0 & 0 & 0 & \frac{1}{3} & \frac{1}{3} & \frac{1}{3}
\end{pmatrix}
$$

[*Ans.* One canonical form is

$$
\begin{pmatrix}
1 & 0 & 0 & 0 & 0 & 0\\
\frac{2}{5} & \frac{3}{5} & 0 & 0 & 0 & 0\\
\frac{1}{2} & \frac{1}{2} & 0 & 0 & 0 & 0\\
0 & 0 & \frac{3}{4} & 0 & \frac{1}{4} & 0\\
0 & \frac{1}{3} & 0 & \frac{1}{3} & \frac{1}{3} & 0\\
0 & 0 & 0 & 0 & 1 & 0
\end{pmatrix}
$$

State 1 is absorbing; all other states are transient.]

13. If a matrix M can be put into the form

$$M = \begin{pmatrix} A & 0 \\ B & C \end{pmatrix},$$

where 0 is the zero matrix then M is said to be *reducible* or *decomposable*. If A and C are square and nonsingular show that

$$M^{-1} = \begin{pmatrix} A^{-1} & 0 \\ -C^{-1}BA^{-1} & C^{-1} \end{pmatrix}.$$

14. Use the results of Exercise 13 to show how a canonical form of a nonnegative matrix can be used to simplify the work of finding its inverse.

15. (a) Show that the Markov chain in Exercise 12 is an absorbing Markov chain.

   (b) Find the matrix Q in canonical form. Show that the matrix $I - Q$ is block triangular.

   (c) Use the results of Exercises 13 and 14 to find $N = (I - Q)^{-1}$.
   [*Ans.* With the canonical form of the answer to Exercise 12, the inverse is

$$N = (I - Q)^{-1} = \begin{pmatrix} \frac{5}{2} & 0 & 0 & 0 & 0 \\ \frac{5}{4} & 1 & 0 & 0 & 0 \\ \frac{10}{7} & \frac{6}{7} & \frac{8}{7} & \frac{3}{7} & 0 \\ \frac{55}{28} & \frac{3}{7} & \frac{4}{7} & \frac{12}{7} & 0 \\ \frac{55}{28} & \frac{3}{7} & \frac{4}{7} & \frac{12}{7} & 1 \end{pmatrix}.]$$

16. Draw the graph of a three-person clique. Also that of a four-person clique. Describe the graph of a clique containing n persons ($n \geq 3$).

17. Verify that the cliques given in Example 3 satisfy the two properties given in the definition of a clique.

18. Let C_1 and C_2 be any two *distinct* cliques of the same communication network.

   (a) Show by examples that $C_1 \cap C_2$ may or may not be empty.

   (b) Prove that the sets $C_1 - C_2$ and $C_2 - C_1$ are *never* empty.

3. STOCHASTIC PROCESSES IN GENETICS

The simplest type of inheritance of traits in animals occurs when a trait is governed by a pair of genes, each of which may be of two types, say G and g. An individual may have a GG combination or Gg (which is genetically the same as gG) or gg. Very often the GG and Gg types are indistinguishable in appearance, and then we say that the G gene *dominates* the g gene. An individual is called *dominant* if he has GG genes, *recessive* if he has gg, and *hybrid* with a Gg mixture.

In the mating of two animals, the offspring inherits one gene of the pair from each parent, and the basic assumption of genetics is that these genes are selected at random, independently of each other. This assumption determines the probability of every type of offspring. Thus the offspring of two dominant parents must be dominant, of two recessive parents must be recessive, and of one dominant and one recessive parent must be hybrid. In the mating of a dominant and a hybrid animal, the offspring must get a G gene from the former and has probability $\frac{1}{2}$ for getting G or g from the latter, hence the probabilities are even for getting a dominant or a hybrid offspring. Again in the mating of a recessive and a hybrid, there is an even chance of getting either a recessive or a hybrid. In the mating of two hybrids, the offspring has probability $\frac{1}{2}$ for getting a G or a g from each parent. Hence the probabilities are $\frac{1}{4}$ for GG, $\frac{1}{2}$ for Gg, and $\frac{1}{4}$ for gg.

Example 1. Let us consider a process of continued crossings. We start with an individual of unknown genetic character, and cross it with a hybrid. The offspring is again crossed with a hybrid, etc. The resulting process is a Markov chain. The states are "dominant," "hybrid," and "recessive." The transition probabilities are

$$
\begin{array}{cc}
& \begin{matrix} D & H & R \end{matrix} \\
(1) \qquad P = \begin{matrix} D \\ H \\ R \end{matrix} & \begin{pmatrix} \frac{1}{2} & \frac{1}{2} & 0 \\ \frac{1}{4} & \frac{1}{2} & \frac{1}{4} \\ 0 & \frac{1}{2} & \frac{1}{2} \end{pmatrix}
\end{array}
$$

as can be seen from the previous paragraph. The matrix P^2 has all entries positive (see Exercise 1), hence we know from Chapter V, Section 7, that there is a unique fixed point probability vector, i.e., a vector p such that $pP = p$. By solving three equations, we find the fixed vector to be $p = (\frac{1}{4}, \frac{1}{2}, \frac{1}{4})$. Hence, no matter what type the original animal was, after repeated crossing we have probability nearly $\frac{1}{4}$ of having a dominant, $\frac{1}{2}$ of having a hybrid, and $\frac{1}{4}$ of having a recessive offspring.

In Example 1 we may ask a more difficult question. Suppose that we have a regular matrix P (as in Example 1), with states $a_1, \ldots, a_n$. The process keeps going through all the states. If we are in a_i, how long, on the average, will it take for the process to return to a_i? We can even ask the more general question of how long, on the average, it takes to go from a_i to a_j.

The average here is taken in the sense of an expected value. There is a probability p_1 that we reach a_j for the first time in one step, p_2 that we reach it first in two steps, etc. The expected value is $p_1 \cdot 1 + p_2 \cdot 2 + \ldots$ (See Chapter IV, Section 12.) This, in general, requires a difficult computation. However, there is a much simpler way of finding the expected values. Let the expected number of steps required to go from state a_i to a_j be m_{ij}. How can we go from a_i to a_j? We go from a_i to a_k with probability p_{ik} in one step. If $k = j$, we are there. If $k \neq j$, it takes an average of m_{kj} steps more to get to a_j. Hence m_{ij} is equal to 1 plus the sum of $p_{ik}m_{kj}$ for all $k \neq j$. To state this as a matrix equation we define the matrix $\overline{M}$ to be the matrix M but with all the diagonal entries m_{ii} being replaced by 0; also let C be the square matrix having all entries equal to 1. Then the equations for m_{ij} can be written in matrix form as

$$(2) \qquad\qquad M = P\overline{M} + C.$$

To see that this is so let us concentrate on the i,jth entry of equation (2). On the left-hand side it is m_{ij}. On the right-hand side it is the i,jth entry of $P\overline{M}$ which is the sum of all products $p_{ik}m_{kj}$ for $k \neq j$ (since the main diagonal of $\overline{M}$ is zero) plus the i,jth entry in C, which is 1. This is the same as before. Let us now multiply (2) by p, the fixed vector of P. Recalling that p is a probability vector we obtain

$$(3) \qquad\qquad pM = p\overline{M} + (1, \ldots, 1)$$

or

$$(4) \qquad\qquad p(M - \overline{M}) = (1, \ldots, 1).$$

But all components of $M - \overline{M}$ except the diagonal ones are 0. Hence our equation simply states that $p_i m_{ii} = 1$ for each i. This tells us that $m_{ii} = 1/p_i$. *The average time it takes to return from a_i to a_i is the reciprocal of limiting probability of being in a_i.* In Example 1 this means that if we have a dominant offspring we will have another dominant in an average of four steps, after a hybrid we have another hybrid in an average of two steps, and a recessive follows a recessive on the average in four steps.

Example 2. A more interesting, and also more complex, process is obtained by crossing a given population with itself, and then crossing the offspring with offspring, etc. Let us suppose that our population has a fraction d of dominants, h hybrids, and r recessives. Then $d + h + r = 1$. If the population is very large and they are mated at random, then (by the law of large numbers) we can expect d^2 to be the fraction of matings in which both parents are dominant, $2dh$ the fraction of mating a dominant with a hybrid, etc. The tree of logical possibilities with branch probabilities marked on it is shown in Figure 18. We use it to compute the fraction of each type. To do this we

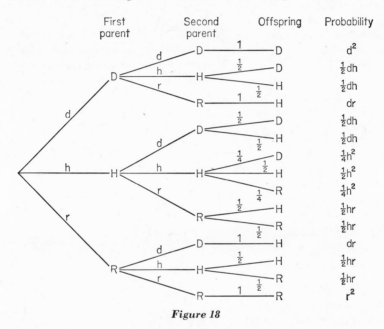

Figure 18

simply add together the path weights of the paths ending in D, in H, and in R. The results are:

D: $\qquad d^2 + 2 \cdot \tfrac{1}{2}dh + \tfrac{1}{4}h^2 = d^2 + dh + \tfrac{1}{4}h^2$

H: $\quad 2 \cdot \tfrac{1}{2}dh + 2dr + \tfrac{1}{2}h^2 + 2 \cdot \tfrac{1}{2}hr = dh + rh + 2dr + \tfrac{1}{2}h^2$

R: $\qquad \tfrac{1}{4}h^2 + 2 \cdot \tfrac{1}{2}hr + r^2 = r^2 + hr + \tfrac{1}{4}h^2.$

If we represent the fractions in a given generation by a row vector, the process may be thought of as a transformation T which changes a row vector into another row vector.

(5) $\quad (d, h, r) \cdot T = (d^2 + dh + \tfrac{1}{4}h^2, \; dh + rh + 2dr + \tfrac{1}{2}h^2, \; r^2 + rh + \tfrac{1}{4}h^2).$

The trouble is that (see Exercise 2) the transformation T is not linear. Nevertheless, we know that after n crossings the distribution will be

$(d, h, r)T^n$, so that, if we can get a simple formula for T^n, we can describe the results simply. And here luck is with us.

Let us compute T^2, i.e., find what happens if we apply twice the transformation specified above. The first generation of offspring is distributed according to the formula (5). We now take the first component on the right side as d, the second as h, and the third as r, and compute $d^2 + dh + \frac{1}{4}h^2$, etc. Here we find to our surprise that $T^2 = T$. Hence $T^n = T$.

This means that $(d, h, r)T = (d, h, r)T^n$, which in turn means that the distribution after many generations is the same as in the first generation of offspring. Hence we say that the process reaches an *equilibrium* in one step. It must, however, be remembered that our fractions are only approximate, and are a good approximation only for very large populations.

For the geneticist, this result is very interesting. It shows that, in a population in which no mutations occur and selection does not take place, "evolution" is all over in a single generation.

To the mathematician the process is interesting since it is an example of a quadratic transformation, a transformation more complex than the linear ones we have heretofore studied.

The next two examples give applications of absorbing Markov chains to genetics.

Example 3. If we keep crossing the offspring with a dominant animal, the result is quite different. The transition matrix is easily found to be

$$
\begin{array}{cc}
 & \begin{array}{ccc} D & H & R \end{array} \\
(6) \qquad P' = \begin{array}{c} D \\ H \\ R \end{array} & \begin{pmatrix} 1 & 0 & 0 \\ \frac{1}{2} & \frac{1}{2} & 0 \\ 0 & 1 & 0 \end{pmatrix}.
\end{array}
$$

This is an absorbing Markov chain with one absorbing state, D. Using the results of Chapter V, Section 8, we have

$$Q' = \begin{pmatrix} \frac{1}{2} & 0 \\ 1 & 0 \end{pmatrix}, \qquad R' = \begin{pmatrix} \frac{1}{2} \\ 0 \end{pmatrix}$$

so that

$$I - Q' = \begin{pmatrix} \frac{1}{2} & 0 \\ -1 & 1 \end{pmatrix}$$

and

$$N' = \begin{pmatrix} 2 & 0 \\ 2 & 1 \end{pmatrix}.$$

The absorption probabilities are

$$B = N'R' = \begin{pmatrix} 2 & 0 \\ 2 & 1 \end{pmatrix} \begin{pmatrix} \frac{1}{2} \\ 0 \end{pmatrix} = \begin{pmatrix} 1 \\ 1 \end{pmatrix}$$

as was to be expected, since there is only one absorbing state. This means that if we keep crossing the population with dominants, then after sufficiently many crossings we can expect only dominants. The mean number of steps to absorption are found by

$$t = N'c = \begin{pmatrix} 2 & 0 \\ 2 & 1 \end{pmatrix} \begin{pmatrix} 1 \\ 1 \end{pmatrix} = \begin{pmatrix} 2 \\ 3 \end{pmatrix}$$

Hence we expect the process to be absorbed in two steps starting from state H, and three steps starting from state R.

Example 4. Let us construct a more complicated example of an absorbing Markov chain. We start with two animals of opposite sex, cross them, select two of their offspring of opposite sex and cross those, etc. To simplify the example we will assume that the trait under consideration is independent of sex.

Here a state is determined by a pair of animals. Hence the states of our process will be: $a_1 = (D, D)$, $a_2 = (D, H)$, $a_3 = (D, R)$, $a_4 = (H, H)$, $a_5 = (H, R)$, and $a_6 = (R, R)$. Clearly, states a_1 and a_6 are absorbing, since if we cross two dominants or two recessives we must get one of the same type. The rest of the transition probabilities are easy to find. We illustrate their calculation in terms of state a_2. When the process is in this state, one parent has GG genes, the other Gg. Hence the probability of a dominant offspring or a hybrid offspring is $\frac{1}{2}$ for each. Then the probability of transition to a_1 (selection of two dominants) is $\frac{1}{4}$, the transition to a_2 is $\frac{1}{2}$, and to a_4 is $\frac{1}{4}$. The complete transition matrix is (listing the absorbing states first)

$$
P'' =
\begin{array}{c}
 \\
a_1 \\
a_6 \\
a_2 \\
a_3 \\
a_4 \\
a_5
\end{array}
\begin{array}{c}
\begin{array}{cccccc}
a_1 & a_6 & a_2 & a_3 & a_4 & a_5
\end{array} \\
\begin{pmatrix}
1 & 0 & 0 & 0 & 0 & 0 \\
0 & 1 & 0 & 0 & 0 & 0 \\
\frac{1}{4} & 0 & \frac{1}{2} & 0 & \frac{1}{4} & 0 \\
0 & 0 & 0 & 0 & 1 & 0 \\
\frac{1}{16} & \frac{1}{16} & \frac{1}{4} & \frac{1}{8} & \frac{1}{4} & \frac{1}{4} \\
0 & \frac{1}{4} & 0 & 0 & \frac{1}{4} & \frac{1}{2}
\end{pmatrix}
\end{array}.
$$

Calculating the fundamental quantities for an absorbing chain, we obtain

$$
Q'' = \begin{array}{c} \\ a_2 \\ a_3 \\ a_4 \\ a_5 \end{array}
\begin{array}{cccc} a_2 & a_3 & a_4 & a_5 \end{array}
\begin{pmatrix} \frac{1}{2} & 0 & \frac{1}{4} & 0 \\ 0 & 0 & 1 & 0 \\ \frac{1}{4} & \frac{1}{8} & \frac{1}{4} & \frac{1}{4} \\ 0 & 0 & \frac{1}{4} & \frac{1}{2} \end{pmatrix}, \qquad
R'' = \begin{pmatrix} \frac{1}{4} & 0 \\ 0 & 0 \\ \frac{1}{16} & \frac{1}{16} \\ 0 & \frac{1}{4} \end{pmatrix}
$$

and

$$
I - Q'' = \begin{pmatrix} \frac{1}{2} & 0 & -\frac{1}{4} & 0 \\ 0 & 1 & -1 & 0 \\ -\frac{1}{4} & -\frac{1}{8} & \frac{3}{4} & -\frac{1}{4} \\ 0 & 0 & -\frac{1}{4} & \frac{1}{2} \end{pmatrix},
$$

and

$$
N'' = (I - Q'')^{-1} = \begin{pmatrix} \frac{8}{3} & \frac{1}{6} & \frac{4}{3} & \frac{2}{3} \\ \frac{4}{3} & \frac{4}{3} & \frac{8}{3} & \frac{4}{3} \\ \frac{4}{3} & \frac{1}{3} & \frac{8}{3} & \frac{4}{3} \\ \frac{2}{3} & \frac{1}{6} & \frac{4}{3} & \frac{8}{3} \end{pmatrix}.
$$

The absorption probabilities are found to be

$$
B'' = N''R'' = \begin{pmatrix} \frac{3}{4} & \frac{1}{4} \\ \frac{1}{2} & \frac{1}{2} \\ \frac{1}{2} & \frac{1}{2} \\ \frac{1}{4} & \frac{3}{4} \end{pmatrix}.
$$

The genetic interpretation of absorption is that after a large number of inbreedings either the G or the g gene must disappear. It is also interesting to note that the probability of ending up entirely with G genes, if we start from a given state, is equal to the proportion of G genes in this state.

The mean number of steps to absorption are

$$
t = N'' \begin{pmatrix} 1 \\ 1 \\ 1 \\ 1 \end{pmatrix} = \begin{pmatrix} 4\frac{5}{6} \\ 6\frac{2}{3} \\ 5\frac{2}{3} \\ 4\frac{5}{6} \end{pmatrix}.
$$

Hence we see that, if we start in a state other than (D, D) or (R, R), we can expect to reach one of these states in about five or six steps. The exact expected times are given by the entries of t. The matrix N'' provides more detailed information, namely how many times we can expect to have offspring of the types $(D, H), (D, R), (H, H)$, and (H, R), starting from a given nonabsorbing state. And the matrix B'' gives the probabilities of ending up in a_1 or a_6. These quantities jointly give us an excellent description of what we can expect of our process.

EXERCISES

1. From (1) compute P^2, P^3, P^4, and P^5. Verify that $P^2 > 0$ and that the powers approach the expected form (see Chapter V, Section 7).

2. Prove that T is not a linear transformation. [*Hint:* Check the conditions on linearity given in Chapter V, Section 9, and show by means of an example that T does not have one of these properties.]

3. Compute T^2 by taking the first component of (5) as d, the second as h, the third as r, and substituting into the formula (5). Making use of the fact that $d + h + r = 1$, show that $T^2 = T$.

4. A fixed point of T is a vector such that $(d, h, r)T = (d, h, r)$. Write the conditions that such a vector must satisfy, and give three examples of such fixed vectors. What is the genetic meaning of such a distribution?

[*Ans.* For example, $(\frac{1}{9}, \frac{4}{9}, \frac{4}{9})$.]

5. In the matrix P the second row is equal to the fixed point vector. What significance does this have?

6. For Example 1 write the matrix M with unknown entries m_{ij}. Write M by replacing m_{11}, m_{22}, and m_{33} by zeros. Then solve the nine simultaneous equations given by (3), to find the m_{ij}. Check that $m_{ii} = 1/p_i$.

[*Ans.* $m_{11} = 4$, $m_{12} = 2$, $m_{13} = 8$.]

7. From the definition of a stochastic matrix (Chapter V, Section 7), prove that $PC = C$.

8. Prove that, if P is a regular $n \times n$ stochastic matrix having column sums equal to 1, then it takes an average of n steps to return from any state to itself. (Cf. Chapter V, Section 7, Exercise 8.)

9. It is raining in the Land of Oz. In how many days can the Wizard of Oz expect to go on a picnic? (Cf. Chapter V, Section 7, Exercise 13.) [*Ans.* 4.]

Exercises 10–15 develop a simpler method of treating the nonlinear transformation T, in the text above.

10. Let p be the ratio of G genes in the population, and $q = 1 - p$ the ratio of g genes. Express p and q in terms of d, h, and r.

[*Ans.* $p = d + \frac{1}{2}h$, $q = r + \frac{1}{2}h$.]

11. Suppose that we take all the genes in the population, mix them thoroughly, and select a pair at random for each offspring. Show, using the result of Exercise 10, that the resulting distribution of dominant, hybrid, and recessive individuals is precisely that given in (5).

$$[Ans. \ (d, h, r)\cdot T = (p^2, 2pq, q^2).]$$

12. If we write $(d, h, r)\cdot T = (d', h', r')$, show, using the result of Exercise 11, that $h'^2 = 4d'r'$.

13. Show that for equilibrium it is necessary that $h^2 = 4dr$.

14. Show that if $h^2 = 4dr$, then $p^2 = d$, $q^2 = r$, and $2pq = h$. Hence show that this condition is also sufficient for equilibrium.

15. Use the results of Exercises 12–14 to show that the population reaches equilibrium in one generation.

16. Prove that in an absorbing Markov chain
   (a) The probability of reaching a given absorbing state is independent of the starting state if and only if there is only one absorbing state.
   (b) The expected time for reaching an absorbing state is independent of the starting state if and only if every state is absorbing.

17. Suppose that hybrids have a high mortality rate; say that half of the hybrids die before maturity, while only a negligible number of dominants and recessives die before maturity.
   (a) In Example 4 above, modify the matrix P'' to apply to this situation.
   (b) What are the absorbing states?
   (c) Verify that it is an absorbing chain.
   (d) Find the vectors d representing the probabilities of absorption in the various absorbing states.

$$[Ans. \ \text{For } a_1, d = \begin{pmatrix} 1 \\ 0 \\ \frac{9}{10} \\ \frac{1}{2} \\ \frac{1}{2} \\ \frac{1}{10} \end{pmatrix}.]$$

   (e) Find N, and interpret.

   (f) Find t, and interpret.
$$[Ans. \ t = \begin{pmatrix} \frac{65}{26} \\ \frac{117}{26} \\ \frac{91}{26} \\ \frac{65}{26} \end{pmatrix}.]$$

The remaining problems concern the inheritance of color-blindness, which is a sex-linked characteristic. There is a pair of genes, C and S, of which the former tends to produce color-blindness, the latter normal vision. The S gene is dominant. But a man has only one gene, and if this is C, he is color-blind. A man inherits one of his mother's two genes, while a woman inherits one gene from each parent. Thus a man may be of type C or S, while a woman may be of type CC or CS or SS. We will study a process of inbreeding similar to that of Example 4.

18. List the states of the chain. [*Hint:* There are six.]

19. Compute the transition probabilities.

20. Show that the chain is absorbing, and interpret the absorbing states. [*Ans.* In one, the S gene disappears; in the other, the C gene is lost.]

21. Prove that the probability of absorption in the state having only C genes, if we start in a given state, is equal to the proportion of C genes in that state.

22. Find N, and interpret.

23. Find t, and interpret.

[*Ans.* $\begin{pmatrix} 5 \\ 6 \\ 6 \\ 5 \end{pmatrix}$; if we start with both C and S genes, we can expect one of these to disappear in five or six crossings.]

4. THE ESTES LEARNING MODEL

In this section we shall discuss a mathematical model for learning proposed by W. K. Estes. We shall not give the most general theory, but only some special cases.

The theory was developed to explain certain kinds of learning which can be illustrated by experiments of the following kind. Suppose for example that a rat is put in a T maze and goes either right or left. The experimenter places food on one side, and if the rat goes to the correct side he is rewarded. This experiment is then repeated many times, using some particular feeding schedule. The interest here lies in trying to predict the behavior of the rat under the different feeding schedules. For instance, if the food is always placed on the right side, will the rat eventually learn this and always go right?

A similar experiment, performed with a human subject, is the following. A subject is given a sequence of heads and tails and each time is asked to guess what the next choice will be. He is to try to get as many right as possible. Again there are various ways that the experimenter can produce his sequences of H's and T's, and the interest lies in how the subject will react to different choices.

In the Estes model it is assumed that there are a finite number of elements, called "stimulus elements." At any given time each of these elements is connected either to a response A_1 or to a response A_2. These connections are allowed to change from experiment to experiment.

In a single experiment there is a certain probability θ $(0 < \theta < 1)$ that any particular stimulus element will be sampled by the subject. To say that an element is sampled is the same as to say that it has an effect upon the subject on that experiment. It is assumed that elements sampled and connected to A_1 influence the subject in the direction of producing an A_1 response, and those sampled and connected to A_2 tend to produce an A_2 response.

The samplings of the various elements are assumed to be an independent trials process (see Chapter IV, Section 8). Thus, for example, if there are three stimulus elements a, b, and c, the probability that a is sampled, b is not sampled, and c is sampled would be $\theta(1 - \theta)\theta$.

We also assume that the experimenter takes one of two possible "reinforcing" actions, E_1 or E_2. This action may be taken before or after the subject's choice, but we assume that the subject learns of the choice of the experimenter only after he has made his own choice. The subject would like to make A_1, if the experimenter makes E_1, and A_2 if the experimenter chooses E_2. We shall say that the subject "guesses correctly" if he matches the choice of the experimenter, i.e., does A_1 when the experimenter does E_1, or A_2 when the experimenter does E_2. In some experiments (e.g., the rat experiment above), he is rewarded if he does guess correctly.

The following two basic assumptions are made.

Assumption A. The probability that the subject makes response A_1 is equal to the proportion of elements *in the set sampled* that are connected to A_1. If no elements are sampled, the responses are assumed to be the same as if all elements are sampled.

Assumption B. If, in a given experiment, the experimenter chooses E_1, then all the elements that were sampled on this experiment, and that were connected to A_2 have their connections changed to A_1. If the experimenter chooses E_2, then all the elements sampled and connected to A_1 have their connections changed to A_2.

Note that in a single experiment only the set of elements that are actually sampled play a role, and these are the only elements whose connections can be changed by this experiment. In general, however, a different set will be sampled on each experiment, so that all the elements will at some time have an effect.

By assumptions A and B it is clear that the future choices of the subject are going to depend upon the choice of the experimenter. Therefore we must describe the method that the experimenter uses to determine his E's. Typical schemes that have been used in actual experiments are the following.

(i)   Choose E_1 with probability p, independent of the choice of the subject.

(ii) Make the same choice as the subject made (i.e., choose E_1 if he chose A_1, E_2 if he chose A_2).

(iii) Choose E_1 if the response of the subject on the previous experiment was A_1. Choose E_2 and E_1 with equal probabilities if his response was A_2.

We can describe a general class of schemes of the above kind as follows: We assume that the experimenter chooses E_2 with probability a, if the subject made response A_1 on the previous experiment, and chooses E_1 with probability b, if the subject made response A_2 on the last experiment. We can represent the choices of the experimenter for each choice of the subject by the matrix

$$
\begin{array}{cc}
 & \begin{array}{cc} E_1 & \quad E_2 \end{array} \\
\begin{array}{c} A_1 \\ A_2 \end{array} & \left(\begin{array}{cc} 1-a & a \\ b & 1-b \end{array} \right).
\end{array}
$$

Thus in the above examples, (i) is the case $1 - a = b = p$, (ii) is the case $a = 0$, $b = 0$, and (iii) is the case $a = 0$, $b = \frac{1}{2}$.

In Figure 19 we illustrate a typical sequence of actions that might occur in a single trial for the case of six stimulus elements. An O_1

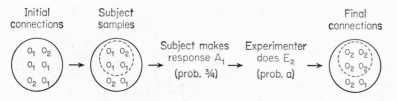

| Initial connections | Subject samples | Subject makes response A_1 (prob. ¾) | Experimenter does E_2 (prob. a) | Final connections |

A Typical Sequence on One Trial

Figure 19

indicates a stimulus element which is connected to A_1 and an O_2 indicates a stimulus element which is connected to A_2.

We note in this case that the subject sampled four of the six stimulus elements. The probability that this particular set of four elements is sampled is $\theta^4(1 - \theta)^2$. Since three of the four elements in the set sampled are connected to A_1, the subject makes response A_1 with probability $\frac{3}{4}$. We assume the subject made response A_1. Then the experimenter chooses E_2 with probability a. We have assumed that the experimenter did choose E_2. All four of the stimulus elements in the set sampled then become connected to response A_2. The final connections for this trial then become the initial connections for the next trial.

We shall now develop a method for studying the response process. We do this by introducing a Markov chain. The states of the chain will be the number of elements connected to response A_1. If there are six stimulus elements, then there are seven possible states: 0, 1, 2, 3, 4, 5, 6. We compute the transition probabilities from the above assumptions.

We shall consider throughout the rest of this section and the next the case of two stimulus elements. The analysis for a larger number of elements is similar but more complicated. Many of the results do not depend upon the number of stimulus elements assumed.

Our states are numbered 2, 1, and 0, indicating the number of stimulus elements connected to an A_1 response. We will illustrate the computation of transition probabilities. For example, let us compute $p_{0,1}$. Since the chain is in state 0, both stimulus elements are connected to response A_2. To change to state 1, exactly one stimulus element must be sampled. The probability for this is $2\theta(1 - \theta)$. If this stimulus element is to change to A_1, the experimenter must do E_1. The probability of this is b. Hence $p_{0,1} = 2\theta(1 - \theta)b$.

A more complicated computation is needed for $p_{1,0}$. In state 1, one stimulus element is connected to A_1 and one to A_2. The former must be sampled, the latter may also be sampled. The response of the experimenter must be E_2, to effect a change to A_2. There are three cases. (1) Only one element is sampled, with response A_1. (2) Both are sampled, with response A_1. (3) Both are sampled, with response A_2. These yield the three terms

$$p_{1,0} = \theta(1 - \theta)a + \tfrac{1}{2}\theta^2 a + \tfrac{1}{2}\theta^2(1 - b).$$

Proceeding in this manner, we obtain the transition matrix

$$P = \begin{array}{c} \\ 2 \\ 1 \\ 0 \end{array} \begin{array}{c} 2 \qquad\qquad 1 \qquad\qquad 0 \end{array} \\ \left(\begin{array}{ccc} (1 - \theta)^2 a + 1 - a & 2\theta(1 - \theta)a & \theta^2 a \\ \frac{1}{2}\theta^2(1 - a) + \frac{1}{2}\theta(2 - \theta)b & (1 - \theta)^2 + \theta(1 - \theta)(1 - a) + \theta(1 - \theta)(1 - b) & \frac{1}{2}\theta^2(1 - b) + \frac{1}{2}\theta(2 - \theta)a \\ \theta^2 b & 2\theta(1 - \theta)b & (1 - \theta)^2 b + (1 - b) \end{array} \right).$$

In the next section we shall study this Markov chain in more detail.

EXERCISES

1. Construct a tree to show the possibilities for the connections after an experiment if the two stimulus elements are both connected to A_1 at the beginning of the experiment. Do the same for the case of no elements connected to A_1 at the beginning of the experiment.

2. Using the trees in Exercise 1, verify that the transition probabilities $p_{0,j}$ and $p_{2,j}$ given above are correct.

3. What is the probability that the subject will make response A_1 if at the beginning of the experiment one element is connected to each response? What is this probability if at the beginning of the experiment both elements are connected to response A_1?   [*Ans.* $\frac{1}{2}, 1.$]

In the following exercises, find the matrix of transition probabilities under the special assumptions given in the problem. State whether the resulting Markov chain is absorbing or regular. Give an interpretation for each of the special cases in terms of the actual experiment. If the process is regular, find the limiting probabilities. If the process is absorbing, find the expected number of steps before absorption for each possible starting state. (See Chapter V, Section 8.)

4. $a = 1, b = 1, \theta = \frac{1}{2}.$ [*Ans.* Regular; $(.3, .4, .3).$]

5. $a = 1, b = 0.$ [*Ans.* Absorbing; $t_2 = (3 - 2\theta)/(2\theta - \theta^2)$; $t_1 = 1/\theta.$]

6. $a = \frac{1}{4}, b = \frac{3}{4}, \theta = .1.$

7. $a = 0, b = \frac{1}{2}, \theta = \frac{1}{2}.$

8. $a = 1, b = \frac{1}{2}, \theta = \frac{1}{2}.$

9. $a = 0, b = 0.$

10. Work out the transition matrix of the Markov chain for the model having a single stimulus element.

11. Assume that $a > 0$ and $b > 0$ for the one-element model. Show that the chain is regular, and find the limiting probabilities.

[*Ans.* $b/(a + b)$, $a/(a + b)$.]

12. Assume that $a > 0$ and $b = 0$ for the one-element model. Find the expected number of steps to absorption. [*Ans.* $1/\theta a$.]

5. LIMITING PROBABILITIES IN THE ESTES MODEL

We wish now to study the limiting probabilities that the subject and that the experimenter will choose each of the possible alternatives.

If our process is in state 0 on a given experiment, then the probability that the subject will make response A_1 is (by assumption A) equal to 0. If it is in state 1, then by symmetry this probability is $\frac{1}{2}$. If it is in state 2, it is (by assumption A) equal to 1.

The matrix P will be regular if and only if the quantities a and b are not zero (see Exercise 1). If the matrix is regular, then there will be a limiting probability for being in each of the states. These probabilities can be represented by a vector $p = (p_0, p_1, p_2)$ and found by solving the equations

$$pP = p.$$

If these equations are solved, we obtain

$$p_2 = \frac{b\theta + 2b^2(1 - \theta)}{(a + b)\theta + 2(a + b)^2(1 - \theta)},$$

$$p_1 = \frac{4ab(1 - \theta)}{(a + b)\theta + 2(a + b)^2(1 - \theta)},$$

$$p_0 = \frac{a\theta + 2a^2(1 - \theta)}{(a + b)\theta + 2(a + b)^2(1 - \theta)}.$$

From these probabilities we can find that the limiting probability that the subject will make response A_1 is

$$1 \cdot p_2 + \tfrac{1}{2}p_1 + 0 \cdot p_0 = \frac{b}{a + b},$$

and that the limiting probability that the subject makes response A_2 is $a/(a + b)$.

To find the probability that the experimenter makes the choice E_1, we must multiply the probabilities for each of the choices of the subject, by the probabilities that the experimenter does E_1 if the subject made the particular choice. Thus the limiting probability that the experimenter makes choice E_1 is

$$\frac{b(1 - a)}{a + b} + \frac{ab}{a + b} = \frac{b}{a + b}.$$

Thus we see that the limiting probability that the subject will make response A_1 is equal to the limiting probability that the experimenter will choose E_1. From the limiting probabilities we can also find the limiting probability that the subject will guess correctly (see Exercise 3).

If we assume that the experimenter makes response E_1 with probability p independent of the choice of the subject, the subject can maximize the expected number of correct responses by always making response A_1 if $p > \frac{1}{2}$ and always making A_2 if $p < \frac{1}{2}$. (See Exercise 5.) The model predicts a less rational choice on the part of the subject. This would not seem disturbing in the case of the rat, but it would be hoped humans would do better. Unfortunately, experiments have borne out that the model's predictions are approximately correct even with human subjects.

The following interesting experiment was performed by W. K. Estes and others with many types of subjects. If the subject does A_1, he is rewarded half the time; if he does A_2 he is never rewarded. One might expect that the subject will learn to do A_1, but this is not the case. What does the theory predict? If A_1 is chosen, reward follows half the time. Hence $a = \frac{1}{2}$. If A_2 is chosen, reward never follows. Hence $1 - b = 0$ or $b = 1$. The theory predicts a limiting probability of $b/(a + b) = \frac{2}{3}$ for the subject to choose A_1, which is in good agreement with experimental results.

We next consider an absorbing case. Specifically, we consider the case $a = 0$ and $b = 1$. This means that the experimenter always does E_1. The matrix of transition probabilities here is

$$
P = \begin{array}{c} \\ 2 \\ 1 \\ 0 \end{array}
\begin{array}{ccc} 2 & 1 & 0 \end{array}
\left(\begin{array}{ccc}
1 & 0 & 0 \\
\theta & 1 - \theta & 0 \\
\theta^2 & 2\theta(1 - \theta) & (1 - \theta)^2
\end{array} \right).
$$

We shall use the methods developed in Chapter V to study this Markov chain. We have one absorbing state, namely, 2. Thus we know that the process will eventually enter this state and remain there. Being in this state means, by assumption A of the previous section, that the subject is sure to make response A_1. Thus being absorbed can be interpreted as the subject "learning" that the experimenter always does E_1.

We have seen that in an absorbing Markov chain it is possible to find the expected number of times that the process will be in each of the states before being absorbed, assuming some given starting state. Let n_{ij} be the expected number of times the process will be in state j if it starts in state i. Before calculating n_{ij} we consider what the knowledge of these quantities would tell us about the experiment. We observe that every time the process is in state 1, the subject chooses A_2 with probability $\frac{1}{2}$ and hence makes a wrong response with probability $\frac{1}{2}$. Every time the process is in state 0, the subject is sure to make response A_2, that is, to make a wrong response. Thus the expected number of wrong responses that the subject will make before learning is

(1) $$\tfrac{1}{2}n_{i1} + n_{i0} \quad \text{for} \quad i = 0, 1$$

assuming that the process starts in state i.

We find the n_{ij} as in Chapter V. We first form the truncated matrix Q obtained from P by omitting the column and the row corresponding to the absorbing state.

$$Q = \begin{pmatrix} 1 - \theta & 0 \\ 2\theta(1 - \theta) & (1 - \theta)^2 \end{pmatrix}.$$

We then find $(I - Q)^{-1}$ to be

$$N = (I - Q)^{-1} = \begin{matrix} & 1 & 0 \\ 1 & \\ 0 & \end{matrix} \begin{pmatrix} \frac{1}{\theta} & 0 \\ \frac{2(1 - \theta)}{\theta(2 - \theta)} & \frac{1}{\theta(2 - \theta)} \end{pmatrix}.$$

Then from (1) we obtain $1/2\theta$ as the expected number of wrong responses if the process begins in state 1, and $1/\theta$ as the expected number of wrong responses if the process begins in state 2.

Of course it is true that in an actual experiment the starting state would not be known. However, it is not unreasonable to assume that on the first experiment the stimuli elements are connected at random. This would mean that the process starts at state 0 with probability $\frac{1}{4}$, at state 1 with probability $\frac{1}{2}$, and at state 2 with probability $\frac{1}{4}$. Thus under this assumption the expected number of wrong responses before learning is

(2) $$\frac{1}{2} \cdot \frac{1}{2\theta} + \frac{1}{4} \cdot \frac{1}{\theta} = \frac{1}{2\theta}.$$

EXERCISES

1. Prove that the matrix P in Section 4 is regular if and only if a and b are different from zero. [*Hint:* Show that if either quantity is 0 the chain is not regular.]

2. Verify that the probability that the subject makes response A_2 is $a/(a + b)$ by finding $1 \cdot p_0 + \frac{1}{2} \cdot p_1 + 0 \cdot p_2$.

3. Show that the limiting probability that the subject's choice agrees with that of the experimenter is

$$\frac{a(1 - b) + b(1 - a)}{a + b}.$$

4. Assume that the experimenter always chooses E_1 with a fixed probability p, independent of the choice of the subject. What proportion would the subject expect to guess correctly?   [*Ans.* $1 - 2p + 2p^2$.]

5. Suppose under the conditions of Exercise 4 that the subject were always to make response A_1. Show that if $p > \frac{1}{2}$, then on the average the subject will do better by this method than by the method predicted by the model.

6. Consider the case $a = \frac{1}{2}$, $b = 0$, and $\theta = \frac{1}{2}$. For each possible starting state find the expected number of times that the process will be in each of the states before being absorbed. [*Ans.* $n_{22} = 3$; $n_{21} = 2$; $n_{12} = \frac{1}{2}$; $n_{11} = 3$.]

7. Do the same as in Exercise 6, for the case $a = 0$, and $b = 0$.

8. In Exercises 6 and 7 find the expected number of incorrect responses that the subject will make, assuming each possible starting state.
[*Ans.* 0, 2, 4; 0, 0, 0.]

9. In Exercises 6 and 7 find the expected number of incorrect responses that the subject will make assuming random connections for the stimuli elements on the first experiment, as in (2).

10. If the subject chooses A_1, he is rewarded with probability p. If he chooses A_2, he is never rewarded. (See the example with $p = \frac{1}{2}$ in the text above.) Find a and b. What is the limiting probability that the subject chooses A_1? How often is he rewarded? How often would he be rewarded if he always chose A_1? Compare these two values for $p = \frac{3}{4}, \frac{1}{2}, \frac{1}{4}$.
[*Ans.* $1/(2 - p)$; $p/(2 - p)$; p.]

11. Compute p_0, p_1, p_2 for the cases given in Section 4, Exercises 4–9. For the regular matrices verify that these are the limiting probabilities there obtained. What do p_0, p_1, p_2 mean for the absorbing chains?

6. MARRIAGE RULES IN PRIMITIVE SOCIETIES

In some primitive societies there are rigid rules as to when marriages are permissible. These rules are designed to prevent very close relatives from marrying. The rules can be given precise mathematical formulation in terms of permutation matrices. Our discussion is based, in part, on the work of André Weil and Robert R. Bush.

The marriage rules found in these societies are characterized by the following axioms.

Axiom 1. Each member of the society is assigned a marriage type.

Axiom 2. Two individuals are permitted to marry only if they are of the same marriage type.

Axiom 3. The type of an individual is determined by the individual's sex and by the type of his parents.

Axiom 4. Two boys (or two girls) whose parents are of different types will themselves be of different types.

Axiom 5. The rule as to whether a man is allowed to marry a female relative of a given kind depends only on the kind of relationship.

Axiom 6. In particular, no man is allowed to marry his sister.

Axiom 7. For any two individuals it is permissible for some of their descendants to intermarry.

Example. Let us suppose that there are three marriage types, t_1, t_2, t_3. Two parents in a given family must be of the same type, since only then are they allowed to marry. Thus there are only three logical possibilities for marriages. For each case we have to state what the type of a son or a daughter will be.

Type of both parents	Type of their son	Type of their daughter
t_1	t_2	t_3
t_2	t_3	t_1
t_3	t_1	t_2

We must verify that all the axioms are satisfied. Some of the axioms are easy to check (see Exercise 1), others are harder to verify. We will prove a general theorem which will show that this rule satisfies all the axioms.

In order to give a complete treatment to this problem, we must have a simple systematic method of representing relationships. For this we use family trees, as drawn by anthropologists. The following symbols are commonly used.

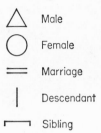

△ Male

◯ Female

═ Marriage

│ Descendant

┌─┐ Sibling

In Figure 20 we draw four family trees, representing the four kinds of first-cousin relationships between a man and a woman.

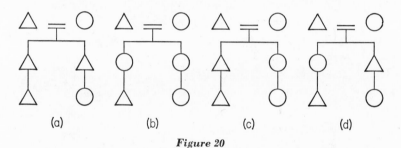

(a)   (b)   (c)   (d)

Figure 20

Example (continued). Does our rule allow marriage between a man and his father's brother's daughter? This is the relationship in Figure 20a. There are three possible types for the original couple (the grandparents) and in Figure 21 we work out the three cases. We find in each

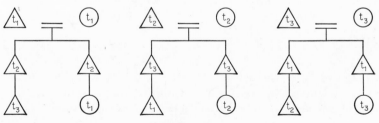

Figure 21

case that the man and woman are of different type, hence such marriages are *never* allowed. Can a man marry his mother's brother's daughter? This is the relationship in Figure 20d. The three cases for this relationship are found in Figure 22. We find that such marriages are *always* allowed.

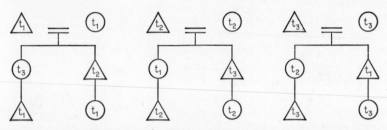

Figure 22

We are now ready to give the rules a mathematical formulation. The society chooses a number, say n, of marriage types (Axiom 1). We call these $t_1, t_2, \ldots, t_n$. Our rule has two parts, one concerning sons, one concerning daughters. Let us consider the marriage type of sons. The parents must be of the same marriage type (Axiom 2). We must assign to a boy a type which depends only on the common type of his parents (Axiom 3). If his parents are of type t_i, he will be of type t_j. Furthermore, if some other boy has parents of a type different from t_i, then the boy will be of type different from t_j (Axiom 4). This defines a *permutation* of the marriage types (see Chapter V, Section 10); the type of a son is obtained from the type of his parents by a permutation specified by the rule of the society. Hence we form the type vector $t = (t_1, \ldots, t_n)$ and represent the permutation in question by the $n \times n$ permutation matrix S. If the type of the parents is component i of t, the type of their sons is component i of tS. By a similar argument we arrive at the permutation matrix D giving the type of daughters.

We have shown that the mathematical form of the first four axioms is to introduce the row vector t and the two permutation matrices S and D. The last three axioms restrict the choice of S and D. This will be considered in the next section.

We have repeatedly seen how the vector and matrix notation allows us to replace a series of equations by a single one. In the present problem this notation allows us to work out a given kind of relationship for *all* marriage types in a single diagram. As a matter of fact, this can be done without knowing how many types there are in the given society, or knowing what the rules are. Let us illustrate this in terms of Figure 22. The couple at the top of the tree is of a given type, represented by our vector *t*. Their son is of type *tS*, their daughter of type *tD*. Then the son of a son is of type *tSS*, the son's daughter is of type *tSD*, etc. We arrive at the single vector diagram of Figure 23. If in this figure we take *t* to have three components, then the diagram is a shorthand for the three diagrams of Figure 22.

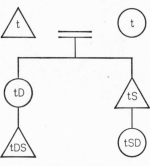

Figure 23

Example (continued). Our *t* vector is (t_1, t_2, t_3) and

$$D = \begin{pmatrix} 0 & 1 & 0 \\ 0 & 0 & 1 \\ 1 & 0 & 0 \end{pmatrix}, \qquad S = \begin{pmatrix} 0 & 0 & 1 \\ 1 & 0 & 0 \\ 0 & 1 & 0 \end{pmatrix}.$$

We know from Figure 22 that a man is always allowed to marry his mother's brother's daughter. Can we see this in Figure 23? The marriage will always be permitted if *tDS* always equals *tSD*, which is equivalent to the matrix equation $DS = SD$. It so happens for our *S* and *D* that this equation is correct. But we can see more from Figure 23. No matter how many types there are, this kind of marriage will be permitted if and only if $SD = DS$, i.e., if the two matrices commute.

We have now seen one example of how the nature of *S* and *D* determines which kinds of relatives are allowed to marry. This question will be the subject of the next section.

EXERCISES

1. In the example above, verify that the rule satisfies Axioms 1, 3, and 4.

2. In the example above, verify that the matrices *S* and *D* given represent the rule given.

3. Construct a diagram for the brother-sister relationship.

4. Using the diagram of Exercise 3, show that, in the above example, brother-sister marriages are never permitted.

5. Find the condition on S and D that would always allow brother-sister marriages.   [*Ans. $S = D$.*]

In the *Kariera* society there are four marriage types, assigned according to the following rules:

Parent type	Son type	Daughter type
t_1	t_3	t_4
t_2	t_4	t_3
t_3	t_1	t_2
t_4	t_2	t_1

Exercises 6–11 refer to this society.

6. Find the t, S, and D of the Kariera society.

7. Show that brother-sister marriages are never allowed in the Kariera society.

8. Show that S and D commute. What does this tell us about first-cousin marriages in the Kariera society?

9. Show that first cousins of the kinds in Figures 20(a) and (b) are never allowed to marry in the Kariera society.

10. Show that first cousins of the kind in Figure 20(c) are always allowed to marry in the Kariera society.

11. Find the group generated by S and D of the Kariera society. (See Chapter V, Section 11.)

In the *Tarau* society there are also four marriage types. A son is of the same type as his parents. A daughter's type is given by:

Parent type	Daughter type
t_1	t_4
t_2	t_1
t_3	t_2
t_4	t_3

Exercises 12–17 refer to this society.

12. Find the t, S, and D of the Tarau society.

13. Show that brother-sister marriages are never allowed in the Tarau society.

14. Show that S and D commute. What does this tell us about first-cousin marriages in the Tarau society?

15. Show that first cousins of the kinds in Figures 20(a) and (b) are never allowed to marry in the Tarau society.

16. Show that first cousins of the kind in Figure 20(c) are never allowed to marry in the Tarau society.

17. Find the group generated by S and D of the Tarau society. (See Chapter V, Section 11.)

7. THE CHOICE OF MARRIAGE RULES

In the last section we saw that the marriage rules of a primitive society are determined by the vector t and the matrices S and D. The axioms make no mention of the number of types, and indeed, we will find that we can have any number of types, as long as $n > 1$. But we will find that the choice of S and D are severely limited. This shows that the rules of existing primitive societies required considerable ingenuity for their construction.

We must now consider the last three axioms. For Axiom 5 we need a simple way of describing a kind of relationship. The family tree is our basic tool, but we want to replace the family tree by a suitable matrix.

Let us consider Figure 23. Instead of starting with the grandparents and finding the types of the grandson and the granddaughter, we could start with the grandson, work up to the grandparents, and then down to the granddaughter. For this we must consider how we work "up." If a parent is of type t, the son is of type tS. Hence, if the son is of type t, then the parent is of type tS^{-1} (see Chapter V, Section 10). Similarly, if a daughter has type t, her parents have type tD^{-1}. In Figure 24 we find the new version of Figure 23.

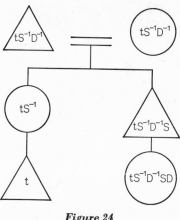

Figure 24

It is easily seen that we can follow this procedure for any relationship. Given a kind of relationship, it determines a matrix M such that if the male of the relationship is of type t, then the female is of type tM. From Figure 24 we see that for "mother's brother's daughter" $M = S^{-1}D^{-1}SD$. We will speak of M as the *matrix of the relationship*. These matrices are all products of S, D, and their inverses, hence each matrix is an element of the group generated by S and D.

Let us consider Axiom 5. Given any kind of relationship between a man and a woman, we form the matrix of the relationship M. The man will be permitted to marry this relation of his if and only if his type is the same as hers, i.e., if a certain component of t is the same as the corresponding component of tM. This means that this component is left unchanged by the permutation M, which proves our first theorem. (See Chapter V, Section 11.)

Theorem 1. A man is allowed to marry a female relative of a certain kind if and only if his marriage type does not belong to the effective set of the matrix of the relationship.

A second result follows from this theorem easily.

Theorem 2. Marriage between relatives of a given kind is always permitted if the matrix of the relationship has an empty effective set; it is never permitted if the matrix has a universal effective set.

Theorem 3. Axiom 5 requires that in the group generated by S and D every element except I is a complete permutation.

Proof. The axiom states that for a given relationship the marriage must always be allowed or must never be allowed. Hence, by Theorem 2, the matrix of the relationship must have an empty effective set or a universal one. The former means that the matrix is I, the latter that it is a complete permutation (see Chapter V, Section 11). Hence the matrix of every relationship must either be I or a complete permutation matrix. The matrices are elements of the group generated by S and D. And given any element of this group, which can be written as a product of S's and D's, we can draw a family tree having this matrix. Hence the matrices of relationships are all the elements of the group. This means that all the elements of the group, other than the identity, must be complete permutations. This completes the proof.

Theorem 4. Axiom 6 requires that $S^{-1}D$ be a complete permutation.

This theorem is an immediate consequence of the fact that the matrix of the brother-sister relationship is $S^{-1}D$.

Theorem 5. Axiom 7 requires that for every i and j there be a permutation in the group which carries t_i into t_j.

Proof. Let us choose two individuals, one of type t_i and one of type t_j. There must be a descendant of the former who can marry a descendant of the latter. Hence the two descendants must have the same type. This means that we have permutations M_1 and M_2 such that t_i is carried by M_1 into the same type as t_j by M_2. Then $M_1 M_2^{-1}$ carries t_i into t_j. Hence the theorem follows.

We have now translated Axioms 5–7 into the following three conditions on S and D: (1) The group generated by S and D consists of I and of complete permutations. (2) $S^{-1}D$ is a complete permutation. (3) For every pair of types there is a permutation in the group that carries one type into the other.

DEFINITION. A permutation group is called *regular* if (a) it is complete, i.e., every element of the group other than I is a complete permutation and if (b) for every pair from among the n objects there is a permutation in the group that carries one into the other.

Basic theorem. To satisfy the axioms we must choose two different $n \times n$ permutation matrices S and D which generate a regular permutation group.

Proof. Conditions (1) and (3) above state precisely that the group generated by S and D be regular. In a regular group every element other than I is a complete permutation; hence condition (2) requires only that $S^{-1}D$ be different from I. Since $S^{-1}D = I$ is equivalent to $D = S$, we need only require that $D \neq S$. This completes the proof.

It is important to be able to recognize regular permutation groups. Here we are helped by a very simple, well-known theorem: A subgroup of the group of permutations of degree n is regular if and only if it has n elements and is complete.

This leads to a relatively simple procedure. We choose n. Then we must pick a group of $n \times n$ permutation matrices which has n elements and is complete, and select two different elements which generate the group. This is always possible if $n > 1$ (see Exercise 11). One of these is chosen as S and one as D. Since there are not very many regular permutation groups for any n, the choice is very limited.

Example. Let us find all possibilities for a society having four marriage types. First of all we must find the regular subgroups of the symmetric group of degree 4, i.e., the groups of permutations on four objects that have four elements and are complete.

Among these we find cyclic groups. Any two of these groups have the same structure and hence lead to equivalent rules. Let us suppose that we choose the permutation group generated by

$$P = \begin{pmatrix} 0 & 1 & 0 & 0 \\ 0 & 0 & 1 & 0 \\ 0 & 0 & 0 & 1 \\ 1 & 0 & 0 & 0 \end{pmatrix}.$$

The group consists of P, P^2, P^3, and I. Either P or P^3 generates the group, and they play analogous roles. We may therefore assume that P is one of the two permutations chosen. This allows us (P, P^2), (P, P^3), and (P, I) as possibilities. We must still ask which is S and which is D. In the second case it makes no difference, since P and P^3 play analogous roles in the group, but there is a difference in the first two cases. This leads to five possibilities:

1. $S = P$, $D = P^2$
2. $S = P^2$, $D = P$
3. $S = P$, $D = P^3$
4. $S = P$, $D = I$
5. $S = I$, $D = P$. This is the Tarau society.

There is only one noncyclic complete subgroup with four elements, consisting of I and the three permutations which interchange two pairs of elements. In this group we have essentially only one case, since all three permutations play the same role.

6.   The Kariera society. (See exercises after the last section.)

Two of these six possibilities are actually exemplified in known primitive societies.

EXERCISES

1. Figure 24 shows the matrix of one of the first-cousin relations. Find the matrices of the other three first-cousin relationships.

2. Prove that marriage between relations of a certain kind is permitted if and only if the matrix of the relation is I.

3. Use the result of Exercise 2 to prove that no society allows the marriage between cousins of the types in Figures 20(a) and (b).

4. Which of the six rules described above (in the example) allow marriage between a man and his father's sister's daughter?   [*Ans.* 3, 6.]

5. Show that all six rules given in the example above allow marriages between a man and his mother's brother's daughter.

6. There are eight kinds of second-cousin relationships between a man and a woman. Draw their family trees.

7. Find the matrices of the eight second-cousin relationships.

8. Are there any second-cousin relationships for which marriage is forbidden by all possible rules?   [*Ans.* Yes.]

9. Test the second-cousin relationships (other than those found in Exercise 8) for each of the six rules given in the example above.

10. For n objects, consider the permutation that carries object number i into position $i + 1$, except that the last object is put into first place. Show that the cyclic group generated by this permutation is regular.

11. Use the result of Exercise 10 to show that a society can have any number of marriage types, as long as the number is greater than one.

12. In the Example of Section 6, prove that S and D generate a regular permutation group.

13. Prove that the following matrices lead to a rule satisfying all axioms.

$$S = \begin{pmatrix} 0 & 1 & 0 & 0 & 0 & 0 \\ 0 & 0 & 1 & 0 & 0 & 0 \\ 1 & 0 & 0 & 0 & 0 & 0 \\ 0 & 0 & 0 & 0 & 1 & 0 \\ 0 & 0 & 0 & 0 & 0 & 1 \\ 0 & 0 & 0 & 1 & 0 & 0 \end{pmatrix}, \quad D = \begin{pmatrix} 0 & 0 & 0 & 1 & 0 & 0 \\ 0 & 0 & 0 & 0 & 0 & 1 \\ 0 & 0 & 0 & 0 & 1 & 0 \\ 1 & 0 & 0 & 0 & 0 & 0 \\ 0 & 0 & 1 & 0 & 0 & 0 \\ 0 & 1 & 0 & 0 & 0 & 0 \end{pmatrix}.$$

14. Prove that the rule given in Exercise 13 allows no first-cousin marriages.

8. MODEL OF AN EXPANDING ECONOMY

The following model is a modification of a model proposed by John von Neumann. It is designed to study an economy which is expanding at a fixed rate, but which is otherwise in equilibrium. The model makes certain assumptions about how an economy behaves in equilibrium. These assumptions are idealizations, and it is to be expected that the model will eventually be replaced by a better model. For the present many economists consider the von Neumann model to be a reasonable approximation of reality. Our interest in the model is purely to illustrate how finite mathematics is used in an economic problem.

The economy is described by *n goods* and *m processes*. A good may be steel, coal, houses, shoes, etc. Goods are the materials of production in the economy. Each good may be measured in any convenient units, as long as the units are fixed once and for all. It is convenient to be able to talk of arbitrary multiples of these units; e.g., we will consider not only 2.75 tons of steel but also 2.75 houses. The latter may be interpreted as an average.

A manufacturing process needs certain goods as raw materials (the *inputs*) and produces one or more of our goods (the *outputs*). As a process we may, for example, consider the conversion of steel, wood, glass, etc. into a house. Of course this process may be used to manufacture more than one house, and hence we have the concept of the *intensity* with which a process is used. One of the basic assumptions is one of linearity, i.e., that k houses will require k times as much of each raw material. Thus we choose an arbitrary "unit intensity" for each process, and the process is completely described if we know the inputs necessary for this unit operation and the outputs produced.

Process number i when operating at unit intensity will require a certain amount of good j as an input. This amount will be called a_{ij}. (In particular, if good j is not needed for process i, then $a_{ij} = 0$.) We will call b_{ij} the amount of good j produced by process i. Here we allow a process to produce several different goods (e.g., a principal output and by-products). But, of course, we allow processes that produce only one good. Then all the b_{ij} for this i will be 0, except for one. The a_{ij} and b_{ij} are nonnegative numbers.

We define the matrix A to be the $m \times n$ matrix having components a_{ij}, and B to be the $m \times n$ matrix with components b_{ij}. Then the entire economy is described by these two matrices.

We must still consider the element of time. It is customary to think of the economy as working in stages or cycles. In one such stage there is just time enough for process i to convert the inputs a_{ij} to outputs b_{ij}. Then, in the next stage, these outputs may in turn be used as inputs. The length of this cycle may be any time interval convenient for the study of the particular economy. It may be a month, a year, or a number of years.

Example. Let us take as our economy a chicken farm. Our goods are chickens and eggs, with one chicken and one egg being the natural units. Our two processes consist of laying eggs and hatching them. Let us assume that in a given month a chicken lays an average of 12 eggs if we use it for laying eggs. If used for hatching, it will hatch an average of four eggs per month. From this information we can construct A and B.

Our cycle is of length one month. Good 1 is "chicken," good 2 is "egg," process 1 is "laying," and process 2 is "hatching." The unit of intensity of a process will be what one chicken can do on the average in a month. The input of process 1 is one chicken, i.e., one unit of good 1. The output will consist of a dozen eggs *plus* the original chicken. (We must not forget this, since the original chicken can be used again in the next cycle.) Hence the output is one unit of good 1 and 12 units of good 2. In process 2 the inputs are one chicken and four eggs, while the output consists of five chickens (the original one plus the four hatched). Hence our matrices are

$$
\begin{array}{c}
\text{Laying eggs:} \\
\text{Hatching eggs:}
\end{array}
\quad
\begin{array}{cc}
\text{Chicken} & \text{Egg} \\
\end{array}
\quad
A = \begin{pmatrix} 1 & 0 \\ 1 & 4 \end{pmatrix},
\quad
\begin{array}{cc}
\text{Chicken} & \text{Egg} \\
\end{array}
\quad
B = \begin{pmatrix} 1 & 12 \\ 5 & 0 \end{pmatrix}.
$$

Suppose that our farmer starts with three chickens and eight eggs ready for hatching. He will need two chickens for hatching the eight eggs, and this leaves him one for laying eggs. Hence he uses process 1 with intensity 1, process 2 with intensity 2. We symbolize this by the vector $x = (1, 2)$. Note that his inputs are the components of xA. His one laying chicken will lay 12 eggs. He will end up with his original three chickens plus eight new ones. Hence he will have an output of 11 units of good 1 and 12 units of good 2. These are the components of xB. Of his 11 chickens only three can be used for hatching, hence he will employ intensities $(8, 3)$. The outputs will be $(8, 3)B = (23, 96)$, as can easily be checked (see Exercise 1). He now has 96 eggs and only 23 chickens, so that some eggs must go unhatched.

On the other hand, suppose that he starts with only two chickens and four eggs. He will then use intensity $(1, 1)$. His laying chicken lays 12 eggs, and with four newly hatched chickens he has a total of six chickens. This result is also given by $(1, 1)B = (6, 12)$. He now has tripled both his chickens and his eggs. He can use intensity $(3, 3)$ on the next cycle, yielding $(3, 3)B = (18, 36)$, which again triples both the chickens and the eggs. Thus he can continue to use the same proportion of the processes, and will continue to triple his output on every cycle. This economy operates in *equilibrium*.

As was seen in the example, the natural way to represent the intensities of our processes is by means of a row vector. Let x_i be the intensity with which process number i is operated, then the *intensity vector x* is $(x_1, \ldots, x_m)$. Matrix multiplication is then an easy way of finding the total amount of each good needed, and the totals produced. Component j of xA is the sum $x_1a_{1j} + \ldots + x_m a_{mj}$; where $x_1 a_{1j}$ is the amount of good j we are using in process 1, $x_2 a_{2j}$ the amount we use in process 2, etc. Hence the jth component of xA is the total amount of good j needed in the inputs. Similarly, xB gives the total amounts of the various goods in the outputs.

We must now introduce prices for the various goods. Let y_j be the price of a unit of good j; this must be nonnegative, but it may be zero. (The latter represents a good that is so cheap as to be "practically free.") It is assumed that k units of good j will cost ky_j. The *price vector y* is the column vector

$$\begin{pmatrix} y_1 \\ \cdot \\ \cdot \\ \cdot \\ y_n \end{pmatrix}.$$

Let us consider the products Ay and By. In Ay the ith element is $a_{i1}y_1 + \ldots + a_{in}y_n$; the product $a_{i1}y_1$ is the amount of good 1 needed for unit operation of process i multiplied by the per unit price of good 1, hence this is the cost of good 1 used in the process, $a_{i2}y_2$ is the cost of good 2 used, etc. Hence the ith component of Ay is the total cost of inputs for a unit intensity operation of process i. Similarly, By gives the cost (value) of the outputs.

Finally, we consider the products xAy and xBy. Since x is $1 \times m$, the matrices $m \times n$, and y is $n \times 1$, each product is 1×1—or a number. An analysis similar to those above shows that xAy is the total cost of inputs if the economy is operated at intensity x, with prices y, and xBy is the total value of all goods produced. (See Exercise 2.)

Example (continued). Suppose that a chicken costs ten monetary units, while an egg costs one unit; then $y = \begin{pmatrix} 10 \\ 1 \end{pmatrix}$. Here

$$Ay = \begin{pmatrix} 10 \\ 14 \end{pmatrix} \quad \text{and} \quad By = \begin{pmatrix} 22 \\ 50 \end{pmatrix}.$$

This means that process 1, laying eggs, multiplies our investment by a factor of 2.2; while process 2, hatching, brings in over \$3.50 for every \$1.00 invested. There will be pressure to use the hens just for hatching—which will create a shortage of eggs, bringing about a drastic change in prices. Suppose now that a chicken costs only six times as much as an egg, i.e., $y = \begin{pmatrix} 6 \\ 1 \end{pmatrix}$. Then

$$Ay = \begin{pmatrix} 6 \\ 10 \end{pmatrix} \quad \text{and} \quad By = \begin{pmatrix} 18 \\ 30 \end{pmatrix}.$$

In this case each process triples our investment, and there will be no undue monetary pressure. Hence the farmer can set up his processes so as to be in equilibrium, and the price structure will be stable.

The remaining factor to be considered is the expansion of the economy. We assume that everything expands at a constant rate, i.e., that there is a fixed *expansion factor* α such that if the processes operate at intensity x in this cycle, they operate at intensity αx during the next cycle, $\alpha^2 x$ after that, etc. There is also something similar to expansion for the money of the economy, namely, that through bearing interest, y units of money in this cycle will be worth βy units after the cycle. We again assume that the *interest factor* β is fixed once and for all in equilibrium. Usually these factors will be greater than 1, but this does not have to be the case. Thus $\alpha = 1$ represents a stationary economy, and $\alpha < 1$ represents a contracting economy.

This completes the survey of the basic concepts. We must now lay down our assumptions concerning the behavior of an economy which is in equilibrium. These assumptions serve as axioms for the system.

First of all, we must assure that we produce enough of each good in each cycle to furnish the inputs of the next cycle. If in a given cycle the economy functions at intensity x, it will function at αx next time. The outputs this time will be xB, while the inputs next time will be αxA; hence we must require:

Axiom 1. $xB \geq \alpha xA.$

(When we write a vector inequality, we mean that the inequality holds for every component.) We will of course have to require similar conditions for the future. For example, in the second cycle the outputs are αxB, and the inputs needed for the third cycle are $\alpha^2 xA$. But when we write the condition that the former be greater than the latter, an α cancels, and we have again the same condition as in Axiom 1. Hence this axiom serves for all cycles.

The first condition assures that it is possible for the economy to expand at the constant rate α. We must also assure that the economy is financially in equilibrium. Suppose that the output of some process was worth more than β times the input. Then we would be prepared to pay interest at a larger rate to someone willing to invest in our process. Hence β would increase. Thus, in equilibrium this must not be possible; no process can produce profits at a rate greater than that given by investment. If we operate processes at a unit intensity, then Ay gives the costs of inputs, while By gives the cost of outputs. The latter cannot exceed the former by more than a factor β for any process.

Axiom 2. $By \leq \beta Ay.$

The next assumption concerns surplus production. If we produce more of a given good than can be used by the total economy, the price drops sharply as merchants try to get rid of their produce. It is customary to assume, for the sake of simplicity, that such goods are free, i.e., to give them price zero. The vector difference $xB - \alpha xA = x(B - \alpha A)$ gives the amounts of overproduction, i.e., the jth component is positive if and only if good j is overproduced. If we assign price zero to these goods, then in the product of the above vector with y every nonzero factor of the former is multiplied by zero; hence the product of the two vectors will be 0.

Axiom 3. $x(B - \alpha A)y = 0.$

Now we turn to the question of whether a given process is worth undertaking. From Axiom 2 we know that no process can yield more profit than investment can. But if it yields any less, it is better not to use it, but rather to invest our money. Hence in Axiom 2 we form the difference $By - \beta Ay$; if the ith component of this is negative, process i should not be used; it must be assigned intensity 0. Similar to the argument used for Axiom 3, this shows that multiplying this vector difference by x must yield zero.

Axiom 4. $x(B - \beta A)y = 0.$

Our final assumption is that something worth while is produced in the economy, i.e., that the value of all goods produced is a positive amount.

Axiom 5. $xBy > 0.$

If for a given economy (given A and B) we find vectors x and y and numbers α and β which satisfy these five axioms, we say that we have found a *possible equilibrium solution* for the economy.

Example (continued). We have already seen that if $x = (1, 1)$, the economy expands at the fixed rate $\alpha = 3$. We can now check that Axiom 1 is satisfied. Actually, xB turns out to equal αxA. Similarly, we have noted a monetary equilibrium if $y = \begin{pmatrix} 6 \\ 1 \end{pmatrix}$, and each process multiplies the money put into it by a factor of $\beta = 3$. We can check that Axiom 2 holds. Actually By is equal to βAy in this case. From these two equations we also know that $x(B - \alpha A)$ and $(B - \beta A)y$ are identically 0; hence Axioms 3 and 4 hold. Finally, $xBy = 48$; the total value of goods produced is positive, so that Axiom 5 holds. Therefore these values of x, y, α, and β represent an equilibrium for the economy. It can also be shown that these are the only possible values of α and β, and that x and y must be proportional to those shown here (which may be thought of simply as a change in the units).

In our example we found one and only one equilibrium for the economy, and we found that $\alpha = \beta$. This raises several very natural questions: (1) Is there a possible equilibrium for every economy? (2) If yes, then is there only one? (3) Must the expansion factor always be the same as the interest factor? In the next section we will establish the following answers: (1) For every economy satisfying a certain restriction (which is certainly satisfied for all real economies) there is a possible equilibrium. (2) There may be more than one equilibrium, though the number of different possible expansion factors is finite. (In the example there is essentially only one possibility for x and y; however this is not true in general.) (3) The interest and expansion factors are always equal in equilibrium.

EXERCISES

1. In the example, for $x = (1, 2)$, verify for three cycles that xA and xB give the correct inputs and outputs.

2. Give an interpretation of xAy and xBy,
   (a) Using the interpretations of xA and xB given above.
   (b) Using the interpretations of Ay and By given above.
   (c) And show that the results in (a) and (b) are the same.

3. In the example suppose that two chickens lay eggs and three hatch eggs. Find x, xA, and xB. Substitute these quantities into Axiom 1, and find the largest possible expansion factor.   [*Ans.* $\alpha = 2$.]

4. In the example, suppose that chickens cost 80 cents and eggs cost five cents. Find y, Ay, and By. Substitute these quantities into Axiom 2, and find the smallest possible interest factor.   [*Ans.* $\beta = 4$.]

5. Show that the x, y, α, and β found in two previous Exercises do *not* lead to equilibrium, by showing that Axioms 3 and 4 fail to hold.

6. Show that if $\alpha = \beta = 3$, then the only possible x's and y's are proportional to those given in the example. [*Hint*: Show that the axioms force us to choose $x_1 = x_2$ and $y_1 = 6y_2$.]

The remaining problems refer to the following economy: On a chicken farm there is a breed of chicken that lays an average of 16 eggs a month, and such that they can hatch an average of $3\frac{1}{5} = \frac{16}{5}$ eggs.

7. Set up the matrices A and B.

8. Suppose that three chickens lay and five chickens hatch. Find x, xA, and xB. What is α?   [*Ans.* $x = (3, 5)$; $xA = (8, 16)$; $xB = (24, 48)$; $\alpha = 3$.]

9. Suppose that chickens cost 40 cents and eggs cost five cents. Find y, Ay, and By. What is β?

10. Verify that the x, y, α, and β found in the previous exercises represent an equilibrium for the economy, by substituting these into the five axioms.

11. Suppose that we start with 16 chickens and 32 eggs. Choose the intensities so that the economy will be in equilibrium, and find what happens in the first three months.   [*Ans.* $x = (6, 10)$; 432 chickens, and 864 eggs.]

12. Suppose that with 16 chickens and 32 eggs (see Exercise 11) we start out by having only five hatching, the others laying. Show that we cannot have as many chickens after three months as we would have in the equilibrium solution.

9. EXISTENCE OF AN ECONOMIC EQUILIBRIUM

We must ask whether the axioms can always be satisfied, i.e., whether the model of the economy allows such an equilibrium.

Of course we are interested only in an economy that could really occur. That means that these goods must be goods that are somehow produced, and that they cannot be produced out of nothing. Hence every process must require at least one raw material and every good has at least one process that produces it. We summarize this:

Restriction. Every row of A and every column of B has at least one positive component.

Theorem. If A and B satisfy the restriction, then an equilibrium is possible.

We will sketch the proof of this theorem. From Axiom 3 we have that $xBy = \alpha xAy$, while from Axiom 4, $xBy = \beta xAy$. Hence $\alpha xAy = \beta xAy$. Furthermore, from Axiom 5 we know that xBy is not zero, hence xAy is not zero. Then $\alpha = \beta$. Hence *in equilibrium the rate of expansion equals the interest rate.*

If $\alpha = \beta$, then Axioms 3 and 4 are equivalent. We can also rewrite the first two axioms (using our result).

Axiom 1′. $\qquad\qquad x(B - \alpha A) \geq 0.$

Axiom 2′. $\qquad\qquad (B - \alpha A)y \leq 0.$

If we multiply the first inequality by y on the right, and the second by x on the left, we see that Axiom 3 (and hence 4) follows from these two axioms. Hence we need only worry about Axioms 1′, 2′, and 5.

The key to the proof is to reinterpret the problem as a game-theoretic one. This is done in spite of the fact that no game is involved in the model. We simply use the mathematical results of the theory of games as tools.

Axioms 1′ and 2′ suggest that we think of the matrix $B - \alpha A$ as a matrix game. We would then like to think of the vectors x and y as mixed strategies for the two players. The vectors are nonnegative, but the sum of their components need not be 1. However, we know that multiplying x by a constant can be thought of as a change in the units of intensities, and multiplying y by a constant is equivalent to a change in the units of the various goods. Hence, without loss of generality, we may assume that x and y have component sum 1, and think of them as mixed strategies. If we do this, the two axioms state precisely that the game has value zero, and that x and y form a pair of optimal strategies for the two players. Thus our first problem is to choose α so that the "game" $B - \alpha A$ has value zero.

Example 1. Let us set up the example of the last section as a game.

$$M = B - \alpha A = \begin{pmatrix} 1 - \alpha & 12 \\ 5 - \alpha & -4\alpha \end{pmatrix}.$$

If we choose $x = (\frac{1}{2}, \frac{1}{2})$ as a mixed strategy for the row player, then $xM = [3 - \alpha, 2(3 - \alpha)]$. If $\alpha < 3$, the components are both positive; hence the game has value greater than zero. If we choose $y = \begin{pmatrix} \frac{6}{7} \\ \frac{1}{7} \end{pmatrix}$ as a mixed strategy for the column player, then

$$My = \begin{bmatrix} \frac{6}{7}(3 - \alpha) \\ \frac{10}{7}(3 - \alpha) \end{bmatrix}.$$

If $\alpha > 3$, both components are negative, and hence the game has negative value. We thus see that the only value of α that could possibly give us a zero value of the game is $\alpha = 3$, and we see from the above that in this case the value really is zero, and x and y are optimal strategies. (See Exercise 1.)

We must now show that the above example is typical in that we can always find an α making the value of $B - \alpha A$ equal to zero. We may write this matrix as the sum $B + \alpha(-A)$, and think of our game as a combination of game B and game $-A$.

By our restriction, every column of B has a positive entry. The strategy vector y for the column player must have at least one positive component. Hence in the product By, one of the components at least must be positive. Hence the value of the game B is positive. Since every row of A has a positive entry, every row of the game $-A$ must have a negative entry. Hence at least one component of $x(-A)$ must be negative, and hence $-A$ has a negative value.

In the combination $B + \alpha(-A)$ the second term is negligible for very small α; hence for these the game has positive value. As α increases, we keep adding larger negative quantities to some of the entries of the game, i.e., we keep decreasing some of these entries. Hence the value of the game decreases steadily. For very large α the first term is negligible, and hence the combined game has negative value. For some intermediate value of α the game must have value zero.

Example 1 (continued). The value of the combined game M is plotted for various α in Figure 25. Since B has value $\frac{15}{4}$ and $-A$ has value -1 (see Exercise 2), at the beginning the game M has value nearly $\frac{15}{4}$, and near the end it has value nearly $2 - \alpha$, which is less than zero (see Exercise 3).

We know that there is at least one α for which the game $B - \alpha A$ has value zero. By choosing such an α together with a pair x, y of optimal strategies, we arrive at a set of quantities satisfying Axioms 1′ and 2′. This still leaves the question of Axiom 5.

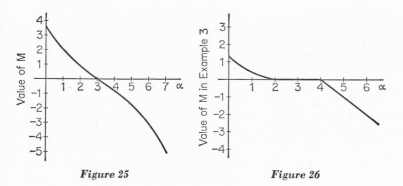

Figure 25   *Figure 26*

If there are two values of α, say $p < q$, for which the game has value zero, every value between p and q also has this property. This is because the value of the game cannot increase as α increases, as we saw above. Hence we must have a situation such as that shown in Figure 26. It can be shown, however, that most of these values represent methods of procedure where nothing worthwhile is produced, i.e., where Axiom 5 fails. For Axiom 5 to hold, different values of α can be achieved only by using at least one new process. Since there are only a finite number of processes, we can have only a finite number of different possible α's on the interval between p and q. If p is the smallest possible expansion rate and q the largest, then p and q are such that Axiom 5 can be satisfied, and there may be a limited number of additional ones in between.

Example 2. In the chemical industry we are interested in manufacturing compounds P, Q, and R. We assume that the basic chemicals are available in plentiful supply, and that their cost can be neglected for this analysis. But to manufacture compound P we must have a unit of both P and Q available, while to manufacture Q we must have P and R available. Compound R is a by-product of both manufacturing processes. The exact quantities are given by

$$\begin{array}{c} \\ \text{Manufacture of } P: \\ \text{Manufacture of } Q: \end{array} \quad A = \begin{pmatrix} P & Q & R \\ 1 & 1 & 0 \\ 1 & 0 & 1 \end{pmatrix}, \quad B = \begin{pmatrix} P & Q & R \\ 6 & 0 & 1 \\ 0 & 3 & 2 \end{pmatrix}.$$

Then

$$M = B - \alpha A = \begin{pmatrix} 6 - \alpha & -\alpha & 1 \\ -\alpha & 3 & 2 - \alpha \end{pmatrix}.$$

Let us choose

$$x = (\tfrac{1}{2}, \tfrac{1}{2}) \quad \text{and} \quad y = \begin{pmatrix} \tfrac{1}{6} \\ \tfrac{1}{3} \\ \tfrac{1}{2} \end{pmatrix}.$$

Then

$$xM = [3 - \alpha, \tfrac{1}{2}(3 - \alpha), \tfrac{1}{2}(3 - \alpha)] \quad \text{and} \quad My = \begin{bmatrix} \tfrac{1}{2}(3 - \alpha) \\ \tfrac{2}{3}(3 - \alpha) \end{bmatrix}.$$

From this we see that if $\alpha < 3$, then the row player has a guaranteed profit, while if $\alpha > 3$, the column player does. Thus $\alpha = 3$ is the only possibility, and for this case the value of the game is zero, and the vectors x and y are optimal strategies, as can be seen from the fact that xM and My have all components zero. Thus there is a unique equilibrium, with $\alpha = \beta = 3$.

We also find that the mixed strategy x is unique, which means that the two processes must be used with the same intensity. However, the strategy y is not unique. We may instead use

$$y' = \begin{pmatrix} \tfrac{1}{2} \\ \tfrac{1}{2} \\ 0 \end{pmatrix} \quad \text{or} \quad y'' = \begin{pmatrix} 0 \\ \tfrac{1}{4} \\ \tfrac{3}{4} \end{pmatrix}$$

or any mixture $ty' + (1 - t)y''$, $0 \leq t \leq 1$. Our y is the case $t = \frac{1}{3}$. Hence we see that different price structures are possible, each leading to the same expansion rate.

Example 3. This "economy" is a schematic representation of the production of essentials and inessentials in a society. Goods are lumped together into two types, E (essential goods) and I (inessential goods or luxury items). For the manufacture of E we need only essential goods (since anything so needed is essential). For the manufacture of I we may need both types of raw materials. Let us suppose that our economy functions as follows.

$$
\begin{array}{cc}
& \begin{array}{cc} E & I \end{array} \qquad\qquad \begin{array}{cc} E & I \end{array}
\end{array}
$$

Manufacture of essentials: $A = \begin{pmatrix} 1 & 0 \\ 1 & 1 \end{pmatrix}$, $B = \begin{pmatrix} 4 & 0 \\ 0 & 2 \end{pmatrix}$.
Manufacture of luxuries:

Then

$$
M = B - \alpha A = \begin{pmatrix} 4 - \alpha & 0 \\ -\alpha & 2 - \alpha \end{pmatrix}.
$$

With a little patience we can determine the values of M for various values of α, and we arrive at the curve in Figure 26. (See Exercise 4.) Hence α must be between 2 and 4. For $\alpha = 4$, we have the optimal strategies $x = (1, 0)$ and $y = \begin{pmatrix} 1 \\ 0 \end{pmatrix}$, which satisfy all our axioms; while for $\alpha = 2$ we have

$$
x = (\tfrac{1}{2}, \tfrac{1}{2}) \quad \text{and} \quad y = \begin{pmatrix} 0 \\ 1 \end{pmatrix}.
$$

For in-between values of α we cannot satisfy Axiom 5. (See Exercises 5–7.) Hence there are two possible equilibria: (1) The society can decide to manufacture only essentials, in which case the production of these will increase rapidly. (2) By putting a high enough value on inessentials, it will arrive at an equilibrium in which both essentials and inessentials are produced, but then the rate of expansion is considerably decreased.

We have now provided complete answers for the three questions raised at the end of the last section, providing a mathematical solution to a series of economic problems.

EXERCISES

1. In Example 1 verify that for $\alpha = 3$ the game M has value 0, and that the x and y given are optimal strategies.

2. In Example 1 solve the 2×2 games B and $-A$, finding their values and pairs of optimal strategies.

3. In Example 1
    (a) Show that the game M is nonstrictly determined for every α.
    (b) Find the value of M for any α. [*Ans.* $(5 + \alpha)(3 - \alpha)/(4 + \alpha)$.]
    (c) Show that the value for $\alpha = .01$ is very near $\frac{15}{4}$.
    (d) Show that the value for $\alpha = 100$ is very near -98.
    (e) Show that the value is 0 if and only if $\alpha = 3$.

4. Find the value of M in Example 3 for $\alpha = 0, 1, 2, 3, 4, 5$, and 6. [*Hint:* Some of these games are strictly determined.]

                                      [*Ans.* 1.33, .60, 0, 0, 0, -1.00, -2.00.]

5. In Example 3, for $\alpha = 4$, verify that the strategies given are optimal, and that Axiom 5 is satisfied.

6. In Example 3, for $\alpha = 2$, verify that the strategies given are optimal, and that Axiom 5 is satisfied.

7. In Example 3, for $\alpha = 3$, find the unique optimal x and y, and show that Axiom 5 is *not* satisfied. Prove that the same happens for every α if $2 < \alpha < 4$.

The remaining problems refer to the following economy: There are four goods and five processes, and the economy is given by

$$A = \begin{pmatrix} 0 & 0 & 1 & 1 \\ 0 & 0 & 2 & 2 \\ 0 & 4 & 0 & 2 \\ 2 & 1 & 1 & 0 \\ 0 & 1 & 0 & 2 \end{pmatrix}, \quad B = \begin{pmatrix} 0 & 0 & 4 & 2 \\ 0 & 0 & 5 & 7 \\ 6 & 5 & 4 & 0 \\ 0 & 4 & 0 & 3 \\ 3 & 0 & 6 & 0 \end{pmatrix}.$$

Also let $\quad x = (\frac{1}{2}, \frac{1}{2}, 0, 0, 0), \quad x' = (0, 0, \frac{2}{5}, \frac{3}{5}, 0),$

$$y = \begin{pmatrix} \frac{1}{3} \\ \frac{2}{3} \\ 0 \\ 0 \end{pmatrix}, \quad y' = \begin{pmatrix} 0 \\ 0 \\ \frac{1}{2} \\ \frac{1}{2} \end{pmatrix}.$$

8. Verify that A and B satisfy the restriction.

9. Compute $M = B - \alpha A$.

10. Compute xM, $x'M$, My, and My'.

11. When will $x'M$ have all positive entries? When will My' have all negative entries? What possibilities does this leave for α?

[*Ans.* $\alpha < 2$; $\alpha > 3$; $2 \leq \alpha \leq 3$.]

12. Show that for the remaining possible values of α the game M has value zero, and x and y are optimal strategies.

13. Show that for the largest possible α the vectors x and y' provide optimal strategies which satisfy Axiom 5.

14. Show that for the smallest possible α the vectors x' and y provide optimal strategies which satisfy Axiom 5.

15. If α is in between its two extreme values, show that
   (a) xM is positive in its last two components, and hence the second player can use only his first two strategies.
   (b) My is negative in its last three components, and hence the first player can use only his first two strategies.
   (c) For these cases it is impossible to satisfy Axiom 5.

16. Process number five is in a special position. Why? [*Ans.* Never used.]

17. Use the results of Exercises 8–16 to show that there are exactly two possible equilibriums for this economy. Interpret each equilibrium, and point out the differences between the two methods of operating the economy.
   [*Ans.* At the price of reducing the expansion rate, the economy can produce a larger variety of goods. To achieve this, the additional types of goods must be valued (relatively) very high.]

10.   COMPUTER SIMULATION

Probabilistic models prevail in the social sciences. While many of them can, in principle, be treated by the methods studied in this book, in practice they frequently are much too complicated to obtain precise theoretical results. In such cases, simulation by a high-speed computer may be a powerful tool.

Simulation is a process during which the computer acts out a situation from real life. Typically, the relevant facts about an experiment are supplied to the computer, and it is instructed to run through a large series of experiments, perhaps under varying conditions. This enables the scientist to carry out in an hour a series of experiments that would otherwise take years, and at the same time all the important information is automatically tabulated by the computer.

Of course, the computer cannot duplicate the exact circumstances of an experiment. The facts fed to it are based on a model (or theory) formed by the scientist, and the value of the simulation depends on the accuracy of the model. Thus the main significance of simulation is that it enables a scientist to study the kind of behavior predicted by his model. For very complicated models this may be the only procedure open to him.

In addition to the use of simulation for theoretical studies, there are two very important types of pragmatic uses of simulation: (1) It can be used as a planning device. If there are various alternative courses of action open, the computer is asked to try out the various alternatives under different conditions, and report the advantages and disadvantages of each course. (2) Simulation may be used as a training device. For example, business schools make increasing use of "business games" in which fledgling executives may try their skill at decision-making under realistic circumstances. Similarly, simulated "war-games" are used to train military leaders.

We will first discuss how machines simulate stochastic processes, and then illustrate the procedure in four examples. To avoid the necessity of lengthy introduction of new models, we shall use three of the games previously discussed, and a Markov chain model. Also, we will describe the simulation so that no previous knowledge of computers is necessary.

How does one introduce a probabilistic element into a high-speed computer? This is achieved by the generation of so-called *random numbers*. In a typical set-up, when an instruction contains the letters "RND," a real number between 0 and 1 is computed that gives rise to fairly good random results.

Actually, the computer is forced to cheat, in that it has only a finite capacity for expressing numbers. So that it may in reality divide the unit interval into a million (or more) numbers, and give them in a pretty random order. When its supply is exhausted, it will start giving the same numbers in the same order. However, if one needs only 100,000 numbers, or even a million numbers, the results are highly satisfactory.

One use of the RND device is to generate an independent trials process with two outcomes. For example, suppose that we wish to have probability .3 for success. Then on each trial we generate an RND, and ask:

$$\text{Is RND} < .3?$$

If yes, we mark it as success; if no, then it is a failure. Since a number picked at random from the unit interval has a .3 probability of being less than .3, we obtain an excellent approximation to the independent trials experiment.

In Figure 27 we show 30 RND's generated by the Dartmouth Computer. If we used these for the above mentioned simulation, we would have success in 8 of 30 trials, only one below the expected number of 9.

Suppose that we wish to simulate an independent trials experiment with more than two outcomes. If the outcomes are equally likely, then the generation of *random integers* is a very convenient device. In this we generate RND's as usual, but reinterpret them as integers.

For example, in Figure 28 we show the result of multiplying the RND's of Figure 27 by 6, and adding 1 to each. Now we have numbers picked at random between 1 and 7. Since such a number is just as likely to lie between 3 and 4 as between 4 and 5, saving the integer part of the number will result in equally likely random integers 1, 2, 3, 4, 5, and 6. This is shown in Figure 29.

.746489	.196691	.053368	.323690	.244322
.625169	.193130	.935845	.445447	.262310
.218802	.783032	.402600	.848350	.558119
.980484	.918514	.873523	.388814	.393435
.545924	.578063	.638623	.637121	.587565
.952204	.985279	.076776	.096170	.736181

Figure 27

5.47893	2.18015	1.32021	2.94214	2.46593
4.75101	2.15878	6.61507	3.67268	2.57386
2.31281	5.69819	3.41560	6.09010	4.34871
6.88290	6.51108	6.24114	3.33289	3.36061
4.27555	4.46838	4.83174	4.82273	4.52539
6.71322	6.91168	1.46066	1.57702	5.41708

Figure 28

5	2	1	2	2	4	2	6	3	2
2	5	3	6	4	6	6	6	3	3
4	4	4	4	4	6	6	1	1	5

Figure 29

Example 1. Craps. Let us simulate the game of craps on the computer. First of all, we must imitate the roll of a pair of dice. We may do this by choosing a pair of numbers from Figure 29, each number representing one die, and letting the sum represent the sum of the two dice. Then we proceed according to the rules of craps.

A flow-diagram for this simulation is shown in Figure 30. If we carry this out for three games, using the numbers in Figure 29 (reading from left to right in successive rows), we obtain the following results: (1) The player rolls 7, and wins. (2) The player rolls 3, and loses.

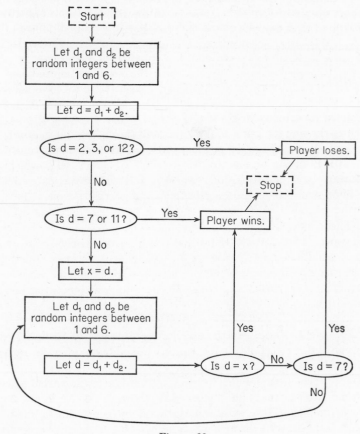

Figure 30

(3) The "point" is 6, but a 7 turns up before a 6, and the player loses again.

Let us use this simulation model to estimate the player's expected value. (In Chapter IV, Section 12, this was found to be $-.0141$.) After 10,000 simulated games the player was behind by \$312, yielding the rather poor estimate of $-.0312$. However, after 250,000 games the estimate was $-.0154$, in good agreement with theory. The total computing time required for 250,000 games of craps was 8 minutes, indicatcating that this is a practical procedure.

The difficult question to answer, in general, is: "When have we run enough simulated games?" However, in the simple case of craps this is not hard to determine. Since the probability of winning is nearly $\frac{1}{2}$, the standard deviation for n games is roughly $\sqrt{n \cdot \frac{1}{2} \cdot \frac{1}{2}}$ or $\sqrt{n}/2$. Suppose that the player wins that many more games than expected. This increases his winnings by $\sqrt{n}/2$ dollars, and decreases his losses by the same amount. Thus there is a net gain of $\sqrt{n}$ dollars. This changes our estimated expected value by $\sqrt{n}/n$, or by $1/\sqrt{n}$.

Thus, running the game 10,000 times will typically result in an error of about .01, which is quite significant compared to the correct answer of $-.0141$. In our simulation we were off by about .017, which is within two standard deviations (which is .020). However, an error of the same size in the opposite direction would actually have yielded a positive expected value. So we can have little confidence in 10,000 simulated games in estimating a number so near to 0.

However, after 250,000 games the typical error is only about .002. Thus from our computed estimate of $-.0154$ we can have considerable confidence that the game is not favorable to the player; and we would estimate that the correct expected value lies somewhere between $-.012$ and $-.019$.

Example 2. Poker. In the exercises of Chapter IV, Section 3, we computed the probabilities for various poker hands. Let us obtain estimates for the same by simulation.

Our problem here amounts to selecting 5 cards at random from a deck of 52 cards. We first of all number the cards from 1 to 52, in any convenient manner. Then we select one card by generating a random integer from the set 1 through 52. (This can be achieved by computing $52 \cdot RND + 1$.) Next we select one of the 51 remaining cards at random, etc. When we have five cards, we determine how good a hand we drew.

This simulation was carried out for 10,000 poker hands on the Dartmouth Computer, requiring about one hour of computing time. The results were as in Figure 31.

Type of hand.	Number of times.
Bust	5046
One pair	4169
Two pairs	508
Three of a kind	191
Straight	43
Flush	11
Full house	25
Four of a kind	6
Straight flush	1

Figure 31

You will be asked, in the exercises, to compare these figures with the expected values.

Example 3. Land of Oz. Models in the social sciences often depend on Markov chain processes. While there are powerful theoretical tools for treating Markov chains, sufficiently complex models may have to be simulated. We will illustrate this for a simple Markov chain, which we have already treated theoretically.

Consider the Land of Oz (Chapter V, Section 7, Exercise 13). Suppose that we wished to find the fraction of times that the weather is "nice," "rain," or "snow," by simulation. We would first pick a starting state, say "rain." We then know that the probability of "rain" is $\frac{1}{2}$, of "nice" $\frac{1}{4}$, and of "snow" $\frac{1}{4}$. We can achieve this by generating an RND; if it is less than $\frac{1}{2}$ we decide on "rain," if it is between $\frac{1}{2}$ and $\frac{3}{4}$ then "nice" is next, while if RND $> \frac{3}{4}$ then "snow" is next.

If we use the RND's in Figure 27, we obtain "nice" for the second day. From here we go to "rain" or "snow," with probability $\frac{1}{2}$ each. Since the next RND is less than $\frac{1}{2}$, we choose "rain." Proceeding in this manner, after the original "rain" we obtain

"nice," "rain," "rain," "rain," "rain," "nice," "rain," "snow."

We carried out this simulation for 10,000 times for each starting state, with the results shown in Figure 32. We note that the results are in excellent agreement with the .4, .2, and .4 long-run distribution predicted by theory, and that the results are pretty much independent of the starting state.

Starting state	Number of "rain"	Number of "nice"	Number of "snow"
"Rain"	4080	2002	3918
"Nice"	3976	1986	4038
"Snow"	3975	1984	4041

Figure 32

Example 4. Baseball. The game of baseball is a good example of a game having a model for which a complete theoretical treatment is not practical, and hence much can be gained from simulation.

How would we build a simulation model for a given team, in order to study the way they produce runs? Fortunately, some very detailed statistics are kept, over long periods, which are ideal for building such a model. Let us suppose that a given batter comes to bat. We know from past experience what the probabilities are for his making an out, getting a walk, or getting a hit of various kinds. We simply generate an RND, and use it to decide what the batter did.

For example, if he has probabilities .1 for a walk, .64 for an out, .2 for a single, .03 for a double, .01 for a triple, and .02 for a home-run, we can generate a random integer from 1 through 100, and interpret it as in Figure 33.

We can then bring the next batter to bat, and arrive at a result based on *his* past performance. The running on the bases may be simulated similarly. For example, we can feed into the machine the probability that a man on first reaches third on a single. Just how realistic we wish to make the model depends entirely on how much work we are willing to do.

Range	Result	Probability
1–10	Walk	.1
11–74	Out	.64
75–94	Single	.2
95–97	Double	.03
98	Triple	.01
99–100	Home-run	.02

Figure 33

It should be noted that we are simulating only the batting of *one* team. We do not here consider the batting of the other team, or questions of defensive play.

Such a model would be most useful in training young managers. The computer could make all decisions (many of them stochastic) having to do with the performance of the players, while the manager could make all decisions normally open to managers. For example, he could call for a hit-and-run play, and the machine would simulate the results. He could call for a steal, or send in a pinch-hitter, or tell a batter to try to hit a long fly ball.

By the use of a computer a new manager could gain an entire season's experience in a few days—and he would not be learning at the expense of his team.

The model is also useful for planning purposes, as we will illustrate here. One important task of the manager is to decide on his batting order. He could feed a variety of batting orders to the computer, have it try each for a season's games (or more), and report back the results.

This was actually done on the Dartmouth Computer.

The team used in the simulation was the starting line-up of the 1963 world champion Los Angeles Dodgers. The line-up of Figure 34 was used throughout.

Line-up	Batting average	Slugging average
1. Wills	.302	.349
2. Gilliam	.282	.383
3. W. Davis	.245	.365
4. T. Davis	.326	.457
5. Howard	.273	.518
6. Fairly	.271	.388
7. McMullen	.236	.339
8. Roseboro	.236	.351
9. Pitcher (average)	.117	.152

Figure 34

An entire season of 162 games was simulated, keeping detailed records for each player. Of course, this simulation differed from the normal year in a few respects. For instance, the first eight players played every inning of every game. Since only the batting was simulated, no allowance was made for defensive play, nor did the game stop after eight innings if the home team was ahead. Games were not called on account of rain, and there were no extra-inning games. But, many important features concerning batting were recreated quite realistically. We will cite a few of the more interesting results.

Seven of the batters ended up with batting averages close to their actual ones, but two did not. Tommy Davis, the league's leading hitter, had an even more spectacular year during simulation: He batted an even 350 (compared with 326 in 1963). On the other hand, Fairly who batted 271 in actuality, had a bad simulated year, batting only 250. This shows how much a batting average can change due to purely random factors.

Howard was far ahead in home runs, with 54. This is much higher than the 28 he had in actuality, but he was only used part time in 1963, while in the simulated year he played all the time. Two of the home runs were hit by pitchers—just as in real life. In one game Howard hit three home runs. But mostly it was the balance of the Dodger team that showed up; there were ten games in which three different players hit home runs.

There were no really spectacular slumps, though Gilliam once went 15 consecutive at-bats without getting a hit. The total number of runs scored was 652, in excellent agreement with the actual 640. On the other hand, the 1352 men left on base compared very poorly with the Dodgers' league-leading performance of leaving only 1034 men on base. Two factors in this were the absence of double-plays and pinch-hitters in the simulation model. But there is probably some other relevant attribute of the team that was missed in the model.

Perhaps the most interesting result is the number of shut-outs. There were 11 in the simulation, as compared to the league-leading performance of only eight shut-outs. In the simulation, two of the shut-outs occurred in the final two games. Thus, if the season ended in 160 games, the simulation would have been off by only one shut-out. This shows how hard it is to get an accurate estimate for a small probability through simulation! And there were four games late in the season, three of which ended in shut-outs. If this had happened in real life, all the Los Angeles papers would have carried headlines about a Dodger batting slump.

To compare various possible batting orders, several line-ups were simulated for ten entire seasons. The seven line-ups are shown in the first column of Figure 35, and the results in the second column. The standard deviation of the average number of runs per game was about .07. Since the difference between the best and the worst line-up is over three standard deviations, one is tempted to conclude that the batting order really makes a difference—though not very much of a difference.

Line-up	Average number of runs per game		
	10 seasons	7 × 10 seasons	Range
1, 2, 3, 4, 5, 6, 7, 8, 9	4.06	4.00	3.91–4.06
1, 4, 2, 5, 6, 3, 8, 7, 9	4.07	4.02	3.92–4.07
4, 5, 6, 1, 2, 3, 7, 8, 9	4.00	3.98	3.90–4.04
2, 1, 3, 5, 4, 6, 8, 7, 9	3.98	4.01	3.95–4.08
1, 4, 7, 2, 5, 8, 3, 6, 9	3.90	3.98	3.90–4.05
9, 8, 7, 6, 5, 4, 3, 2, 1	3.89	3.82	3.72–3.89
9, 6, 3, 8, 5, 2, 7, 4, 1	3.83	3.83	3.76–3.92

Figure 35

However, this simulation—though time-consuming—is not conclusive. We may still entertain the hypothesis that any line-up averages about 3.95 runs per game, and all seven outcomes are within two standard deviations of this. We are forced into an even more substantial simulation run.

The simulation was repeated; this time every line-up had seven sets of ten entire seasons simulated. The newly computed averages are shown in column three of Figure 35, while the maximum and minimum values obtained for a set of ten seasons are shown in the last column. Since we have simulated seven times as many games for each line-up, the standard deviation is reduced by a factor of $\sqrt{7}$, to less than .03. The differences in the averages now look more significant. Also we note that the ranges obtained for the first five line-ups don't overlap (or hardly overlap) the ranges for the last two line-ups. We may therefore conclude that we have five "good" and two "poor" line-ups. And this hypothesis stands up under more sophisticated tests.

What characterizes the poor line-ups? Most noticeably, the pitcher is first, rather than being last. But also we note that the Dodgers had three weak hitters (numbers 3, 7, and 8), and two of these are near the top of the bad line-ups. We therefore conclude that poor hitters should be near the end of the line-up. But little else can be concluded.

We should also note that the difference between best and worst is surprisingly little, and drastic changes in the "best" have practically no effect. Thus we conclude that the importance of the batting order has been greatly exaggerated.

One additional remark may be of interest: The first line-up in Figure 35 is, of course, the one chosen by the coach. The last five are simply permutations chosen according to simple patterns. However, the second line-up was chosen by one of the authors, a Dodger fan, as his attempt to "coach" the team. He was most pleased that it turned out best! Of course, .02 is only $\frac{2}{3}$ of a standard deviation, which represents about three runs per year, and is not significant.

EXERCISES

1. Use the RND in Figure 27 to simulate an independent trials process with probability .4 of success, for 30 trials. How many successes do you obtain? [*Ans.* 11.]

2. In Example 1 three games of craps were simulated, using Figure 29. Check these, and then simulate one more game.

3. From Chapter IV, Section 3, Exercises 18, 19 compute the expected number of bust, one pair, two pairs, and three-of-a-kind hands in 10,000 poker hands. Also compute the standard deviation for each. Do the figures given in Example 2 for the simulation look reasonable?
[*Partial Ans.* Bust: expect 5012; off by less than one standard deviation.]

4. Consider an independent trials process with probability p for success. Show that if p is very small then the standard deviation $\sqrt{npq}$ is very close to the square root of the expected number of successes.

5. Use the results of Chapter IV, Section 3, Exercise 11, together with the result of Exercise 4 (above), to check the simulated values for the rarer poker hands in Example 2.

6. Use the results of Exercises 3 and 5 to discuss how far one can rely on the simulated probabilities obtained from 10,000 poker hands.

7. Use the RND in Figure 27 to simulate 30 days' weather in the Land of Oz, following a rainy day.   [*Ans.* "Rain" 10, "Nice" 7, "Snow" 13.]

8. Change the RND in Figure 27 to random integers from 1 through 100.

9. Suppose that we have a team each of whose batters performs according to the simulation scheme in Figure 33. Use the random integers obtained in Exercise 8 to simulate the performance of the first 30 batters on one team. How does the team stand after 30 men have come to bat?

[*Ans.* End of six innings, four runs scored.]

10. In 1951, Gil Hodges of the Brooklyn Dodgers was officially at bat 582 times, and hit 40 home runs. Estimate his probability of hitting a home run each time he was at bat. How large a fluctuation in his annual home-run output is attributable to pure chance?

11. From 1949 through 1959, Gil Hodges had the following number of home runs: 23, 32, 40, 32, 31, 42, 27, 32, 27, 22, 25. Is there a case for his having had "good" and "bad" years, or may we assign the differences entirely to chance fluctuations? [*Hint:* Estimate the expected value from the data, and use Exercise 10.]   [*Ans.* Explainable as chance fluctuations.]

SUGGESTED READING

Harary, F., R. Z. Norman, and C. C. Cartwright, *Structural Models*, Wiley, New York, 1965.

Gardin, J. C., et P. Garelli, "Étude des établissements assyriens en Cappadoce par ordinateurs," Annales Économies, Sociétés, Civilisations, **16** (1961) pp. 837–876.

Neyman, J., *First Course in Probability and Statistics*, Holt, New York, 1950, Chap. III.

Estes, W. K., and C. J. Burke, "Application of a Statistical Model to Simple Discrimination Learning in Human Subjects," *J. Exptl. Psychol.*, **50** (1955), pp. 81–88.

Bush, R. R., and F. Mosteller, *Stochastic Models for Learning*, Wiley, New York, 1955.

Bush, R. R., and W. K. Estes, *Studies in Mathematical Learning Theory*, Stanford University Press, 1959.

Weil, André, "Sur L'Étude de Certains Types de Lois de Marriage (Système Murngin)," in Appendice à la Première Partie, *Les Structures Elementaire de la Parente*, by Claude Levi-Strauss, Presses Universitaires de France, Paris, 1949, pp. 278–285.

Kemeny, John G., Oskar Morgenstern, and Gerald L. Thompson, "A Generalization of the von Neumann Model of an Expanding Economy," *Econometrica*, **24** (1956), pp. 115–135.

Index